FLORIDA'S HURRICANE HISTORY

JAY BARNES

FOREWORD BY STEVE LYONS

The University of North Carolina Press

Chapel Hill

FLORIDA'S
HURRICANE
HISTORY

SECOND EDITION

The paper in this book meets the
guidelines for permanence and
durability of the Committee on
Production Guidelines for Book
Longevity of the Council on Library
Resources.

Library of Congress
Cataloging-in-Publication Data
Barnes, Jay.
 Florida's hurricane history /
Jay Barnes; foreword by
Steve Lyons.—2nd ed.
  p. cm.
 Includes bibliographical
references and index.
 ISBN-13: 978-0-8078-3068-0
(cloth : alk. paper)
 ISBN-13: 978-0-8078-5809-7
(pbk. : alk. paper)
 1. Hurricanes—Florida—History.
 1. Title.
 QC945.B35   2006
 551.55'209759—dc22
 2006028183

11 10 09 08 07   5 4 3 2 1

Title page: The Royal Palm Park in downtown Miami was littered with boats and debris after the September hurricane of 1926. (Photo courtesy of Special Collections, University of South Florida Library)

Page v: A weary Pompano Beach resident searches through wreckage after the 1948 hurricane. (Photo courtesy of Noel Risnychok)

Page vii: Tampa's cigar district was among the areas most affected by wind during the hurricane of 1921. These children gathered on Fifth Street after the storm. (Photo courtesy of Special Collections, University of South Florida Library)

Page xiii: Hurricanes strike Florida more frequently than they strike any other state. (Photo courtesy of NOAA)

CONTENTS

119
116
147
150

FOREWORD

In June 1972, I was a graduating senior in high school in southern California. Living just a few miles inland from Huntington Beach, I became an avid surfer and follower of hurricanes off Mexico's Pacific Coast. I knew they brought huge waves, and I rode many of them. That June, as I became interested in hurricanes and how waves grow, Hurricane Agnes meandered across the Florida Panhandle. Agnes's right-front quadrant struck a very vulnerable portion of Florida's coast near Cape San Blas. I read in the newspaper about high water there and the subsequent catastrophic flooding in the northeastern United States, both a result of Agnes. That news started me thinking that hurricanes were far more complex than just storms at sea that made big waves. So my meteorological career began when I flew off to the University of Hawaii. There was no better place for a surfer to go to learn about hurricanes and waves!

While at college, I studied tropical cyclones and their global impact. I soon learned of Hawaii's vulnerability and that Honolulu was a sitting duck for a major hurricane disaster (it still is). But news about hurricanes always seemed to focus on Florida. Its extensive coastline, uniquely flat land, shallow coastal waters, and large Lake Okeechobee make it extremely prone to hurricane surge. Much of its existing land was originally swamp. Perhaps that's the way we should have left it—pristine, remote, full of wildlife, and very vulnerable to hurricanes. But it's too late for that now.

Most of the land in Florida is within sixty miles of the ocean, making it and everything built on it extremely vulnerable to the ravages of hurricane winds. Gusting winds coming from the ocean don't get much chance to slow down over Florida's flat, smooth, swampy landscape before impacting residents and their property. And Florida's coastline is the most densely populated area of the state. Unfortunately hurricane waves have pounded every portion of Florida's coast. Today costly beach restoration is needed to fight the constant erosion caused by tropical storms and hurricanes.

Florida's hurricanes have long been a significant factor in the overall vitality of the state. At times, hurricanes have literally changed the course of Florida's history and development. The first changes likely occurred when Florida's native peoples learned to adapt their living conditions to the threat of hurricanes. Unfortunately European settlers were not as successful. Many of Florida's economic woes have been associated with big hurricanes. In modern times, Florida's agricultural and tourist industries have sometimes faltered with the passage of major hurricanes. In 1992 Hurricane Andrew temporarily crippled the state's home insurance industry by inflicting $30 billion in damages, causing many insurers to pull out of Florida.

Florida has experienced many great storms. Some have been deadly, others have left horrific damage, but all have tested the spirit and resolve of the people they affected. Some have passed namelessly into meteorological history. Each storm has brought a distinctive wrath, though at times only to a limited region. We know Floridians can adapt and recover. After Andrew, Miami's motto was "We will rebuild." Much of the state was challenged by the destructive 2004 and 2005 hurricane seasons, requiring a recovery effort that is likely to take years. Florida recovers, but the price of recovery continues to rise.

Florida's exploding population is a major concern for hurricane planners. Nearly all of the state's residents live in a "coastal zone," which exacerbates the hurricane threat. By 2025 Florida's population is estimated to exceed 27 million, compared to 5 million in 1960. Huge population increases, mostly in large cities, make hurricane evacuations more difficult because they take longer to orchestrate. Many lives could be lost in Florida if a major hurricane rapidly developed and then rushed shoreward overnight toward a large city while the residents slept, leaving no time for evacuation. Thousands could be trapped in their cars as the big one hit, stuck in traffic with no way out.

Efforts to educate the public about hurricanes and their life-threatening impact must be a priority. That's what we try to do at the Weather Channel. In Florida, understanding the threat is important for new residents as well as for older ones who may develop "hurricane amnesia" after a few years without a storm. Schools and the media must help in the hurricane education and preparedness process.

The importance of our appreciation of the power of these storms was made very clear during the devastating 2005 hurricane season. Hurricane Katrina became the nightmare we meteorologists have been talking about for years. After Katrina crossed Florida, it strengthened and flooded New Orleans, in some places with more than twenty feet of water. Some people who failed to evacuate waited helplessly on rooftops to be rescued; others drowned. The city succumbed to bedlam amid filth, rancid water, and looting. For days some were stranded in floodwaters that resulted from failures in a levee system built to protect against such disasters. The levee system had given a false sense of security to hundreds of thousands of residents that many paid for with their lives. Hurricane Katrina hit a city below sea level and a surge-vulnerable Mississippi coast with enough power to make Andrew's death and damage statistics fade quietly into the meteorological record books. But could Tampa be just as vulnerable?

Florida is extremely vulnerable for a variety of reasons. Many residents have moved to Florida from cool northern climates and have never experienced a hurricane. They are unaware of the potential destruction of a strong hurricane or slow-moving tropical storm. During much of the hurricane season, the state is inundated with tourists, many of whom are not prepared for an encounter with a hurricane. And many of Florida's sun-seeking residents are elderly and generally more vulnerable during hurricane evacuations because they may have serious health concerns that require constant monitoring. Most Florida residents have never experienced sustained hurricane-force winds, though many think they have because a hurricane passed within fifty miles of their home. Over the last several decades, Florida's coastline has filled with development. There is now far more property to damage, fewer undeveloped areas, and no decline in development in sight. This means costlier hurricane events. In 2004 the combination of Hurricanes Charley, Frances, Ivan, and Jeanne resulted in widespread damage across Florida, making it the most expensive year for hurricanes in U.S. history up to that time. After this devastation, the cost of property in Florida continued to increase, housing demand remained high, and Florida's coast continued to grow more vulnerable. Florida has some of the strictest building codes in the nation, but considering the magnitude of the damage in 2004, it has a long way to go before it becomes hurricane resistant—as demonstrated in 2005 by the large number of power outages from tropical storm Katrina.

The accuracy of forecasting hurricanes has improved tremendously over my meteorological career. On average, a five-day track forecast today is more accurate than a three-day forecast was in 1972. Better data collection and advances in computer modeling are two key reasons for these track improvements. Unfortunately improved accuracy in forecasting hurricane intensity (especially rapid changes in intensity) has proven more difficult to achieve. And forecast improvements really don't make much difference if emergency-management plans to protect the public are inadequate or the public's response is lacking.

Here in the pages of Jay Barnes's fascinating book, readers can experience for themselves the deep history of a state with a stormy past. They can compare the great disasters, read the personal stories, study the facts and figures, examine the photographs, and gain a valuable new appreciation for the force of hurricanes in Florida's past. In years to come, if another great hurricane strikes Tampa–St. Petersburg or Miami, those who take action because they read *Florida's Hurricane History* may very well save their own lives. And the rest of us will marvel at the unleashing of nature's fury on a state destined for yet another hurricane disaster.

Steve Lyons
Hurricane expert
The Weather Channel

FLORIDA'S HURRICANE HISTORY

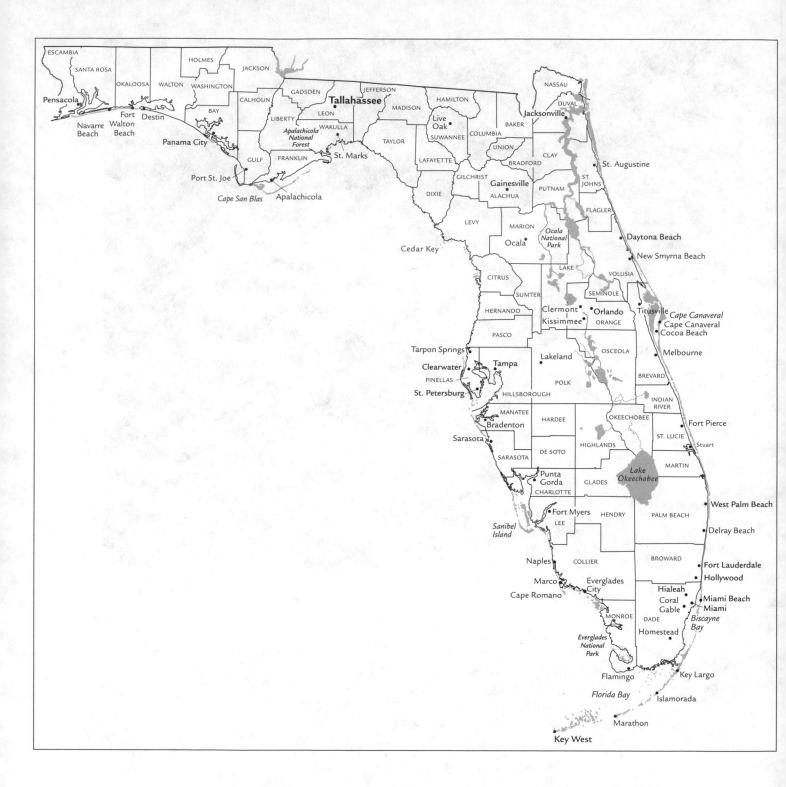

INTRODUCTION

It has become a ritual of every summer season. From half a world away, we tune in the local news or the Weather Channel and watch by satellite for embryonic tropical storms. We plot their growth, give them names, and track their every movement across the sea. With each new hurricane season, we wonder if this will be the year of *the* storm on *our* beach in *our* neighborhood.

For some Floridians, fears about such a storm have become nightmarish realities in recent years. In 1992 Hurricane Andrew blasted the southern end of the state and left an epic disaster in its wake. The 1995 season brought another round of storms ashore, including two hurricanes and two tropical storms. Then all hell broke loose in 2004 when four hurricanes struck Florida in succession—followed by three more in 2005. Thanks to Charley, Frances, Ivan, Jeanne, Dennis, Katrina, and Wilma, a whole new generation of Florida residents have experienced the core of a destructive hurricane. Our attention remains focused on these recent events, but Florida has had a long and brutal hurricane history. Countless tropical cyclones have overwashed its Atlantic and Gulf shores and scarred its interior counties. Through the centuries, thousands of Floridians have lost their lives in the desperate struggle against the waves and winds of hurricanes.

Dipping into the Gulf of Mexico like a toe extending into a warm bath, the Florida Peninsula is a balmy paradise for millions of residents and vacationers. In many ways, climate has played a major role in its history and development. Early settlers were plagued by severe autumn storms and mosquito-borne fevers. But by the late nineteenth century, a new wave of developers touted the beneficial effects of Florida's tropical climate and built extensive railroads and resorts to host droves of annual tourists. Agricultural interests found wealth in Florida's long, favorable growing seasons. Hunters and naturalists enjoyed a bounty of wildlife unlike the range of wildlife found in any other state. Florida prospered because of its latitude and its great natural beauty. Today millions are drawn to its almost winterless weather and the relaxed life-style that comes with it. Its mild climate and seemingly endless beaches are two of its most inviting physical resources. Unfortunately these same features make it a frequent target for dangerous tropical weather.

Florida's extensive ocean shoreline stretches over 1,300 miles and among the states is second only to Alaska's in length. Facing both the Atlantic Ocean and the Gulf of Mexico, its irregular coast is made up of barrier islands, sandy cusps, and keys broken and segmented by inlets, estuaries, rivers, and bays. Even though Florida covers more than 65,000 square miles, no part of the state is more than seventy miles from Atlantic or Gulf waters. Its low-lying terrain, in some areas only a few feet above sea level, extends miles inland from the coast. Its many rivers, lakes, and glades are prone to flooding from heavy rains. Along with its position in a near-tropical sea, these physical features contribute to Florida's great vulnerability to the recurring effects of hurricanes and tropical storms.

The rapid growth Florida has experienced in recent years has increased its vulnerability to destructive hurricanes. From the building boom of the 1920s through the explosion of growth in the last few decades, many of Florida's residents have come to live and work in hurricane-prone areas near the coast. Between 1960 and 2000, the state's population more than tripled, and by 2005 more than 18 million people called Florida home. With this increase in population came more homes, highways, and structures of all kinds that could suffer from the advances of a major hurricane. Powerful storms that swept the peninsula in the early 1800s caused little damage; the risks today are much greater. The next great hurricane could cause tens of billions of dollars in property damage and place millions of people in harm's way.

When we ponder the risks and consequences of Florida's hurricanes, our thoughts are drawn to recent events. In 2004 bouts with Charley, Frances, Ivan, and Jeanne focused new attention on the state's unique vulnerability to destructive tropical weather. Then in 2005, after Dennis struck the Panhandle, Hurricane Katrina crossed South Florida, slammed into the Louisiana and Mississippi coasts, and went on to become our nation's single greatest natural disaster. The record-setting season also featured Wilma, an October storm that knocked out power to over 6 million Floridians.

Even though the state and federal response to Katrina in New Orleans was widely criticized, our ability to respond to and recover from hurricane disasters has actually shown dramatic improvement in recent years. The experience with Andrew in 1992 was somewhat of a turning point. In the aftermath of Andrew, those involved in the recovery effort faced enormous challenges. Issues ranging from building code enforcement to the pre-positioning of federal aid were targeted for revamping. Federal, state, and local emergency planners learned hard lessons from everything that went wrong. Hurricane readiness in Florida has improved significantly since that time, but responders have been challenged by the economic and human impact of the flurry of recent storms. Each hurricane is a learning experience, and the government, church, and nonprofit agencies involved continue to improve their capabilities. But the stakes remain high. Experts agree that we can expect more multibillion-dollar hurricane disasters in the years to come.

Among the many South Florida residents whose lives were rocked by Andrew, little in these pages will surprise or amaze. Because of its incredible intensity and destruction, Andrew remains a milestone in our national hurricane experience. Those who endured the 2004 and 2005 seasons now have their own hurricane stories to tell. But many hurricane disasters have occurred in Florida's past, some long ago and others in recent decades. This book attempts to piece together that history and chronicle the significant hurricanes known to have battered the Sunshine State.

Since Florida has such a long hurricane history, it is no surprise that it is often identified with these great storms. Athletic teams at the University of Miami bear the name "Hurricanes," as do little league teams throughout the state. The term *hurricane* is also applied to everything from nightclubs to water-park rides. And, of course, Hollywood has strengthened the connection by including hurricane scenes in countless movies set in Florida, such as John Huston's *Key Largo*. Ernest Hemingway wrote about them, and the National Aeronautics and Space Administration (NASA) frequently is forced to plan around them. Hurricanes and tropical storms come with the territory in Florida, as any longtime resident will tell you. The events chronicled here, which include some of the state's greatest tragedies, offer further evidence of that.

Accounts of hurricanes are scattered throughout the history of Florida, beginning with the first known report of a great storm in 1559. This September gale wrecked the fleet of Spanish explorer Tristán de Luna as he was attempting to establish a settlement at Ochusa, known today as Pensacola. For the next few hundred years, the many tropical storms that affected the Florida region were scarcely documented due to the small number of European settlements and the vast portions of uninhabited coastline. Storm accounts were sometimes recorded in the journals of sailors at sea, but complete records of these early storms are rare. Surely dozens of powerful hurricanes swept over the peninsula during this period for which no records exist. Nevertheless, through centuries of settlement and countless battles among the Spanish, British, French, and Seminoles, hurricanes played an important role in shaping the geography and development of the Florida territory.

During the last quarter of the nineteenth century, reports of hurricanes in Florida became more complete, thanks largely to the creation of the U.S. Weather Bureau and the efforts of weather reporters and newspapers throughout the region. At least twenty hurricanes buffeted the state during this time. Then from 1900 to 2005, a total of sixty-seven hurricanes made landfall in Florida, far more than in any other state during this period. Some of the more powerful storms struck in the first half of the twentieth century, during a time when tropical meteorology was becoming better understood. But until Andrew hit in 1992, Florida had actually suffered little from hurricanes in recent years, as few major storms made landfall in the 1960s, 1970s, and 1980s.

There were, however, a few notable exceptions. Hurricane Donna, which swept the middle Keys in September 1960, was one of the twentieth century's most powerful hurricanes and is well remembered by longtime South Florida residents. Others may recall the visits of Betsy and Dora or perhaps Eloise and Elena. But unlike the relative calm of the late twentieth century, Florida was continuously battered by tropical weather in the 1920s, 1930s, and 1940s. Between 1941 and 1950 alone, eleven hurricanes made landfall in the state. Some of the most potent storms known to have affected Florida occurred during these early years, including the Miami hurricane of 1926, the Okeechobee hurricane of 1928, the Long Key hurricane of 1929, the Labor Day hurricane of 1935, the Fort Lauderdale hurricane of 1947, the Delray Beach hurricane of 1949, and Hurricane King in 1950.

Florida's Hurricane History was first published in 1998, and since that time a handful of new storms have struck the state. Most notably, the grueling hurricane season of 2004 was one for the record books, with four hurricanes tracking across Florida in just a matter of weeks. Hurricanes Charley, Frances, Ivan, and Jeanne hammered much of the state and delivered unprecedented disaster to dozens of beachfront communities as well as inland cities like Orlando. Across Florida, one in five homes was damaged, and the resulting costs surpassed the one-year record of almost $30 billion set after Andrew. Never before since record-keeping began had four hurricanes struck the state in one season. In 2005 the storms kept rolling in, with three more hurricane landfalls in Florida. This recent flurry of activity adds many new pages to this book and will long be remembered as one of the most active hurricane periods in Florida's history.

This journal does not attempt to report every hurricane or tropical storm in Florida's history but instead offers a chronological account of the significant storms on record. It was compiled from a wide variety of sources but relies heavily on National Weather Service records and numerous works by other weather historians. Newspaper and magazine reports, historical publications, letters, and personal interviews were also essential sources used to compile this history. These references, which are listed in the acknowledgments section of this book, offer valuable details concerning the meteorology, damages, and other accounts of the storms. Photographs that document the impact of Florida's great hurricanes are historical treasures, and those taken prior to the 1920s are rare. The images reproduced here were collected from museums, newspapers, libraries, government agencies and archives, relief organizations, businesses, and family albums. In addition to these sources, many individuals graciously contributed to the completion of this work.

Florida's Hurricane History may be of most interest as a photographic scrapbook of great hurricanes and the unusual events that accompanied them. Hopefully, by taking a look at the storm experiences of the past, we can gain some insight into the nature and recurrence of our hurricane risk. Perhaps we can then better prepare for the next great hurricane that strikes the Florida coast.

BIRTH OF A HURRICANE

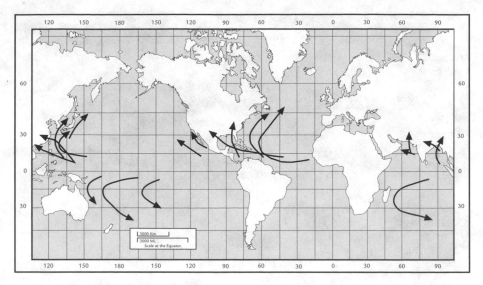

Tropical cyclone development around the world.
(Adapted from Atlantic Hurricanes, *by Gordon Dunn and Banner Miller)*

As old as the oceans themselves, hurricanes are born each year from the heat of the Tropics. They begin as innocent thunderclouds and evolve into massive storms with violent winds and torrential rains. They may live for days or for weeks, and most die off harmlessly over cooler waters. Some track dangerously close to land before veering away just beyond the shoreline. Occasionally these storms make landfall with a violent blast of wind, rain, and tide. Other storm systems may be larger and tornadoes sometimes pack more violent winds, but nothing in our atmosphere can match the broad-scale destructive force of hurricanes. These seasonal cyclones and their counterparts around the globe are the greatest storms on earth, killing more people worldwide than all other storms combined.

They are called *hurricanes* in the Western Hemisphere, a term probably derived from "Hurukan," the name of the Mayan storm god, and other similar native Caribbean words translated as "evil spirit" or "big wind." In the western Pacific, they are known as *typhoons,* and in the Indian Ocean, they are called *cyclones*. These terms all describe the same phenomena—cyclonic storms that form in all tropical oceans except the South Atlantic and Southeast Pacific.

As the intense rays of the summer sun warm the ocean's surface, evaporation and conduction transfer enormous amounts of heat and moisture into the atmosphere, fueling the birth of tropical cyclones. Warm vapors rise, cool, and condense, forming billowing clouds, scattered showers, and thunderstorms. Newborn thunderstorms grow and multiply, many produced in passing *tropical waves*—low-pressure troughs that drift westward through equatorial waters.

(Page 5)
Hurricane Elena swirls over the Gulf of Mexico in 1985, as viewed by astronauts aboard the space shuttle. (Photo courtesy of the U.S. Geological Survey, EROS *Data Center)*

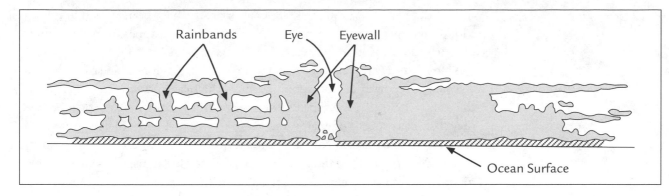

Cross section of a severe hurricane.

Some waves become *tropical depressions* as thunderheads build, pressures drop, and low-level circulation develops. If conditions are favorable, a depression can intensify until sustained winds reach 39 mph, at which time it becomes a *tropical storm*. Once the tropical storm's rotation becomes well organized, its central pressure falls, and sustained winds reach 74 mph, a hurricane is born.

Satellite images of fledgling tropical systems give meteorologists the opportunity to watch these storms develop over a period of hours and days. Forecasters look for signs of rotation and organized convection in emerging storms, which indicate the potential for strengthening. The earth's spin produces the *Coriolis effect*, which causes winds within a tropical depression to spiral around the central low pressure. These winds encounter surface friction that causes them to spiral inward, helping to intensify the storm by bringing warm, moist air to recharge the growing thunderstorms. Once the circulation completely surrounds the center, a relatively calm *eye* sometimes develops, from which massive rainbands spiral outward for many miles. The storm's most intense winds are found at the edge of the eye in the *eyewall*. It is usually here that the hurricane delivers its greatest destruction.

In order for a tropical storm to develop and intensify, it must encounter minimal *vertical shear*. Shearing winds, like those produced by upper-level lows, sometimes blow the tops off developing storms, never allowing a convective "chimney" to form. In the absence of strong shear, storms can more readily strengthen. Once a storm becomes a well-developed hurricane, it may cover thousands of square miles as it tracks across the ocean's surface. Whether it maintains its strength and direction or stalls and dissipates depends on the effects of the atmosphere that surrounds it. Rivers of air push and steer the hurricane, while nearby low-pressure troughs and high-pressure domes can either draw or block the storm. High-altitude steering currents and low-level trade winds influence the hurricane's course, and the combination of these forces can produce erratic storm tracks. Some hurricanes have been known to track in a loop (like Hurricane Easy in September 1950). Others appear to wobble, much like a child's top spinning precariously across a table.

As long as they remain over warm water, tropical cyclones can strengthen. To intensify, they need a good supply of fuel—the heat and moisture available in the atmosphere at sea. As they move over relatively cooler waters or over land, they lose their source of energy and begin to weaken. Nevertheless, hurricanes and tropical storms can sometimes track deep inland before fully dissipating. Some, like Opal in 1995 and Ivan in 2004, can cause extensive damage to areas many miles from the coast. In Florida many hurricanes that make landfall on one coast cross the peninsula only to reenter the warm waters on the other side, where they sometimes regain their strength. Like Donna in 1960 and Andrew in 1992, many of Florida's most infamous storms have swept the state from coast to coast before eventually making landfall a second time in another state.

During the long, hot days of late summer, ocean temperatures reach their peak, and tropical storm activity increases. August, September, and October are the prime months for hurricanes in the Atlantic, but the official hurricane season runs from June 1 through November 30. Hurricanes have been documented in the Atlantic in the months before and after the official season, but the majority of tropical cyclones occur from June through November. The earliest hurricane ever to strike the U.S. coast was Alma, which hit the Florida Panhandle as a minimal hurricane on June 9, 1966. The latest hurricane known to make landfall in the United States, an unnamed storm on November 30, 1925, also struck Florida, near Tampa.

Although Andrew came in August, September is clearly the most dangerous month for tropical cyclones in Florida. Over 60 percent of the major hurricanes to strike the state in the twentieth century occurred during this month, many within the first two weeks. Most of Florida's worst hurricane disasters occurred in September, including the great hurricanes of 1926, 1928, 1935, 1945, and 1947, as well as Donna in 1960, Betsy in 1965, Eloise in 1975, and Ivan in 2004.

Early-season hurricanes that strike Florida most often make landfall on the Gulf coast. In August and September, *Cape Verde–type storms* (born from African waves near the Cape Verde Islands) form in the eastern Atlantic and track toward the west. These hurricanes are often very severe and have battered Florida's Atlantic coast many times through the years. Hurricanes affecting Florida early or late in the season often emerge from the western Caribbean and the Gulf of Mexico and can strike either the Gulf or the southeastern coast. During the winter months, severe and damaging storms called *nor'easters* sometimes brew off Florida's coasts, but these storms are not true hurricanes. They are known to meteorologists as *extratropical cyclones*, and they lack the warm central air mass and well-defined eye of a hurricane.

Even so, nor'easters have been known to cause major destruction. The Ash Wednesday storm of March 1962 was perhaps the biggest Atlantic extratropical storm of the twentieth century. For three long days, this nor'easter stalled off the Atlantic coast, during a time of high spring tides and full moon, and battered the coastline from Florida to New England. Florida experienced considerable damage, but the storm's worst floods and most concentrated destruction occurred from North Carolina to New York. The Lincoln's Birthday storm of 1973 and the March superstorm of 1993 are two other notable nor'easters of recent years. Residents along Florida's east coast regularly experience nor'easters and other winter storms and sometimes endure coastal flooding and severe beach erosion from them.

Each year, about sixty tropical waves form in the Atlantic, Caribbean, and Gulf of Mexico. On average, only about ten reach tropical storm intensity, and only about six become hurricanes. The U.S. coastline will be struck by an average of more than three hurricanes every two years, anywhere from Texas to Maine. Almost 40 percent of all U.S. hurricanes hit Florida. According to the statistical averages, hurricanes battered Florida in about three out of every five years during the twentieth century. But statistics can be misleading in any attempt to determine what to expect in the future. And few hurricane seasons seem *average* in Florida.

HURRICANE EFFECTS

Hurricanes strike Florida more frequently than they strike any other state. (Photo courtesy of NOAA)

In recent years, national media coverage of major hurricanes has provided ample evidence of the violence unleashed by these storms. Powerful and destructive hurricanes like Andrew, Charley, Ivan, and Katrina have redefined our perceptions of hurricane disasters. Storms like these produce high winds that can leave homes and businesses with the bombed-out appearance of a war zone. A surging ocean and unyielding rain inundate coastal communities and inland rivers, flooding homes, highways, and farmlands. The combined natural forces of wind and water sometimes bring property losses in the billions of dollars and take the lives of the unprepared.

So how does the hurricane machine deliver this kind of destructive force? All hurricanes are not alike; some are small and some are large, some weak and some strong. Each may affect a region differently, but every hurricane has the

potential for deadly flooding and damaging winds. Meteorologists look carefully at the measurable components of storms to try to build an understanding of their power and direction.

STORM INTENSITY

We have seen the aftermath of great hurricanes in recent years; the unbelievable destruction left by Katrina in 2005 is still fresh in our memories. The awesome natural forces that created the Andrew disaster were some of Mother Nature's most violent. But more often than not, hurricanes strike with lesser winds and more moderate tides. Not all hurricanes are created equal, and their fickle natures often bring about changes in intensity with each news update. These changes can be critically important to coastal residents and forecasters who must make judgments about warnings and evacuations. *All* hurricanes are dangerous, but clearly some bring a greater potential for disaster than others.

Over the past few decades, hurricane forecasters have used the *Saffir-Simpson scale* to rate hurricane intensity. On this relative scale of 1 to 5, a minimal hurricane with wind speeds of 74–95 mph is considered a category 1 storm. At the other extreme, a category 5 hurricane is a monster with sustained winds that exceed 155 mph and a tidal surge of over eighteen feet.

In the Atlantic basin, a hurricane reaches category 5 intensity on average once every three years. Fortunately, however, landfalls by these dangerous

CATEGORY	EXAMPLE	WINDS & TIDES	EFFECTS
1	Erin (1995)	Winds 74–95 mph; surge 4–5 feet above normal	No damage to building structures; most damage to unanchored mobile homes, trees, and signs. Coastal-road flooding and minor pier and boat damage.
2	Cleo (1964)	Winds 96–110 mph; surge 6–8 feet above normal	Some damage to roofing materials, doors, and windows. Considerable damage to mobile homes, trees, signs, piers, and small boats. Some coastal evacuation routes flooded.
3	Wilma (2005)	Winds 111–30 mph; surge 9–12 feet above normal	Structural damage to some buildings; mobile homes destroyed. Coastal structures damaged by floating debris. Substantial regional flooding along beaches and rivers.
4	Charley (2004)	Winds 131–55 mph; surge 13–18 feet above normal	Extensive structural damage with some complete roof failures. Major damage to lower floors of structures near the shore. All terrain lower than 10 feet above sea level may be flooded, requiring massive evacuation of residential areas in all low-lying areas. Intense winds continue into inland areas.
5	Labor Day storm of 1935	Winds greater than 155 mph; surge more than 18 feet above normal	Complete roof failures on many residences and buildings. Some complete building failures. Major damage to all structures located less than 15 feet above sea level. Massive evacuation of all residents for many miles inland. Intense winds continue far into inland areas.

Source: National Weather Service

storms are extremely rare; only three struck the United States in the twentieth century. The Labor Day storm of 1935 swept over the upper Florida Keys on September 3, claiming 408 lives and punishing those islands with winds estimated at 200 mph. This small but deadly cyclone established a new record for intensity and gave South Florida its third major hurricane disaster in ten years. Hurricane Camille first struck Biloxi, Mississippi, in August 1969 before sweeping northward through Tennessee, Kentucky, and Virginia. This superstorm brought a devastating tidal surge of twenty-five feet at Pass Christian,

Mississippi, winds estimated at over 175 mph, and a death toll of over 250. Its barometric pressure bottomed out at 26.84 inches. As the remnants of Camille tracked through Virginia, twenty-seven inches of rainfall in eight hours caused flash floods to race across the state, killing 109.

After Hurricane Andrew blasted through southern Dade County in August 1992, forecasters rated the violent storm as a strong category 4 on the Saffir-Simpson scale. Andrew's maximum sustained winds were thought to exceed 145 mph, and gusts over 175 mph were reported. It delivered a storm surge of almost seventeen feet and brought unprecedented destruction to the state and to the nation. Ten years later in 2002, a group of top hurricane meteorologists gathered to reassess Andrew's intensity. They found that at landfall, Andrew's winds were actually sustained at 165 mph, making it the third and last category 5 storm to strike the United States in the twentieth century.

Meteorologists use barometric pressure as one of the primary measuring sticks for hurricane intensity—the lower the pressure, the more intense the storm. Reconnaissance flights into hurricanes by National Oceanic and Atmospheric Administration (NOAA) aircraft, weather data buoys, and ship reports provide pressure readings from storms at sea. Once a hurricane has made landfall, any good barometer in the storm's path can supply a reading. Historically, these measurements have been recorded in inches of mercury, and thus this standard is used consistently throughout this text. Today, however, meteorologists prefer to measure pressure in millibars. Conversion can be made as follows: 1 millibar equals 0.0295 inch.

During the Labor Day hurricane of 1935, a pressure of 26.35 inches was recorded at Craig, Florida, between Lower Matecumbe Key and Long Key. This reading established a new record for atmospheric pressure that stood for fifty-three years as the lowest in the Western Hemisphere. This incredibly intense hurricane was relatively compact; it is estimated that at one point during the storm, there was a pressure difference of one inch of mercury over just six miles!

In 1988 Hurricane Gilbert, also a category 5, struck Cozumel, Mexico, with incredible force. Prior to this hurricane's landfall, reconnaissance aircraft recorded a barometric pressure of 26.22 inches, establishing a new record. On the other side of the globe, a new *world* record for low pressure had been recorded during supertyphoon Tip in October 1979. A reconnaissance aircraft used a *dropsonde* (a sounding instrument released from a plane) to obtain an atmospheric pressure of only 25.69 inches! Fortunately category 5 hurricanes are not common; less than 5 percent of Atlantic tropical storms ever reach that level of intensity.

Many great hurricanes have buffeted Florida through the years; in fact, five of the eight most powerful to hit the United States since 1850 have struck here. In addition to two category 5 storms (September 1935 and Andrew), category

Hurricane Andrew's winds tossed a one-by-four board through the trunk of this royal palm. (Photo courtesy of NOAA, National Hurricane Center)

4 hurricanes blasted the state on seven occasions during this period. They are the September hurricane of 1919 (which had a pressure of 27.37 inches), the Lake Okeechobee hurricane of 1928 (27.43), Hurricane Donna in 1960 (27.46), the Miami hurricane of 1926 (27.61), the Florida-Georgia hurricane of 1898 (27.70), the September hurricane of 1947 (27.76), and Hurricane Charley in 2004 (27.79). A table comparing and ranking the most intense hurricanes to strike the United States from 1851 to 2006 is included in the appendix of this book.

WINDS

The "evil winds" feared by the ancient Mayans are the same destructive forces we most often associate with hurricanes. By definition, a tropical storm becomes a hurricane when its constant wind speeds (one-minute sustained winds at a

The gusting winds of Hurricane Donna ripped away the roof over most of this hotel near Marathon. (Photo courtesy of the Florida State Archives)

height of ten meters) are determined to be 74 mph or greater. At this minimal intensity, modest damage may occur to trees, signs, roofs, windows, and small structures. Wind *gusts* may be higher and may bring somewhat heavier damages to isolated areas. Major hurricanes, corresponding to categories 3, 4, and 5, pack sustained winds in excess of 110 mph and cause much more widespread and significant damage. Winds surpassing this intensity could severely damage thousands of homes, even those that comply with local building codes.

Since its invention in the mid-1800s, meteorologists have used the *anemometer* to measure and record wind speeds. These instruments were installed at weather-observation sites around the country throughout the late nineteenth century and have provided helpful wind data on many storms. (It is useful to note that four-cup anemometers used prior to 1928 are believed to have reported higher readings than the three-cup models used since that time.) Unfortunately, during severe hurricanes, some weather stations lose these instruments, as they are blown down or damaged by high gusts. And because of the distance between weather-observation sites, even anemometers that survive a hurricane may not record its top winds if their location does not fall within the powerful eyewall where the winds are greatest. For these reasons, accurate wind records do not exist for some of the highest winds of the greatest storms.

And *great* storms do occur. Category 5 hurricanes develop constant wind speeds of over 155 mph and gusts that may exceed 200 mph. Although these

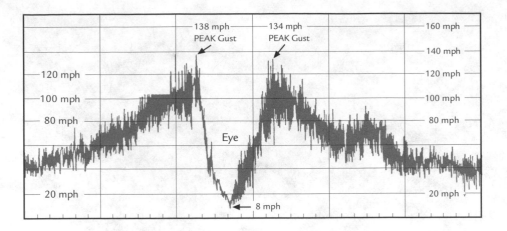

worst-case hurricanes have rarely hit the coast, they are the hurricanes that forecasters and emergency planners fear most. Even substantial structures can be leveled by winds of this force, which can actually *exceed* the velocities in most tornadoes! (Less than 3 percent of tornadoes have winds that exceed 206 mph.) Hurricane Camille was such a storm. Camille's winds were estimated to be over 175 mph, although meteorologists concede that such extreme winds are difficult to verify. In some areas, gusts along the Mississippi Gulf coast probably topped 200 mph.

Florida has also seen its share of extreme hurricane winds. During the Labor Day hurricane of 1935, no wind instruments survived as this small but deadly storm swept the upper Keys. Engineers who studied the resulting damages estimated that sustained winds in the storm were likely near 200 mph. By recording the lowest barometric pressure and using a pressure-gradient formula, scientists were able to support the 200 mph estimate.

Hurricane Donna also brought high gusts to the Keys, estimated at 175–80 mph. One anemometer, at Tavernier, would only record up to 120 mph. After it reached its upper limit, it was reported in the *Naples Daily News* that "the needle was solid against the pin for 45 minutes" during the storm. Other extreme winds have been reported in Florida through the years, including a one-minute reading of 155 mph at the Hillsboro Lighthouse in September 1947 and a one-minute sustained reading of 153 mph at the Jupiter Lighthouse in August 1949. Gusts of 150 mph or more were either recorded or estimated during the Miami hurricane of 1926, the Lake Okeechobee hurricane of 1928, the September storm of 1929, and Hurricane King in 1950.

Hurricane Andrew's winds blasted the homes and businesses of many thousands of people in the Bahamas, Florida, and Louisiana. Initial analyses of the storm's winds showed a sustained speed of 145 mph as it entered South Florida, but after later review, it was determined that sustained winds of 165 mph buffeted a small area on the shores of Biscayne Bay. Gusts in this region were significantly higher. Ironically, the National Hurricane Center was located at the time in Coral Gables, just north of the storm's path. There, at 4:48 A.M. on August 24, the Hurricane Center's anemometer recorded a peak gust of 164 mph before it was disabled. Near Homestead, an isolated gust of 212 mph was reported, though that measurement was later corrected downward. This gust could have come from what scientists call a *suction vortex*, a swirl of very high winds less than one mile wide, embedded within the eyewall. This phenomenon may have occurred in some areas of high wind damage, creating the ghastly sight of shredded trees and houses. Few tornadoes were thought to have been associated with Andrew's winds in Florida.

In severe hurricanes, wind-related property losses are often substantial and widespread. Signs, stoplights, porches, and awnings are usually among the first casualties. The roofs of homes are sometimes peeled back by the winds or blown away altogether. Unprotected glass windows and doors are shattered by flying debris and by shear wind force. Even closed garage doors are no match for the uplifting power of extreme gusts.

Wherever severe hurricanes strike land, broken, uprooted, and fallen trees are commonplace. And when trees fall, they often land on power lines, homes, automobiles, and people. Utility poles can bend, sway, and snap in a hurricane's violent gusts. As the poles go down, they usually bring with them a tangled web of hot electric cables, cutting power to entire communities and threatening unsuspecting storm victims with the risk of electrocution. Utility companies are always challenged by major hurricanes, as line crews must work around the clock to restore power to thousands or even millions of customers.

Tree branches, road signs, and even beach sand become airborne in strong hurricane winds. Lawn furniture, lumber, and other household items turn into deadly projectiles when launched by over 100 mph gusts. Those caught outside in the fury of a hurricane find their lives in jeopardy. After the storm passes, cleanup efforts may take weeks or months because churning winds can leave tons of debris scattered over many miles.

Hurricane-force winds affect structures to varying degrees, depending on the velocity of the wind, the exposure of the building, and the materials and methods used in the construction process. As hurricane winds increase, their destructive energies grow *quadratically*. The force exerted by the wind does not increase proportionally with the wind's speed but with the *square* of the speed. Therefore, a hurricane gust of 140 mph would exert about four times as much force as a 70 mph gust.

Modern building codes require the addition of metal straps, truss braces, and other devices to minimize the damaging effects of high winds. Good roof design can help reduce potential damage, as can many other beneficial design practices. Roof failures can still occur during severe hurricanes, al-

Although they remained inside the garage, these two vehicles were flipped by Hurricane Andrew's winds. This home was located west of Whispering Pines near Eureka Drive. (Photo courtesy of NOAA, National Hurricane Center)

though proper construction techniques will limit roof damage in moderate storms. Storm shutters or properly attached plywood should be used to protect windows and glass doors (the application of tape does nothing to prevent breakage). Garage doors should be reenforced to prevent hurricane winds from penetrating the home through the garage. Local building inspectors and emergency-management coordinators often provide detailed recommendations for methods of home protection. But when all is said and built, experts agree that homeowners should not feel that their well-built homes are "hurricane-proof."

Sometimes hurricane winds can be devastating to inland areas many miles from the coast. In 1989 Hurricane Hugo struck the South Carolina beaches near Charleston and blazed a trail through the state to Charlotte, North Carolina, where thousands of massive trees were downed and homes damaged. Opal had a similar effect in 1995 as it barreled inland near Pensacola Beach and continued on, bringing flash floods and destructive winds to several states, including portions of the Blue Ridge Mountains in North Carolina and Tennessee. Numerous other historical accounts detail hurricane damage in the interior portions of the United States. During colonial times, those who ventured into the impenetrable wilderness beyond the original colonies sometimes found river valleys choked with fallen trees, presumed to have been downed by hurricane winds.

High hurricane winds have been responsible for a number of amazing feats. On July 26, 1825, during a hurricane gust at Guadeloupe, a wooden plank one

inch thick was driven completely through the trunk of a palm tree sixteen inches in diameter. Similar occurrences, with various objects piercing trees and posts, have been reported in Puerto Rico, in Havana, and in Dade County during Hurricane Andrew. At one point during Andrew, a massive concrete and steel beam measuring eighteen feet in length, with part of a roof section still attached, was carried through the air more than 150 feet. In the same storm, a possible vortex near the Hurricane Center lifted cars off the ground and dropped them onto other cars. In other hurricanes, railroad boxcars are known to have been blown uphill, and photographs and personal items have been carried dozens of miles. Also, automobiles have had their paint completely stripped away—down to bare metal by wind driven sand.

Throughout history, many chilling accounts of hurricane winds have been recorded. In Lieutenant Colonel W. Reid's *Law of Storms*, a letter from Sir George Rodney described the Great Hurricane of 1780 in Barbados: "The strongest buildings and the whole of houses, most of which were of stone, and remarkable for their solidity, gave way to the fury of the wind, and were torn up to their foundation; all the forts destroyed, and many of the heavy cannon carried upwards of a hundred feet from the forts. Had I not been an eyewitness, nothing could have induced me to have believed it. More than six thousand persons perished and all the inhabitants were entirely ruined." During this same hurricane in Barbados, it was reported that the bodies of cattle and men were lifted off the ground by high winds and carried several yards.

A storm surge floods Lummus Park during the Miami hurricane of September 1926. (Photo courtesy of Noel Risnychok)

Pleasure craft of all sizes are often among the first victims of the storm surges of approaching hurricanes. (Photo courtesy of the Florida State Archives, copyright the Miami Herald)

STORM SURGE

Even though hurricanes are most often feared for their tempestuous winds, a more deadly force is delivered with the crushing tides of the *storm surge*. The ocean's rapid rise peaks near the time the storm makes landfall and drowns all low-lying areas in several feet of water. Monstrous wind-driven waves ride atop the elevated seas and add to the destructive force. The surge may overwash exposed beaches, but when it strikes the coast, it sometimes heads inland, flooding estuaries and rivers far beyond their banks. Peak surges are frequently measured away from the coast, near the headwaters of an open bay. And, as expected, the more powerful the storm, the greater the storm surge.

As a hurricane churns across the open sea, the combined effects of the storm's lowered barometric pressure and strong, inward-spiraling winds create a deep, swirling column of water beneath the ocean's surface. This effect causes the sea level to rise in the vicinity of the storm, creating a dome of water that may be a few feet high in the center and a hundred miles wide. This dome of water and underlying circulation advance with the hurricane, and when the storm thrusts toward land, the gradually shallowing seafloor forces the water dome to rise dramatically. Powerful hurricanes produce surges that can exceed twenty feet above sea level, bringing total devastation to all beachfront structures. Under these extreme conditions, it is not difficult to understand why nine out of ten hurricane-related deaths are attributed to drowning.

The first signs of the surge effect can be seen in the days before the storm's arrival, as huge swells travel great distances and build along the shore. As their size increases, they crash onto the beach and produce a roar that can be heard for miles inland. Although the skies may be clear and sunny, the ominous spectacle of evenly spaced, ten-foot swells spanning the horizon offers warning of the hurricane's approach. The bulging ocean begins to pile up several feet of water in front of the storm, and coastal flooding may occur at times of high tide. As the storm approaches the coast and makes landfall, the sea level surges upward and great destruction occurs.

Although powerful storms sometimes produce massive surges, many hurricanes strike with modest tides and little destruction. In each storm, various factors contribute to the severity of the resulting flood. The hurricane's intensity and forward speed, as well as the coincidental timing of normal astronomical high tides, determine the measured effect of the surge. Geographical factors such as the size and shape of bays and rivers and the topography of the seafloor can alter the surge's impact by either dispersing the water dome or concentrating its destructive energy.

Historically, storm tides around the world have produced epic tragedies. Nowhere on earth has this phenomenon been more deadly than in Asia, especially in the low delta region of Bangladesh. Here, the death tolls from cyclones have reached biblical proportions. The fertile soils at the mouth of the Ganges River attract millions who farm the low islands, called *chars*, which are little more than mud flats at high tide. The extremely low elevation of the entire region offers little escape from approaching storm tides. Cyclones sweeping northward through the Bay of Bengal have repeatedly focused their energies here with devastating consequences. The Hooghly disaster struck on October 7, 1737, when a storm "wave" estimated at forty feet swept up the mouth of the Hooghly River, killing 300,000. Other great disasters occurred near the mouth of the Ganges in 1789, 1864, and 1876. A disastrous cyclone struck the region on November 13, 1970, producing a storm tide in excess of twenty feet that claimed at least 300,000 lives. Eleven thousand more perished in a cyclone that struck the region in 1984, 15,000 died in 1985, and another 139 were killed in 1991.

Great loss of life in storm surges has occurred in the West as well. The Great Hurricane of 1780 killed 22,000 in Martinique, St. Eustatius, and Barbados, although it is not known how many of those deaths can be attributed to storm surge. In August 1893, a powerful hurricane surprised residents of the coastal islands of South Carolina, where almost 2,000 persons were lost to the rapidly rising storm tide. In October of that same year, 2,000 more drowned when a storm swept over the Mississippi Delta region.

Wind-driven waves crash against a seawall on Biscayne Bay during Hurricane Cleo in 1964. (Photo courtesy of NOAA)

Hurricane Opal's powerful surge destroyed this section of U.S. 98 linking Okaloosa Island to Destin in 1995. (Photo by David Lee Hartlage, courtesy of the Northwest Florida Daily News*)*

Just as a hurricane's churning winds can pile up waters along the coast, they can also pull water away from shore, dropping the water to below sea level. According to Weather Bureau records, during one hurricane in the Keys, a boat owned by the U.S. Army Corps of Engineers was anchored about a half mile offshore in six to seven feet of water. As the storm whisked by, strong offshore winds drove the water out to sea and grounded the vessel. The crew of the ship was then able to climb down and walk across the ocean floor to the beach.

Although the storm surge is most often described as building over a period of minutes to hours, extremely rapid surges have occurred that have produced great tragedies. One example of this took place in the Galveston hurricane of 1900, which claimed over 8,000 lives—more than any other U.S. hurricane. Most of these deaths were attributed to the spectacular rise in sea level as the storm made landfall. In his book *Hurricanes: Their Nature and History*, Ivan R. Tannehill relayed the report of Galveston weather observer I. M. Cline: "The water rose at a steady rate from 3 P.M. until about 7:30 P.M., when there was a sudden rise of about 4 feet in as many seconds. I was standing at my front door, which was partly open, watching the water which was flowing with *great rapidity from east to west*. The water at this time was about 8 inches deep in my residence and the sudden rise of 4 feet brought it above my waist before I could change my position."

Florida has also experienced tragic hurricane floods. Storm surges ranging up to fifteen feet or more above mean sea level have been reliably reported.

The highest, estimated to be at least eighteen feet, occurred during the Labor Day storm of 1935. Other extreme tides took place during Andrew in 1992 (16 feet), the Tampa Bay hurricane of 1848 (14 feet), Opal in 1995 (14 feet), Donna in 1960 (13 feet), the Miami hurricane of 1926 (10.9 feet), and the 1921 Tampa hurricane (10.5 feet). During the 1926 hurricane, the Miami River was the scene of a *bore*—a high, abrupt tidal wave that sweeps through narrow channels. This phenomenon occurred with the shift of the wind as the eye passed over the city, and it wrecked dozens of boats that had sought safe anchorage in the river. It was not the surge of the ocean, however, that was responsible for Florida's greatest flood disaster. Instead, it was the waters of Lake Okeechobee, which were driven by hurricane winds over a levee in September 1928, drowning over 2,000 persons.

RAINFALL

The turbulent rush of the storm surge is not the only source of flooding associated with hurricanes. Torrential rains are dumped from the skies all along the storm's course, causing localized flooding in some areas and dangerous flash floods in others. These rains may pour for hours or for days, depending on the forward speed, size, and orientation of the storm. On average, six to twelve inches of rain can be expected as a hurricane passes nearby.

Heavy rains associated with decaying hurricanes have caused dreadful floods in areas many miles from the coast. Soon after Hurricane Agnes made landfall near Panama City in June 1972, it lost its hurricane status. But as Agnes churned its way up the east coast and into Pennsylvania, it unleashed unprecedented rains that caused rivers to crest at record levels from North Carolina to New York. The resulting floods claimed 122 lives and caused over $2 billion in damages.

More recently, tropical storm Alberto made landfall near Destin, Florida, on July 3, 1994, briefly disrupting Fourth of July activities with little initial impact. But for the next four days, the storm lingered over western Georgia and eastern Alabama, and record rains inundated the countryside. Widespread flooding occurred on the Flint and Ocmulgee Rivers, and many residents in Georgia, Alabama, and Florida were forced out of their homes. Twenty-one inches of rain fell in Americus, Georgia, during a twenty-four-hour period. In all, Alberto's rains were responsible for over $500 million in damages and the deaths of twenty-eight people in Georgia and two in Alabama.

Rainfall amounts are not necessarily linked to storm intensity. Some of the heaviest rains have resulted from tropical storms of less than hurricane strength. In October 1941, a weak tropical storm drifted out of the Gulf and onto the Florida coast near Cedar Key. As it moved inland near Gainesville, it stalled for nearly two days, dumping tremendous amounts of rain on the re-

Although it was only a category 1 hurricane, the October storm of 1947 dumped heavy rains over a broad region, causing extensive flooding. (Photo courtesy of Noel Risnychok)

gion. At Trenton, thirty miles west of Gainesville, almost thirteen inches fell in six hours, and the two-day total for that location was thirty-five inches. Ironically, just two weeks later, a hurricane striking South Florida passed directly over Miami, where it deposited only 0.35 inch of rain.

Until 1979, when tropical storm Claudette dumped forty-two inches of rain on Alvin, Texas, the twenty-four-hour rainfall record for the entire nation was established on the west coast of Florida on September 5–6, 1950. This was during Hurricane Easy, one of the first hurricanes to be designated by name in the United States. Much like the 1941 storm, Easy drifted in circles as it deluged the coastline just south of Cedar Key. The rains lasted for three days, and the astonishing one-day record at Yankeetown was 38.70 inches. This twenty-four-hour record still stands in Florida and was made less than fifty miles south of where the previous record was made in 1941.

When hurricanes and tropical storms track over Florida, heavy rains often cause serious problems. Depending on the rainfall amounts, agricultural interests can be either grateful during times of drought or devastated because their crops are drowned and washed away. Most cities in Florida are laid out on flat terrain, making the rapid removal of water difficult. Also, many areas are covered with impermeable surfaces—streets, highways, roofs—that help to concentrate floodwaters. Traffic is often disrupted in periods of heavy rain, and municipal water supplies are sometimes threatened by overflowing sewers

and septic systems. Fortunately much of Florida is sand and limestone, so floodwaters are usually absorbed rapidly after the passing of hurricanes.

TORNADOES

As if damaging winds and floods weren't enough, tropical cyclones can sometimes spawn deadly tornadoes. Unlike the broad, sweeping winds of a hurricane, tornadoes create narrow paths of concentrated destruction that can be even more lethal. Homes can be leveled, cars overturned, and large trees uprooted and broken, all within seconds. Hurricane-spawned tornadoes are not usually found near the cyclone's core; they strike more frequently on the fringes of passing hurricanes, many miles from the eye of the storm.

Florida is frequently battered by tornadoes, averaging forty-four twisters a year—more than Kansas averages annually. Many occur during severe thunderstorms throughout the seasons and are not associated with any tropical storm or hurricane. Some, known as *waterspouts*, form over water and sometimes threaten boaters and coastal structures. Waterspouts are generally less severe than tornadoes and usually dissipate harmlessly after dancing about on a lake or sea. But unlike waterspouts, tornadoes race across the land, where they tear through forests and grasslands and sometimes rip through populated areas.

In Florida dozens of tornadoes have been reported in association with tropical storms and hurricanes. Although not as vicious as their midwestern cousins, these twisters have brought substantial damage to houses, mobile homes,

Tornadoes and waterspouts sometimes develop during hurricanes. (Photo courtesy of NOAA)

A tornado ripped through this trailer park on Big Coppitt Key during Hurricane Agnes in 1972, damaging more than eighty trailers. (Photo courtesy of AP/Wide World Photos)

and structures of all kinds. Early documentation of tornadoes occurred in the Florida hurricanes of September 1919, September 1929, and September 1933. In June 1972, Hurricane Agnes spawned fifteen tornadoes in Florida as it tracked up the Gulf and came ashore near Panama City. Agnes caused 9 deaths and 119 injuries in Florida, more than half of which were attributed to tornadoes. And as so regularly happens, one tornado during Agnes sliced through a mobile home park on Big Coppitt Key, destroying over eighty homes. The greatest property loss occurred in Brevard County, where a trio of tornadoes brought $4 million in damages. But no Florida hurricane can match the tornado production of Hurricane Beulah, which set a record when it struck the coast of Texas in 1967 and spawned over 150 twisters across the Texas countryside.

OTHER FACTORS

Wind, storm surge, and rain are the essential elements of a hurricane's destructive power. Hurricane intensity, as measured on the Saffir-Simpson scale, may determine how extreme these conditions are. But other factors contribute to the severity of a storm's impact on a given location. The orientation, forward speed, and diameter of an approaching hurricane may critically influence how severe conditions become. The timing of lunar tides and the geographical features of the region can also alter a storm's effects.

The flight deck of the USS Bennington was buckled by massive waves during a typhoon in the Pacific in 1945. (Photo courtesy of the National Archives)

In the Atlantic Ocean and the Gulf of Mexico, the *right-front quadrant* of a tropical cyclone has the greatest potential for destruction. The combined effects of the storm's forward speed and counterclockwise rotation produce the strongest winds and greatest tidal surges in areas of the coast that are hit by this portion of the storm. Hurricanes striking Florida's east coast typically move westward and therefore deliver their highest tides and strongest wind gusts just north of the center of landfall, where the right-front quadrant of the eyewall comes ashore. Beaches and bays on Florida's west coast are typically hit by eastward-moving storms, with the strongest impact just south of landfall; northward-moving storms striking the Panhandle region are generally more severe on their eastern side. Occasionally, hurricanes will flirt with the Florida coast and never make landfall but still deliver destructive winds and tides as they pass. Depending on a storm's orientation to the coast, the right-front quadrant and its more intense winds could envelop the shoreline, or they could remain at sea while the hurricane sweeps by. In 1985 Hurricane Elena battered the Florida Gulf coast with tides ten feet above normal at Apalachicola and wind gusts to 92 mph in Pensacola, even though the storm's eye never came closer than thirty-five miles offshore. Elena carved a loop in the Gulf of Mexico and forced the evacuation of more than a million people before eventually sweeping back to strike the Mississippi coast.

The forward momentum of a hurricane as it crosses the coastline also contributes to the storm's severity in any given area. The measured speed of the hurricane's winds could be thought of as a combination of the rotational winds and the contribution, either positive or negative, of the translational forward speed of the storm. Consequently, fast-moving hurricanes may bring higher winds to locations in the right quadrant and reduced winds on the left side of the storm. Slow-moving hurricanes, on the other hand, may have lesser winds but may typically dump larger amounts of rain.

Usually hurricanes track across the tropical ocean at about 8–15 mph. As they enter more temperate latitudes, they often increase in forward speed and have been known to race northward at speeds of 30–50 mph. Fortunately most hurricanes that affect Florida average about 15 mph, and their forward speed has little impact on their severity. This is not the case in the northeastern states, including New England, where fast-moving hurricanes have caused tremendous destruction to coastal areas through the years.

TRACKING THE STORMS 3

June—too soon.

July—stand by.

August—look out you must.

September—remember.

October—all over.

—Mariner's poem, cited in

NOAA technical report

It has become a given that residents of Florida's low-lying coastal areas will occasionally be asked to leave their homes and businesses to avoid the lashing winds and rising tides of approaching hurricanes. Costly preparations and late-night evacuations will be required of thousands or even millions of residents and vacationers. Mad scrambles to avoid incoming hurricanes can be expensive and frustrating, especially when fickle storms abruptly change course or intensity and leave targeted areas unharmed. But at least today's coastal residents enjoy the benefits of forewarning. Only a few decades ago, hurricane forecasts and communications were poor, and coastal areas were exposed and vulnerable. Early hurricanes usually barreled ashore without warning, often with dire consequences. Through the years, thousands of Floridians have perished in fast-moving hurricane tides that have risen without warning, leaving little opportunity for escape.

Long before warning systems were available, sailors and coastal residents relied on the lore concerning a hurricane's approach. They watched the skies carefully, looking for double moons, sun dogs, and the scarlet aura of a summer sunrise. They discovered truth in the adage "Red sky at morning, sailors take warning; red sky at night, sailor's delight." They read the weather in the clouds and developed their own forecasts: "Mare's tails and mackerel scales make tall ships take in their sails." Mare's tails are cloud formations usually seen after the passing of a cold front, while a mackerel sky, resembling the scales of a fish, often precedes a warm front. Their observations were reasonably effective for day-to-day use but left them vulnerable to approaching tropical storms.

Soothsayers had their own language for catastrophes. It was once widely believed that the position and alignment of the stars and planets foretold impending hurricane tragedies. Comets, meteors, and certain planetary alignments were all troublesome omens that were thought to bring about great weather disasters like tropical hurricanes. Animal behavior was also believed to be a key indicator of severe weather. In the Caribbean cats could supposedly foretell hurricanes by displaying nervous tail twitching and unusual behavior. It was also said that shorebirds gather and livestock wander in the days preceding a hurricane. Some animals are extremely sensitive to variations in air pressure, and others possess a keen sense of hearing. When the pressure falls prior to a storm, swallows and bats were said to fly closer to the ground to help equalize the pressure in their ears. Geese and ducks fly low and often become very vocal, and bees return to their hives. Dolphins and porpoises, however, are sometimes seen at play on the ocean's surface prior to a severe storm, which is why they were unwelcome company for ancient sailors, who considered them to be evil omens.

For centuries, these questionable forecasting methods and meager communications left the residents of Caribbean islands and coastal communities vulnerable to the ravages of hurricanes. The first European to report encounters

(Page 31)
Developing tropical storms and hurricanes in the Atlantic, Caribbean, and Gulf of Mexico are monitored closely by reconnaissance aircraft. (Photo courtesy of NOAA, National Hurricane Center)

with tropical cyclones was Christopher Columbus, who managed to avoid the worst storms on his early visits to the New World. Perhaps the first significant advancement in the study of storms came in November 1743, when Benjamin Franklin observed a "nor'easter" in Philadelphia that obscured an expected eclipse of the moon. Because he later learned that the eclipse had been seen in Boston but was followed by a gale, he theorized that the nor'easter had actually moved from the southwest, even though the storm's surface winds had come from the opposite direction. Six years later, Franklin was able to track the progress of a hurricane from North Carolina to New England and verify his theory that the storm had moved from one place to another.

William Redfield was perhaps the first American to devote much time to the study of hurricanes. In 1831 he published an article in the *American Journal of Science and the Arts* that described these storms as "whirlwinds" with a rotary form, in which winds blow from all directions around a slowly moving center. He was also the first to track the paths of hurricanes from the West Indies to the east coast of the United States. Later, the Englishman Henry Piddington was sent to India to study the catastrophic tropical storms of that region and coined the term "cyclone" (from the Greek word meaning "coils of a snake").

But perhaps the person who did the most to advance the early understanding of hurricanes was Benito Viñes, a Jesuit priest who was director of the College of Belen in Havana, Cuba. Until his death in 1893, Father Viñes was devoted to the study of hurricanes and to the creation of an elaborate warning system throughout Cuba. He utilized hundreds of volunteer observers, gathered ship reports, issued telegraph warnings to nearby islands, and even developed a "pony express" between isolated villages to warn residents of approaching hurricanes. In addition to his extensive warning system, Father Viñes contributed more solid scientific evidence to the study of hurricanes than perhaps any other person of his century.

In 1870 President Ulysses S. Grant signed a proclamation giving the U.S. Army Signal Service the responsibility of gathering weather information and issuing storm warnings throughout the United States. Weather maps were created by using information from far-reaching locations. In 1891 the U.S. Weather Bureau was formed under the Department of Agriculture. During this time, a number of devastating hurricanes swept across the U.S. coastline, killing thousands. But it was not until the Spanish-American War of 1898 that a comprehensive hurricane forecasting service was established. President William McKinley was said to have had a greater fear of hurricanes than of attack from the Spanish navy. The warning service was extended to include shipping interests and numerous ports throughout the Caribbean, with a forecast center located in Havana. In 1900 a horrific hurricane struck Galveston, Texas, killing over 8,000 people. Soon afterward, in 1902, the Weather Bureau's hurricane forecast office was moved to Washington, D.C. After the devastating Labor Day hurricane

During the 1930s, the U.S. Coast Guard dropped floating hurricane-warning messages from airplanes over remote portions of the Florida Keys. (Photo courtesy of Jerry Wilkinson)

of 1935, the office was moved to Jacksonville, Florida, where it remained until 1943.

Weather observers in some locations used inventive methods to warn residents of approaching storms. The flying of hurricane flags to signal a storm alert was common practice at most stations, and local residents kept a keen eye out for the "raising of the red and black." Other techniques for local warnings included criers on horseback, the pealing of church bells, and the firing of rockets and flares. Concerned about the approach of an offshore cyclone, a Weather Bureau observer filed this notice in an August 1899 edition of the *Tampa Morning Tribune*: "When you see the storm rocket, get ready for a hard blow. . . . I am keeping in close communication with Washington, and as soon as there are bulletins that threaten danger to Tampa and this immediate section, I will fire hurricane rockets from the roof of the Knight building. I see no reason at present, however for any undue apprehension."

In spite of the government's efforts to protect its interests, deadly storms kept coming, and hurricane forecasting and warning were tragically ineffective in the early part of the twentieth century. During the 1920s and 1930s, several powerful storms struck Florida and other areas along the east coast, claiming hundreds of lives. Forecasts often came with short notice, if they came at all. Remote communities sometimes never knew of approaching hurricanes, and even large cities endured major storms with little warning.

The great tragedies that resulted from numerous poorly forecast hurricanes challenged scientists to better understand these weather phenomena. During World War II, when Allied forces were scattered around the globe, military weather forecasters gained valuable experience with tropical storms, especially in the Pacific Ocean. In 1943 Colonel Joseph P. Duckworth and navigator Ralph O'Hare guided a light, single-engine plane through the eye of a storm in the Gulf of Mexico and recorded various weather data. This was the first intentional aircraft flight into a hurricane to gather information on wind speeds, direction, and barometric pressure. Duckworth later received the Air Medal for his effort. Reconnaissance flights of "hurricane hunters" continue today and still provide the most valuable and timely information available to forecasters.

Also in 1943 the Weather Bureau's forecast office in Jacksonville was moved to Miami, where a joint hurricane forecasting center with the air force and navy was created. When the air force and navy withdrew from this location after the war, the facility remained the Weather Bureau's hurricane forecast office (later the National Hurricane Center), which had the responsibility to track and forecast all tropical storms and hurricanes in the Atlantic Ocean, Caribbean Sea, and Gulf of Mexico.

During the 1950s, several technological advances occurred, including the creation of a network of coastal radars developed to track hurricanes. By the early 1960s, satellites were positioned in space to provide images from above. Communications improved, warnings became more accurate, and scientists began to use computers to study the storms. Forecasters at the Hurricane Center improved their skills, and lives were saved. For many years, the National Hurricane Center was located in Coral Gables, just outside Miami, until Hurricane Andrew struck the area in 1992. Soon afterward, the center was moved to the campus of Florida International University in Miami.

Today the organization is called the Tropical Prediction Center (TPC). The National Hurricane Center is the forecast division of the TPC and still functions as the nerve center for the nation's hurricane-warning system. Technological advances over the last several decades have transformed hurricane forecasting into an accurate, timely, lifesaving service. The advent of radar, television, computers, weather-watching satellites, and regional evacuation planning has improved the system dramatically. As a result, coastal residents can tune their televisions in to the unfolding drama of an approaching hurricane days before it strikes. This early-warning system clearly has been effective in saving lives, as casualties from modern hurricanes have shown a steady decline in the United States.

Hurricane research and forecasting are now entering a new frontier. Powerful new techniques are being used to study these storms, including supercomputer atmospheric modeling, Doppler radar systems, high-altitude jet aircraft reconnaissance, and global weather studies to predict seasonal trends. But even with the recent advances in technology, the business of predicting exactly when and where hurricanes will strike remains a tentative one. The unpredictable nature of some fast-moving storms can still leave coastal residents with very little time to evacuate vulnerable areas. Densely populated coastal cities and remote islands like the Florida Keys still find their roads jammed with vacationers and residents scrambling to avoid approaching hurricanes. And even with today's advanced warning system, those who refuse to evacuate face the same perils endured by coastal residents a hundred years ago.

THE NAMING OF HURRICANES

Alma and Betsy broke my heart,
Camille made me cry,
Donna swept me off my feet,
And left me high and dry,
Eloise was a tease,
She made me run and hide,
These ladies won't leave me alone,
I'll never turn their tide.
—Untitled poem in *The Marketeer*, 1975

Radar was a useful tool for tracking hurricanes in the 1950s. This unit in Pensacola was one of five in Florida at the time. (Photo courtesy of the Florida State Archives)

Reconnaissance aircraft called "hurricane hunters" began flying missions into hurricanes during the 1940s to gather information on storm position, movement, and intensity. Today NOAA also uses this Gulf Stream IV jet to gather data from high altitudes. (Photo courtesy of NOAA, National Hurricane Center)

As each hurricane season begins in the Atlantic, forecasters offer daily updates and watch for the first storm of the year to earn a name. A name is assigned once a tropical depression's winds reach 39 mph and a tropical storm is born. Throughout the season, a predetermined list provides the names for the storms, in alphabetic sequence. Attaching a proper name to a tropical cyclone may seem a bit frivolous, but the practice actually serves several beneficial purposes for forecasters and emergency planners.

During the first few centuries after the discovery of the New World, great hurricanes were often reported in letters, ship logs, and other documents. Although there was no system for naming storms through these early years, some severe hurricanes were given names. Word spread about these great storms, and they became known for the islands they devastated, the ships they sank, or the religious holidays nearest the time of their approach. The Santa Ana storm of 1825, Racer's Storm in 1837, the Cuba hurricane of 1870, and the San Ciriaco storm in 1899 are examples of early hurricanes that were given names. A deadly and destructive hurricane that swept the island of Dominica in September 1834 came to be called the Padre Ruiz hurricane because its arrival interrupted funeral services for a priest of that name who had passed away in Santa Barbara. But most of the great storms of the past few centuries are known only by

The Tropical Prediction Center/National Hurricane Center, currently located on the campus of Florida International University in Miami, is the nation's nerve center for hurricane tracking and forecasting. (Photo courtesy of NOAA, National Hurricane Center)

the date of their occurrence or the location of their greatest damages—like the Great Storm of 1780 or the Galveston hurricane of 1900. Since few early hurricanes were identified by name, it was difficult for those who kept historical records to make references and comparisons.

Through the nineteenth century, in the early days of hurricane tracking, storms were identified by their position at sea—the latitude and longitude of the latest ship report. Although this method allowed hurricanes to be graphed on maps, describing their location by their numerical coordinates was confusing. It was especially confusing when several tropical storms or hurricanes were active at the same time. During the late 1800s, hurricane tracking became more comprehensive. It was during this time that Clement Wragge, an Australian meteorologist, began the practice of using women's names for tropical storms. But throughout the early years of the twentieth century, hurricanes were officially referred to by number rather than by name. For example, the fourth tropical storm of the 1933 season was known as hurricane number 4.

Eventually, military weather observers began using code names from a phonetic alphabet to identify storms—Able, Baker, Charlie, and so on—which made storms easier to distinguish and track. In 1950 the Weather Bureau officially began using this method to aid in the forecasting and warning of hurricanes. After George R. Stewart used a woman's name for a hurricane in the 1941 novel

Storm, the practice continued during World War II. Air force and navy meteorologists who tracked the movements of typhoons across the wide expanses of the Pacific frequently assigned female names to storms. This system became official in 1953, when the Weather Bureau began using female names for storms in the Atlantic. It continued through the late 1970s, until women's groups and several countries lobbied the World Meteorological Organization to change the naming system. In 1979 men's names and names of international origin were added to the lists.

Today the National Hurricane Center assigns each emerging tropical storm a name from a predetermined list. Six different lists of names are used on a rotating basis; the cycle repeats every six years. Each year's list consists of twenty-one names, from A through W, and each year the first name on the list alternates between male and female names. No hurricane names begin with Q, U, X, Y, or Z because few names begin with those letters. Separate lists of names are used to identify tropical storms that form in the Pacific. The 2005 Atlantic hurricane season was the most active ever recorded, with twenty-seven named storms. For the first time ever, all twenty-one names were used, forcing officials to name the next storm of the season Alpha—the first letter in the Greek alphabet. Amazingly, the storms kept coming, and Beta, Gamma, Delta, Epsilon, and Zeta soon followed. Prior to 2005, the busiest season on record was 1933 with twenty-one storms (though none were given names), followed by 1995 with nineteen.

A name is retired from the list if it was given to a hurricane that caused great destruction or loss of life. It is replaced by another name that begins with the same letter. Andrew, Charley, Ivan, and Katrina are recent examples of hurricane names that will never be used again.

This international system for naming tropical cyclones has proven effective in eliminating confusion and promoting awareness throughout the many regions affected by hurricanes. Although the names don't always seem to fit the "character" of the storms, many hurricanes are fixed in our memories with a name attached—like the horror of Andrew or the anxious arrival of Opal. Names help hurricane forecasters track storms, alert and involve the general public, and provide historical reference. As years go by, names are easier to remember than dates and numbers. Also, for some, it may be helpful to be able to focus the angst and frustration felt in the wake of a destructive storm on an entity with a name. This personification of disaster has become part of our hurricane experience.

EARLY FLORIDA HURRICANES, 1546–1799

Eyes never beheld the seas so high,

angry and covered by foam.

We were forced to keep out in this

  bloody ocean,

seething like a pot of hot fire.

Never did the sky look more

  terrible;

for one whole day and night it

  blazed like a furnace.

The flashes came with such fury

  and frightfulness

that we all thought the ships

  would be blasted.

All this time the water never

  ceased to fall from the sky.

—*Letter from Christopher*

  Columbus to Queen Isabella

  of Spain, 1494, cited in

  The Hurricane Handbook,

  by Sharon Carpenter and

  Tonie Carpenter

(Page 39)
*Early Florida map by Giovanni
Maria Cassini, 1797. (Courtesy
of the R. M. Strozier Library,
Florida State University)*

Long before Christopher Columbus sailed into Caribbean waters in search of a new route to the Orient, hurricanes and tropical storms battered the islands, bays, and continental shorelines of the New World. Geologists who have studied sediment samples from West Florida and other areas along the Gulf coast have found evidence of great storm surges and freshwater flooding thousands of years ago. Native civilizations certainly endured devastating storms for centuries, well before the first European settlements. Then, late in the fifteenth century, along with their discovery of the New World, Europeans discovered the tempestuous wrath of hurricanes.

Columbus provided the earliest account of a hurricane in a letter to Queen Isabella in 1494. His first exploration in the fall of 1492 was apparently hurricane-free, and he encountered a strong winter storm in the Azores on his voyage the following year. But it is believed that he experienced his first true hurricane on July 16, 1494, about which it was written that "nothing but the service of God and the extension of the monarchy should induce him to expose himself to such dangers." In June of the following year, Columbus was hit by what was probably a hurricane while anchored at the European settlement of Isabella on Hispaniola. As the tides and waves rose, two of his ships capsized and sank; only the *Niña* survived. Crude island huts were blown to pieces by the storm's winds, and great trees were twisted out of the mud. Spanish historians later reported that this hurricane was God's judgment on the town's residents for their brutal treatment of the native inhabitants.

On his fourth and final voyage in the summer of 1502, Columbus arrived in Hispaniola in time to see the signs of an approaching storm. The seasoned admiral sent his captain ashore to warn the island's governor, Nicholas de Ovando, and request safe harbor. The boorish Ovando ignored the warning and denied shelter to Columbus and his ships. He then arrogantly ordered his own large fleet of ships, carrying slaves and gold, to sail to Spain immediately. The hurricane soon overcame the expedition; 20 ships and over 500 lives were lost in the violent seas. Santo Domingo was leveled by the hurricane, as it would be by many storms to come. Columbus, experienced in the ways of the sea, safely rode out the hurricane under anchor in a nearby island cove.

Stories of great storms are spread throughout the early centuries of New World explorations. Our knowledge of hurricanes from the past comes from the pioneering efforts of several weather historians who researched and collected information on scores of storms through the years. In his 1952 book *Hurricanes: Their Nature and History*, Ivan R. Tannehill offered a list of past hurricanes, based on the 1856 work of an early meteorologist, Andreas Poëy of Havana. Poëy's list of hurricanes was compiled from the accounts contained in over 450 books and periodicals, including the writings of William Redfield, an early American meteorologist. Although it became a valuable resource for Tannehill and many others who have studied hurricane history, Poëy's list included storms that occurred throughout the calendar year, many of which were not true hurricanes. In 1963 the definitive record of America's early bouts with tropical weather was written by weather historian David M. Ludlum for the American Meteorological Society. In *Early American Hurricanes, 1492–1870*, Ludlum chronicled hurricanes through more than 350 years of colonial development. Ludlum, who died in 1997, penned numerous other articles and books on weather history, many of which were consulted in the writing of this book.

These well-researched historical collections provide the primary background for the early history of hurricanes in Florida. As with many historical writings, a great debt is owed to those like Poëy, Tannehill, and Ludlum whose original research became the foundation for later compilations. Along with the publications mentioned above, many other valuable references were used to compile this early history, including newspaper accounts, ship logs, letters, government reports, and numerous historical articles and publications. Although these sources offer specific reports of storms affecting Florida, it is likely that countless hurricanes have battered the Sunshine State over the centuries for which no record exists.

In 1513 Juan Ponce de León completed the first recorded cruise along the Florida coast and came ashore near present-day St. Augustine to claim Florida for Spain. Famous for his unsuccessful search for a Fountain of Youth, he might have discovered Florida earlier had it not been for the ravages of hurricanes. In August 1508, he was struck by two hurricanes within two weeks. The first drove his ship onto the rocks near the port of Yuna, Hispaniola, and the second left his ship aground on the southwest coast of Puerto Rico.

Soon after Hernando Cortés found treasures of gold and silver in the newly discovered lands of the West, expeditions to retrieve the riches of the New World for Spain began in earnest. In 1525 Cortés lost the first ship he sent to Mexico in a severe hurricane, along with its crew of over seventy. But the dangers of stormy seas did not dissuade the Europeans from returning to conquer native tribes and plunder their gold. Soon annual treasure fleets were returning to Spain loaded with gold, silver, and slaves. Each year the ships would gather in Havana for a scheduled March return, but their mission was usually distracted by the many fiestas, banquets, and religious ceremonies that began in the spring and lasted through the summer. Not wanting to miss out on a good party, they often postponed their departure until August or September—the height of the hurricane season. As a result, many of the ships that left port in Havana never made it to Spain. Because of the frequency of hurricanes, it was said that "a ship was sunk for every lonely mile of the unexplored Florida coast."

The officers and crews of the Spanish fleets knew the risks of hurricanes and would only set sail once their ships had been blessed by local priests. These religious ceremonies were performed against a backdrop of pealing cathedral bells and burning incense. Because safe passage at sea depended so much on good weather in October, the month dedicated to St. Francis of Assisi, various legends and lore soon developed regarding St. Francis and his connection with nature, including tropical weather. It was believed that he used the knotted cord around his waist to fend off the evils of hurricanes. The "cord of St. Francis," a small piece of rope with three knots of three turns apiece, was displayed in homes, churches, and shipboard cabins to protect against storms during hurricane season. Some descendants of African slaves in the West Indies still tie knots in the leaves of certain trees and hang them in their homes to ward off hurricanes.

Hurricanes were sometimes pivotal events in the early history of Florida. In her book *Hurricane*, Marjory Stoneman Douglas describes with stunning detail Florida's early hurricanes. She first gives the account of Domingo Escalante Fontaneda, a thirteen-year-old shipwrecked in a hurricane on the Florida Keys in 1546. He was captured by a native tribe and taken northward to a river and a place called "Mayaimi," named for the tribal chief. There he was held prisoner along with other shipwrecked souls, but he learned the native language and saved himself from sacrificial execution. In later years, he was rescued from the Glades tribe and returned to Spain, where he wrote his account of these early Floridians. Time and again after hurricanes and tropical storms, these natives scavenged the wrecks of Spanish ships for metals, cookware, and tools, as well as gold bars, silver ingots, ornaments, and jewels. They captured prisoners and profited from the unfortunate Europeans.

Douglas also describes the grim tale of an enormous fleet carrying a thousand passengers that was lost in a hurricane during this period. The storm swept the fleet northward along the west coast of Florida, sinking the ships and their treasures and drowning most of the passengers. About 300 survivors made it to shore and began a gruesome march along the Gulf coast toward Panuco. Many were soon killed by natives, and most of the others died of exposure, starvation, or drowning. The only survivor was a priest who was rescued by a friendly tribe.

When Philip II became king of Spain, he decreed that both Florida coasts would be settled by the Spaniards. The new ports would harbor naval ships and provide protection from French pirates and hurricanes for his gold-laden galleons. In 1559 he dispatched Tristán de Luna to the New World as admiral of his fleet and governor of Florida. On the western coast, de Luna was to establish a suitable port for Spain. On June 11, he left Veracruz, Mexico, with thirteen vessels, all well stocked with supplies and over 200 horses. On August 14, de Luna and his fleet sailed into Ochusa, which he thought would make a fine port. There he claimed Florida for Spain and began efforts to establish a town. His plans were short-lived, however, as just a week later a powerful hurricane swept over de Luna and his men, devastating the newborn settlement. Hundreds were killed, and all plans for creation of a town were dashed. The port of Ochusa was located at present-day Pensacola, which, if not for the ravages of this great hurricane, might have been the first city in America.

King Philip changed his mind after de Luna's failure and sent him a message to give up all ideas of settlement on the Gulf coast because the hurricanes there were too lethal. He ordered him to sail to Florida's east coast instead and establish a stronghold for Spain at Santa Elena. In desperation, de Luna patched together a trio of vessels and sent them out under the command of his inexperienced nephew. This small fleet never found Florida's east coast and was lost in a hurricane in the Gulf of Mexico. In 1993 archaeologists found what was believed to be the wreckage of one of de Luna's ships near the Florida coast. De Luna was one of many early adventurers who found their plans for New World colonization thwarted by hurricanes.

In 1565 another hurricane brought about a notable change in the course of Florida history. The French had set out to challenge the Spaniards' ownership of the New World, and Jean Ribault led the expedition to claim territories for France. Late in 1564, Ribault and his aide, René de Laudonnière, built Fort Caroline as a French stronghold on the Atlantic coast near present-day Jacksonville. In the following summer, Ribault learned that a Spanish fleet led by Pedro Menéndez de Avilés was nearby. Menéndez had just established St. Augustine to the south, which posed an obvious threat to France's territorial claim. Ribault and his armada chased Menéndez down the Florida coast to the harbor at St. Augustine, where both fleets encountered a terrible storm on September 22.

The hurricane's high winds dismasted and wrecked Ribault's ships, whereas Menéndez wisely grounded his vessels and took his men on a course over land. They walked northward along the coast, through swamps and thickets and across rivers, until they finally reached the unguarded Fort Caroline. The Spaniards then captured the garrison and executed its male inhabitants. Meanwhile, Ribault and his men were shipwrecked by the storm south of St. Augustine. Menéndez eventually found Ribault and had him promptly beheaded. Because of this turn of events during the hurricane of 1565, the French lost their bid to control the Atlantic coast of North America and the future of Florida.

Pedro Menéndez Marqués, Menéndez's nephew, was the first to survey the Florida coast. In 1574 his ship went aground in a hurricane at Cape Canaveral. From there, he and seventeen of his crew were forced to walk the beaches northward to St. Augustine. As they crossed over swamps and inlets, they were followed by a threatening band of Native Americans. Marqués was able to save himself and his men from harm by mesmerizing the natives with his ardent gestures and elaborate speeches. The Native Americans trailed them all the way to St. Augustine, listening respectfully all the while.

Another useful publication offering reports of early tropical storms and hurricanes is *The Deadliest Atlantic Tropical Cyclones, 1492–1994*, a National Hurricane Center technical memorandum published in 1995. In this well-researched report, Edward N. Rappaport and José Fernández-Partagás chronicle the most costly Atlantic hurricanes in terms of loss of life. Their records suggest that at least three more severe hurricanes battered the Florida coast in the sixteenth century. A storm in 1571 wrecked two ships—the *Santa Maria de la Limpia Concepcion* and the *San Ignacio*—and left few survivors. In 1589 a hurricane on Florida's east coast sank one of Perez de Olesbal's ships, killing all but forty of its crew. Just two years later, a severe storm sank twenty-nine ships, many of which were lost off the coast of Florida. Undoubtedly, many other hurricanes swept over the Florida Peninsula during this period but were either never encountered or never recorded by Europeans.

In the seventeenth century, the French, Spanish, and English continued their quest for dominance in the New World. And although European adventurers became more skilled at navigating the waters of the West, hurricanes and tropical storms continued to batter their ships and settlements. For a number of years, though, the Spanish treasure fleets were spared the scourges of pirates and hurricanes, and Philip III became increasingly dependent on the riches they delivered.

Then in September 1622 another hurricane blasted the Spaniards. In *Hurricane*, Douglas describes two great processions of ships that were affected by the storm. Both fleets were loaded with silver and bound for Havana when they were swept northward into Florida waters. Thirty-nine days later, most of the ships struggled into the harbor at Havana, including the *Candelaria*, which "was discovered to be overrun with rats that fouled the drinking water, ate the supplies and bit the sleeping people." Another fifty vessels that departed from Havana for Spain were also rocked by the hurricane. The storm then swept over Havana, filling its streets and harbor with debris. One week later, eighteen of the battered and weed-hung vessels limped back into harbor, their masts broken and splintered. The remaining ships were scattered by the storm. Fifty survivors had washed up on the Dry Tortugas, and sixty more were found floating on planks and debris along the Florida coast. One man was found adrift on a hatch cover off the Florida Keys and was said to have survived by eating a seabird that had landed on his head.

Few of the original expedition ever saw the coast of Spain, as hurricanes evidently chased the fleet westward. As many as nine Spanish ships sank in Florida waters, several west of the Tortugas. From these, 550 sailors were either drowned or killed by sharks. Among the most famous of these ships were the *Margarita* and the *Atocha*, which sank near Matecumbe Key. The *Atocha* was one of the ships from which famed treasure hunter Mel Fisher retrieved many artifacts in the 1980s.

Other hurricanes wrecked ships in Florida during the following decades, including storms in 1641 and 1695. Then, it was probably a hurricane in September 1697 that marooned Jonathan Dickenson on Florida's Atlantic coast. Dickenson, a Quaker merchant, had sailed out of Jamaica on the barkentine *Reformation* with his family and servants, bound for Philadelphia. Their ship was driven by the storm onto the beach near Jupiter Inlet, which he later described as "wilderness country looking very dismal," as Douglas reports in *Hurricane*. Dickenson and his storm-beaten family, having survived the battering of the storm's waves, were soon captured by Native Americans who were by no means friendly to the English. They were forced to march northward along the beach to St. Augustine, a distance of some 200 miles. He later wrote about the hurricane waters that flooded the Indian River.

By the end of the seventeenth century, new settlements were under way in several regions along the American coast, and hurricanes throughout the following decades continued to hamper their growth and development. The eighteenth century was a critical period for growth in the New World, as Spain, France, and England all struggled to maintain settlements in an effort to gain political and military advantages. Hurricanes frequently wrecked new towns, in many cases forcing the settlements to be relocated or abandoned. The storms brought losses to crops, livestock, dry goods, and shipping cargoes and threatened the very survival of the earliest European settlers.

The West Florida region, which at the time stretched as far west as the Mississippi River, was one area where great storms were frequently encountered. Accounts of hurricanes during this period became more regular, perhaps not so much because of an increase in tropical activity as because of the emergence of a more widespread population to observe them. An excellent compilation of hurricane history from this era is found in the article "A History of Hurricanes in Eighteenth Century West Florida" by Thomas Muir Jr., published in *Pensacola History Illustrated*. Muir summarizes the effects hurricanes had on the region: "The Eighteenth Century in West Florida began with the Spanish taking claim to Florida, the French to Louisiana. The earliest establishments, Pensacola, Mobile and New Orleans, were often times suspicious of each other, but were forced to cooperate occasionally for survival despite the political climate in Europe. Although well-acquainted with them from experiences in the previous century, Europeans still greatly feared the storms. Hurricanes at that time came without warning; there was no escape from destruction, and no one around to give immediate aid to the victims."

Through the early 1700s, the Spanish flotas continued the annual voyages from Havana they had made for decades, spiriting away the riches they had harvested from Mexico, Colombia, and Peru. Late in June 1715, a fleet of fifteen ships commanded by Admiral Don Juan de Ubilla sailed from Havana through the Straits of Florida, loaded with some 14 million pesos worth of gold, silver, and jewels. The Spanish flagship *Capitana* alone carried 1,300 chests of treasure, including a small strongbox filled with jewels intended for the queen of Spain. On July 31, the fleet was overcome by a hurricane that wrecked all but one of the ships along the coast between St. Lucie Inlet and Cape Canaveral, with a loss of over 700 lives. The fleet's precious cargo was sunk with the storm, but the Spaniards returned to the area the following spring and established a salvage camp just south of Sebastian Inlet. Using primitive methods, they reportedly retrieved much of the sunken treasure. But plenty remained below, and twentieth-century salvors and amateur treasure hunters have been successful in recovering artifacts and gold from the lost fleet. In 1970 the McLarty State Museum was constructed near the site of the old salvage camp, and today the museum displays more than $1 million worth of gold and artifacts from the expedition. Perhaps more than any others, these ships downed by the hurricane of 1715 have given this portion of Florida the nickname "treasure coast."

On the other side of the peninsula, in a letter to the king of Spain in 1716, the governor of Pensacola recommended that the settlement at Santa Rosa Island be moved because the "frequent hurricane characteristics of the region pounded away at the bastions, keeping them in a constant state of disrepair and unsuitable for defense." In August 1716, Diego Peña departed from St. Augustine on an expedition to Apalachicola, but his mission was delayed by a hurricane. In a notation made at the "Ocklocknee River" on September 10, cited in Muir's "History of Hurricanes," Peña described the turn to bad weather in late August and said that "God sent us a 'Uracan' of force that closed the road to us."

A strong September hurricane in 1722 blasted New Orleans, causing the Mississippi River to rise eight feet and leaving devastation from Natchez to Mobile. Over thirty-five houses, a church, and a hospital were destroyed in New Orleans. According to Muir's account in *Pensacola History Illustrated*, New Orleans would have been abandoned if all of the ships in port had not been wrecked by the storm. In a letter contained in Ludlum's *Early American Hurricanes*, it was reported that "great numbers of Cattle, Horses, Hogs, and some people were drowned. The deer were found frequently lodged on high trees." This hurricane likely swept the settlement at Pensacola as well. The French had occupied Pensacola in 1719 and held it briefly, but the Spanish were on their way to retake it when the hurricane of 1722 struck the area. The Spanish expedition dispatched for this mission, led by Don Alejandro Wauchope, encountered the three-day hurricane in the Gulf. When they arrived on the Florida coast in November, they found only a "dilapidated hut" still standing on Santa Rosa Island. Although it was reported that the French had destroyed the settlement, the September hurricane may have left little for them to burn.

As had happened so many times before, another large Spanish treasure fleet was wrecked in an Atlantic hurricane in July 1733. Led by Admiral Don Rodriguez de Torres, this fleet of twenty-one heavily loaded vessels and several armed galleons was wrecked on the reefs near Upper Matecumbe Key. According to her account in *Hurricane*, Douglas reported that Don Rodriguez "saved his galleon, thirteen ships and a great deal of silver, but he was forced to burn all the other wrecks to keep their cargoes from the Bahama pirates." Three of the best known of these vessels were the *San Jose*, the *San Pedro*, and the *Infante*. Once again, the ravages of wind and waves had spoiled the Spanish harvest of riches from the New World.

In the following years, several hurricanes apparently swept the northwestern Florida coast and blasted the Pensacola region. The Spanish settlement at Santa Rosa Island, so often hammered by tropical disasters, was "swept away" by a hurricane in 1736. Muir noted that most of the island's inhabitants were drowned in the storm. Just four years later, in September 1740, two hurricanes struck near Mobile within seven days. The first arrived on the eleventh and destroyed houses, drowned over 300 head of cattle, and "carried half of Dauphine Island away." It also blasted Pensacola just as the Spaniards were rebuilding their outpost. Then another storm came ashore on the eighteenth that flooded all of the rivers and bays of the region. Of greatest concern was the loss of the flour supply, which was washed away by the twin hurricanes. It was later reported that the storms brought famine to the surviving residents of the fledgling colony. Although England and Spain were essentially at war during the 1740s, it was said that more ships were lost to hurricanes during this period than to the perils of battle.

Over thirty shipwrecks in the Atlantic and Gulf of Mexico were attributed to a hurricane in October 1752, twelve of which were reported in the "Gulf of Florida"—the region between Florida and the Bahamas. The tenacious Spaniards had once again refortified their settlement on Santa Rosa Island when another fierce hurricane swept it away on November 3, 1752. Only two buildings were left standing; the garrison, village, and all of the island's dunes were washed away. After the storm, survivors scattered all around the bay. Some remained to try to rebuild on Santa Rosa and others moved inland to higher ground, but the hurricane had left the Pensacola settlement in disarray. With so many disasters in the colony's brief history, the king and his military advisers considered abandoning all plans to rebuild. But in 1757 the decision was made to continue the settlement on the mainland near the site of a Native American mission called San Miguel. Fort Miguel, the present site of Pensacola, was designated as the new presidio. Within a few short years, this new encampment was also tested by a hurricane. On August 12, 1760, another cyclone battered the Spanish colony. Every structure in the town lost its roof, and half the stockade was destroyed. It seemed that no matter where or how the Spaniards built their fortress, it was destined for destruction by hurricanes.

In 1759 a fierce hurricane apparently washed over the Florida Keys and was said to have "swept sea water over every bit of land from the Dry Tortugas to Key Largo." According to Douglas, an English ship called the *Ledbury* was caught by the hurricane and forced to drop anchor in Hawk's Channel. After the storm passed the following morning, the *Ledbury* was found high in the mangroves of Elliott Key, more than four miles away.

The Seven Years' War between England and France ended in 1763, and the terms of the treaty involved land trades with Spain. Florida became the property of Great Britain, and Spain acquired Louisiana and regained Cuba. In August 1763, the English took over the settlement at Pensacola, which had been merely a storm-worn outpost for the Spaniards. The English had plans to further colonize Florida and create new settlements. In November of that year, the Spaniards were preparing the garrison at Apalachicola for evacuation and British rule when another hurricane struck. Just before midnight on the sixteenth, as the storm's eye moved ashore, the winds changed direction and "increased to hurricane force." It may have been this hurricane that brought down the Spanish ship *Perdido*, drowning all of its crew. The *Perdido* is thought to have sunk near the mouth of the river on the Florida-Alabama border that now bears its name.

In 1766 several hurricanes were documented throughout the West Indies and the Gulf of Mexico. An October hurricane swept through the Gulf and wrecked a Spanish treasure fleet along the Texas coast before curving eastward through New Orleans. On October 22, the storm struck Pensacola and wrecked two brigs, four schooners, and several sloops in the bay. In a letter to General Thomas Gage, Colonel William Taylor reported the effects of the storm: "In a storm last night, rain came through the doors, walls, and roof; soldiers' huts were unroofed, conditions are intolerable." The tide at St. Marks was twelve feet above normal, suggesting a storm of considerable strength.

Under British rule, Florida was divided into two parts—East Florida and West Florida. The population of Pensacola was growing, and the English built more substantial housing for the soldiers. But just as the settlement had suffered through terrible hurricanes for more than a century of Spanish rule, the English also experienced the hardships brought by the storms. In *A Concise Natural History of East and West Florida*, Bernard Romans provides a detailed account of a hurricane that struck West Florida in 1772. According to Romans, the storm lasted from August 30 until September 3, and it "destroyed the woods for thirty miles from the sea in a terrible manner." At Pensacola all but one jetty was washed away, boats were driven ashore, and houses were destroyed.

The destruction was also severe at Mobile, where houses were blown down and ships and debris were washed into the streets. As had happened in many storms before, the colony's food supply was destroyed and survivors risked famine in the hurricane's aftermath. Romans reported that "vegetables were burned up by the salt water which was carried over the town so as to fall like rain at a distance of a half mile." He added: "The most extraordinary effect of this hurricane was the production of a second crop of leaves and fruit on all the mulberry trees in this country, a circumstance into which I very carefully enquired, but could not learn from the oldest and most curious observers that this had ever happened before. This tardy tree budded, foliated, blossomed, and bore ripe fruit with the amazing rapidity of only four weeks time immediately after the gust, and no other trees were thus affected."

A series of hurricanes battered the West Florida coast during the period of the American Revolution. In 1778, 1779, 1780, and 1781, storms brought destruction to ships, fortifications, crops, and the cargoes of war—and in some cases, they altered the course of battle. On the morning of October 9, 1778, Pensacola was rocked by a hurricane that sank over fourteen ships of the Royal Navy and caused extensive destruction to the wharves and buildings of the strategic port. The British governor wrote in the minutes of the Florida House of Assembly that a hurricane of "irresistible fury and violence" had prevented the assembly from meeting for more than a week and was "the severest hurricane ever felt or known in this part of the world since West Florida has belonged to the crown of Great Britain."

In August 1779, another severe hurricane swept over the West Florida region and hit New Orleans particularly hard. Loyalist William Dunbar, one of the first scientists to study the Gulf coast area, was under house arrest when the hurricane arrived. In "Remarks of the Climate of Mississippi," he wrote that the center of the storm passed over New Orleans and afterward not a single vessel could be seen on the river. More than half the houses lost their roofs or were blown down. It was also in New Orleans that Spanish governor Bernardo de Gálvez had assembled his forces for an attack on the British at Manchac and Fort New Richmond at Baton Rouge. According to Muir's account in *Pensacola History Illustrated*, de Gálvez had planned the assault for August 22, but in the early-morning hours of the eighteenth, the hurricane wrecked his fleet. Provisions for the expedition were ruined, and de Gálvez was forced to delay his plans. He later gathered the few ships that had survived the storm and successfully drove the British out of the Mississippi area.

The year 1780 is regarded as the most treacherous year for hurricanes in the eighteenth century, if not in the recorded history of the Western Hemisphere. At least eight hurricanes swept through the Atlantic, Caribbean, and Gulf of Mexico during the year, five of which came in October. Strange occurrences throughout the year preceded the deadly tide of tropical cyclones. Muir, in "A History of Hurricanes," reports that in Pensacola a chaplain wrote about the unusual events of February 6, which included "an earthquake shock so severe that in the barracks the weapons fell off the walls and furniture was overthrown in the rooms. Chimneys fell down. . . . Houses had tumbled down, and people buried underneath were crying for help. There was a tidal wave and lightning and thunder without ceasing." On May 19, the northeastern colonies from Pennsylvania to Maine were cast into darkness by the thick smoke of distant forest fires. Many believed the world was ending because the sun emitted such an eerie glow throughout the region. But these events were of minor consequence compared to the great hurricanes that would later boil out of the tropical Atlantic.

The hurricanes of 1780 are known for their great destruction and for the unparalleled numbers of deaths attributed to them. Because of their widespread damage to European navies, some may have altered the course of history. Even though most of the eight storms did not strike Florida, they had great political consequences for the region. The first was an August storm that made landfall near New Orleans—the third to do so in three years. Louisiana historian Charles Gayarré recorded that on August 24, 1780, "as if intended to be the last pound of weight wanting to break the camel's back, a hurricane, much more furious than the one that had prevailed the year preceding . . . destroyed all crops, tore down houses, and sank many vessels." Another report cited in Leslie R. Crown's *Hurricane Survival Guide* claimed that the storm "sank every ship in the Mississippi Delta." An American cargo vessel loaded with gunpowder capsized in the storm, diminishing the American war effort against the British on the Illinois frontier.

The first of the October storms was dubbed the Savanna-la-Mar hurricane for the Jamaican town it razed on October 3. This storm turned northward over Cuba and then overcame several large British fleets—one off the Florida coast, one near Cape Hatteras, and then one in the waters off Rhode Island. The hurricane sank at least thirteen British warships east of Daytona Beach, among them the *Phoenix* and the seventy-four-gun *Thunder*. The storm brought many others down as it curved to the north, dealing a staggering blow to the Royal Navy.

Just a week later, the most deadly hurricane of record in the Western Hemisphere swept through the eastern Caribbean on its way to Bermuda. It has come to be known simply as the Great Hurricane. In 1874 Elisee Reclus published *The Ocean*, which includes a description of the storm of October 10–18, 1780:

> Starting from Barbados, where neither trees nor dwellings were left standing, it caused an English fleet anchored off St. Lucia to disappear, and completely ravaged this island, where 6,000 persons were crushed under the ruins. After this, the whirlwind, tending toward Martinique, enveloped a convoy of French transports, and sunk more than 40 ships carrying 4,000 soldiers; on land the towns of St. Pierre and other places were completely razed by the wind, and 9,000 persons perished there. More to the north, Dominique, St. Eustatius, St. Vincent and Puerto Rico were likewise dev-

astated, and most of the vessels which were on the path of the cyclone foundered with all their crews. Beyond Puerto Rico the tempest bent to the northeast, toward Bermuda, and though its violence had gradually diminished, it sunk several English warships returning to Europe.

At Barbados, where the cyclone had commenced its terrible spiral, the wind was unchained with such fury, that the inhabitants hiding in their cellars did not hear their houses falling above their heads; they did not feel the shocks of the earthquake which . . . accompanied the storm.

It is believed that the Great Hurricane of 1780 killed 22,000 on its awesome week-long rampage. In the NOAA technical memorandum *The Deadliest Atlantic Tropical Cyclones, 1492–1994* by Rappaport and Fernández-Partagás, records show that the Great Hurricane "exceeds the cumulative loss in any year (except 1780) and, in fact, in all other decades." Although the largest numbers of people killed were island natives, the storm wrecked dozens of European settlements and killed thousands of people at sea.

Once again, the British navy was diminished by an October hurricane. In *Hurricane* Douglas summarized the scene: "This is the first hurricane in history which may be today traced in the painstaking day-to-day logbooks of those unhappy British ships which felt it to their shuddering oaken hearts. By masts lost, men lost, sails ripped to rags, rudders gone, deck houses and boats stove in, rigging parted, leaks, strains and breakages, the hurricane left a track thousands and thousands of sea miles long."

Even though neither of these October storms of 1780 directly affected Florida or the original colonies, they may have aided the American Revolution. By scuttling the prized British fleet across the Caribbean and the Atlantic, the two storms greatly diminished Great Britain's military advantage at sea. And the hurricane season wasn't over.

A third October hurricane came just as Field Marshal de Gálvez sailed out of Havana to attack Pensacola and reclaim Florida for Spain. His war fleet was led by Admiral Don Jose Solano, who took his flagship, the *San Juan*, seventy-four ships, and nearly 4,000 men out to sea on the sixteenth. Within two days, the seas began to pitch and a strong northeast gale blasted the fleet. De Gálvez's ship was battered and blown to New Orleans. Many others were rocked by the high seas and dismasted by the wind. One ship lost its figurehead to the high surf, and others jettisoned medical equipment, cannon, and horses to stay afloat. It is believed that over 2,000 sailors were lost in this storm.

Solano, separated from his fleet altogether, boarded another less tattered ship and sailed on to Pensacola. When he arrived, he found no other Spanish vessels and was forced to abandon his plans for ambush and return to Havana, where he rendezvoused with de Gálvez. Much later the English commanders in Pensacola learned how the storm had thwarted the attack. Because English historians used Solano's logbook to document the storm, it is known as Solano's Hurricane. It was the last of the tumultuous 1780 season.

Not to be extinguished by the weather, de Gálvez's passion to retake Florida inspired another expedition in May of the following year. But even the spring siege of Pensacola was not without an interruption by a storm. On May 6, 1781, a "great storm" blew into the area, forcing the Spanish fleets to pull up anchor and sail away. Troops on land saw their tents destroyed and were forced to stand in trenches of waist-deep water. Although it was probably not a hurricane, this storm brought a brief delay in the fighting, which resumed the following day. Solano was again a key figure in the voyage and attack, and ultimately he and de Gálvez were successful in reclaiming West Florida for Spain. With the signing of the Treaty of Paris in 1783, the Spanish regained rule of the Florida Peninsula.

Few other significant tropical storms or hurricanes are known to have affected Florida throughout the remainder of the eighteenth century. There was, however, one last storm in 1799, according to Muir's article in *Pensacola History Illustrated*. Muir reported that in September of that year, a controversial Englishman named William Augustus Bowles was wrecked in a hurricane off St. George Island while traveling aboard the British ship *Fox*. Bowles was on his way to Apalachicola when the storm hit. The *Fox* broke apart and sank near an area now known as Fox Point. The storm apparently lasted for three days, and the islands were reported to have been "covered with two feet of water." Bowles survived the ordeal, and the next year, he went on to declare war against Spain on behalf of the Creeks and create the State of Muscogee.

NINETEENTH-CENTURY STORMS,
1800–1899

The early part of the nineteenth century was a relatively quiet period for hurricanes in Florida. The political changes, however, were swift. During the War of 1812, Pensacola became a British naval base, but it was captured in 1814 by American troops. Then in 1819 Spain agreed to transfer possession of Florida to the United States, which formally took control two years later. During this period, hurricanes battered the Pensacola region and tested the Americans, just as they had the Spanish and the British. A September storm in 1819 made landfall somewhere between New Orleans and Apalachicola and dumped heavy rains for many miles inland. Two years later, another September hurricane struck the same area in much the same way. Damages to ships and structures were heavy in New Orleans and Mobile. In Pensacola damage to structures was not severe, but six brigs and schooners were driven ashore. At Fort St. Marks high waters flowed into the soldiers' quarters to a depth of two feet.

A powerful September hurricane is believed to have bounced off the South Florida coast in 1824 as it continued on a long and destructive journey. Hurricane historian Donald Gaby did the sleuthing on this storm and pieced together its probable path. Gaby, former manager of NOAA's Satellite Field Services Station in Miami, took clues about the storm from a number of different sources, including Andreas Poëy and David M. Ludlum. He was able to document the first signs of the hurricane in Guadeloupe on September 7 and then traced it to western Puerto Rico on the tenth, the Lower Bahamas on the twelfth, and the Miami area on the fourteenth.

Gaby found an intriguing reference in the pages of *Florida Wild Life*, a book by Charles Torrey Simpson published in 1932. Simpson was a retired Smithsonian botanist who resided on Miami's Biscayne Bay. After he lost countless trees on his property in the terrific hurricane of 1926, he studied their condition. As Simpson was clearing the damaged oaks and pines from the woods near his home, he counted their rings and found that they were all about a hundred years old. He theorized that a great hurricane must have leveled the forest sometime just before 1826.

Gaby discovered a letter in the National Archives that provided additional evidence of an 1824 hurricane off the Florida coast. In the *Lighthouse Letters*, it was reported that the storm sank the ship carrying Samuel B. Lincoln, who was under contract to build lighthouses in Florida. The loss of construction materials aboard the ship delayed the construction of the Cape Florida and Key West Lighthouses for a year. Gaby found another record of the storm in its final fury, when it apparently made its second landfall on September 16 at St. Simons Island on the Georgia coast. There the hurricane's storm surge delivered heavy destruction and drowned eighty-three people; more people were killed farther up the coast.

Newspaper reports about the storm referred to it only as a "gale," a common reference at that time. Weather records from St. Augustine during this period did not mention a storm, even though a shift of wind occurred there on the fifteenth. From this, Gaby has deduced that the hurricane struck Florida first near Miami, curved back into the Atlantic, slid past St. Augustine while at sea, and turned inland again over Georgia. The precise course of the hurricane of 1824 may never be known, but it would appear that parts of the Florida coast were involved.

Andrew Jackson, who served briefly as provisional governor of Florida in 1821, was occupied with battling the Seminoles and running for the presidency during the 1820s. In August 1827, a devastating hurricane swept through the Caribbean and left heavy damages in the West Indies. Hardest hit were Anguilla, St. Kitts, Nevis, and the Virgin Islands. Although the storm never struck the Florida coast, Jackson became involved in the trade-policy debate that followed the storm. President John Quincy Adams had prohibited trade with the British West Indies, but after the storm, the badly damaged island ports were opened to free trade for three months. Jackson's protests against closing the island ports to American ships drew support from several powerful shipping interests and helped him win the presidency in 1828.

William Redfield, one of the earliest Americans to study tropical storms and hurricanes, reported on two hurricanes that struck Florida in 1830—one on August 15 and the other a week later on August 22. Both storms apparently curved along the Florida coast, then went on to hit Charleston, South Carolina, on their way toward Nova Scotia. The following year, Redfield recorded another hurricane that was first seen in Barbados on August 10, then crossed over Cuba on the fourteenth, swept over the Keys the next day, and finally bashed New Orleans on the sixteenth. In 1831 Redfield wrote in the *American Journal of Science and the Arts* that this powerful storm had a devastating effect from the Caribbean to America, "destroying property valued at a half a million and causing the death of 5,000 individuals. In the Barbados, no fewer than 1,477 persons perished within seven hours!"

The first "documented" hurricane to strike Key West arrived in September 1835. The *Key West Enquirer* reported that the "severe gale" lasted for two days. It also stated that a British navy officer had forecast that 1835 would be filled with "gales of wind and other atmospheric phenomena" due to the expected appearance of Halley's Comet. During the storm, waters near Cape Florida were of "astonishing height" and "many of the islands were completely overflowed; and at Key Biscayne the water was four feet deep around the light house premises, carrying away the keeper's stock of poultry." According to Donald Gaby's article "Historic Hurricanes in South Florida" in *Update*, this storm was also responsible for creating Norris Cut. Up the coast at Ponce de León Inlet, a newly erected brick lighthouse was undermined and toppled by the storm, just days before the scheduled arrival of its first order of lamp oil.

The storm entered the Gulf of Mexico and recurved to the northeast, where it struck the Tampa area the following day. At Fort Brooke on Tampa Bay, the weather was "very stormy" on the night of the sixteenth. Damage estimates for the area amounted to $200,000—a considerable sum for an area with little development. After spinning across the West Florida coast, the hurricane then tracked northward through Georgia and the Carolinas and was reported to have caused damage "all the way into New England."

By the late 1830s, the towns along Florida's northwest coast were growing steadily, even though a financial depression was gripping the nation. Residents of Pensacola, Apalachicola, St. Marks, and St. Joseph were busy building new shops, wharves, and homes. As steam railways spread throughout the region and cotton exports grew, fierce competition developed among these ports of trade. Their prosperity continued to be disrupted, however, by the recurrence of destructive tropical weather.

The hurricane season of 1837 was very active, with at least eleven tropical storms or hurricanes of record. In his *Law of Storms*, published in England in 1838, Lieutenant Colonel W. Reid of the Royal Engineers described three hurricanes affecting Florida in 1837. The first struck north of the Miami area on July 30 and then crossed the peninsula into the Gulf. Ludlum surmised that it may have been this same hurricane that hit St. Marks on Apalachee Bay on August 7. At the lighthouse, waters were six feet above normal, and in town, floodwaters were two feet deep in the streets.

The second hurricane followed a few days later, making landfall south of St. Augustine on a northwest course through Tallahassee. The third was born in the Gulf and made landfall east of Apalachicola on August 30. Damage from this hurricane was severe, as ships were wrecked and homes and wharves were washed away. In St. Joseph a three-story building was "razed to the ground." The damages in Apalachicola were first estimated to be $200,000, but that figure was later reduced. The editor of the *Apalachicola Gazette* summarized the scene: "I write from the midst of ruins."

One other hurricane of the 1837 season is known to have struck western Florida in early October. Dubbed "Racer's Storm" after its encounter with the British sloop *Racer* in the Yucatán Channel, this storm would become one of the most infamous hurricanes of the nineteenth century. Its path and history were also reported in the writings of Lieutenant Colonel Reid. Racer's Storm was first spotted in late September southeast of Jamaica, where Kingston was inundated for two days. On October 4, it completely destroyed Brazos Santiago on the Mexican coast, then curved northward with destructive force through Brownsville and Galveston. The hurricane followed the coast eastward and passed over New Orleans and Mobile and just north of Pensacola. On October 8, the storm tracked across South Carolina and returned to sea near Charleston. Heavy damages were reported in dozens of cities and towns along the storm's destructive course, which was more than 2,000 miles long.

As the hurricane moved into the Atlantic, it wrecked the new paddle-wheel steamer *Home* off of Cape Hatteras. Only 40 of the ship's 130 passengers were saved; the rest, mostly women and children, drowned in the violent seas of the storm. The ship had been equipped with only two life preservers. As a result of this great tragedy, Congress passed a law requiring all American vessels to carry one life preserver for each passenger—a law that has saved countless lives since that time.

One of the most bustling ports in West Florida during this period was St. Joseph. In this city of over 4,000, land speculation was rampant and parties and balls filled the taverns and hotels. Its fast-spending cotton traders, coarse sailors, and easily found liquor earned the town a reputation for wickedness. But in 1841 an epidemic of yellow fever swept through West Florida, and Apalachicola and St. Joseph were ravaged by the disease. Out of fear of becoming infected, many people left the coastal towns, never to return. By late summer, the population of St. Joseph was reduced by death and desertion to fewer than 500 people. The newspapers of both Apalachicola and St. Joseph suspended publication. Then, as if Mother Nature sought to make an example of the town, St. Joseph was "completely destroyed" by a hurricane in September. Little is known about the storm, except that not much was left of the once lively port. For many years afterward, Florida circuit riders preached that the plague and the hurricane were a judgment from God for the sins of the town.

Late in October 1841, a Caribbean-born hurricane swept northward through Havana and into the Florida Keys. According to the local press, the storm tide in Key West harbor was the highest remembered by the oldest inhabitants. Many ships were run aground, especially at Mango Key, nine miles east of Key West. The storm then apparently moved northward and struck near Punta Rassa, where it crippled Fort Dulany, killed two people, and floated the steamship *Isis* into the middle of the camp.

In *Early American Hurricanes, 1492–1870*, Ludlum documented three hurricanes that affected Florida in 1842. The first was named "Antje's Hurricane" by Redfield because it was first spotted north of Puerto Rico by the crew of the HMS *Antje* on August 30. On September 4, the storm hit Key West, although the wind caused little damage to shipping. Nearby islands were not so lucky, however. Ludlum reported that "half of Sand Key blew away. The light tender's house was demolished. The storm tide also washed away the Dove Key Beacon nearby."

Pensacola was struck by a storm that may have been of less than hurricane strength on September 22, 1842. The winds were described as "severe," but little damage was reported. Then, in late September, a hurricane was born deep in the Bay of Campeche that tracked across the Gulf of Mexico in early October. It was reported that many seabirds were later found dead in the waters of the Gulf, as the storm's winds prevented them from finding safe haven. This powerful hurricane swept inland in the extreme northeastern Gulf near St. Marks in the early-morning hours of October 5.

According to Ludlum, at Apalachicola the storm was "thought to be one of the severest gales on record." The lighthouse at East Pass was heavily damaged when it lost almost thirty feet of its height to the storm's winds. The keeper's house was "swept off the island," and his wife and many other island residents were drowned. Many houses in Apalachicola were unroofed by a gust of wind that came around 4:00 P.M. on the fifth. At Tallahassee initial damage estimates totaled $500,000, as homes and businesses lost roofs and windows to the high winds. Ludlum reported that "roads in all directions from the Florida capital were blocked with thousands of fallen trees." At Cedar Key "the water is stated to have risen twenty feet above low water mark, and within six feet of covering the island." According to the *Florida Herald*, St. Augustine experienced "the greatest gale ever remembered, at least for 15 years." As the hurricane re-entered the Atlantic and swept northward, stormy conditions were reported in Savannah, in Charleston, and near Cape Hatteras.

As railroads continued to be built along the West Florida coast, land developers offered lots for sale in new communities throughout the region. Port Leon was established in 1838 on the banks of the St. Marks River, about two miles below St. Marks. Within a few years, the new village had numerous shops, dwellings, docks, and warehouses and a small weekly paper. The highest elevation in town was not more than a few feet above sea level.

On the morning of September 13, 1843, residents of Port Leon awoke to a fresh breeze from the southeast, which gave way to a gale by afternoon. By midnight the wind was of hurricane force, and the entire town was washed over by a "tidal wave," which inundated the area in seven to ten feet of water. Newspaper accounts later exclaimed: "Our city is in ruins!" In his report of the destruction of Port Leon in *Florida Historical Quarterly*, historian T. Frederick Davis wrote:

Every warehouse in the town was laid flat with the ground, except that of Hamlin and Snell's, and a part of that also was demolished. Nearly every dwelling was thrown from its foundation and many of them crushed to atoms. The merchants took what precautions they could for protection against high wind and water before the height of the storm, by moving their goods, as they thought, out of danger. But the surging water and furious blasts were irresistible, and the goods in the stores were either destroyed or badly damaged. The store of Daniel Ladd was the least injured of any, although the water there was three feet above the counters; this building had the highest elevation of any in the town. Every dwelling house and store that was not demolished was left in a wretchedly shattered and filthy condition.

Miraculously, only one life was lost in Port Leon. The railroad that had brought the city into existence was washed away to a point north of St. Marks. All of the warehouses and most of the dwellings in St. Marks were also destroyed, but no lives were lost there. All of the resort cottages near the lighthouse below Port Leon were washed away, and "seven white occupants and five negro servants" drowned.

After the storm had passed, the dazed citizens of the devastated Port Leon assembled to discuss the fate of their town. Their unanimous decision was to not rebuild but instead relocate to higher ground farther up the St. Marks River. They salvaged what they could from the wreckage of their town and found a suitable site on the banks of the river four miles above St. Marks. There they established Newport in October 1843. This was not the first or the last time a Florida settlement was removed from the map by a hurricane.

In September 1844, a "tremendous gale" was reported in Apalachicola's *Commercial Advertiser*. On the evening of the eighth, the storm blew to a "perfect hurricane" and damaged trees, ships, and buildings. The tin roofs of the town's brick stores were peeled off and "flying through the air like scraps of paper." No lives were lost, however, and damage estimates were only about $20,000. The residents of Tallahassee were by now accustomed to late-season hurricanes, as evidenced by a comment in the following day's *Tallahassee Sentinel*: "Last night our annual September gale came in all its fury."

Redfield made careful study of a large storm in October 1844 he called the "Cuban Hurricane." This storm swept over Cuba, just eighty-five miles east of Havana, on the fifth. Although its track probably remained east of the Florida coast, its passing along the Keys left substantial destruction. The local paper in Key West, the *Light of the Reef*, reported that "houses, fences, trees, vessels, and almost everything in its course was leveled to the earth or borne off with frightful velocity." Key West recorded almost ten inches of rain on October 5. At Indian Key, much closer to the center of the storm, all homes were blown down and the wharves washed away. As the hurricane tracked to the north, great flood tides and severe winds were reported at Jupiter Inlet and St. Augustine.

After Florida became the twenty-seventh state in March 1845, one of the most significant hurricanes of the nineteenth century struck the state—the Great Hurricane of 1846. This storm was first detected south of Jamaica on October 6 and then went on to strike Cuba on the tenth with full hurricane force. Havana was hit hard by the storm, as homes and structures of all kinds were demolished by the fierce winds. Of the 104 vessels in the harbor at the time, all but 12 were either sunk, wrecked, or dismasted. The lowest barometric pressure reported was 27.06 inches, suggesting a storm of extreme intensity. Hundreds of lives were lost in Cuba.

The storm moved northward along the 82 degree meridian with very little loss of energy, and its effects began to be felt in Key West in the early-morning hours of October 11. By midday the winds were at full hurricane force, and the surging tide completely filled all of the town's streets to a depth of several feet. Colonel S. R. Mallory, a customs agent in Key West at the time, described the wind in a letter to the U.S. Secretary of Treasury: "At this time slates from roofs, boards and even heavy pieces of timber were driven through the air like straws, and one piece of plank, nine feet by fourteen inches wide came from a distance like an Indian arrow and penetrated through the weatherboards and ceiling into one of the Customs House rooms."

From noon on the eleventh until dawn of the following day, water stood three feet above the floors of most of the buildings along Duval Street and adjacent streets. Heavy timbers and debris choked every alley, most of which came from the collapse of nearby structures and the loss of all of the wharves. Apparently, only 8 of the 600 houses that stood on the island escaped destruction or damage from the storm.

The violence of the hurricane was at its peak during late afternoon and was witnessed by a Lieutenant Pease who was aboard a small naval vessel in Key West harbor. He wrote: "At 4 P.M. the air was full of water, and no man could look windward for a second. Houses, lumber, and vessels drifting by us—some large sticks of lumber turned end over end by the force of the current, and the sea running so high and breaking over us brought lumber, casks, &c. on board of us and across our decks."

The northeast side of the island was said to have been covered by 7.5 feet of water. It was here that Lafayette Salt Company and a military cemetery were washed away. Another burial ground on the southern side of the island was unearthed by the flood, and the dead were scattered through a forest, "many of them lodged in trees." This terrible scene was reported in a later edition of *Florida Historical Quarterly*: "The graveyard which was on the southern shore, was wholly uncovered, and bones, and skeletons, and coffins, dashed about, and scattered far and wide. After the storm subsided, one coffin was found standing upright against the bole of a tree, the lid open, and the ghastly tenant looking out upon the scene of desolation around, as if in mingled wonder and anger that its rest had been so rudely disturbed."

Two nearby lighthouses were destroyed in the hurricane. The Key West Lighthouse, built in 1825 to a height of eighty-five feet, was swept away by the awesome tide, and with it fourteen of the keeper's family and staff. The Sand Key Lighthouse was also toppled in the storm, killing the female keeper, Rebecca Flaherty, and her family. The tremendous tide also caused the "total disappearance of Sand Key." Soon after the storm, the Key West Lighthouse was relocated farther inland and rebuilt to a height of sixty feet. About forty years later, its height was increased by twenty feet.

Of a total population of some 2,000, only about 50 people in the Key West vicinity were lost to the storm. It was reported that many survivors swam or waded through streets of chest-deep water to gather at a point of high land about seventeen feet above sea level. Even at this location, they were nearly washed away by wind and waves.

The 1846 hurricane continued northward through the Gulf along Florida's west coast until it made landfall again near Cedar Key. As it passed along the west coast on October 14, a Manatee County plantation owner was drowned while crossing a river on horseback. According to an account by Karl H. Guismer in his book *Tampa*, Hector Braden was returning to his plantation from Tampa when the storm reached its peak. Both he and his horse went under while crossing the Little Manatee River. Supposedly, Braden's body "was found some days later still upright on his horse. The gruesomeness of the picture was accentuated by the fact that his eyes were wide open and in his hands were clenched the bridle reins and his riding whip." From there, the monster storm rolled through the Piedmont regions of Georgia, the Carolinas, and Virginia into Maryland, Pennsylvania, and New York. High winds and flash floods left a trail of destruction throughout the East.

Until the 1840s, Florida's bouts with hurricanes were experienced only in the cities and ports along the northwest coast, the east coast, and the Keys. But new settlements on the southwest coast would soon experience destructive storms. The "small village" of Tampa was bashed by a major hurricane in 1848. The town was built around Fort Brooke, an army garrison that occupied all of the land south of Whiting Street. On September 25, the hurricane piled waters into Tampa Bay, and a massive flood overcame Fort Brooke and the shops and homes of Tampa. A low-pressure reading of 28.18 inches was measured at the fort. The tide in the bay reportedly rose fifteen feet above the normal low water mark.

Guismer offered a detailed description of the 1848 hurricane in his book *Tampa*: "Early Monday morning the wind shifted to the south and finally to the southwest, blowing with dreadful fury. The rain fell in torrents. Water from the Gulf was blown into the bay and the wind kept sweeping it northward. Great waves began crashing in. The islands in the bay were covered and so was almost all of Interbay Peninsula. The garrison was almost entirely inundated, with mad waves pounding at the buildings. Up the river only the tops of trees could be seen through the driving rain. The wind was so fierce that people could move through it only by crawling on the ground."

According to Guismer, the worst of the hurricane was suffered by W. G. Ferris, an army sutler and store proprietor in Tampa. During the onslaught of the storm, Ferris carried his family to the Palmer house and then returned to his shop through chest-deep water and driving wind and rain. He narrowly escaped being crushed or drowned when a nearby warehouse crashed into the store; both buildings were swept away by the storm surge. At the Palmer house, the tide rose quickly and entered the first floor, where Ferris's family had gathered. Furniture began to float. In their escape, Josiah, the proprietor's son, "swam through the front door with a young girl in his arms." The family was able to retreat to higher ground and was eventually reunited with the battered storekeeper.

In the days following the storm, Ferris and the other merchants of Tampa searched through piles of debris for any goods they could salvage. Among the missing fixtures was Ferris's strongbox, which contained over $3,500 in gold and silver coins. The coins were to be used to pay survey crews employed in the area by the federal government. Because the store and its contents were washed into the river, it was feared that the coins would never be found. After several days of searching, the strongbox was finally recovered, with the cash still in it, at the foot of Washington Street.

In *Tampa*, Guismer also described the ordeal suffered by the keeper of the Egmont Key Lighthouse, who is said to have resigned his post after the storm:

> Down at Egmont Key, the lighthouse built during the Seminole War was badly damaged and so was the lighthouse keeper's home. When the keeper, Marvel Edwards, saw that waves were going to wash over the island, he placed his family in a boat and waded with it to the center of the island and tied it to cabbage palms. During the night the boat was lashed by the raging wind and on Monday the high water lifted it close to the tops of the trees. By the time the wind died down, the members of the family were almost exhausted. But they all survived the ordeal. When the water subsided the family returned home to find that all its possessions had been washed away or ruined by the water. The lighthouse was later rebuilt at a cost of $16,000, this time strong enough to withstand any storm.

After the hurricane, Tampa was a scene of devastation. Magnificent old oaks were toppled by the hurricane's winds. At Fort Brooke the barracks, horse sheds, and other structures were gone. The pine forest north of the garrison was filled with wreckage and debris. The hurricane's powerful surge had shifted sand all along the coast and reshaped many of the keys near Tampa Bay. Navigation routes were filled in and closed, making charts of the area produced before 1848 almost useless after the hurricane. In terms of intensity and destruction, the 1848 storm remains perhaps the greatest in Tampa's history.

Just two weeks later, on October 11, another hurricane emerged from the Gulf to strike Florida's west coast. This storm was not of the same intensity as the September hurricane, but its effects were felt over a broad area of coastline from Cape San Blas to Tampa Bay. Fort Brooke again experienced a very high tide, although this time the waters were some five feet less than the recently established record. Several ships endured the storm in the Gulf, one of which "had her lee rail under water for eight hours." Tallahassee and Jacksonville both reported being hit by the storm, which was the last of the many October hurricanes that battered Florida in the 1840s.

Another powerful Gulf storm charged into Apalachicola on August 23, 1850. Destruction along the wharves was significant, as this hurricane also carried with it a massive storm tide. Like so many times before, warehouses were flooded and trade ships damaged and sunk. The *Commercial Advertiser* reported that the storm tide covered Water Street, Commerce Street, and the upper end of Market Street. Water Street was filled with the trunks of trees and other debris that rendered it impassable. No significant damage was reported at St. Marks or Newport, but the Wakulla River bridge was carried away by the flood.

As the storm rolled inland, it dropped enormous amounts of rain on Georgia, the Carolinas, and Virginia. Major flooding occurred along the banks of numerous rivers, including the Dan in Virginia, which rose twenty feet above normal in some areas. Flash floods and high winds continued throughout the Northeast, and damage was reported across New England.

The Great Middle-Florida Hurricane of August 1851 was one of the most savage and destructive storms in the history of Apalachicola. It was first sighted east of the Windward Islands on August 16, and from that location, it tracked on a steady west-northwest course south of Puerto Rico, across Haiti and Cuba, and into the Gulf of Mexico. On August 22, it turned to the north and then the northeast, curving directly onto the Florida coast near Cape San Blas. The *Commercial Advertiser* reported that it was "the most destructive storm it [Apalachicola] has ever witnessed." The wind apparently blew for more than twenty hours, leveling houses of all sizes. Extremely high tides washed away warehouses and stores and all of their contents, "leaving the inhabitants without shelter and almost without food." All of the buildings on Water Street were destroyed, and "every house on Front or Commerce Street is in ruins." The steamer *Falcon* was driven upriver by the tide, where it capsized on an island. The Presbyterian and Episcopal churches were demolished, and "all three lighthouses were blown down or washed away." Five lives were lost at Dog Island, and several more people perished at Cape San Blas.

In Tallahassee the storm raged from about six o'clock in the evening of Friday, August 22, until sunrise on Sunday, August 24. The rain poured in torrents, and gusting winds caused significant damage. The *Tallahassee Sentinel* reported that "tall forest oaks were uprooted or rudely snapped asunder; China trees stood no chance, fences were prostrated, tin roofing peeled up like paper, roofs torn up, brick bats flying; and altogether such a general scatteration taking place as is not often seen." The winds were aptly described as "howling, hissing, whistling, moaning and groaning."

At St. Marks the water rose higher than all previous water marks on the old fort. Portions of the fortifications were swept away with the tide, and the storm waters destroyed all of the buildings and quarters inside the fort. The tide was said to have been at least twelve feet above normal water levels. Floodwaters were two feet deep in the warehouses, which caused goods including salt, cotton, and rosin to be washed away or destroyed. As the hurricane's tide rose in the streets of St. Marks, the townspeople were forced from their places of refuge and had to swim or float on planks to the safety of some railway baggage cars, which were positioned on high ground in a pine forest. Merchants, sailors, children, and slaves all huddled together during the ordeal and safely rode out the storm.

The 1851 hurricane was large and powerful. Its forces were felt in Key West, Fort Brooke, and Pensacola, even though the storm never directly struck these settlements. The hurricane wasn't finished when it left Florida; it went on to bring high winds and heavy rains to Georgia and the Carolinas before it returned to the Atlantic near Norfolk, Virginia.

The following year, two more hurricanes occurred in West Florida—one in August and another in October. The first made landfall near Pascagoula, Mississippi, around midnight on August 24. Mobile experienced, according to the *Mobile Tribune*, "the highest and most disastrous flood" it had ever known. Water filled numerous streets, including Front, Commerce, and Water Streets, in some places to a depth of ten to twelve feet. The hurricane's flood and high winds delivered damage typically seen along the Gulf coast: large trees downed everywhere, fences flattened, tin roofs peeled back, and shops and warehouses overflowing with ruined goods.

In *Early American Hurricanes*, Ludlum reported that Pensacola, on the eastern side of the storm, shared the same fate as Mobile. The winds in Pensacola were said to have been "force 10" on the Beaufort scale (hurricane-force winds are considered to be force 12) on the evening of August 24, and heavy rains poured over the town. A rain gauge there measured 13.20 inches between the twenty-third and the twenty-sixth, but "there was much more rainfall than indicated by the gage. The driving wind prevented the gage from holding the water, and at night the water was blown out when less than partly full, at least 18 inches fell during the storm."

The August hurricane moved northward into Alabama and Georgia with "great fury." High winds and heavy rains battered areas many miles from the coast. On the twenty-seventh, many bridges were washed away near Columbus, Georgia, and at Augusta two large bridges over the Savannah River were destroyed. Like many other Gulf hurricanes before it, the August storm of 1852 caused widespread destruction as it tracked northward across the Deep South.

In October 1852, just two months after the dreadful August hurricane, another storm swept through the Gulf and onshore. This storm made landfall east of Apalachicola, and the greatest destruction was reported in St. Marks and Newport. On the afternoon of the ninth, the fast-moving cyclone came ashore and its winds rapidly increased to hurricane force. In Newport the tides were seven feet above "ordinary spring tide," and considerable damages to wharves and warehouses were reported. At 2:00 P.M., the western end of the courthouse was blown down, and by 3:30 P.M., the entire structure was leveled. Judge William Council, who was in his chambers at the time, narrowly escaped being crushed by the collapse of the building.

In Tallahassee the storm lasted only six hours. High winds again leveled large trees, but the most notable damage occurred to the state capitol. A gust from the hurricane blew down a large chimney, which crashed through the roof and onto the floor of the senate chamber. Cotton crops were severely damaged in the surrounding counties and across Georgia. The storm tracked over northern Florida and exited into the Atlantic between Jacksonville and Savannah. Damages were widespread but were said to have been somewhat less than those from the August hurricane.

By the mid-1850s, Florida was becoming known as a haven for the well traveled, a respite for invalids, and a paradise for adventurers who came to hunt and fish. Many who visited in 1856, however, left with a less than enthusiastic report on the favors of the climate. The winter had been unusually cold and rainy—a Pensacola man apparently froze to death in an open boat on Lake George in February. But once again, as if playing a broken record, a late-summer hurricane battered the upper Gulf coast and chased away many who were seeking rest and recreation.

The 1856 Gulf hurricane was first noted as it passed through the Straits of Florida on August 27. Fort Dallas, on Biscayne Bay, reported strong winds, and Key West saw a heavy gale and a barometric low of 29.77 inches. The storm was apparently many miles to the south and west of the Keys, on a northwest course into the Gulf. For the next two days, numerous ships throughout the eastern Gulf of Mexico were beaten by the storm, including the SS *Florida*, which was blown ashore in St. Joseph Bay, a complete loss. At around midnight on the thirtieth, the center of the hurricane struck the coast somewhere west of Cape San Blas, near Panama City.

Apalachicola took another pounding from this "gale." In the early-morning hours on the day the storm hit, rising waters submerged the town's docks. By noon the waters reached the streets, and by dusk the winds reached full hurricane force. At 7:00 P.M., the tide rushed into the stores on Water Street, but the flood continued to rise until it reached its peak at three or four o'clock in the morning. Commerce Street was submerged to a depth of 3.5–4 feet. A report from the Apalachicola dispatch in the *New Orleans Daily Crescent* compared the storm to that of 1851: "As regards the violence of the gale, it approximates nearer to that of 1851 than any other—the gale was more protracted than that of 1851, though the water was not quite so high."

The center of the storm moved inland and passed over Marianna, which was considered "a wreck." Very high winds and heavy rains caused severe damage for miles inland. Ludlum's account of the storm suggests that unlike some of its predecessors, this hurricane maintained great energy after it continued inland. Many communities in the interior of Alabama and Georgia reported "their heaviest storm in many years." In Columbus, Georgia, streets and sidewalks were barricaded in every direction by fallen trees. Angry floods washed away countless bridges across Georgia and broke several factory dams. The corn and cotton crops suffered in the storm, and agricultural losses were extensive. The hurricane's trail of destruction continued through the Carolinas and Virginia. Blustery wind and rain were reported in Augusta, Savannah, Columbia, Charleston, and Norfolk, where the storm was said to have been "unequaled since 1846."

By 1860 the population of Florida had grown to 140,000. Even though they were often swept by great storms, the ports along the Panhandle coast were growing, as were the cities of Jacksonville and Tallahassee. Large plantations grew cotton, corn, sugar, and rice and shipped them on the railways that crisscrossed northern Florida. Trade ships loaded and unloaded their goods in ports all along the coast and delivered imports from other harbors. The shipping trade was never better—until a few hurricanes and a civil war disrupted it.

No less than three hurricanes hit the Louisiana coast during the 1860 season, and all three had a significant impact on cities and towns along the Gulf shore. The first came on August 11 with a twenty-foot surge at the Mississippi Delta south of New Orleans. The second occurred a month later, on September 14. Flooding in Mobile came within nineteen inches of the record for high water established there in August 1852. The third dreadful storm to strike the region took place in October and delivered high winds to New Orleans and the inland reaches of Mississippi and Alabama. During all three hurricanes, Pensacola and the western sections of Florida felt the shoulders of the storms, with high tides and gusting winds. Although the hurricanes' greatest impact was to the west, Florida residents were once again bruised by tropical weather.

After the outbreak of the Civil War, Florida separated from the Union on January 10, 1861, and joined the Confederacy. Most of Florida's coastal towns were captured by Union forces early in the war, but Tallahassee remained under Confederate control. A number of skirmishes were fought on Florida soil, including the Battle of Olustee, which took place in 1864 and was one of the last Confederate victories. Amazingly, after so many dreadful storms so far in the century, few significant hurricanes hit the Florida coast through the war years and the rest of the 1860s.

In 1870 President Ulysses S. Grant signed a proclamation giving the responsibility for weather forecasting and warning to the U.S. Army Signal Corps. Meteorological information from twenty-four stations could be collected by telegraph, including long-distance reports of hurricanes. Under orders from General Albert J. Myer, the first simultaneous gathering of weather data occurred on November 1, 1870. Weather maps for the nation were created with the data received. The number of reporting stations grew quickly to more than a hundred. Unfortunately the fragile nature of the early telegraph system caused frequent breakdowns in transmissions, especially during the critical time of a hurricane's landfall.

Just as the Signal Corps' weather program was getting off the ground in the fall of 1870, three hurricanes hit Florida—one near Pensacola and two near Key West. The first was a July storm that landed at Mobile, pushing water deep into the streets and unroofing houses. According to the *Mobile Daily Register*, it moved quickly through the city, lasting only two hours, yet dropped the barometer there to a low of 27.50 inches! Its impact on Pensacola, though not thoroughly documented, was likely to have been similar to that of other hurricanes that had struck nearby.

In October "twin" hurricanes lashed the Florida Keys in a period of less than two weeks. The first passed over Cuba on the seventh and dragged up the east coast of Florida at a snail's pace. Observers in Key West reported that winds near hurricane force lasted for four consecutive days. Northeast winds were recorded as force 10 at 9:00 P.M. on October 8 and 9. At 9:00 P.M. on the tenth, winds were still force 10 but from the north. By 2:00 P.M. the following day, they had shifted to the northwest but remained at force 10.

Just nine days later, a second storm crossed Cuba and passed west of the Keys. The wind in Key West was strongest from the southeast, and it blew at hurricane force for a short time on the morning of October 20. Significant damages to buildings and vessels were reported in the local press. But the two storms were not the worst Key West had seen. Ludlum wrote that in these two hurricanes "no major structural damage occurred and there were no unusual inundations."

In 1871 the Signal Corps' weather program recruited college graduates interested in serving as reporters in the field. A network of observers was developed, including several who watched for hurricanes along the Atlantic and Gulf coasts. This network would later become the U.S. Weather Bureau. In June 1872, the *Monthly Weather Review* made its debut; it continued to provide the official word on weather in the United States for many decades. In 1873, however, the observation program was curtailed due to budget cutbacks, and the Signal Corps instead relied on the dependable hurricane information provided by Father Benito Viñes of the College of Belen in Cuba. Throughout the 1870s, Father Viñes's hurricane reports were quite valuable to the United States. But his expenses for weather equipment and telegraph operations were greater than his budget, and he was given no financial support from the U.S. government.

Later, however, shipping interests, insurance companies, merchants' associations, and chambers of commerce helped pay for the expenses of operating his warning network.

Because of the organization of the weather program, more precise storm information was recorded after 1871. Its creation brought a new era in the documentation of hurricane histories, and this is reflected in numerous publications used as references in the completion of this book. One useful compilation of hurricane information is included in *Florida Hurricanes and Tropical Storms, 1871–2001*, by John M. Williams and Iver W. Duedall. This collection of storm reports from the Florida region was originally published by Sea Grant in 1994.

Another comprehensive listing of tropical storms and hurricanes is available in *Tropical Cyclones of the North Atlantic Ocean, 1871–1995*, by Charles J. Neumann, Brian R. Jarvinen, Colin J. McAdie, and Joe D. Elms, published by NOAA through the National Weather Service. This excellent year-by-year look at past hurricanes is updated annually and offers the track histories of every storm of tropical origin known to have moved through the Atlantic, Caribbean, and Gulf of Mexico. In addition to providing a time frame for each storm's movements, it is also the primary source for the tracking maps used in this book.

OCTOBER 6, 1873

At about the time the Signal Corps cut back its network of weather observers in September 1873, a major hurricane drifted westward from the Leeward Islands across the Caribbean into the Yucatán. On October 2, it reentered the lower Gulf and stalled off the Mexican coast. From there it recurved to the north and then almost due east, backtracking across the warm waters of the Gulf toward Florida. On the morning of October 6, the hurricane swept inland on Florida's southwest coast and completely inundated the small village of Punta Rassa. The town was destroyed by the hurricane's fourteen-foot storm surge. Little other information is available on this hurricane, except that it exited on Florida's east coast near Melbourne.

SEPTEMBER 27–28, 1874

In 1874 another September storm came from the Gulf and crossed the Florida coast near Hog Island, just north of Cedar Key. Few reports of local damage are available, but this hurricane had a life beyond the borders of Florida. After passing south of Lake City and exiting the coast near Jacksonville, the storm system curved out to sea and followed the Gulf Stream toward the north. It went on to disrupt shipping and down trees in North Carolina, Virginia, and several more states to the north. According to an article by Patrick Hughes in *Weatherwise* titled "Hurricanes Haunt Our History," this was the first hurricane ever seen on a weather map. The Signal Corps map of September 28, 1874, showed the storm over the coastal waters between Jacksonville and Savannah.

1876

The hurricane of September 1876 first left its mark on Puerto Rico on the thirteenth. NOAA's track of the storm shows it moving rapidly through Haiti, over Cuba, up Florida's east coast, and into the central North Carolina coast. The official track shows that the eye of the storm never made landfall in Florida but remained twenty to thirty miles off the coast from Palm Beach to Melbourne. In *Florida Hurricanes and Tropical Storms, 1871–2001*, the authors contend that the storm actually did come ashore in Florida, citing a letter written by G. W. Homes, who lived in Eau Gallie, now part of Melbourne. Homes reported that the wind was "from the east at over one hundred miles an hour" and that the hurricane's eye passed over Melbourne. He wrote: "The vortex [the eye] came on us for about four hours, during which not a leaf stirred. We began to look for our boats when all at once with a tremendous roar the wind came from the west, with equal violence in the early part of the night."

In mid-October, a second hurricane turned toward Florida. From the seventeenth through the nineteenth, it swept through the Grand Caymans and western Cuba, where it made landfall with 120 mph winds. Because of its severity, throughout the region it became known as "Huracan de Gran Cayman–La Habana." It weakened after passing over Cuba and continued north toward the Keys. It struck Florida's southwest coast on the twentieth with winds over 90 mph. By the following day, the storm had crossed the peninsula and exited the coast near Melbourne.

OCTOBER 3, 1877

In 1877 three hurricanes passed through Florida in September and October, but the most significant was the hurricane of October 3. Like many other long-lived storms of the nineteenth century, its destruction was spread from the Caribbean to Canada. On September 21, the hurricane was first reported east of Grenada. Its low trajectory carried it through Curaçao, where the loss of life was great and damages caused by high waves and mudslides were estimated at $2 million. In *West Indian Hurricanes*, author E. B. Garriott reported that the storm curved slowly northward into the Gulf of Mexico on September 28 and finally struck the Florida coast near Cape San Blas at 11:00 P.M. on October 2. At St. Marks the wind was measured at 66 mph the following morning, and the tide rose twelve feet above normal.

Damages along the coast were typical—vessels were driven ashore and wharves washed away. Cotton and rice crops were destroyed, and some banks offered special "hurricane loans" to bail out farmers whose harvests were lost. Like many other powerful storms, the 1877 hurricane buffeted inland communities with high winds when it tracked through Georgia. The forward speed of the once slow-moving hurricane increased dramatically once it turned inland. Gale-force winds along the North Carolina coast pushed high waters into Albemarle Sound, and bridges and wharves were swept away. Similar flooding occurred in Virginia, and several ships were wrecked in the Chesapeake and Delaware Bays. Passenger trains in Pennsylvania, New Jersey, and New York were reportedly "wrecked by washouts, resulting in great loss of life and property." Eventually, the storm passed Cape Cod on a path just off the coast of Newfoundland. More vessels were lost, and few survivors were found.

1878

The next year, two significant hurricanes swept out of the Tropics and onto American soil, only one of which passed over Florida. On September 7, 1878, the first storm just missed Key West on a due-north course that would take it into the Everglades. By this time, the storm had already claimed hundreds of lives in Cuba, Haiti, and Trinidad, where it was labeled the "severest storm in forty years." For the next four days, its slow drift over Florida unleashed tremendous rains. Its path over the state was not typical, as it danced north-ward along the southwest coast at a snail's pace, then turned westward into the Gulf north of Tampa. There it reintensified, turned back to the east, and returned to the Atlantic north of St. Augustine on September 11 after giving the entire peninsula a thorough soaking.

The storm made landfall again on the South Carolina coast below Charleston on the twelfth. It quickly gained forward speed and cut a path through the Carolina Piedmont into the Virginias. The usual problems plagued communities in seven states—namely, bridge and railway washouts, downed trees and telegraph lines, flooded farmlands, and wrecked ships.

The "Autumn Gale of 1878" that came in October was the second notable storm of the year. Its eye remained about forty miles offshore when it passed along Florida's east coast on the morning of the twenty-second. Although its impact on Florida was not great, it caused significant disruption to shipping throughout the region. Over a dozen vessels were driven aground from the Straits of Florida to Cape Canaveral. Ships also went down in Chesapeake Bay and in New England, and the newly established U.S. Life-Saving Service was put to the test rescuing the survivors of the wrecks. The storm had a forward speed of over 30 mph when it made landfall in North Carolina. It went on to set new wind-speed records in dozens of cities in the Northeast; some of these records still stand today.

In his book *Weather Is Front Page News*, Ti Sanders described the effects of the 1878 storm: "Along the coast, life saving squads were kept busy for several days, pulling out one survivor after another from the life-engulfing waves which swooped in to shore at an estimated twenty-five to thirty feet high." Sanders also noted the terrific winds that accompanied the storm. Among the cities hardest hit by the wind was Philadelphia, where some 700 buildings were destroyed and nearly 50 churches lost their spires. The storm cruised through New England and then curved back to sea on a southeastern course. Winds in Portland, Maine, were measured at 70 mph before the anemometer cups were blown away.

According to Sanders's account of the 1878 gale, residents along the Gulf coast to New Orleans were thankful for the storm: "In the Southland, in the vicinity of New Orleans, a Yellow Fever epidemic was rampant from early July until the latter days of October, and had already claimed 4,000 lives and prostrated another 12,000 people. The Gulf Coast was anxiously awaiting the season's first frost, to put an end to this still mysterious disease. In the wake of the hurricane that passed to their east, enough Canadian air penetrated the bayous, and their wishes were granted."

AUGUST 29–31, 1880

During the early 1880s, an era of rapid economic growth began in Florida. Large tracts of swampland were drained and converted to farmland where citrus groves were planted. Great deposits of phosphate were discovered, which were mined and transported on the new railroads that covered the state. New tourist resorts were built, and the railroads delivered hoards of visitors from the North. Florida's first boom was under way, led primarily by developers Henry M. Flagler (1830–1913), Henry B. Plant (1819–1899), and Hamilton Disston (1844–1896). On many occasions, however, hurricanes in the latter part of the century would wreck their plans and slow the economic growth of Florida.

Florida's central east coast was hammered by a strong hurricane in August 1880. *Florida Hurricanes*, a Weather Bureau report first published by Richard W. Gray in 1933 and then updated by Grady Norton in 1949, lists the 1880 storm as a "Great Hurricane" (with winds over 125 mph). It slammed head-on into the coast somewhere between Palm Beach and Cocoa Beach at 6:00 A.M. on August 29. A large surge of water flooded all nearby rivers and bays and submerged the barrier beaches. From there it slowly dragged across the state, dumping heavy rains and downing countless trees. Just south of Cedar Key, it moved out over the warm waters of the Gulf and then swept Apalachicola and Pensacola. Losses to crops were significant after the hurricane's rains and high tides "turned garden vegetables into seaweed." On one Florida ranch, it was reported that "the cattle were blown down in the fields." A total of sixty-eight lives were reported lost in the storm.

SEPTEMBER 9–10, 1882

By the late 1870s, the Signal Corps' efforts to monitor storm reports by telegraph were paying off. The network was especially important to shipping interests in the Northeast, who could harbor their vessels at the warning of an approaching hurricane from the south. This proved to be the case during the hurricane of September 1882. This storm passed over Cuba on the fourth and fifth and curved into the Gulf toward Pensacola. It made landfall east of Pensacola around midnight on the ninth. Losses at Cedar Key were estimated at $100,000, and extensive crop damage occurred throughout the state's northern counties. Devastation of docks and warehouses was widespread from Louisiana to Apalachee Bay. The storm moved at a relatively slow pace, which aided the Signal Corps in the completion of its mission—a timely forecast. Warnings of the hurricane's approach were issued, and ships throughout the eastern states remained in harbor. In addition to untold numbers of lives, the Signal Corps later reported that $13 million in potential losses to shipping was saved because of the early warning.

AUGUST 23–24, 1885

The 1885 storm season was especially active in the northern Gulf of Mexico and along the southeast coast. Five separate tropical weather systems moved over Florida between August and October. Three of the storms hugged the Panhandle coast and eventually passed near Tallahassee within one five-week period. The most significant storm, however, never made landfall in Florida but still had a terrific impact on the state.

In late August, a major storm took a right turn above Cuba and then went on to sideswipe Florida, curving northward and hugging the central east coast near Cape Canaveral. On the morning of August 24, its eye passed within twenty miles of the beach, and a powerful surge and high winds pummeled the coast. It may be that the storm's eye remained offshore, but its effect on nearby beaches and towns was significant. According to Glenn Rabac's book *The City of Cocoa Beach: The First Sixty Years*: "The hurricane that hit in 1885 discouraged further settlement. The storm pushed the ocean waves over the barrier island (elevation ten feet), flooding out the homesteaders. The beach near the Canaveral Light House was severely eroded, prompting President Cleveland and the Congress to allot money for an effort to move the tower one mile west."

1886

The Florida coast from Apalachicola to Cedar Key was hit hard by three unusually early hurricanes in the summer of 1886. All three storms were born in the same spot in the western Caribbean, south of Cuba. And all three took a similar path, curving northward toward the far corner of the Gulf of Mexico. The first came ashore near Apalachicola on the summer solstice, June 21. It caused destruction throughout northern Florida and southern Georgia. Ships were driven aground, and floodwaters filled the lower streets of all surrounding coastal towns. Most of the property losses occurred in Apalachicola and Tallahassee. Winds were reported to have been well over 100 mph. In the Weather Bureau report *Florida Hurricanes*, Grady Norton listed this June storm as a "Great Hurricane."

Then, nine days later, a second hurricane struck just east of Apalachicola with tremendous force. Tallahassee was hit hard again by heavy rains and damaging winds on June 30. Winds there were measured at more than 80 mph, and more large trees were downed, adding to the destruction of the week before. Crops were heavily damaged, and railroad cars were said to have been blown down their tracks by the winds. Several lives were reported lost in the Apalachicola area, and one man was killed in Jefferson County.

On July 18, a third Gulf hurricane came ashore just south of Cedar Key. Little is known of this storm's effects on the Florida coast, as the highest tides and greatest winds struck an area with little population. Its track carried it across the Florida Peninsula, and it exited the coast near Jacksonville. From there it disrupted shipping along the coast off Savannah, Charleston, and beyond. Early-season hurricanes are not unusual in Florida, but the fact that these three storms struck so close together in time and in location during the early portion of the summer makes the 1886 season unique in Florida's hurricane history.

1888

Two hurricanes struck Florida during the 1888 season. The first came in August and was listed by Norton in the category of great hurricanes. First observed north of Haiti on August 14, this powerful storm passed over the lower Bahama Islands and took dead aim on the tip of Florida. It made landfall on the morning of the sixteenth near Miami and crossed over to Fort Myers, where it entered the Gulf of Mexico. The storm's surge was reported at fourteen feet on the beaches near Miami. Damages in South Florida were widespread, although few communities were established there at that time. The August 1888 edition of *Monthly Weather Review* contained a report of the storm from Sebastian Inlet: "High northeast wind prevailed in the afternoon and evening, the wind reaching an estimated velocity of seventy-five miles per hour at 1:30 P.M.; trees and telegraph poles were prostrated, and many small boats were blown ashore; orange groves and other fruit trees sustained damage to the amount of several thousand dollars." On August 19, the hurricane struck again when it came ashore on the Louisiana coast west of New Orleans. Severe flooding was reported throughout the Mississippi River Delta region.

The second storm formed deep in the Gulf of Mexico on October 8 and followed a direct course toward Florida's upper west coast. On the afternoon of the tenth, the storm's eye passed directly over Cedar Key on its way inland toward Jacksonville. Few details of damages are available, but it is likely that the storm was of minimal intensity. Nine deaths occurred in the Cedar Key area.

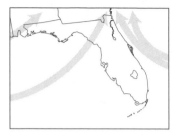

1893

The hurricane season of 1893 was one of the most tragic in U.S. history. In that year, six hurricanes made landfall in the United States between June and October. Four battered the northeastern states with high winds, heavy rains, and flash floods. Two great storms also came ashore on American soil—one from the Atlantic in August and one from the Gulf in October. Each of these two storms would be responsible for killing over 2,000 people, making the 1893 hurricane season the second most deadly in the United States since record keeping began.

The first hurricane of the season was born in the Bay of Campeche on June 12. It developed a steady northeasterly course that carried it across the Gulf and onto the Florida coast near Cedar Key on the fifteenth. Winds were not particularly destructive, but heavy rains were dumped across the northern counties, flooding fields of summer crops. This minimal hurricane crossed into the Okefenokee Swamp by late afternoon and continued through the Carolinas and up the northeastern coast. Total damage estimates were not significant. On August 24, a second hurricane hit the coast near New York City.

The season's two most deadly storms passed just to the east and the west of Florida. The Sea Islands hurricane struck near Savannah on August 27 with a devastating storm surge that drowned thousands of unsuspecting coastal residents. The tremendous surge delivered great destruction to properties all along the Georgia and South Carolina coasts. According to Ti Sanders's book *Weather Is Front Page News*, "Residents of the Northeast had no way of knowing that yet a third hurricane was churning northward from the Caribbean that was destined to kill over a thousand people, mostly blacks, on a trail of destruction from Titusville, Florida, to Wilmington, North Carolina." The great tragedy of the storm was amply described in the *Harper's Weekly* of September 16, 1893: "Hundreds of corpses were strewn along the farms, unknown save to the vultures which flocked about them. Whole families were wiped out in some places. The coroner has sworn in an army of deputies and these are hunting for the dead."

The year's other deadly hurricane landed near New Orleans on October 2, with an equally destructive storm tide. In Louisiana another 2,000 lives were lost. The wind was thought to be at least 100 mph, strong enough to destroy all of the Weather Bureau's wind instruments in the region. Damages were severe for many miles east of the storm; Mobile and Pensacola lost waterfront properties, and railways were washed away. According to E. B. Garriott's account in *West Indian Hurricanes*, "The storm was accompanied by a tidal wave which engulfed everything before it, explaining the great loss of life reported, one local account placing it as high as 2,000. The canning interests suffered severely, and there was immense destruction to shipping, the property losses in the aggregate footing up millions of dollars. There was great suffering among the living in many localities, and in some instances, as on the islands, it was necessary to use for food dead animals and poultry that had perished in the storm."

Yet another October hurricane tracked just east of Florida's Atlantic coast on Columbus Day, on its way toward the Carolinas. Although this storm didn't make direct landfall in Florida either, its passage nearby pushed a storm surge of several feet onto the east coast from Palm Beach to Jacksonville. High tides combined with heavy rains to inundate numerous coastal communities, including St. Augustine, where water was "deep in the streets." Winds at Sebastian were reported at 90 mph. The hurricane made landfall near Charleston and swept through the Northeast on the thirteenth, where it delivered significant damage to numerous states. In Florida and South Carolina, twenty-eight people died in the storm.

The storm's effects along the coast were severe. They were remembered in a report in the *Stuart Times* of October 1913: "Twenty years ago last Saturday a hurricane of big dimensions swept the coast and did a lot of damage all along the shore. . . . The high winds knocked the foundation out from under Mr. Kitching's store at Sebastian and blew the building plumb into the Indian River. The stock at that time was valued at $5,000 and was almost a total loss. John Michael, a relative of Mrs. Walter Kitching, wife of the Stuart storekeeper, sent Sylvanus Kitching a check for a case of tomatoes which he picked up in his banana patch six miles away and across the Indian River."

1894

Two hurricanes struck Florida in 1894—one hit Key West and then Sanibel Island, and the other came ashore near Apalachicola. The first storm traveled the length of Cuba on September 23 and then turned northward toward the Florida Keys. As the hurricane churned by on the twenty-fifth, winds at Key West were clocked at 104 mph. It continued northward onto the Florida coast below Sarasota and delivered high tides throughout the region. A weather station in Clermont, in Lake County, recorded 12.50 inches of rain in twenty-four hours with the passing of the storm. In the *Monthly Weather Review*, an observer in Jacksonville wrote: "The hurricane of Sept. 24th to 26th did considerable damage to the orange and vegetable crops and caused the destruction of much property of all kinds. Great damage was done to houses and railroads by the unprecedented downpours of rain besides what was done by the wind."

In October another hurricane swept up from the lower latitudes and into the Gulf on a course toward the West Florida coast. Landfall occurred near Apalachicola on the morning of the eighth, and extreme tides and winds were reported from numerous weather-observation sites. Although the highest winds measured by the Weather Bureau were only 68 mph (from the northeast) at Pensacola and 62 mph (from the southeast) at Jacksonville, the storm passed directly between these two locations, and higher winds were likely encountered. A Weather Bureau summary described the hurricane: "The hurricane of Oct. 8th and 9th, which passed over the western and extreme northern portion of the State caused the loss of many lives along the Gulf coast and the destruction of much property. Every city and town between Jacksonville and Pensacola was damaged more or less. Considerable loss was sustained by the farmers. Unpicked cotton was leveled to the ground and tangled together. Sugarcane was blown flat and the crop almost ruined. Fences and trees were blown down and oranges and pecans shaken from the trees, etc. This storm was the most violent one which has passed near Jacksonville during the past 23 years."

As the storm tracked northward through Georgia and the coastal plains of the Carolinas, it continued to deliver heavy rains that washed away bridges and damaged crops in the field. It briefly entered the Atlantic off the Virginia coast and struck again through the heart of New England. Winds up to 84 mph were recorded, and the storm was said to have been "very severe" at Narragansett and Block Island, Rhode Island. Once again, timely warnings from the Weather Bureau kept many vessels in port and saved many lives.

1896

By 1896 the Weather Bureau had established a network of almost fifty meteorological reporting stations across Florida. The bureau itself had stations in Pensacola, Jacksonville, Tampa, Jupiter, and Key West. More than forty other voluntary meteorological stations and numerous "forecast display stations" completed the network. Weather data was recorded more consistently than ever before across major portions of Florida. The greatest concentration of stations was in the counties north of Tampa; with the exception of Key West, South Florida had few recording stations. Through this network, weather information was gathered and used to warn of southern storms. Telegraph lines out of Florida routinely carried the news of approaching hurricanes to ports along the coast in the mid-Atlantic and northeastern states. Unfortunately the network was not as beneficial to the coastal residents of Florida, who rarely enjoyed the advantage of forewarning.

The hurricane season of 1896 was a busy one for the Weather Bureau and for Florida residents, as three storms struck the Gulf coast during the year. The first came ashore just east of Pensacola on the morning of July 7. Although the city was on the weaker side of the storm, a maximum wind of 72 mph was recorded there at 11:45 A.M. The winds and tides caused "much damage," especially near the harbor. Nine fishing boats and countless small craft were sunk, two barks were badly damaged, and a brig dragged its anchor across the harbor and washed ashore. About thirty-five houses were unroofed, and high winds downed trees, telegraph poles, signs, smokestacks, and windmills. According to a summary report of the storm in the *Monthly Weather Review*, "The property loss has been estimated as high as $400,000 in Pensacola alone, but that statement seems excessive. Probably $100,000 would be nearer the true figures." On July 8 and 9, the decaying hurricane moved northward over Alabama, Georgia, Tennessee, Kentucky, and Ohio. On the eastern edge of the storm, tornadoes spawned in North Carolina and Virginia killed and injured several people.

The September hurricane of 1896 was a tragic and powerful storm. It probably originated as a Cape Verde–type hurricane that was first spotted in the Windward Islands on September 22. Its westward movement carried it south of Jamaica and Cuba, but when it entered the Gulf of Mexico on the twenty-seventh, it recurved to the northeast on a path toward Florida. At about 3:30 A.M. on the twenty-ninth, the small but powerful storm made landfall at Cedar Key and raced northward to Canada. This inland course was accomplished in less than twenty-four hours, as the storm moved at an average forward speed of 46 mph. Although it left a trail of death and destruction through nine states, its most grievous damages occurred in Florida. The September 1896 storm was later classified by Norton as one of Florida's great hurricanes.

After landfall on the coast, the storm moved inland on a north-northeast track. The Weather Bureau reported that the width of the storm's destructive path was unusually narrow: "Places 50 to 100 miles on either side of the central path were not exposed to winds of unusual severity." But in the narrow band of the hurricane's track, particularly in Florida, the storm was deadly. At least 68 Floridians died (some estimates exceeded 100) as the cyclone tore through Levy, Lafayette, Alachua, Bradford, Suwannee, Columbia, Baker, and Nassau Counties. The two counties hit hardest were Lafayette and Suwannee. The storm surge in the vicinity of Cedar Key was ten feet. The entire northeastern portion of the state was left reeling, with total property damages of over $3 million. The estimate for loss of pine timber alone was over $1.5 million. The Weather Bureau reported that "during the early part of the storm the trees were torn up by the roots, but as the force of the wind increased they were broken and twisted off and thrown forward in a confused mass."

As the hurricane sped northward, its severity lessened through the Carolinas. But once it reached Virginia at around 9:00 P.M., it apparently increased in

Wreckage at Cedar Key after the passage of the hurricane of September 1896. (Photo courtesy of Noel Risnychok)

intensity until it passed through Pennsylvania at midnight. It was one of the worst storms on record in the District of Columbia. In Washington the winds were recorded at 66 mph for five minutes and averaged 56 mph from 10:40 to 11:40 P.M. Damaging winds were reported throughout northern Virginia, Maryland, and Pennsylvania. Harrisburg, Pennsylvania, recorded winds of 72 mph, even higher than the winds measured in Washington. The hurricane's rapid forward speed contributed significantly to the extreme winds in the northern states. In all, the storm shattered wind records in numerous cities, including Harrisburg, Washington, Savannah, and Jacksonville, Florida, where a reading of 76 mph remained the highest speed measured until 1964.

As the hurricane raced past Washington, a weather observer reported in the *Monthly Weather Review* an unusual sighting in the storm: "The form and color of the clouds as observed in Washington during the early part of the storm greatly resembled ground fog driven by high wind. They were very low, scarcely above the house tops, and of pure white. With the shift of wind from southeast to south to southwest the form and color of the clouds changed, but the darkness soon became so intense that further observations could not be made. The display of atmospheric electricity was almost continuous, and in the form of broad, diffuse flashes, though not of marked brilliancy or intensity. The flashes were very similar to the well known phenomenon of sheet lightning in summer."

The storm was reported to have experienced a second lull through northern Pennsylvania and central New York, but then it accelerated and caused severe damages in New York's Cayuga and Cortland Counties. From there it entered the St. Lawrence Valley as a large rainstorm with heavy winds. Like so many hurricanes over the years, it had spent its destructive energies through countless communities many miles from the nearest ocean waters.

In addition to the 68 known deaths in Florida, the storm killed 25 in Georgia, 5 in Virginia, and 8 in Maryland. In all, at least 114 people died in the United States. The total estimated property damages exceeded $7 million, making the 1896 hurricane one of the most expensive in the United States up to that time. The Weather Bureau gathered statistics on deaths and damages as part of its new role in the aftermath of major storms.

Several days after the hurricane passed through the Gulf of Mexico, the pilot boat *Glance* came to port in Key West with ten exhausted sailors whose ship had gone down in the storm. The Norwegian bark *Saturn*, bound from Belize to Scotland with a load of timber, had capsized and sunk, tossing its crew into the stormy seas. Many drowned in the ordeal, but some survivors clung to floating timbers and other debris. They reported that in the days following the storm, gruesome shark attacks had killed several of their shipmates.

A little more than a week later, on October 9, the third storm of the 1896 season swept over Florida. This weaker storm struck a less populated portion of the state, and damages were not severe. It made landfall near Punta Gorda, where localized flooding was reported, then crossed the state and exited the coast near Sebastian. Few areas reported major damages, except for north of the storm in Lake Butler, where a tornado apparently touched down and destroyed several homes.

1898

Soon after the American battleship *Maine* exploded and sank in the Havana harbor on February 15, 1898, the United States declared war on Spain. With the prospect of increased naval maneuvers throughout the hurricane-prone waters of the Caribbean, concerns arose over the safety of American vessels during the approaching hurricane season. Willis L. Moore, chief of the Weather Bureau, paid a visit to President William McKinley to urge the establishment of a hurricane-warning network throughout the West Indies. Moore's presentation was apparently convincing, as McKinley was later said to have been more afraid of the threat of a hurricane than he was of the Spanish navy. Moore was ordered to immediately establish the warning system, which was hastily assembled prior to the season's first storm.

The events that happened next were described by Patrick Hughes in "Hurricanes Haunt Our History" in *Weatherwise*: "A battle fleet left Spain steaming westward. Concern spread along the east coast of the United States. Observation posts were hurriedly built at key points[,] . . . emergency plans made—all for nothing. The Spanish fleet was trapped in the harbor at Santiago, Cuba, and destroyed. The war ended. Not a single hurricane had appeared. . . . No American ships or men had been lost. The hurricanes came late that year, or they might have played a role in the drama that marked the end of Spanish power in the New World as they had at its beginning, four centuries before."

Two hurricanes eventually did impact Florida that year—one in August and one in October. The August storm began as a tropical low in the Atlantic east of the Bahamas and then passed over the state on a course from Jupiter to Tampa on the morning of August 2. As the storm entered the Gulf, it probably increased in strength before slamming the coast near Apalachicola later that day. According to Weather Bureau reports, it had a "comparatively narrow track," and it "wrought havoc with several tug-boats, scows, dredges and fishing smacks, causing the loss of a dozen or more lives and a property damage exceeding $100,000." Among the losses were the tug *Keyser*, which sank fifteen miles off Cape San Blas, killing three people, and the dredge *Herndon*, which foundered and sank after it was cut adrift from the *Keyser*.

The greatest inland damage was reported to have occurred between the Apalachicola and Choctawhatchee Rivers, where fierce winds over 80 mph knocked down fences, forests, and crops. The most severe damages took place in Franklin, Calhoun, Washington, and Jackson Counties. Crawfordville recorded 7.51 inches of rain during the twenty-four-hour period of the storm's passing. For several days after the hurricane, heavy rains continued to affect the region; a weather reporter near St. Andrews Bay recorded 18.29 inches during the week of the storm. The month's rainfall totals at several West Florida stations were the greatest recorded to that date.

Exactly two months after the passing of the August storm, another hurricane struck, although this October cyclone never actually made landfall in Florida. It formed in late September somewhere east of the Leeward Islands and charted a course to the northwest that eventually brought it toward Jacksonville. On the morning of October 2, it barreled ashore on the Georgia coast just south of Savannah, pushing a tremendous storm tide onto the barrier beaches. Newspaper headlines around the country told of the great flood: "Savannah is Sunk! Heavy losses are feared on the sea islands, owing to the submerged country and the isolated location of the islands, no news can be had from them until the water subsides. For eight miles north of Savannah, the entire country is a lake, with only the hummocks visible."

The storm surge along the Georgia coast was powerful and deadly. The Weather Bureau reported that the tide was eighteen feet above mean high water at Sapels Lighthouse and thirteen feet at Darien and that the business section of Brunswick was under four to eight feet of water. Throughout the region, scores of people were drowned by the tide. At Campbell Island as many as fifty lives were lost, and ninety-seven black laborers were drowned on one rice plantation on the Ogeechee River.

In Florida the large and powerful storm caused extensive damage, even though the region was hit by the storm's weaker southern side. Fernandina was "nearly destroyed," according to the Weather Bureau observer in Jacksonville. Damages were heavy as far south as Mayport, particularly to boats and structures near the water. The storm tide in Mayport was eight to ten feet above normal. The Weather Bureau's report of the storm described the scene: "The damage to Fernandina and vicinity was very great. It is conservatively estimated at $500,000. Nothing escaped damage, and a great deal was absolutely destroyed. Giant oaks were snapped off at the base, houses blown down, and vessels blown inland by an irresistible in-rush of water. The wind signal display man Major W. B. C. Duryee, who has resided in Fernandina more than thirty years, states that no previous storm was so severe."

Once again, the Weather Bureau's early forecast of the storm was widely distributed and well heeded. Early on the day before the hurricane's arrival, warnings of "dangerous shifting gales" were issued to all ports from Key West to Norfolk. On the morning of October 2, just hours before the storm hit, new warnings were sent out by telegraph that the storm was of hurricane force. Numerous ships were kept in port along the Atlantic coast, and many lives were

saved, facts that the Weather Bureau eagerly reported. In the summary report issued from Jacksonville, the bureau noted that ten ships from Florida ports with crews totaling fifty-six and cargoes valued at $380,000 were saved by its timely warnings.

1899

Two August hurricanes affected Florida in 1899, but only one made landfall in the state. A small but severe storm struck near Carrabelle on August 1 and drove dozens of ships aground on the Panhandle coast. The Weather Bureau reported that "the diameter of the storm was not more than 40 miles, and its force was spent before it progressed 50 miles inland." Even though the hurricane was not large, it wrecked Carrabelle, "where not more than a score of unimportant houses withstood the storm." The barometer reached a low of 28.90 inches when the eye passed over the town. Recent National Weather Service reports list this storm as having been of category 2 intensity on the Saffir-Simpson scale.

Along the coast, maritime losses were tremendous. Fourteen loaded barks, forty smaller boats, and three pilot boats were wrecked or dismasted. Among the losses were vessels from Norway, Russia, and the United States, including the *Hindos, Jafnhar, James A. Garfield, Latava, Mary E. Morse, Vivette, Vale,* and *Warner Adams.* The value of the lost cargo was $375,000, and property losses in Carrabelle and other nearby towns totaled $200,000. Six people died in the storm, including a couple from Tampa who were found near the Cape St. George Lighthouse aboard their capsized sloop. They were later buried on the beach.

On the day after the hurricane passed, hundreds of sightseers, reporters, and others traveled by train into the area of destruction. After excursion parties surveyed the damages at Carrabelle, newspaper reports stated that it was remarkable that the hurricane had not taken more lives. The *Tampa Morning Tribune* reported that "the people of Carabelle [*sic*] are appealing for aid. They need it. Some of them lost all their clothes in the storm." Some aboard the train came prepared to help and worked to clear boats from the streets and provide assistance. The *Morning Tribune* noted that "the people of Apalachicola and Tallahassee came down on Sunday and opened their pocketbooks for those who are in need."

Another more powerful storm nearly struck the east coast just a few days later. This great hurricane, dubbed "San Ciriaco" after a particularly deadly visit to Puerto Rico on August 8, went on to pass close to Florida on the thirteenth and strike North Carolina's Outer Banks a few days later. Few significant damages were reported on the Florida coast. The Weather Bureau's observation station at Jupiter recorded an extreme wind of 63 mph and a barometric pressure of 29.22 inches, as the storm remained well offshore.

On the same day as the passing of the San Ciriaco hurricane along the coast at Jupiter, Pensacola and Key West also experienced severe storms. Because of the numerous storm reports filed within a short period from Pensacola, Carrabelle, Puerto Rico, Key West, and Jupiter, newspaper editors expressed confusion about the location of the hurricanes. The *Morning Tribune* attempted an explanation: "Have we missed the storm? Judging from the dispatches received by the local office of the Weather Bureau and by the *Tribune* last night, the West Indian hurricane has divided itself into several separate storms, and they seem to all be playing hide and seek around the coast of Florida."

A few days after the storms had passed, the same paper commented on the great apprehension felt by residents in Jacksonville: "Thanks to a kind Providence, the fury of the wind was spent before reaching land and Florida escaped unharmed. There have been many storms in this state, but never before was there as much anxiety expressed as during the past week in this vicinity. This is indicated by the numerous storm-risks issued by insurance companies, the failure of some people to sleep, and the general alarm. . . . How thankful we should be for this deliverance and how glad we should be that we live in Florida, where few hurricanes come, no floods, no droughts, famines and pestilence."

HURRICANES IN THE SUNSHINE STATE,
1900–1949

A storm victim sifts through the rubble of his Pompano Beach home after the hurricane of September 1948. (Photo courtesy of Noel Risnychok)

By the beginning of the twentieth century, Florida's first development boom was well under way; its economy was growing rapidly, and its population surged upward. The charge was led by the aggressive development of Henry Flagler on the east coast and Henry Plant on the west coast. Their railroad ventures stretched farther and farther south, opening up Florida for the creation of new settlements and tourist destinations. Citrus farms and other new industries also spread farther south, and business prospered. Towns became cities. Florida was connected by a growing network of telegraph lines, railroad tracks, and roads. Railways aided the growth, but trade remained brisk at all of Florida's major ports, and large cargo ships still sailed the Gulf and the Atlantic. But unfortunately for Florida, deadly hurricanes continued to stir the same waters.

SEPTEMBER 11–14, 1903

A category 1 hurricane struck the Florida coast fifty miles south of Jupiter on the evening of September 11, 1903. Winds were up to 84 mph at the Weather Bureau office in Jupiter, and the barometer dropped to 29.63 inches. The storm sliced across the state and into the Gulf and then reentered the coast near Apalachicola. At St. Andrews the pressure dipped to 29.08 inches, and the winds were estimated at 75–80 mph. The storm surge was about eight feet at Jupiter and ten feet at Apalachicola. Once the hurricane moved inland, its winds diminished and it swept into eastern Alabama as a tropical storm, then curved back toward the Atlantic over South Carolina.

Ships were driven ashore near Jupiter and Apalachicola, and losses totaled $500,000. Crop losses were significant, but structural damage was not extensive at any location. At least fourteen deaths were reported in Florida. In newspapers across the East, this modest storm was overshadowed by a more deadly hurricane that struck the Jersey shore just three days later, killing fifty-seven.

SEPTEMBER 27, 1906

The 1906 hurricane season was a deadly one in Florida. The most significant hurricane of the year actually made landfall near the Alabama-Mississippi border, but western Florida was caught in the ferocious right-front quadrant of the storm. Classified as a "Great Hurricane" by Grady Norton, it roared ashore on the morning of September 27 after building strength for a week in the western Caribbean and the Gulf of Mexico. At Pensacola it was heralded as the worst storm in history—or at least the worst since the village of Pensacola on Santa Rosa Island was swept away 170 years before.

At the time of the hurricane's arrival, Pensacola was just recovering from other calamities. Yellow fever had gripped the town throughout the previous year, claiming the lives of numerous prominent residents. Then a disastrous fire blazed through the business district. Reconstruction of many of the city's burned buildings was completed just prior to the hurricane's visit. Fortunately, since Guglielmo Marconi had introduced wireless telegraphy in 1902, the Weather Bureau was able to use this new technology to transmit warnings quickly and efficiently—some twenty-four hours before the storm's landfall. But as the warnings were released, a great anxiety swept the town, based on a renewed fear of hurricanes brought on by the well-known disaster that had befallen Galveston, Texas, in 1900. The Weather Bureau reported that "during the early morning hours the people of the city were panic-stricken, many believing that a repetition of the Galveston disaster was imminent, and large numbers of people took refuge in the higher portion of the city, braving the high winds and the stinging sand-filled rain in the hope of reaching a place of safety."

When the hurricane did strike, it brought record flooding in numerous ports along the coast. At the height of the storm, between 3:00 and 4:00 A.M., the storm tide reached its peak in Pensacola of 10 feet above normal, and at Mobile the flood was 9.9 feet above normal, both setting new records for high water. The highest wind reports ranged from 83 to 94 mph, even though several stations lost their anemometers before the hurricane's peak.

At Pensacola the entire waterfront area was inundated, and many houses were carried away. The large Muscogee wharf was broken into two parts, and railroad tracks on both sides of the docks were washed away, taking two engines and thirty-eight freight cars loaded with coal with them. Some of the cars were later found buried in deep sand. The south side of West Main Street

was washed away, and flooding to a depth of ten feet was reported north of Intendencia Street. Waves broke through second-story windows in houses along the waterfront. Afterward, homes along the bayshore from Barcelona Street to Perdido were "in ruins," and masses of timbers, vessels, and wreckage were "jammed upon the beach in a torn and twisted mass." A new inlet was cut through Santa Rosa Island east of the life-saving station; the station itself was washed away. It was later reported that the station's crew were found "without money or clothing."

Pensacola was a scene of devastation. Of the fifty or sixty large ships and sailing vessels in the harbor before the storm, all but five or six dragged their anchors far up onto the shore. Great iron ships of 3,000 tons were driven through large houses on the waterfront. When the hurricane was at its peak, a fire broke out in a large mill in the business district, adding to the confusion of the morning. At least thirty miles of the Louisville and Nashville Railroad tracks were washed away. Over 5,000 houses were damaged or destroyed, and at least 3,000 Pensacola residents were left homeless. Gallant rescues took place around the city. According to the *Tampa Morning Tribune*, "It is known, however, that many houses in that section are now under from five to ten feet of water and many women have been taken from second story windows and carried to safety in boats."

Pensacola harbor, September 1906. (Photo courtesy of the Florida State Archives)

The Weather Bureau included the following in its report from Pensacola:

Wharfmaster Cox stated that the tide was fully ten feet above normal high tide along the city waterfront and twelve feet at Bayou Grande, based upon the reckonings of five reliable men. The sea swells entering the slip between Palafox and Baylen streets were from seven to twelve feet high between midnight and 7:00 A.M. and were about one hundred yards apart, lifting wharf timbers and boards as they rolled thru the slip and splashed over Cedar street. Oyster boats, launches, steamers, tugs, lighters, timbers and wreckage of all description are jammed together at the corner of Cedar and Baylen streets; the launch Wolverine, a boat 40 by 9 feet, past [*sic*] over Cedar street and entered the lot at the northeast corner of Baylen and Cedar streets, followed by other wreckage mentioned above. Trees fully exposed to the easterly gale in all parts of the city were blown down, the chinaberry and sycamores suffering most. All weak chimneys that were broadside to the east were tumbled to the westward. Whenever the wind got under a tin roof, it rolled it off.

At Mobile the hurricane was also of record proportions. A low-pressure reading of 28.84 inches was recorded at 6:30 A.M., but the flooding arrived a little later. At 6:00 A.M., the water was about two feet below the top of the wharf; within a half hour it reached the top of the wharf; by 7:45 it had flowed into the

third street from the river; and at 10:00 it reached its maximum stage, exceeding by about a foot the previous record set in 1893. The Weather Bureau also noted that in Apalachicola rainfall was measured at 10.12 inches; that the tidal surge in Galt, in Santa Rosa County, was fourteen feet; and that at St. Andrews "a tidal wave swept this place; the water was higher than any time during the past 19 years."

The total financial losses in Pensacola were well over $2 million, a considerable sum for that time. Thirty-two deaths in the city were attributed to the storm. In the broader area of destruction from Mississippi to Apalachicola, the death total was 134. In the days following the disaster, martial law prevailed, and there were accounts from Mobile and Pensacola of looters and thieves who were caught and beaten to death. One good bit of news was reported in the *Pensacola Journal* after the hurricane: "The storm brought in great schools of fish and the beach fishermen are reaping a rich harvest."

After the storm swept inland near Mobile on September 27, it tracked northward across Mississippi and entered northeastern Arkansas as a tropical storm on the twenty-eighth. Heavy rains poured across the land, as typically occurs with great hurricanes, and rivers and streams filled beyond their banks. One last tragedy blamed on the storm occurred when a northbound passenger train encountered a washed-out bridge over the Cumberland River in central Tennessee. The engine, baggage car, and mail car went into the river, taking seven

Louisville and Nashville Railroad employees with them. Miraculously, the passenger cars broke free and no passengers were killed.

OCTOBER 17–18, 1906

Throughout the 1880s and 1890s, financier and developer Henry Flagler planted the seeds of future growth along Florida's entire eastern shore. His Florida East Coast Railway steadily grew southward, from St. Augustine to Palm Beach to Miami. Along the way, Flagler built elegant resorts like the Ponce de León Hotel in St. Augustine, his first, which opened in 1888, and the Royal Palm Hotel in Miami, which opened in 1897, just a year after his railroad reached the city. These grand resorts attracted wealthy and adventurous northerners who brought further development to Florida's growing cities. But Flagler's most astonishing feat was yet to come. Extending his railway southward to Key West was his next great ambition, and this massive engineering effort began early in 1905. The isolated existence of the Keys pioneers was about to be changed forever with the construction of the Overseas Railroad.

Building the railroad was a huge undertaking. Hundreds of workers cut through thick mangrove forests and hardwood hammocks and dumped millions of cubic yards of rock and fill into the shallow waters that surrounded the Keys. The project was sure to take years, even if the weather cooperated. But Florida's second great hurricane of 1906 dealt a major setback to Flagler and his miracle railway.

On October 11, the cyclone was first observed as a tropical storm near the Windward Islands. Within a few days, it was rounding the western tip of Cuba as a hurricane, blasting Havana with heavy rains and high winds, and turning toward the Straits of Florida. The storm was already starting to blow as Flagler's workers went to bed on the night of the sixteenth aboard the large houseboats they lived on at Long Key. They got very little sleep. Early on the morning of the seventeenth, the hurricane roared up the Keys and swept through the labor camps that housed the men. Almost all of the houseboats were swept out to sea in the storm, and at least 124 laborers were killed.

One of the most tragic events was the sinking of *House Boat No. 4*. The *Tampa Morning Tribune* printed a firsthand report from one of the wreck's survivors, W. P. Dusenbury:

Mr. Dusenbury estimates the damage done four large work barges and four fine launches at between $50,000 and $60,000. At 5 A.M. on the morning of the hurricane, with 150 men, he was aboard *House Boat No. 4*. This boat was moored to six pilings that were driven into solid rock to a depth from 6 to 8 feet. This mooring was lost at 5 A.M. by the breaking of the chain, which was felt no more than if a thread had been popped. The vessel drifted in a southeasterly direction into the Gulf Stream and toward the Bahamas. One hour after reaching the Gulf Stream, with seas breaking over her 50 to 60 feet high and combing in water of 900 fathoms, the craft was beaten to pieces. The men were then left to fare for themselves. The lumber of the houseboat was very light and most durable and in view of the fact many found rest and safety clinging to wreckage. Other men before his eyes, while not drowned, were cruelly beaten to death by timbers hurled against them. Thus far of the 150 men that were with him, only 73 have shown up, and as far as he knows, only 77 out of 210 workmen have been accounted for.

RESCUED. This survivor was in the water about 11 hours. Ten of these he was seated on a piece of wreckage. The other hour he was swimming and clinging to the plank for dear life. The greatest number picked up at any time was 13, who had improvised a raft out of the side of the vessel. Mr. Dusenbury was discovered by the Austrian steamer *Jennie* and landed at Key West. Today he will go to St. Petersburg for a stay of a week with his family. He will then return to his duties. The work, while temporarily delayed, will not be seriously embarrassed.

Nineteen survivors on another raft were picked up by the British steamship *Alton* and taken to Savannah. All of the men were later treated for numerous cuts, bruises, and broken bones suffered during their ordeal at sea. One survivor was said to have saved "only a ring on his finger." A few men were picked up by the steamer *Colorado* and taken to Mobile; others were rescued by the British steamer *Heatherpool* and taken to Norfolk. They were said to have been found standing on a raft that was waist deep in water. Numerous other vessels were lost in the hurricane, including the *Elmora*, the *Peerless*, and the steamer *St. Lucie*, from which 35 of its 100 passengers were drowned.

The storm apparently cut a narrow path across the Keys. The hurricane's eye passed over Long Key, where groves of coconut trees were split to pieces and destroyed, whereas in areas twenty miles to the east and west, trees were not damaged. Winds near the storm's center were estimated to have been over 100 mph. The wind at Key West was measured at 77 mph, with a barometric low of 29.30 inches. At Sand Key the wind speed was 72 mph. Initial reports from Miami stated that the telegraph office was flooded by two feet of water, the wires were down, and the streets were impassible. The barometer there dropped to 28.55 inches. Damage was reported at Jupiter, which had 70 mph winds, and at St. Augustine, which had its highest storm tide in ten years. Considering the combined losses from the Keys, the Florida coast, and Cuba, the October hurricane of 1906 was a truly tragic storm. A Miami newspaper reported that the hurricane's death toll would exceed 400. The *Monthly Weather Review* later reported that "in 1906 many hundreds of laborers were drowned." According to NOAA's *Deadliest Atlantic Tropical Cyclones, 1492–1994* by Edward N. Rappaport and José

Fernández-Partagás, the storm was responsible for at least 193 deaths, most of which were men sent to build Flagler's Overseas Railroad. In 2005, after reviewing data from the storm, researchers at NOAA's Hurricane Research Division reclassified the October 1906 hurricane as a category 3, or major hurricane.

OCTOBER 11, 1909

The hurricanes of 1909 also left death in their wakes at numerous locations around the Gulf of Mexico. A July storm killed at least 41 in Texas, a hurricane in late August claimed 1,500 lives in northeastern Mexico, and a September hurricane killed 353 in Louisiana and Mississippi. A hurricane in early October killed at least 34 in Cuba and the United States. Although it killed only about 15 in the Florida Keys, it was one of the most intense storms ever recorded in Florida until that time.

On the morning of October 10, the hurricane passed over western Cuba, and the Weather Bureau issued warnings that a storm was on the way. During the day, the barometer at Key West fell gradually, reaching 29.80 inches by 9:00 P.M. The following morning, the hurricane drew closer and the pressure fell remarkably fast, from 29.52 inches at 6:00 A.M. to 28.52 inches at 11:40 A.M. The storm passed over the Keys on a northeastern track that carried it over the northern Bahamas on the morning of the twelfth.

At Sand Key, about eight miles southwest of Key West, the Weather Bureau maintained an observation station. At 8:30 on the morning of the storm, the station was abandoned, and the weather instruments and supplies were taken to the nearby lighthouse. At that time the wind was 75 mph. Shortly thereafter, the anemometer cups were blown away by winds estimated at 100 mph. Within the next hour, all trees and fences were blown down, and the storm's tide swept over the island. At about 10:30 A.M., the Weather Bureau building was swept out to sea and destroyed. The lowest barometer reading obtained from Sand Key was 28.36 inches, which a report in the *Monthly Weather Review* boldly (and incorrectly) proclaimed was "believed to be the lowest atmospheric pressure ever observed in the United States." At Knight's Key an even lower pressure of 28.26 inches was measured.

At Key West winds were clocked at 94 mph and 6.13 inches of rain fell within two hours and fifteen minutes. Several locations in the Keys and South Florida recorded eight to ten inches of rain as the hurricane passed. Key West was hit hard by the storm; about 400 buildings were either swept away by the tide or collapsed by high winds. High tides floated many structures off their foundations, placing them in city streets and on vacant lots. A large concrete cigar factory was heavily damaged by high winds. Along the waterfront and in Key West harbor, over 300 boats were totally destroyed. Damage estimates for the city were placed at $1 million.

Telegraph poles were toppled
along Duval Street in Key West
after the hurricane of October
1909. (Photo courtesy of Jerry
Wilkinson)

Duval St. Looking South

KEY WEST'S WORST STORM, OCT. 11, '09

In Miami the damage was not nearly as severe. The highest winds only lasted for an hour, but some buildings were unroofed and porches and signs were flattened. One of the casualties was the New March Villa, a new hotel that was nearly completed. The storm's winds razed the structure. Flooding along the waterfront damaged docks and vessels of all kinds. Shade trees in the city and coconut trees on the beach were blown down as the storm passed nearby.

Flagler's Overseas Railroad suffered considerable damage from the storm; it was reported that portions of track, trestles, boats, and equipment were carried away. The Weather Bureau stated that "had not the company been fully forewarned of the coming storm the loss of property and life would have been much greater."

OCTOBER 17–18, 1910

Hurricane forecasters were baffled by the mysterious data they received about a mid-October hurricane in 1910. Initial reports suggested that it was actually two separate storms, but it was later identified as a single cyclone that stalled out near western Cuba and carved a shallow loop before continuing northward into Southwest Florida. This "loop hurricane" was a first for the Weather Bureau, and its true path was the subject of much debate at the time. As a result of the observations of this storm, other looping hurricanes in years to come were better understood.

The storm's origins can be traced to the extreme southern portions of the Caribbean, where it first developed on October 10. On the fourteenth, it barreled ashore in western Cuba and then entered the warm waters of the Gulf

of Mexico. It drifted away from the Cuban coast and then back again, nearing the island's western tip on the sixteenth. Over two and a half days, while under the influence of a large high-pressure system over the central United States, the storm spun in a counterclockwise loop, all the while building intensity. As it moved toward Florida on October 17, its forward speed increased; its eye passed just west of Key West, and it eventually moved inland near Cape Romano. Once it was over land, it lost hurricane strength and moved northward through central Florida as a tropical storm. From there it turned toward the Atlantic and hugged the coastlines of Georgia and the Carolinas on its way out to sea.

At Sand Key the barometer fell to a low of 28.40 inches, and winds were estimated to have reached 125 mph. The Weather Bureau's observer reported that

at noon the wharf and woodpile were washed away and the lighthouse shook and swayed in the wind. Great trouble was experienced in keeping the doors closed. The force of the wind drew large nails from the doors. The sand was all washed from sight by this time, and monster waves broke over the whole island, reaching nearly up to the water tanks. Spray from the waves mingled with the rain and made it impossible to see more than 200 feet. . . . After the storm was over the island was completely covered with water about 2 feet deep at its shallowest point, and about 5 feet deep under the lighthouse.

Some conception of the force of the wind may be gained from the following. The windows and doors were all kept closed, but two panes of glass were blown out on the windward side. The air that was forced in through these holes increased the pressure at the opposite side of the house by about 0.05 inch. When the door was opened to let the air go through the barometer fell about 0.05 inch and when the door was closed it immediately rose again.

At Key West it was reported that gusts reached 110 mph, the pressure dipped to 28.47 inches, and the storm tide measured fifteen feet. Sea swells were described as "unusually high." By 3:00 P.M. on the seventeenth, the rising flood had filled the basement of the Weather Bureau station to a depth of seven feet. Several docks were broken apart, and their debris crashed into a U.S. Army office building. Fifteen-foot waves broke against the building's windows. A number of small schooners were wrecked, and the French steamship *Louisiane* went ashore at Sombrero Light with 600 passengers aboard. All were safely rescued by the revenue cutter *Forward*. There was great apprehension about the 1,500 workers still engaged in building Flagler's Overseas Railroad to Key West, but because of ample warnings and careful preparations, none of the laborers were lost. In all, the $250,000 in damages suffered throughout the Keys was considerably less than the damages from the hurricane of the previous year.

At Tampa the storm's winds were felt from the northeast, which had the effect of blowing the water out of Tampa Bay to the lowest point ever recorded. According to the weather observer stationed there, "In the Hillsboro [*sic*] River at Tampa, the water fell 9 feet below mean tide, the usual depression being about 1 foot. Forty vessels were counted at daylight on the morning of the 18th aground in the river. Little damage resulted, except in the case of the small bay steamer *Mistletoe*, which rolled over on the bank so far as to fill with water as the tide returned."

Destruction was spread throughout Southwest Florida. The barometer dropped to 28.40 inches at Fort Myers. Seven men drowned in the wreckage of four Cuban fishing schooners at Punta Gorda, and a one-armed man and a baby were drowned in the vicinity of Thousand Islands. Buildings at Flamingo were destroyed, and great waves battered the coast from there to Cape Romano. These waves were said to have reached a great distance inland, and the survivors "could only escape by climbing trees." The total number of deaths that resulted from the hurricane in Cuba, Florida, and the waters of the Gulf and the Atlantic was estimated to have been at least 101.

Along Florida's east coast, damages were not severe, but offshore winds and the storm's relentless rains caused many problems. The American schooner *Harry T. Hayward*, bound from Baltimore to Knight's Key, was blown ashore and wrecked near Boca Raton. Three of its crew were drowned; the rest were saved after clinging to the ship's rigging for twelve hours. The Weather Bureau's observer at Jupiter reported that "the rainfall at this point did more damage than the high wind. It had rained every day from the 3d to the 13th, with a total fall of 5.96 inches, and the creeks and flat woods were full of water when the first storm began. From the 14th to the 18th, inclusive, 14.27 inches more fell. The inlet being closed the rivers rose 8 feet above normal high water, which in a flat country like this, puts practically all land under water from 1 to 8 feet. Fortunately the sea remained low and comparatively smooth, so that it was possible to open the inlet and let the water out."

SEPTEMBER 4, 1915

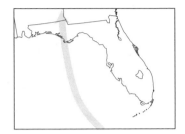

The category 1 hurricane that made landfall near the mouth of the Apalachicola River on September 4, 1915, was not a significant storm in Florida history. Much like a category 1 storm that struck Pensacola in August 1911, its impact on the coast was minor when compared to the great storms of the past. Its arrival was nevertheless unwelcome to the people of the Apalachicola region, who endured winds of 70 mph and damages that totaled $100,000. Numerous boats and wharfs were wrecked, including several vessels from the sponge fleet. In all, twenty-one deaths were attributed to the "modest" hurricane.

Even with the loss of twenty-one lives, this hurricane was easily overshadowed by two incredible storms that struck the United States during the same season. The first was an August hurricane that spawned in the Cape Verde Islands and eventually struck the Texas coast with awesome fury. Tides were twelve feet above normal at Galveston, winds were 120 mph, and the destruction totaled $50 million. Even though the Weather Bureau warned Texas residents twenty-four hours before the hurricane struck, 275 lives were lost. Including the losses in Cuba, Jamaica, and the Gulf of Mexico, the total number of deaths exceeded 400. This powerful storm was, according to Ivan R. Tannehill in *Hurricanes: Their Nature and History*, "probably the greatest hurricane of the century, up to that time, in diameter and intensity."

The second terrible storm of the year had a marginal effect on West Florida, as landfall occurred on the Louisiana coast. On September 29, this hurricane rushed ashore south of New Orleans and swept inland over the city and up through the Mississippi River region. The impact on Mobile and Pensacola was not extreme, but portions of Louisiana were devastated. At New Orleans a barometric pressure of 28.11 was recorded, which was reported by Tannehill as "the lowest of record in the United States at that time." Extreme winds were measured at 130 mph in New Orleans and 140 mph at Burrwood, Louisiana. Many towns and cities were said to have had 90 percent of their buildings destroyed. According to Tannehill, property losses totaled $13 million, and 275 deaths occurred in Louisiana and Mississippi.

JULY 5, 1916

The 1916 hurricane season was one of the most active of record. Eleven hurricanes moved through the Atlantic and Caribbean during the year, and two had an impact on Florida's westernmost counties. The first of these was an early-season storm that moved inland on the Mississippi coast at 5:00 P.M. on July 5. The barometer dropped to 28.92 inches in Mobile, and high winds buffeted the coast. The maximum wind velocity at Mobile was 106 mph, the highest ever reported at that station. According to an account in the *Monthly Weather Review*, "The high tides were responsible for the major portion of the coastal damage. At Mobile the tide was somewhat more than 2 feet above the previous highest tide of 9.87 feet above mean tide in September, 1906, and the entire business district was inundated."

At Pensacola the maximum wind was 104 mph, which also established a record for that location. The Weather Bureau observer on duty, William F. Reed Jr., climbed to the roof of the American National Bank Building to check his instruments periodically as the storm worsened, tying a rope to his waist for security. Reed later commented on the storm's winds: "When the wind passed the 80-mile rate people could not stand at the cross streets, and when they attempted to cross were thrown down and had to creep if they could not hold on to something. Automobiles could not make headway against the wind and had to seek shelter or be blown around at the mercy of the wind; a few were turned over."

Fortunately the storm surge at Pensacola was not as great as that at Mobile; it measured several feet less than the hurricane flood of 1906. At about 2:00 P.M., the rising tide flooded the engine room of the Pensacola Electric Company's power plant, shutting off electricity to the city. The winds were less forgiving; houses were unroofed, chimneys were toppled, trees were blown down and split, and small boats were wrecked and destroyed. A row of large trees on Chase Street was leveled, and traffic was blocked on many city streets. Seven canvas hydroplane hangars were blown down at the "aeronautic station," though the planes and their pontoons had been moved to brick buildings. But even though the peak winds in Pensacola were much greater than those in the 1906 hurricane, less building and structural wind damage was observed. This was attributed to the fact that the 1906 storm had removed many of the older roofs and trees around the city, leaving fewer weak targets for the later storm. No lives were lost in Pensacola.

As the hurricane progressed inland, its forward speed slowed, and it stalled over the interior counties of Mississippi and Alabama. For five days, the decaying hurricane drifted over the Deep South with no real direction and dumped tremendous amounts of rain over several states. The heavy rains overfilled rivers and streams and turned farmlands into lakes. Crop damages were enormous in

Mississippi, Alabama, Florida, and Tennessee. In Florida four lives were lost to the storm, and property damages approached $1 million; across the South, the hurricane killed thirty-four and left $3 million in damages.

OCTOBER 18, 1916

A few months later, an October hurricane paid a visit to Pensacola, the second significant storm to strike the area during the year. This hurricane formed in the western Caribbean and passed over the Yucatán Peninsula on the fifteenth and sixteenth. As it turned northward into the Gulf of Mexico, it accelerated and charged toward western Florida on the morning of the seventeenth. Ship reports of the storm's location were radioed to shore, and the Weather Bureau issued "northeast warnings" along the Gulf coast from Carrabelle to Bay St. Louis, Mississippi. All interested parties were urged to take precautions, and ships were held in port. By 8:00 A.M. on October 18, ship reports placed the hurricane just off the Alabama coast, and hurricane warnings were issued from Apalachicola to New Orleans. At 10:30 the eye of the storm moved directly over the city of Pensacola.

The winds in Pensacola were even higher than the record winds measured in July. At 10:12 the wind reached a five-minute velocity of 114 mph from the southeast, with an extreme of 120 mph within the next minute. At 10:14 the anemometer was blown away, just prior to the dramatic cessation of wind that occurred when the eye passed over the city. The eye moved quickly, and the high winds soon returned, estimated to have been from the west at 120 mph. But the hurricane's eyewall was relatively small, and by 11:00 the winds had again subsided to "less than a gale." The lowest pressure reading in Pensacola was 28.76 inches. In Mobile the pressure was not as low, but the winds were of equal strength. Winds there were measured at 115 mph at 8:25 A.M., with an extreme velocity of 128 mph at 8:28.

Because of the relatively small size of the hurricane and its rapid forward speed, little storm surge was experienced along the Pensacola waterfront. As the eye came over the city, the tide was only three feet above normal. Rainfall near the center of the storm was also light, although regions farther out from the eye received heavy downpours; Burrwood, Louisiana, recorded almost twelve inches of rain. Because of the timely warnings issued by the Weather Bureau and the lack of significant flooding, little damage was reported from the storm. Property losses in the Pensacola-Mobile area totaled $100,000. Almost all of the damages resulted from gusting winds, which delivered typical destruction to trees, fences, signs, and roofs. In Pensacola oak trees that had withstood the July storm were blown down; in all, about 200 trees were toppled in the city.

No deaths were reported in Florida from the hurricane, although some twenty lives were lost when a ship went down in the extreme western Caribbean. As the storm sped northward through the interior sections of the United States, a remarkable redevelopment occurred over Indiana and Illinois, bringing strong gales to the Great Lakes region and the New England coast. According to the *Monthly Weather Review*, on October 20 the storm caused "several casualties to shipping, attended by considerable loss of life."

SEPTEMBER 28–29, 1917

Pensacola was the scene of yet another hurricane in 1917, following closely on the heels of the two storms of the previous year. This hurricane was quite possibly a Cape Verde–type storm, although it was first identified near the Leeward Islands on September 21. From there it tracked westward through Jamaica and Cuba, where destruction was substantial. Its northwesterly course through the Gulf of Mexico would have taken it into western Louisiana, but on the twenty-seventh, it veered to the north and then northeast and made landfall near Pensacola on the afternoon of the twenty-eighth.

In the hours before the storm approached Pensacola, residents heeded the Weather Bureau's early warning that a hurricane was on the way. As it drew closer, other signs were noted by the meteorologist at the Pensacola station,

William F. Reed Jr.: "The roar of the hurricane surf could be heard in Pensacola, which is six miles from the Gulf coast, by 12 midnight on the 26th, when the center of the storm was still some hundred miles distant. . . . Flocks of small seagulls were observed flying inland between 6 A.M. and 7:30 A.M. seeking places of safety at the heads of the bayous. Upon inquiry I found that old residents considered this a sure sign of the immediate approach to our coast of a hurricane, and that these small gulls flew inland in large flocks just previous to the storm of September 26–27, 1906."

Even though the eye of the storm was believed to have passed some fifty miles south of the city, Pensacola still caught the brunt of the hurricane. The lowest barometer reading was measured at 28.51 inches, which established a new record low for that station. The five-minute wind velocity was recorded at 103 mph, with an extreme velocity of 125 mph. The storm tide was reported to have been about 4.5 feet above normal. A little farther east near Valparaiso, tides were 7.5 feet and the pressure dipped to 28.29 inches.

Damages at Pensacola were generally reported to have been more severe than damages in the October hurricane of the previous year. A number of small craft were grounded and wrecked, including the USS *Quincy*, which came ashore in the harbor. As would be expected, considerable damages occurred to wharves, docks, boat houses, and other structures near the shore. In his summary report, Reed counted the losses in the vicinity of Pensacola. "Damages by wind, $100,000; damages by wave action and water, $50,000; and damages to small craft, $20,000; damage total, $170,000." No deaths were reported in Pensacola.

Losses were said to have been heavy in Santa Rosa and Okaloosa Counties, where high winds damaged timber, crops, and numerous homes and other structures. Five lives were lost at Crestview, about forty miles northeast of Pensacola. Soon after the storm moved inland, it dissipated over southern Georgia and had little further impact.

SEPTEMBER 9–10, 1919

The Great Hurricane of September 1919 was one of the largest and most powerful hurricanes ever encountered by the U.S. Weather Bureau. Its large diameter caused it to affect much of the Gulf region, and its extreme intensity and large death toll place it among the worst American hurricanes. Although it did not pass directly over Florida, its impact on the Keys was disastrous, and it later made landfall with continued tragedy on the Texas coast.

The origins of the hurricane can be traced to the eastern Caribbean, where a tropical disturbance was observed south of Puerto Rico on September 3. Once the storm moved over the eastern Bahamas, it apparently strengthened. The Weather Bureau called for reports from its Nassau station, but on the afternoon of the seventh, no report was issued. The evening report was not sent until 9:00 A.M. on the eighth. By this time, the Miami station was experiencing winds of 26 mph and a steadily falling pressure. With little time to prepare, warnings were ordered for the Florida coast from Jupiter to Key West and along the southwest coast to Fort Myers.

On the afternoon of September 9, it became apparent that this powerful storm was passing through the Straits of Florida, and additional emergency warnings were issued. Around midnight the hurricane slowly passed about thirty or forty miles south of Key West on a west-northwest track, pounding the lower Keys with some of the most extreme weather in Florida history. In his official report for the Weather Bureau, Key West observer H. B. Boyer wrote of the severity of the storm:

> The storm that passed over Key West on September 9 and 10 was, without question, the most violent experienced since records at this station began. While the minimum barometric pressure reading, 28.81 inches, was not as low as that recorded in 1909 (28.52) and in 1910 (28.47), the violence of the wind was undoubtedly greater. It is to be regretted that owing to the vibrations of the tower supporting the wind instruments the anemometer cups were shaken loose and blown away at 7:30 P.M. on the 9th in gusts ranging between 75 and 80 miles an hour, and thereafter until 3:35 P.M. of the 10th the wind velocity record was lost. The wind-vane was blown away at 12:45 A.M. of the 10th during the winds of greatest intensity, and at 3:16 A.M. the collector of the recording rain-gage was blown off and the door forced open.
>
> . . . In the terrific gusts that prevailed during the height of the storm stanch brick structures had walls blown out and large vessels, firmly secured, were torn from their fastenings or moorings and blown on the banks. Notwithstanding the great loss, estimated at $2,000,000, the official in charge has been the recipient of many congratulations on the splendid service rendered by the Bureau.
>
> The usual phenomena preceding, accompanying, and following storms of tropical origin were present in this one; and while no thunder was heard, diffuse lightning was noted at intervals for several hours before the maximum force was reached.

The storm's slow movement prolonged the period of damaging winds. At Key West winds of at least gale force were continuous from 7:00 A.M. on the ninth to 9:30 P.M. on the tenth—a period of more than thirty-eight hours. The highest winds at that location were estimated to be 110 mph, and virtually every structure was damaged to some degree. The Weather Bureau building and grounds suffered extensive damage, and many homes were unroofed. Of the $2 million in losses, more than a third was attributed to destruction at the "air station." Over thirteen inches of rain fell during the storm, and at least three deaths were caused by drowning.

At Sand Key the Weather Bureau's observation station was once again abandoned prior to the arrival of the storm. All of the station's instruments, records, equipment, bedding, and so on were moved to the lighthouse during the early-morning hours of the ninth. As the storm worsened later in the day, the entire island was covered with water, and large waves rolled through the government compound. At 10:00 P.M. the station's eighty-five-foot instrument tower was buckled by gusting winds and collapsed onto the bureau office. The station's anemometer and rain gauge were lost early in the evening, so no records exist for peak winds or total rainfall.

As the storm reached its climax just after midnight, the barograph recorded a low-pressure reading of 28.35 inches. Sand Key is about eight miles southwest of Key West and about twenty miles north of where the hurricane's center was believed to have passed. Amazingly, over a distance of only eight miles between the two stations, the lowest pressures differed by almost one-half inch, suggesting that the pressure near the storm's center must have been much lower. Numerous ships caught in the hurricane recorded extreme low-pressure readings, including the steamship *Fred W. Weller*, which measured a low of 27.37 inches in the vicinity of the Dry Tortugas on September 9. Because of this extreme low, the 1919 storm was ranked by the National Hurricane Center as the third most intense U.S. hurricane of the twentieth century, until Hurricane Andrew in 1992 bumped it back to fourth place.

As the hurricane moved slowly into the Gulf of Mexico, it was not clear to forecasters which direction it would take. Storm warnings were issued for the Florida Panhandle and the southern portions of Alabama, Mississippi, and Louisiana. By the afternoon of September 12, warnings were extended along the northern Texas coast, but the bureau suggested that the hurricane would probably reach the Louisiana coast during the night. Because of its large diameter and extreme intensity, the hurricane delivered moderately high tides and winds to numerous coastal locations around the Gulf, including Tampa, Pensacola, and the Louisiana coast. Because of its slow movement and the lack of radio reports from ships in the Gulf, forecasters could only offer general warnings. Residents throughout the Gulf region agonized for several days as they waited for news of the hurricane's next move.

Along the Texas coast, warnings were issued well in advance of the storm, even though it was not known when or even if it would arrive. The people of Galveston took all storm warnings seriously, however, and trains were filled to capacity carrying people, livestock, and grains out of harm's way. At Corpus Christi similar precautions were taken. But even with this early warning and time for preparation, the storm's final impact was devastating. The hurricane finally made landfall just south of Corpus Christi on the fourteenth, where a low barometric pressure of 28.65 inches was recorded. The tide there rose sixteen feet above normal, and hundreds of homes, wharves, and structures of all kinds were bashed by the rolling tide. All of the 900 beach homes along one stretch were destroyed, "most of them beyond a trace." The property losses in Corpus Christi alone topped $20 million. Most tragically, 284 people were killed in the vicinity of Corpus Christi, most of them victims of the hurricane's incredible tide.

The hurricane's impact on the Florida Keys and South Texas was truly severe, but the greatest disasters of the storm occurred at sea. At least ten major vessels went down during the storm's protracted eight-day course from the Bahamas to Texas, and another twenty-five smaller ships were wrecked or sunk. One of the casualties was the Ward Line steamship *Corydon*, which sank on September 9 in the Straits of Florida. Of the crew of thirty-seven, twenty-seven, including the captain, went down with the ship. Ten survivors escaped in a lifeboat, nine of whom were picked up two days later at Cape Florida. The tenth man apparently went "insane" on the lifeboat and was washed overboard and lost.

The greatest tragedy, however, was the loss of the *Valbanera*, a 400-foot Spanish steamship that left Spain on August 21 with over 1,000 passengers and a crew of 88. Its voyage included stops in Puerto Rico and Santiago, Cuba, where hundreds of passengers who had purchased tickets to Havana unexpectedly got off the ship. Rumors of a hurricane nearby may have prompted their early departure. On September 9, with a passenger list of 400 and the same crew of 88, the steamer approached Havana and requested a harbor pilot. The seas were too rough for safe docking, so the ship's captain probably decided to ride out the hurricane at sea. The *Valbanera* was never heard from again.

One week after the hurricane, a search for the lost ship began along the northern coast of Cuba and around the Florida Keys. On September 19, a U.S. Navy ship spotted a mast sticking up out of the water about forty miles west of Key West; it turned out to be the *Valbanera*. Mysteriously, divers later found that the ship was nearly intact; the davits showed that no one had tried to lower the ship's lifeboats, yet none of the passengers or crew were ever found. It was rumored that the ship's safe was taken soon afterward by a sponge fisherman, but the rest of the vessel remained largely untouched until 1996, when a historical salvage expedition was organized. In the Keys, the *Valbanera* became known as the "Wreck of Whores" because several prostitutes were supposedly on board when it went down. Historians are quick to point out, however, that many passenger vessels of this era carrying poor immigrants were likely to have some prostitutes on board.

The exact number of deaths attributed to the hurricane remains unknown. The losses from the *Valbanera* and *Corydon*, when combined with the deaths in Corpus Christi, bring the total to almost 800. According to the NOAA report *The Deadliest Atlantic Tropical Cyclones, 1492–1994*, the September hurricane of 1919 was responsible for 600–900 deaths. This total makes it the third most deadly hurricane of the twentieth century in the United States.

As the hurricane passed below Florida on September 10, a tornado was reported at Goulds, a small town twenty miles southwest of Miami. Reports of this tornado provided the first authenticated account of a tornado occurring within the immediate area of a hurricane. The tornado first formed over Biscayne Bay as a waterspout and then cut a narrow path of destruction toward the west-northwest, following the southeast winds that prevailed in the area at the time. It crossed a three-mile-long section of marsh, carved a 600-foot-wide path through the woods near Goulds, and eventually disappeared over the Everglades, about fourteen miles from where it first touched land.

At Goulds nineteen buildings were damaged and six were totally destroyed. There were no deaths, but several people were injured by flying debris. It was reported that "the absence of fatal accidents was due to the fact that the occupants of all buildings that were demolished heard the approaching storm in time to escape into the open, where they threw themselves upon the ground." One man tried to outrun the tornado in his car, but he was quickly overtaken by the storm and flying debris. A large piece of airborne sheet metal sliced the top off his vehicle, apparently without injuring the man or the rest of his car.

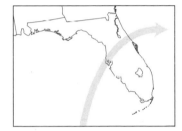

OCTOBER 25, 1921

In the fall of 1921, one of the most explosive periods in America's real estate history was under way in Florida; it would later be called the "Big Boom." At the end of World War I, Americans were bursting with new capital. Factory workers made good salaries, farmers became wealthy, and bankers and industrialists made millions. It seemed that everyone was experiencing the newfound American Dream with money to spare. Northerners discovered they could afford vacations, and they headed south to the bright sunshine of Florida. They traveled in private railroad coaches, shiny new yachts, and caravans of newly purchased automobiles. Those who traveled by car packed tents and boxes of canned food and headed for Florida's rapidly sprawling resort camps, where they earned the nickname "Tin Can Tourists." Wealthy and middle-class visitors quickly bought up cheap land, and some made magical profits by reselling it within days at much higher prices. They poured millions of dollars into the state; across the nation, "Florida fever" was spreading fast.

The wild speculation was especially rampant on the east coast, but in 1921 the growth in Tampa was just beginning. In October of that year, Tampa experienced its worst hurricane in over seventy years. The destruction was not as great as in other Florida hurricanes of the period, but many feared that news stories about the hurricane would frighten winter tourists away from the west coast and thwart development in the Tampa area. This was not the case, however; the boom was under way, and this hurricane couldn't stop it.

Like many October hurricanes, this storm was born in the far reaches of the western Caribbean. It passed through the Yucatán Channel on the twenty-third, where the schooner *Virginia* recorded a minimum pressure of 27.80 inches. At noon on the twenty-fourth, hurricane warnings were issued from Key West to Apalachicola. In the early afternoon of October 25, the storm made landfall near Tarpon Springs and then crossed the Florida Peninsula and headed into the Atlantic.

The Weather Bureau station in Tampa recorded a barometric low of 28.81 inches, the lowest to date for that location. According to NOAA's *Deadliest, Costliest, and Most Intense United States Hurricanes of This Century* by Paul J. Hebert, Jerry D. Jarrell, and Max Mayfield, the storm's lowest pressure in Florida was 28.11 inches. The recorded rainfall was 8.53 inches, but according to the observer, "much more probably fell and was blown out of the gage." Winds reached a maximum velocity of 68 mph, resulting in limited wind damage, but the greatest destruction was caused by the hurricane's angry tides. At about 2:00 P.M., the tide reached its highest point, later measured by the U.S. Corps of Engineers at 10.5 feet above mean low water. This was by far the highest tide measured in Tampa Bay since the flood in 1848, which was reported to have been 15 feet. Tides ran high not just in Tampa but all along the coastal region. According to the official report in the *Monthly Weather Review*, "Egmont and Sanibel Island: Both were practically covered by water. Fort Myers: Tide was 12 to 18 inches higher than previous records for 30 to 35 years. Punta Gorda: Tide was 7 feet above normal high tide at 3 P.M. of 25th; water was in the streets of the city. Punta Rassa: Tide was 6 feet above normal high water. Boca Grande: Tide 5 feet 4 inches above normal high tide at 7:15 A.M. Clearwater: Tide 5 feet above normal high tide, 1:30–4 P.M. St. Petersburg: Tide 8 feet 5 inches above mean low water at 2 P.M."

In Tampa the tide swept over the seawall along Bayshore Drive and into some of the finest homes in the city. The flooding was even more severe at Palmetto Beach, Edgewater Park, and DeSoto Park, where no seawall offered protection. These areas suffered the greatest damages; some houses had water lapping at second-story windows, and many were demolished by breaking waves. At Palmetto Beach at least fifty houses were destroyed by the missilelike bashings of a fleet of storm-tossed cedar logs. The logs, many still chained together, had been rafted off the beach while in route to the Tampa Box Company on Twenty-second Street, where they were to be made into cigar boxes. Large waves drove them onto the waterfront, where they smashed through the walls and doors of sturdy houses along the shore. Some of the logs were later found split open, revealing hollow chambers that held demijohns of bootleg rum, illegally smuggled into the country in violation of Prohibition.

Odd occurrences were reported from locations around the bay. One resident said his home at Sunset Beach began to float down the street during the storm, and he and his family abandoned it for the safety of a small raft. Another man,

caught in the rushing tide on Twenty-second Street, began swimming, only to have a stray pig climb on his back. Other livestock struggled to escape the rising water; some were said to have climbed into houses. Debris of all kinds was strewn among the treetops, including one family's piano, which was later discovered high in the crotch of a pine tree. Also found in the hurricane's aftermath were numerous streetcars, washed off their tracks and buried in sand up to their windows. At St. Petersburg Beach several residents survived the ordeal by lashing themselves to nearby palm trees after consuming significant amounts of bootleg whiskey at a "hurricane party." At Rocky Point seventy-year-old J. D. Wilder clung to his eighty-five-year-old wife and a cabbage palm for most of the night, as the storm waters rose around them. In the early-morning hours of the hurricane's arrival, the wind and tide intensified, and Wilder's wife was swept away with the flood. According to the *Tampa Morning Tribune,* "The two had clung to the tree through the long night hours, Mr. Wilder for the last several hours holding his wife. At last the strain was more than the aged man could bear and in a moment of inadvertent relaxation of his grasp, the end following."

At St. Petersburg all four downtown piers were badly damaged or destroyed. Many vessels of all sizes and descriptions were wrecked in the storm, including the Home Line's *Genevieve* and the trawler *Hypnotist,* which crashed into the Atlantic Coast Line pier, dashing its crew of seven into the raging waters. The steamer *Pokonoket* was washed ashore high on the grounds of the Tampa Bay

Hotel, and the Wilson Line's steamer *Favorite* was also driven ashore and totally wrecked. One story that received much attention was the adventure of Carrie Green, who had accompanied her husband to secure a motor launch near Ballast Point. While assisting her husband, who was attempting to repair the vessel's inoperative engine, Carrie boarded an adjacent ten-foot skiff, only to lose her moorings and be set adrift in the boiling seas, her husband helpless to reach her. She lost one oar and was swept into the bay with only the remaining oar. Tossed about in the storm, she guided the boat through the waves by shifting her weight and finally washed ashore some ten miles away at Delaney Creek. The *Tampa Morning Tribune* described her arrival: "Upon reaching the eastern side of what would ordinarily have been the bay's confines, Mrs. Greene's skiff kept right on going, driving into the woodland, which was six or eight feet in water at the time. Inevitably, the skiff crashed into a pine tree and overturned. Mrs. Greene, clinging to the upturned boat, swam for about a mile, pushing the little craft along until she could reach bottom. She then waded ashore and walked for another two miles, until she located a light in the residence of the Moyer family, where she arrived at 4:30 A.M., eleven hours after her boat went adrift on the Bayshore waterfront."

Soon after the storm's arrival, a rumor circulated that a tidal wave had completely "wiped out" Pass-a-Grille and drowned over a hundred residents. All communications were cut off, power was out throughout the bay area, and bridges were washed away, so it would take a while for search crews to make their rounds to sort out the losses and recover the dead. The following day,

a De Sota Park Bungalow
after Hurricane
Oct 25-1921

Red Cross officials loaded relief supplies and dozens of pine caskets aboard a U.S. Navy subchaser to take to Pass-a-Grille. Fortunately the rescue ship discovered that no lives had been lost there and the rumored devastation had not occurred. A pier and a casino at the Pass-a-Grille Hotel were destroyed, and the hotel itself was heavily damaged. At the fifty-room St. Petersburg Beach Hotel and Casino at Blind Pass, employees swam amid floating furniture in the lobby as they made their way toward a stairway to safety. The hotel later collapsed.

At the *St. Petersburg Times* office at Fifth Street and First Avenue South, the staff worked by lantern light throughout the night of the storm. But with no electricity to run the typesetting machine, they had no way to assemble their stories for print, until they got some help from Otis Beard. Beard, who ran a nearby motorcycle shop, connected a two-cylinder motorbike to their Linotype machine, allowing them to set the copy for the morning's edition. A small-job press that required no electricity was used for the printing, and the "Motorcycle Extra" brought the first news of the storm to the streets.

The hurricane's impact was spread beyond the shores of Tampa Bay and the west coast. Significant losses were reported to crops and farms in the inland portions of the state as the hurricane crossed over to the Atlantic. One steamer, the *Vann*, was lost off the east coast near Jupiter, and several other schooners were reported to have capsized in the Atlantic as the storm passed off Florida's shore. Fortunately, though, the losses to shipping were relatively light due to adequate warnings by the Weather Bureau. The total number of deaths attributed to the hurricane is not known, but it was reported that at least eight died on the west coast. In Tampa two people were drowned, and three were electrocuted when they came in contact with downed wires. In St. Petersburg one man was crushed under a fallen roof, and one died of a heart attack while working to prepare his home for the storm. The eighth death occurred near Punta Gorda when the operator of an icehouse drowned in the hurricane tide. Total financial losses from the storm exceeded $3 million.

SEPTEMBER 15, 1924

Two hurricanes struck the Florida coast in 1924, both of category 1 intensity. The first came ashore near Port St. Joe on September 15, with winds of 75–80 mph near the storm center. Wind damages were not significant, but heavy rains flooded fields and washed away acres of crops. The heaviest rainfall was measured at Quincy, in Gadsden County, where 12.93 inches were recorded within twenty-four hours. The Suwannee and Aucilla Rivers were far above flood stage, and thousands of acres were submerged. The heaviest damages occurred to cotton, corn, sugarcane, peanut, sweet potato, and pecan crops.

OCTOBER 20–21, 1924

A little more than a month after the September storm of 1924, another hurricane struck the state, but this storm made landfall farther south, near Cape Romano. Prior to its arrival in Florida, it was one of the most severe on record in western Cuba. At Jutias City a barometric pressure of 27.22 inches was recorded aboard the SS *Toledo* on October 19. Fortunately the hurricane weakened considerably prior to its arrival on Florida's southwestern coast the following day. Winds at Marco Island were estimated at 90 mph, and the barometer there measured 28.80 inches. Remarkably, the Weather Bureau reported a twenty-four-hour rainfall total of 23.22 inches during the passing of this storm, which established a new one-day rainfall record in Florida. Most of the rains fell across the vast unpopulated expanses of the Everglades, so damages to homes and property were not significant.

NOVEMBER 30–DECEMBER 1, 1925

The 1925 hurricane season was unusually quiet—only two tropical storms emerged in the Atlantic basin, and only one of those became a hurricane. On November 29, a tropical system formed in the western Caribbean and quickly moved northward into the Gulf. On the evening of the following day, it became a category 1 hurricane, and its path would take it onto the Florida coast between Sarasota and Tampa. Its impact on the immediate coastline was not significant, and it crossed the Florida Peninsula as a tropical storm. But once it entered the Atlantic near Daytona Beach on December 1, it regained strength and threatened the U.S. east coast as a hurricane.

STORM
St. Petersburg Times
EXTRA

St. Petersburg, Fla., Wednesday Morning, Oct. 26, 1921

TROPICAL STORM SWEEPS CITY

Property Damage May Reach $5,000,000; Two Men Die

RUMOR PASS-A-GRILLE WIPED OUT

With property loss estimated at $5,000,000, and two known dead, the water front a sea of debris and sunken ships, St. Petersburg Tuesday was swept by the worst tropical storm in the history of the West coast, striking about 3 o'clock in the morning and lasting until late in the afternoon, unroofing hundreds of hotels, apartment houses and homes, tearing down power lines and isolating the city completely from the outside world.

Communication was completely cut off from Pass-a-Grille, where reports estimated the loss of life from 15 to 150, with the resort under five feet of water.

TWO MEN DIE

J. W. McLean, 75, living at Twenty third street and First avenue south, dropped dead from excitement early Tuesday morning while closing the windows and doors of his home to guard against the rain.

Ferrel C. Wolfe, 18, son of W. H. Wolfe, living in the Chappael apartments was killed when caught under a falling roof at Seventh street and Central avenue. First reports were that another man had been killed in the crash, but examination of the wreck failed to disclose his body.

HEAVY PROPERTY LOSS

Heavy losses were reported as follows:

Complete ruin of the county's citrus crop estimated at $1,000,000.

Spa bathing pavilion, reported complete loss; $100,000.

A. C. L. pier; $100,000.

Municipal pier swept out; loss $100,000.

Biaff pier, $10,000. Detroit pier, $10,000.

DAMAGE IN BAYBORO

Damage in Bayboro harbor including the shipping and flooding of shops and factories totalled more than $200,000. Included in this was $10,000 damage to the naval radio station according to Chief H. Kidder.

The Seaboard Air Line bridge at Seminole went out early in the day.

The highway bridge at Seminole followed the railroad bridge.

SEVEN MEN RESCUED

All seven members of the crew of the yacht Hypnotist which sank early Tuesday afternoon after striking submerged pilings off the railroad pier were saved according to information received at 5 o'clock. After the boat had sunk and after three of the men had been washed from the boat, Hubert Caufield with Arthur Herbert, captain of the life saving corps of New York city and George Gamble went to the rescue in Caufield's yacht Sheerwater. The men were brought ashore and given first aid on board the U. S. Sub Chaser 60 in the yacht harbor.

The three men who had been washed from the boat drifted from the railroad pier to the Municipal pier and after clinging to the piling were carried out on the bay.

Herbert Ballard accompanied by two other men rescued one member of the crew three miles out in the bay. The man was apparently lifeless when dragged from the water but later was revived at the city hospital. He was unable to give his name.

Two other members of the crew washed ashore near Coffee Pot, more than two miles from where they entered the water.

The Ballard launch went dead after the rescue and drifted three hours before the engine was started. J. H. Commers and Bob Ely happened to be at Coffee Pot when the launch landed and rushed the men to the hospital.

The two men who floated to within a few yards of shore along North Shore were rescued by Deputy Sheriff James Hance, Fred F. Davis, V. J. Clark, and J. M. Quinn who waded out to pull them in.

STORM SUBSIDES

At 9 o'clock Tuesday night, the storm had passed. Incoming water on the waterfront which had reached Beach Drive had subsided.

The city was in complete darkness Tuesday night. Chief of Police Eidamen swore in a large force of deputies to guard the streets.

Bayboro was a sea of water with scores of residents being rescued in small boats. Other parts of the city were inundated.

FEW CASUALTIES

Despite the intensity of the storm, which hurled roofs into the street, sent signs down, crashed trees to the street, and sent sheets of tin bowling down the streets, few casualties were suffered.

At a late hour Tuesday night only two known were dead, and but one of these was killed in an accident.

PIERS DESTROYED

Only a few pilings remain where the Municipal pier stood. The refreshment stand at the end of the pier and all wooden structure, including the piling was washed away.

All that remains where the railroad pier stood is the building of the Hibbs Fish company and the water tank. All other buildings and pilings went out.

The Fountain of Youth Pier entirely disappeared during the storm. This pier went out first.

Braff pier at the foot of Fifth avenue north was entirely destroyed.

CARRIES OUT NEWS

The A. C. L. passenger train left at 8:30 Tuesday night taking the first word of the damage done here by the storm to the outside world. A special message was sent to the Associated Press at Jacksonville by the Times. Previous efforts to get in touch with other points were made by means of wireless but were fruitless, the local plant going dead at 4 o'clock Tuesday afternoon. Messages were being received but none could be sent out.

The Western Union offices were swamped by scores of persons anxious to get word to relatives telling them of their safety. A Western Union man, bearing several hundred telegrams, boarded the A. C. L. passenger with instructions to wire the messages at the first available telegraph station. There was no word as to how far inland the storm had hit.

GAS AND WATER

The city was assured of gas and water, according to R. E. Ludwig, director of Public Utilities. One smoke stack was blown down at the city water plant, but an emergency stack was available and the power house will continue to run. No considerable damage was done to the gas station. Both plants have sufficient fuel and supplies to keep going for two weeks, according to Ludwig.

A large force of men were put to work late Tuesday afternoon clearing up the wires in order that power may be turned on. No damage was done to the power house, Ludwig said, and juice can be furnished as soon as the lines are cleared. The earliest possible time that power could be restored was late this afternoon by udwig. He was not able to estimate the loss.

NO INSURANCE

The city carried no hurricane insurance on the three piers. Ludwig announced and the total loss on the waterfront of approximately $250,000 must be borne by the city.

The storm slackened about 3:30 Tuesday afternoon and hundreds of persons flocked to the waterfront by automobile and on foot to see what the storm had done. Scores were out when the storm was at its height.

WIRELESS ACTIVE

Chief Kidder, of the naval wireless station reported Tuesday night that his communication by wireless with the outside world was cut off at 4 a. m. Tuesday. He has been able to receive during the day.

Wireless from Key West reported that that city was 200 miles east of the storm path said to have been 50 miles wide. Clearwater was hit hard but Tarpon Springs was undamaged reports said.

Weather report from Key West Tuesday afternoon were to the effect that the storm would turn and that northeast gale warnings should be posted from Key West to Apalachicola.

PASS-A-GRILLE DESTROYED?

Rumors from Pass-a-Grille at 8 o'clock were that 150 persons had been drowned and that the water was five feet deep in the street.

Oliver Eady, proprietor of the fishing tackle store on the railroad pier estimated his loss at $2,000.

The Pass-a-Grille bridge, Seminole bridge and S. A. L. railroad bridge to Clearwater went out in the storm. The damage here was estimated at more than $800,000.

To prevent looting through the city more than 15 extra patrolmen were sworn in Tuesday night by E. J. Eidaman, police chief.

ATTEMPT RESCUE

After rumors had been heard that 150 had been drowned at Pass-a-Grille, George M. Lynch, head of the Red Cross, made an attempt to form a rescue party but no boat could be found to make the trip.

Capt. W. S. Sweat, of the Gulfport-Pass-a-Grille boat line reported that Pass-a-Grille was under five feet of water. He reported that the yacht New York which he had sent to Pass-a-Grille Tuesday morning had not been heard from.

CLEARWATER REPORT

W. T. Hood, Tampa, and B. Carlstromer, Philadelphia, came through by automobile from Clearwater at 5 o'clock. They made the trip via Largo. Hood and Carlstromer reported heavy damage in both Clearwater and Largo. At

HOW WE DID IT

This miniature issue of The Times was made possible through the efforts of every member of the newspaper's force and the assistance of Otis Beard, 143 Second street north, who furnished a motorcycle which was used as power for the operation of the linotype machine. Beard is a member of Beard Bros., automobile mechanics 827 Baum avenue. Credit for rigging up the machinery is due J. J. Martin, superintendent of service for the Clark-Quinn Motor company, distributors of Oldsmobiles, together with Fred F. Davis, sales manager, who gave his help and advice.

The St. Petersburg Times published its famed "Motorcycle Extra" after the October 1921 hurricane. Because the city was without electricity, the Times was forced to borrow a two-cylinder motorcycle and attach a belt to its rear wheel to power a Linotype machine in order to produce the issue.

On December 2, the *USS Patoka* measured a barometric pressure of 28.90 inches while caught in the storm some 100 miles southeast of Wilmington, North Carolina. Ultimately, the hurricane lost some of its fury before sweeping over North Carolina's Outer Banks as a tropical storm. In Florida and along the coastal waters of the eastern states, over fifty lives were lost to the storm, and damages totaled more than $1.6 million. But this hurricane is most notable for its tardiness; by making landfall in Florida on November 30, it is recognized as the latest hurricane known to have struck the United States in the history of the Weather Bureau.

JULY 27–28, 1926

The Atlantic hurricane season of 1926 was both active and deadly. Eight hurricanes were recorded, four of which caused significant loss of life. In addition to a July storm that killed more than 287 in Puerto Rico, the Dominican Republic, the Bahamas, and Florida, an August hurricane killed 25 in Louisiana, the Great Miami Hurricane in September killed a total of 372, and a deadly October storm killed 709 in Cuba and the waters near Bermuda. Warnings and forecasts issued by the Weather Bureau did save lives, but many people either never received the warnings or greatly underestimated the power of these deadly storms.

The July hurricane was the first of two to strike Florida during the year. It was first sighted east of the Leeward Islands on July 22. As it progressed on a rather typical northwest course, it grew in strength and passed near Puerto Rico, Haiti, and the Bahamas. On the morning of the twenty-sixth, the storm's eye was near Nassau, where residents reported that it was the most severe hurricane in many years. It continued on a north-northwest course until it reached the Florida coast near Jupiter on the afternoon of July 27. Winds along the coast were about 90 mph, and the minimum pressure at the Jupiter station was 28.80 inches. The Weather Bureau reported on the effects of the storm: "The Center was near Palm Beach on the morning of the 27th, then north-northwestward. The high winds and seas sweeping before them boats, docks, boat houses and other marine property on the ocean front as well as that on the Indian River. Trees were uprooted, including citrus trees; houses were unroofed or otherwise damaged. The observer at Merritt Island remarks that there was a tremendous wave and with the high wind all boats, docks, and other property from the river front were swept ashore."

As the storm swept through the north-central portions of Florida, high winds leveled trees, farm buildings, and crops. In Jacksonville it was regarded as one of the greatest storms in recent years, although no deaths were reported. The storm weakened considerably as it tracked into Georgia and Alabama, but heavy rains caused serious flooding and considerable losses to summer crops.

In Florida damages of over $2.5 million were reported, and the storm total for the United States surpassed $3 million.

SEPTEMBER 18–21, 1926

When Henry Flagler's Florida East Coast Railway rolled into Miami in the spring of 1896, few could have guessed the future of the city carved out of the mangroves. Over the next thirty years, steady growth followed, and the city blossomed. In the early 1920s, Florida's great boom was most explosive in Miami and its environs. From 1923 to 1925, the speed-of-light prosperity that enveloped the city was at its peak, as frenzied speculation sent sprawling growth in all directions.

At Miami Beach few mangroves remained; they had been replaced by hotels, casinos, palatial homes, shops, and streets surrounded by grass lawns and built over pumped-in sand. In Miami new subdivisions pushed westward toward the Everglades, and bordering communities were invented, marketed, and sold, with names like Coral Gables and Hollywood. In 1925 alone, Miami saw over $60 million worth of new construction, making it the "fastest growing city in the country." Newborn millionaires strolled the sidewalks, and every week Flagler's railroad brought fresh arrivals to this glamorous city in the sun. By the end of the year, the population of the sprawl from Fort Lauderdale to southern Dade County topped 300,000. The growth was so rapid that shortages of materials and labor sometimes caused delays in the construction of new homes, forcing new settlers to live for months in camps of tar paper shanties that sprang up around the edges of several Miami suburbs.

But by the spring of 1926, the boom was beginning to fade in Miami, and the real estate market dropped. The summer was a time for regrouping, and many realtors, licensed or not, developed plans for how to rejuvenate their properties for the upcoming fall season. The July hurricane that had passed to the north added to the nervousness of a volatile market but left the beaches unscathed. Unfortunately for the people of Miami, the July storm did little to prepare them for the storm that would follow. It would later be called the "Great Miami Hurricane" and was largely responsible for turning Miami's boom to bust.

It began, like so many other awesome Atlantic hurricanes, as a Cape Verde–type storm, far away from the casinos and bungalows of Florida's shores. It was first spotted as a tropical disturbance on September 11, some 1,000 miles east of the Leeward Islands. On the afternoon of the sixteenth, it rapidly passed by the Turks Islands, where winds were at least 150 mph. The storm apparently passed north of Puerto Rico with little fanfare, and its rapid forward speed (19 mph) brought it through the Bahamas on the afternoon of September 17.

At the Weather Bureau's Miami office, chief meteorologist Richard W. Gray was at an extreme disadvantage with little information available on the storm

other than a 1:00 P.M. report from Nassau on the seventeenth. In Miami blue skies were accompanied by light breezes, and no blood-red skies or long swells had been seen on the previous day. On the morning of the seventeenth, the *Miami Herald* featured a four-inch story about the storm on page 1, but the editors added that it was not expected to hit Florida. By afternoon the *Miami Daily News* reported that the Weather Bureau had hoisted storm warnings at noon, that the storm was expected to strike Nassau, and that "destructive winds" were anticipated by late evening. The word "hurricane" was not used in the story, and the citizens of Miami ended their Friday with no concept of the turmoil that was about to overtake them. Even into the evening, little concern was felt, except by Gray, who watched his barometer fall rapidly at his office on Northeast First Street and First Avenue. Finally, as the storm's first squalls raked the Florida coast at 11:30 P.M., Gray raised the red and black hurricane flags, but his warning was too little and too late.

Over the next twelve hours, Miami was pummeled by the most severe hurricane conditions in Weather Bureau history. The eye of the storm swept directly over the city, and thousands awoke to the wind's horrifying roar. The storm's awesome winds, rains, and tide swept through the streets of Miami and its neighboring towns, delivering massive destruction to buildings and vessels of all kinds. The ferocious winds ripped at structures of all sizes, from downtown skyscrapers to tourist-camp huts. On Miami Beach an anemometer on the roof of the Allison Hospital recorded a wind velocity of 128 mph (true wind 123) for five consecutive minutes beginning at 7:30 A.M. on September 18. At 7:40, a two-minute reading of 138 mph (132 true) was recorded. The wind continued at a rate above 120 mph until 8:12, when the instrument was blown away. Gray later estimated that the "extreme velocity of one mile of wind" was 150 mph. According to the Weather Bureau's account that followed the storm, this wind speed was the "highest ever recorded in the United States."

The severity of the storm was also measured by Gray's barometer in Miami. At about 10:00 P.M. on the seventeenth, the pressure began to fall rapidly from 29.20 inches and continued to fall at a rate of about 0.25 inch per hour through the early morning. From 5:30 to 6:10 A.M., the pressure dropped 0.40 inch and finally reached a low of 27.61 inches at 6:45. At about this time the hurricane's eye was directly over the central and southern parts of the city. At least eight inches of rain fell (no exact figure is available since the rain instruments were destroyed), and a storm surge that measured 11.7 feet above mean low water struck Biscayne Boulevard. Gray estimated the surge in Coconut Grove to have been 14 or 15 feet and called it "the greatest ever caused by a storm on the coast of the United States."

The waterfront in Miami was flooded two to three blocks from the bay, and most sections near the Miami River were under several feet of water. Water filled the first floors of hotels, shops, and residences all around the bay to a depth of three to five feet. The storm tide pushed a destructive tidal wave, or *bore*, up the Miami River, wrecking scores of boats that had retreated there for safe anchorage. All along the bayfront, boats of all shapes and sizes were tossed into the streets, from small launches to large schooners, yachts, and barges. At least 150 ships were driven onto land or sunk in Biscayne Bay. Among the losses was the *Nohab*, once owned by ex kaiser Wilhelm and considered "one of the finest yachts afloat." It capsized in the bay during the storm, and only one member of its crew was saved. Other ships in the mass of wreckage were the steamer *Jacksonville*, the five-masted schooner *Rose Mahoney*, and a large barge that broke its anchor lines and rode the tide across Biscayne Boulevard, crashing over palms and streetlights in its path.

Perhaps the greatest tragedy occurred at the time the storm's center crossed Miami. After hours of ever-increasing gusts, an eerie silence fell over the city just after 6:00 A.M. The eye of the hurricane had arrived, but few knew what it was. Thousands fled their houses, apartments, and hotel rooms and poured into the streets to survey the damage. Some were seen kissing the earth and praying aloud with their faces turned upward toward the boiling gray skies. It was said that the air pressure was so low that breathing was difficult. Within minutes, a stream of cars began racing across the causeway from Miami Beach. But Gray knew the coast was not clear. According to the *Miami Herald*, he threw open the door to his Weather Bureau office and shouted to those in the street: "The storm's not over! We're in the lull! Get back to safety! The worst is yet to come!"

At 6:45 A.M., less than thirty-five minutes after Gray's earnest plea, the "second storm" struck Miami with an even more vicious fury. Scores were trapped in the littered streets with no protection from airborne debris. The cars on the causeway never made it to the other side. All around the Miami area, people

Many cottages and homes on Miami Beach were torn open by the combination of water and wind in the September 1926 storm. (Photo courtesy of the Florida State Archives)

Miami Beach was blasted by the September 1926 storm. Many buildings lost their roofs, and deep sand filled the lobbies of hotels and casinos along the strand. (Photo courtesy of Noel Risnychok)

were caught outside of shelter and, in some cases, away from their loved ones. Many whose houses were severely damaged by the earlier winds were crushed when the winds shifted and their homes collapsed. Within the next hour, the gusts grew more intense until they reached the top speed measured at the Allison Hospital. Most who experienced the "lull" had no concept of the hurricane's rotational forces. Many marveled at how the storm had managed to stop and then "change direction."

After the storm had passed Miami, survivors slowly staggered into the streets to witness the destruction. In an official report on the storm, Gray wrote: "The intensity of the storm and the wreckage that it left can not be adequately described. The continuous roar of the wind; the crash of falling buildings, flying debris, and plate glass; the shriek of fire apparatus and ambulances that rendered assistance until the streets became impassable; the terrifically driven rain that came in sheets as dense as fog; the electric flashes from live wires have left the memory of a fearful night in the minds of the many thousands that were in the storm area."

Perhaps the most dramatic account of the 1926 hurricane can be found in *Florida Hurricane and Disaster 1926*, a pictorial diary of the storm by L. F. Reardon. Although Reardon's eyewitness account only covers the first nine days of

the storm's aftermath, he provides graphic evidence of the hurricane's fury. In it he chronicles the structural damages and recovery efforts in the many affected communities in the Miami area. In 1986, on the sixtieth anniversary of the storm, Miami historian Arva Parks reprinted Reardon's journal to bring the story of the 1926 disaster to a new generation of Floridians. Among Reardon's most moving accounts was this passage he wrote after emerging from his shelter:

> Few people were to be seen. Are they all dead? Those we did see were either laughing hysterically or weeping. One grocer stood calmly back of his cash register, his entire store naked to the lowering Florida skies. There were no customers. As we approached Miami along Eighth Street sights of desolation that met our eyes were heart-rending. Whole sides of apartment blocks had been torn away, disclosing semi-naked men and women moving dazedly about the ruins of their homes. Houses, stores, and shops lay sprawled. How many dead are under them? Everybody was looking for a drink of water—and there was none to be had. People were pouring into the street—most of them in bathing suits. Ambulances rushed in every direction, their wailing sirens reminiscent of the storm. There's a boy covered with blood running blindly across the street. Where are his parents? We must turn here as a building has spread itself across the trail. Is that wind rising again?

I am too tired to write any more now. We got to the Everglades Hotel after circling the business district where, for several blocks, the water was four feet deep and laden with wreckage. The lobby is full of refugees from the storm. Third street is strewn with twisted automobiles. Along Biscayne Boulevard large yachts and barges weighing hundreds of tons have been deposited in front of the McAllister and Columbus Hotels.

We are in a soggy apartment now—and we have had a drink of water. We must sleep; or have I been dreaming a terrible dream?

Reardon's vivid description of the Miami streets illustrated the shocking nature of the disaster. Wreckage was everywhere. No building in the downtown district was undamaged. The seventeen-story Meyer-Kiser Bank Building was said to have rocked, swayed, and "danced the Charleston" in the hurricane's high winds and was left leaning precariously over the street. Few plate glass windows in the entire city remained intact. Flagler Street was filled with debris, and virtually every street-level shop was spilling over with soaked goods. Electricity was out all over town, all radio and telegraph communications were cut off, and the city's newspapers were unable to print the news. Word did get out, however, as *Miami Tribune* reporter Al Reck was able to push through the debris on the Dixie Highway and take the first news of the storm to West Palm Beach on Saturday evening.

The hotels, casinos, and large stately homes of Miami Beach caught the full brunt of the hurricane. According to witnesses who survived the storm surge, water was six feet deep on Meridian Avenue at the height of the hurricane. South Beach was perhaps the hardest hit; according to Reardon, "Hardee's and Smith's Casinos might as well have been under a barrage of cannon for days." The Million Dollar Pier was heavily damaged, and the South Beach Casino, Charley's Grill, and the Ritz Restaurant were virtually destroyed. Sand was two feet deep on Ocean Drive from Fifth Street northward to the Snowden estate. Trees that had once provided a great canopy over the streets were swept away, and in the days after the storm, longtime residents had difficulty recognizing landmarks as they explored the destruction. Homes of some of the most prominent and wealthy citizens in Florida were laid to waste within a matter of hours. Among the mounds of wreckage that filled the streets and canals were pieces of European statuary, half-buried grand pianos, twisted wrought iron, and scattered dead fish. One couple, knocked off their feet as waves broke through their home on Collins Avenue, abandoned their house in haste with the tide. Soon afterward, a huge wave apparently cast them into a coconut tree, where they hung for four hours until the storm subsided.

In her 1958 book *Hurricane*, Marjory Stoneman Douglas wrote of the perils of Miami Beach businessman George W. Woollard, whose stylish oceanfront offices were overtaken by the storm's incredible tide:

Hardee's Casino on the south end of Miami Beach was heavily damaged in the September 1926 storm. (Photo courtesy of Noel Risnychok)

Miami's streets were flooded with water and traffic after the September 1926 hurricane passed. (Photo courtesy of Noel Risnychok)

His candle went out. In pitch blackness he heard all the windows crash open as two waves, one from the street and one from the ocean, filled the room with swirling sea water to his waist. Some dark object rolled against his knees. It was a half-drowned policeman. For hours they stood on a table in water to their hips, roofed with the extraordinary howling-crashing-roaring of wind and rain and sea.

Winds from the September 1926 hurricane destroyed homes, warehouses, and farming equipment many miles from the coast. (Photo courtesy of Noel Risnychok)

Boats and vessels of all sizes were washed out of Biscayne Bay and into the streets and yards of Miami in the September 1926 storm. (Photo courtesy of the Florida State Archives)

By the whiteness of waves they saw dimly the grand piano carried out through the door. Roofs over the windows collapsed, but not on them. The Roman Pool next door split in two, adding five hundred thousand gallons of fresh water to the ocean that rose around them. At dawn they hung to a chandelier, lifting and falling with the waves.

Woollard and the policeman were eventually rescued after spending ten hours in the flooded office. Like so many fortunate survivors of the hurricane, they managed to be spared even when the walls around them came crashing down.

The costly estates of Coconut Grove suffered a similar fate. The main highway through town, proclaimed by the late President Warren Harding as the most beautiful in the United States, was blasted by wind and tide. The graceful Australian pines that lined the roadway were toppled. Prior to the storm, many of the nation's most respected names in art, literature, music, science, and industry gathered in this community each winter, and Reardon noted that in the hurricane's aftermath, their "artistic and literary penchants are directed towards shoveling fallen plaster and drying out rugs."

In Hialeah, which had been spared the terror of rising ocean waters, the greatest damages resulted from the hurricane's incredible winds. It was reported that seventeen people died while huddled together in one building when the structure's walls and roof spontaneously collapsed. Hundreds of working-class homes were razed; the official estimate was that 70 percent of Hialeah's homes were severely damaged or destroyed. On the day after the storm, the streets were impassable. Large piles of wreckage, bedding, appliances, and trees choked the thoroughfares. Children were seen wandering naked, sifting through the rubble in search of treasures. Hialeah's famed racetrack was blasted; the massive grandstand roof of the Miami Jockey Club was stripped off and scattered over the Everglades. At the dog track, the kennels were blown down, and racing hounds were chased away by the winds. At the Tropical Radio Station, communications with the outside world were lost at about 3:00 A.M., just as families from the surrounding area arrived at the station seeking shelter. At 4:30 A.M., all five of the station's towers crashed to the ground with a deafening roar— four were 439 feet high, and the fifth was 460 feet. Luckily, the station's crew and the refugees were unharmed.

Of all the areas affected by the hurricane, the small community of Moore Haven paid the highest price in lives lost. Situated on the southwestern side of Lake Okeechobee, this village of 1,200 was one of south-central Florida's truck-farming communities. In the years prior to the hurricane's arrival, the state had undertaken a massive reclamation project to drain the Everglades' vast grasslands for farming. Heavy rains in 1922 and 1924 had caused the lake's level to rise, and the citizens of Moore Haven had built a muck dike to protect themselves from future floods. But the state of Florida and the people of Moore Haven had underestimated the awesome impact a major hurricane could have on the waters of Okeechobee.

After the 1926 storm swept over Miami on a northwesterly course, it streaked across the Everglades toward the Gulf of Mexico. Its churning winds whipped up the waters of Lake Okeechobee, sending a massive flood of wind-driven water toward the southern end of the lake. The dikes near Moore Haven were no match for the flood. Reardon's account best describes the scene:

> With the wind at more than 100 miles per hour, the mad waters rushed over the too-low protection, through the great gaps and breaks of the broken dykes, and swept over Moore Haven and its helpless populace to a depth of fifteen feet. Scores of men, women, and children were drowned like rats in a trap in the first rush of the flooding waters, which came like a wall through and over the dykes. Those caught in their beds had not a chance for life as the crazed elements drove the very lake through their windows and doors. . . .
>
> To the roofs! That was the only place of refuge in Moore Haven; and that is where the frightened, hysterical, terror-crazed people tried to go. It was dark—dark as pitch—black as ink. Fathers and mothers trying to get to the roofs of their homes, or seizing floating wreckage, whipped and buffeted by wind and water, weak and terror-stricken, saw their children torn from their arms and swirled away in the raging torrent.

When the first relief train finally arrived in Moore Haven late Saturday evening, mud-soaked survivors fell in fatigue onto the floors of the coaches. Many others insisted they would not leave until they found their loved ones and had to be forced onto the train by the National Guard. The entire town was evacuated. The actual number of dead in Moore Haven was never verified, but it was estimated that more than 150 corpses were scattered in the mire. Some estimates ran as high as 300. Many of the dead were swept out into the far reaches of the Everglades, and flocks of vultures were said to have patrolled the skies for days after the storm. The cleanup and recovery of the dead took weeks and was described as among the most gruesome work ever undertaken by any rescue party in the country. Three weeks after the hurricane had passed, water was still two to three feet deep in the streets of Moore Haven.

Many other South Florida communities experienced losses from the storm—far too many to list. At Fort Lauderdale tall buildings were gutted by winds, and countless yachts were sunk along the banks of the New River. The storm surge there was measured at 12.58 feet above mean low tide. The roof of the Broward County courthouse was sheared away, and at least twenty-six lives were lost. In all, 3,500 structures sustained major damage in a town that had a population of only 12,000 at the time. In Hollywood hotels and casinos were blasted by water and wind, and scores were killed. Seminole chief Tony Tommy told the *Hollywood News* that the hurricane was the "worst in the history of the Seminoles in Florida." Up the coast at Cocoa Beach, the storm unearthed an old Spanish ship near First Street South. Down at Goulds, houses were said to have been lifted off their foundations and spun ninety degrees. Boxcars on the Florida East Coast Railway were blown over; some rolled more than 100 yards downwind from the tracks. It was also reported that streets in Goulds were littered with hundreds of dead birds.

As the storm passed inland, its effects stretched far beyond the Miami area and the waters of Lake Okeechobee. Terrific winds buffeted citrus groves across the state, tossing fruit onto the ground. The storm was felt as far north as Seminole County, where the 165-foot "Big Tree," the tallest cypress east of the Rockies, was reduced in height by more than 30 feet by hurricane-force winds. Farther south, at Tampa, Fort Myers, and Naples, high winds blew out store windows and toppled trees and utility poles. In Tampa no deaths were reported and damages were only about $100,000, even though the waters of Tampa Bay and the Hillsborough River had spilled high over their banks. As the hurricane approached the town of Everglades City in Collier County, high winds from the north blew the water out of the Barron River and Chokoloskee Bay, but when the storm passed and the winds shifted, an eight-foot surge of water inundated the town. Those who had not evacuated watched from second-story windows of the Everglades Inn as houses rose from their foundations and sailed across town. According to the *Naples Star*, automobiles parked in the streets were "filled with muddy saltwater and sea creatures. Those animals trapped in cars later died when the water subsided leaving a stench that lingered for weeks."

Like many other great hurricanes that have affected South Florida through the years, the 1926 storm crossed the peninsula and entered the warm waters of the Gulf of Mexico. Its exercise in destruction was not ended; from there it took aim on the northern Gulf coast. By sunrise on September 20, the hurricane's eye was just south of Pensacola, and the storm was slowing down. Its gradual turn toward the west just before landfall took it inland near Gulf Shores, Alabama, around mid-morning. But its slow movement along the coast delivered prolonged devastation to the region around Pensacola. The Weather Bureau recorded winds of hurricane force for more than twenty consecutive hours; winds of over 100 mph were recorded for five hours. Pensacola recorded 8.61 inches of rain; Bradenton measured 8.76 inches. The barometer at Pensacola dropped to 28.56 inches. The harsh weather finally broke on the afternoon of the twenty-first when the diminished storm drifted over Louisiana.

Almost every pier, wharf, boat, and warehouse on Pensacola Bay was destroyed. The storm tide reached a peak of 9.4 feet above normal at Pensacola, 10.4 feet at Fort Pickens, and 14 feet at Bagdad. Large vessels were cast into the streets, including the *William Harbison*, which rode the tide across Navy Boulevard. The Bayou Chico drawbridge had been opened to allow boats into the safety of the bayou, but strong winds twisted it into a mass of tangled metal. No deaths were directly attributed to the hurricane in the Pensacola area, but the number of deaths from malaria and pneumonia increased significantly in the months after the storm. The total damages in the city were estimated at $4.3 million.

After the September 1926 hurricane blasted Florida's east coast, it crossed the peninsula and entered the Gulf of Mexico on a path toward Pensacola. Along the way, it generated huge storm waves that broke through this beachfront home at Boca Grande. (Photo courtesy of Noel Risnychok)

Although it is usually referred to as the Miami hurricane of 1926, this storm also caused much destruction in Pensacola. High tides ripped through the city's harbor district and left ships and debris scattered about. (Photo courtesy of the T. T. Wentworth Jr. Collection, Historic Pensacola Preservation Board)

Trapped by the rapid rise of water, a young serviceman rode out the September 1926 storm aboard a floating timber at the Naval Air Station in Pensacola. (Photo courtesy of the U.S. Naval Historical Center)

Along with numerous other vessels in the area, the USS SC-159 was driven ashore near Pensacola by the hurricane of September 1926. (Photo courtesy of the U.S. Naval Historical Center)

Although the storm in Pensacola had also been severe, the nation's attention was focused on Miami. As with any great disaster, tales of amazing feats of survival and bizarre tragedies were often repeated after the 1926 hurricane. A small home in Fort Lauderdale collapsed during the first hours of the storm, pinning its owner underneath heavy beams and a mass of wreckage. The man's wife tried desperately to pull her still-conscious husband from the debris, just as floodwaters began to reach the floor of the home. She did not have the strength to free him, and no help was available as the storm reached its peak. While kneeling beside him, she did her best to hold his head above the rising waters until she herself was almost submerged. The winds remained furious, and the waters continued to rise. Finally, with torn emotions, she kissed him farewell and scrambled away to safety.

Tragedy also struck Mr. and Mrs. Elmer Crawley of Fort Lauderdale. Tossed into the raging New River when their houseboat capsized, they struggled to make their way to safety in the predawn darkness. Because his wife could not swim, Crawley made several attempts to carry her in his arms through the waves to shore. After finally reaching the riverbank, Crawley realized that she had fainted—or so he thought. As the storm reached its peak, he tied her to a nearby tree while he went for help. Upon his return, he discovered that his wife was dead.

As the tidal surge swept over the Venetian Islands, a group of three men and two women found themselves submerged in neck-deep water when the house they occupied was crushed by waves. They quickly tied themselves together with bed sheets and drifted with the currents across the islands, ever in fear of being swept into the bay. For more than two hours, they rafted together before eventually grasping another house that offered safety.

Reardon described a most unusual wedding that occurred during the height of the storm. Ted Yates was supposed to be married on Friday evening, the night of the storm, but rising waters prevented his arrival at the Hollywood Hotel, where his bride-to-be was staying. He tried several times to reach her, but waters rushed up the boulevard as far as the Dixie Highway, and he was forced to return uptown. The next morning, during the "lull" that most thought was the hurricane's end, he donned a bathing suit and waded to the hotel. His bride, also wearing a swimsuit, met him in the lobby. The hotel staff secured a refugee minister, and the couple were wed in the hotel lobby "while Arnold Johnson and his famous orchestra, clad in surf-suits, played the wedding march."

Funeral homes around the Miami area were stacked with corpses after the hurricane. So many dead were collected and so many survivors were busy with recovery efforts that few formal funerals were held. One service that did occur, for Thomas Gill of Hialeah, ended with a strange twist. The service took place at Combs' Undertaking, where a handful of friends gathered to pay their respects to Gill, who had been working on a dredge in Biscayne Bay when the storm broke. The service was under way and the minister was reading the Twenty-third Psalm when Gill himself walked in. He explained that during the storm, he had abandoned the dredge and had swum to shore. The following day, divers had recovered a body in the wreck of the vessel, which Gill's shipmates had identified as his. This was not the only case of misidentification of the dead that occurred in the hurricane's aftermath.

Numerous stories were told of the storm's effects on animals. A Fort Lauderdale woman who lived in a fourth-floor apartment draped her canary's cage with a towel as the storm worsened on Friday night. She later abandoned her apartment for safer quarters, returning the following day to recover her belongings. The apartment building had been razed by the winds, and many of her possessions were destroyed. But about 150 yards away, she spotted the bird's cage suspended from the limb of a tree. The towel was still in place, and the canary had not lost a single feather. Many pets did not fare so well, however, as thousands of dogs and cats became hopelessly separated from their owners or did not survive the storm.

In the wake of the hurricane, Miami gathered itself together and dealt with the greatness of the disaster. The Florida East Coast Railway offered free passage to those who wanted to leave, and many did. Those hospitals not destroyed by the storm were overflowing with hundreds of injured residents, and numerous large hotels, schools, and public buildings became temporary hospitals. Water was in short supply, but the city quickly implemented a rationing plan. In some areas, apartment dwellers were reported to have carried buckets of water up seventeen floors to flush toilets. Once the roadways were cleared, cars were often seen with hand-painted signs that read: "Boil Your Drinking Water." At least 200 children were found whose parents were missing. City Manager Frank H. Wharton issued a proclamation that all food supplies would be seized for the good of the people and that any establishment engaged in "profiteering" would be closed and the proprietor arrested. Martial law was declared in Miami, and at least eleven people were shot for looting.

Aid for the people of South Florida poured in within days. The Cuban government sent a battleship loaded with 250 tons of provisions as well as 50,000 doses of typhoid vaccine. After President Calvin Coolidge asked the nation for assistance, the Red Cross raised more than $3 million. Benefit performances staged in theaters around the country generated funds for the relief effort. Henry Baker, national disaster director for the Red Cross, narrowly escaped disaster himself on his way to visit the hurricane-torn area when his plane went down in an Alabama swamp. Fortunately he and the pilot managed to escape unharmed. In addition to the Red Cross, many other relief organizations worked diligently to aid the hurricane victims. Hundreds of Boy Scouts cleared debris, escorted ambulances, and carried messages throughout the city. The *Chicago Herald-Examiner* dispatched a train to Florida loaded with doctors, nurses, medicine, food, and milk. Legionnaires, Knights of Columbus, and members of countless other civic and religious groups provided food, clothing, and medical treatment to storm victims.

The Great Miami Hurricane of 1926 remains one of Florida's most tragic and destructive storms. It is difficult to calculate the number of deaths and the financial losses in such a great disaster, and not surprisingly conflicting reports abound. According to NOAA's account by Hebert, Jarrell, and Mayfield, *The Deadliest, Costliest, and Most Intense United States Hurricanes of This Century*, 243 lives were lost in the storm, and the destruction totaled $112 million. Other NOAA reports suggest there were 372 deaths. An official report released by the Red Cross on October 9, 1926, placed the number of dead at 373, with 6,381 injured, 43,000 homeless, and $159 million in property losses. That death toll excluded 811 people who were missing and presumed dead, many of whom were transients whose whereabouts had not been documented. But whatever the actual numbers, the hurricane remains one of Florida's greatest tragedies.

Its effects extended far beyond the crushed homes, sunken houseboats, and splintered lives of the people of Miami—the great boom that had turned South Florida into a showcase had been virtually shot down overnight. Unfinished subdivisions were leveled, and profits of the previous years were whisked away with the winds. Land that sold for $60,000 in 1925 was soon available for $600. Some believed that the storm had struck because of the "wickedness" of the great prosperity. Historian Arva Parks wrote about the events in *Miami: The Magic City*: "A lot of people who'd come down to speculate left because of the hurricane. It squished the boom and started our depression three years early."

AUGUST 7–8, 1928

In the aftermath of the great hurricane of 1926, the people of Florida's southeast coast gained a new respect for the awesome forces of these storms. After a very quiet season in 1927, the first of two hurricanes in 1928 was taken very seriously. Even though it was a modest category 2 storm that eventually landed up the coast from the Miami–Fort Lauderdale area, great apprehension gripped coastal residents throughout the region when the first storm warnings were issued on August 6. Many scrambled to board northbound trains or otherwise escape the area in advance of the storm.

It had been tracked since the first of the month as a tropical disturbance and then as a developing tropical storm. On August 4 and 5, it churned over Haiti, never reaching full hurricane status until it arrived in the Bahama Islands on the morning of the sixth. Its path at the time might well have led it onto the Florida coast near Miami, but a gradual curve to the north-northwest brought the storm's eye over land just north of Fort Pierce. Winds were close to 100 mph, and the Weather Bureau's barometer measured a low pressure of

28.84 inches. Property damages were heaviest from southern Brevard County to St. Lucie County. According to the Weather Bureau's report of the storm, "Substantial houses were unroofed and frail ones were razed. Highways were flooded and badly washed. Many bridges were undermined requiring replacement. Many citrus trees were uprooted, the loss of fruit estimated at 1,000,000 boxes. Large oaks, sentinels of a century, were uprooted."

The losses resulting from damage to timber, railways, small craft, docks, and wharfs were never fully estimated. Of the total estimated losses of $250,000, at least $100,000 involved damages to "dwellings, outhouses, and other buildings." Two deaths were reported in Florida, both in the vicinity of Indian River.

Although the storm lost its hurricane status almost as soon as it made landfall, it tracked slowly toward Tallahassee and into Georgia over the next two days, spilling tremendous rains on numerous inland counties. The decaying tropical storm turned toward the northeast and out to sea near the Virginia coast on August 12. In South Carolina, North Carolina, and Virginia, river levels rose well beyond flood stage as more than six inches of rain fell during the two-day period. As additional tropical moisture swept into the region on August 15, more heavy rains fell on the already saturated soils of several states. Some rivers set new high-water marks, including the Broad and Congaree in South Carolina. Dams burst under the pressure, and floods covered acres of farmlands and washed away numerous bridges. Although warnings were issued regarding river flooding, several hundred thousand dollars in additional damages were reported.

SEPTEMBER 16–17, 1928

The Great Okeechobee Flood—in the telling of Florida's hurricane history, no other hurricane disaster can compare to its toll of at least 1,836 dead in Florida, as well as another 1,575 in the Caribbean. At the time of the catastrophe, many in South Florida said the actual death count there was over 2,300; some said it may have been as high as 3,500. Whichever figure is correct, it ranks among the United States' worst natural disasters; only the Great Galveston Hurricane of 1900 (over 8,000), the Johnstown flood of 1889 (2,200), and the two hurricanes of 1893 (2,000 each) are likely to have caused more deaths on American soil. It arrived on the coast near Palm Beach on the night of September 16, 1928, just two years after the Great Miami Hurricane, and like its predecessor, it cast its most sinister blow on those who lived on the southern edges of Lake Okeechobee.

It began in the far eastern Atlantic, near the Cape Verde Islands, where it was first reported by the crew of the SS *Commack* at latitude 17 degrees north and longitude 48 degrees west. At the time, this was the most easterly radio report regarding a hurricane in the Atlantic ever received. The storm undoubtedly developed significant strength well before it reached its first target—the island of Guadeloupe. The eye of the storm crossed there at noon on September 12, with a barometric low of 27.76 inches. Guadeloupe, St. Kitts, and Montserrat were devastated. By the morning of the next day, the hurricane was southwest of St. Croix, where the SS *Matura* recorded a low pressure of 27.50 inches. After delivering significant destruction to the Virgin Islands, it crossed Puerto Rico on Thursday, the thirteenth, the Day of San Felipe. The blast to Puerto Rico was incredible; according to Tannehill in *Hurricanes: Their Nature and History*, "Wind there was the highest, rainfall the heaviest, and destruction the greatest of record in recent years." At least 300 lives were lost, and many more died in the following weeks due to starvation and disease. Damages in Puerto Rico were estimated at $50 million, and over 200,000 people were left homeless. Because of its horrible consequences on this date, the September 1928 hurricane is often referred to as "San Felipe."

In his 1984 book *Weather Is Front Page News*, Ti Sanders included this vivid description of the storm's terror in Puerto Rico:

> Many deaths were caused by zinc roofs flying through the air like scythes. Sand was hurled from the beaches to homes a mile inland and came through the windows and blinded people's eyes. In the hilly country water was pouring down in streams through red sand which was so brilliant, it "looked like a river of blood." Oxen ran wild through the country, some of them still yoked, fighting and snorting in an effort to gain freedom. Lightning flashed constantly, and there was the continual roar of thunder and the crash of falling debris. The waves which swirled high in the air contained sand and mud and fell heavily on the shore. Then another one would leap and bound, and a reflection of fire in the sky could be seen in the ocean.

The greatness of the tragedy in Puerto Rico slowly made the news in the United States, just about the time Florida residents were receiving their first warnings of the powerful storm offshore. On September 15, it swept through the Bahama Islands, dashing away anemometer cups before they could record the highest winds. Residents along the Florida coast did what they could to prepare; some secured their homes, and others fled. In the early hours of the sixteenth, San Felipe was poised 200 miles southeast of Miami, and already this large and powerful storm was being felt along the coast, which was battered by gale-force winds and rolling surf.

By nightfall the hurricane made its lunge over the Florida coast near West Palm Beach. Experiencing the awesome power one would expect from a category 4 storm, Palm Beach County was rocked by a large tidal surge and winds estimated at over 150 mph. A minimum barometer reading of 27.43 inches was taken at 7:00 P.M., which fell just short of establishing a new record low for the United States (a reading of 27.37 inches had been measured in 1919). West Palm

Beach recorded a total of 18.42 inches of rain during the week of the storm, over 10 inches of which fell as the hurricane passed through. Witnesses reported that the "lull" lasted about forty minutes, and the storm was moving at a forward speed of about 14 mph.

As in the Miami hurricane two years before, the once prosperous resorts and palatial homes of the Palm Beach area were reduced to rubble. Damages were heavy all along the coast from Fort Pierce to Boca Raton. The total damage estimate for the region was placed at $25 million, far less than was seen in the Miami hurricane. But the local destruction was heavy; in West Palm Beach 1,711 homes were destroyed, and another 6,363 were damaged. In *Pioneers in Paradise: The First One Hundred Years of West Palm Beach*, Jan Tuckwood and Eliot Kleinberg quoted local officials as they described the scene. County coroner T. M. Rickards said, "The street was shoulder-deep in debris. The suffering throughout was beyond words. Individual tales of horror, suffering and loss are numberless."

Up the coast at Jupiter, many residents, both black and white, took refuge in the schoolhouse, which weathered the storm much better than did their homes. One cement-block house collapsed during the storm, crushing several members of a family the only reported deaths in Jupiter. The Jupiter Lighthouse, the red brick sentinel that had witnessed many storms, was said to have swayed a remarkable seventeen inches "as mortar squeezed from between bricks like toothpaste." Prior to the hurricane, the light had been converted from oil burners to electricity. As the storm reached the coast, all power lines were downed, and the lighthouse auxiliary generator failed to work. Captain Seabrook, the keeper, refused to let the light go out and scrambled to reinstall the old oil burners. Without electricity, the light's mantle had to be turned by hand, and Seabrook, who was suffering from blood poisoning at the time, was prepared to push the apparatus around all night. His son Franklin, noticing the bright red streaks on his father's arm, stepped in to work the mantle, continuing to near exhaustion. As a result, the light shone through one of the century's most dreadful storms, and later the younger Seabrook was officially commended for his heroism.

All along the coast, piers, docks, and waterfront structures were lifted by the tide and carried for hundreds of yards. In some instances, houses were raised from their foundations and spun ninety degrees, their porches and stairs twisted into tangled arrangements. Trees were knocked down on virtually every street, wrapped in webs of electric cables. Throughout the area, the problems faced by the storm survivors were similar to those endured by survivors of the Miami hurricane—they lacked food and water, thousands of homeless were in need of shelter, and they suffered the emotional wounds of having to cope with disaster. At least twenty-six lives were lost on the coast.

On Tuesday morning, September 18, thirty-six hours after the hurricane's arrival, headlines around the nation summarized the calamity: "Florida De-stroyed! Florida Destroyed!" The initial news of the disaster at West Palm Beach was just beginning to emerge when a far more ominous catastrophe was discovered—the mind-boggling massacre on the edges of Lake Okeechobee.

Lake Okeechobee is the fourth-largest natural lake in the United States, and its shape is like that of a saucer—shallow and round. With a diameter of forty miles and a depth of no more than fifteen feet, it served as the catch basin and primary water supply for central Florida. Over the previous decade, canals had been dug and dikes built to "control" the flow of water in the region and to drain portions of the vast Everglades for farming. A land boom ensued in which hundreds of acres of what was once wet saw grass were sold as black-soil farmland. Soon huge fields of beans, celery, carrots, and sugarcane stretched for miles around the lake. Tractor towns grew up along the lake's edge, where supply stores and juke joints provided life's necessities to landowners and their imported laborers. Engineers designed dikes around the lip of Okeechobee to restrain floodwaters and protect the farming communities. But as was seen in Moore Haven in 1926, the dikes were never engineered to match the fury of a great hurricane.

By noon on the day of the storm, many of the people around the lake had heard of the approaching cyclone. In South Bay several men took the initia-tive to drive the maze of roads around the lake to spread the news and to urge people to seek shelter. Many women and children gathered on a large barge anchored in the lake. But as the afternoon progressed and the great storm grew nearer, hundreds of families, landowners, and laborers went about their work on the broad, flat terrain with no idea of what was about to occur.

Normally, the water level in the lake was maintained slightly above the level of the land so that water could be drained off as needed. In the weeks before the storm, heavy rains had kept the lake level high and filled the ditches and canals around the glades. By September 10, the lake level had risen three feet in thirty days, and the ten or more inches of rain that fell during the storm added to the burden. But it was the intense hurricane winds, estimated at over 150 mph at Canal Point, that lifted the waters of Lake Okeechobee and tossed them southward, completely washing away entire communities and the dikes that were supposed to protect them. According to some reports, the waters rose from four to six feet in the first hour of the storm, and still-water marks in some buildings were almost eight feet above the ground. Few were able to sur-vive this incredible wall of water. In the darkness of the next few hours, Florida experienced its greatest recorded tragedy.

A detailed and vivid account of these events is chronicled in Lawrence E. Will's book, *Okeechobee Hurricane and the Hoover Dike*. In it, Will relives the storm and writes of the great irony of the disaster: "This calamity occurred within a few miles of a large city and of a world famous resort, yet so isolated was the

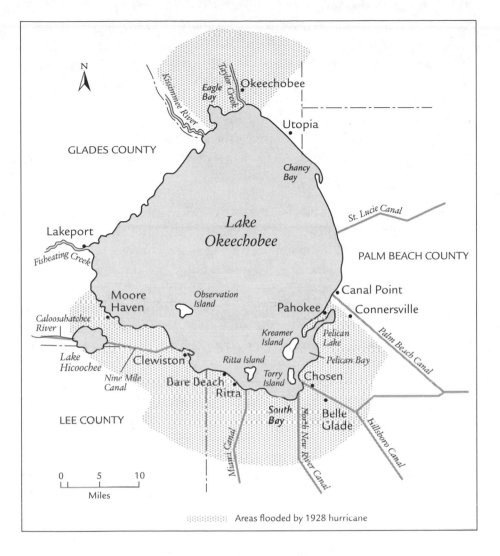

location that not until three days later did the state's own governor learn of its enormity. So extended and so difficult was the terrain that after six weeks the search for bodies was discontinued with many still unrecovered."

Kreamer Island was one of the first areas to feel the effects of the rushing flood. Here, as in most of the communities around the lake, the majority of the people chased by the rising waters were black Bahamian laborers, brought to the fertile Okeechobee region to work the fields. As news of the storm first spread on the island, laborers and landowners, women and children, both black and white, gathered together in any shelter they could find. In some homes, twenty to thirty people took refuge and were forced to stand on tables and chairs above the rising waters. Many of these homes were lifted off their foundations and bashed into rows of pines, and others were swept more than half a mile. Amazingly, only one drowning occurred on the island.

On Torry Island residents tried to escape to the mainland when word spread of the hurricane, but by this time, the causeway was already under water. In desperation, twenty-three people returned to John Aunapu's packinghouse, where they perched on tractors, trucks, and stacks of field crates. According to Will, the sturdy structure rocked and swayed in the ferocious winds, and driving rain on the tin roof "as of a hundred fire-hose streams, effectively discouraged conversation." Floodwaters soon covered the structure's dirt floor and chased them upward into the rafters. After the structure was battered by uprooted custard apple trees, it heaved and then folded into the dark waters of a nearby canal.

One man kicked out a gable near the roof of the structure just before it sank and escaped into the branches of a tree, pulling his fiancée from the building as well. They soon were swimming in the pitch-black torrent and, after several minutes, were fortunate to grab onto the frame of a large floating dredge. Several others from the packinghouse miraculously found safety on this same dredge. Others were swept far beyond the dredge. Margaret BeaDer was swept into the Belle Glade bridge, where she badly injured her knee, and then onto a dike, a total distance of some three and a half miles. Unclothed by the wringing waters and unable to walk because of her injury, she was not found for two days. Some of the Torry Island survivors were swept into treetops, and one woman successfully tied herself to a stationary telegraph pole. A teenage boy outdistanced everyone when he was carried some eight miles to the Experiment Station. Ten of the twenty-three people in the packinghouse were drowned, some of the first victims of the Okeechobee flood.

Will's chronicle of the storm recounts many incredible feats of survival: "A colored family of two men and a woman on Jess' farm, after the roof had left their house, took refuge in a pop ash tree. The tree bent before the gusts, nearly drowning them in the waves, but rebounding long enough to give them a breath of air before immersing them again. Nearly all the trees on the island were uprooted, but by good fortune, theirs remained and all three survived."

At Chosen the small frame house owned by Pat Burke provided shelter for nineteen. Knowing that the rising water was soon to sweep through the structure, they all hustled into the attic, where the men labored to break a hole through the roof. Tearing through the corrugated iron and sheathing was no easy task, but they managed to create an opening through which most of the group crawled out into the stinging rain and wind. Just as they had gathered on the roof, the lake broke through the dike and sent a massive wave that rolled the structure over on its side. Only two of the nineteen survived.

Twenty Chosen residents took refuge in Isaac West's store, which lost its roof during the storm. They managed to survive by cramming into a bathroom "like sardines." Another house full of people was floated by wind and flood for half a mile. Its journey was apparently so gentle that those inside were unaware of its movement until it crashed into a railroad embankment. Those caught in the storm without shelter were fortunate to find any high ground. Chosen's Indian mound was one of the few elevated sites, and it provided escape for thirty-one residents and laborers. Throughout the night, this group clutched the grasses on the lee side of the mound to avoid being blown or washed off into the dark waters below. Amazingly, this entire group survived. The mound was reported to have been eight feet ten inches above the surrounding land, and at the peak of the flood, water was two feet above the crest of the mound.

At Belle Glade, the largest community affected on the lakeshore, the destruction and loss of life were immense. Many town residents took refuge in two hotels. In houses throughout the area, residents fought the storm by frantically chopping through ceilings with axes to provide escape into their attics. In many cases, families survived by hanging onto attic rafters with their faces just above water.

Will described the incredible ordeal of one group of eleven people who took refuge in the "storm-proof" home of Mahlon Eggleston. As floodwaters lifted the structure off the ground, it soon crashed into another errant home. It was discovered that two women and a man were clinging to a windowsill on the outside of the Eggleston house, having been dashed into the waters after some earlier collapse. The occupants broke a windowpane and brought the three people inside the drifting home. The house soon crashed with a thud into some unknown object, pitched to one side, and came to a stop. The two rooms on one side of the house rolled under the water, and the pressure broke out half the windows. In one of these rooms was Mrs. Eggleston, her six-year-old daughter, and her infant son. Their quarters submerged in the flooded darkness, they could only survive by breathing the air trapped near the ceiling of the room.

Immediately after the house came to a stop, Ray Browne, Mrs. Eggleston's nephew, struggled through the house to their door. Without hesitation, he dove through the submerged doorway and swam up to the air pocket where the threesome were trapped. He then proceeded to rescue the two children, one at a time, by swimming back through the doorway while clutching them under his arm. But when he returned for his aunt, she flatly refused to swim through the doorway in the darkness. She finally allowed Ray to rescue her after Ray's father agreed to swim before them with a flashlight. Similar rescues followed in another submerged room of the house, and soon all were gathered in the attic, the only remaining refuge. Because they feared the house might collapse and sink in the howling storm, they decided to cut a hole through the roof to allow their escape. Once again, Ray swam down into the house in search of tools for the job, but none could be found. Instead, the men proceeded to cut through

the gable end of the house with a pocketknife, a task that took them three hours. As they peered out the opening, they saw that the house was lodged on the opposite bank of the canal, over a quarter of a mile from where it had originally stood.

At South Bay, as news arrived of the fast-approaching hurricane, many took to the safety of Huffman's barge. Nearly 200 people survived the storm aboard this vessel, working through the night on a bucket brigade to bail out the vessel's hold. Some residents foolishly abandoned their homes when the waters first approached and sought shelter in their automobiles. Most were soon thrown from the vehicles into the raging waters, where they struggled to grasp any available floating debris. Stories abound, as in many other hurricanes, of survivors sharing rafts of flotsam or treetop branches with water moccasins.

At Sebring Farm one house became a shelter for sixty-three residents and laborers, who, according to Will, were "crouched in the black darkness of the attic, the white people in one end waiting in tense silence, while in the other end the negroes wailed and prayed and wept." Soon they chopped a hole through the metal roof with an ax, but the first man through the hole was swept away by the wind. Before the others could attempt to escape, a surging wave hit the house and the roof collapsed on the crowd. A few managed to free themselves from the wreckage and were washed three miles into the saw grass.

Perhaps the greatest tragedy of the storm took place at Pelican Bay, where hundreds of bodies were later recovered. Most were black laborers who had ventured out from their camp at Tishomingo during the eye of the storm. Think-

As the waters of Lake Okeechobee flooded Belle Glade in the September 1928 storm, the roof of this home floated over nearby electric lines. (Photo courtesy of the University of Florida Archives)

Floodwaters remained high in Belle Glade long after the September 1928 storm passed. (Photo courtesy of the University of Florida Archives)

ing that the worst was over, they began to walk the dike toward Pahokee when the hurricane resumed, the winds increased, and the lake quickly spilled over the dike.

As the storm moved on and the sun emerged the following day, few relief agencies rushed to the aid of the survivors at Okeechobee. In fact, most attention was first placed on the destruction along the coast. Soon, however, word spread of a great disaster, the scope of which it would take many days to realize. Dead bodies were scattered everywhere, decomposing in the Florida sun with each passing day. Many of those who had managed to survive had been swept for miles into the saw grass and were forced to walk or wade back to whatever recognizable roadway they could find. Some, too weak or injured to stand or walk, sat for days in hopes of being spotted by passersby. Some who survived the storm are believed to have perished later as they wandered the vast Everglades.

Five days after the storm, Governor John W. Martin toured the region with his aides. The horror of the scene is revealed in the governor's description of the body count:

> In six miles between Pahokee and Belle Glade I counted twenty-seven corpses in water or on the roadside but not taken from the water. Total dead on roadside and not buried and counted but not in plank coffins was one hundred and twenty-six. In six additional miles over five hundred and thirty-seven bodies were already interred. Fifty-seven additional bodies were hauled out of this area today in trucks and tonight four truck loads of bodies were brought from adjoining areas by boat, loaded and sent to West Palm Beach for burial. One military officer reported to me that while in Belle Glade today for thirty minutes, ten bodies were brought in and added to the piles of bodies, thirty-seven in one pile and sixty in the other.

In the days following the disaster, help was slow to trickle in to the Okeechobee region. Only one route to West Palm Beach was open, and most roads were covered with huge mounds of debris. No cars in the area could operate, and food and drinking water were nonexistent. William J. Buck, the only physician on the south end of the lake, took command of the immediate cleanup effort by issuing a radical order—he sent all of the surviving women and children away from the area on foot. Even though West Palm Beach was forty-two miles away, walking there was seen as their only chance of survival. Over 100 women, carrying their babies and necessary belongings, set out on the arduous journey. Most made it only as far as the Experiment Station, and some went on to Six Mile Bridge, where they were later greeted by the Red Cross. The remaining men, haggard and emotionally drained, slowly began sifting through mounds of wreckage in search of loved ones.

The unsettling task of recovering the dead went on for days. Efforts to identify loved ones, however, were rapidly abandoned. Because of the deterioration of the corpses, it soon became impossible even to determine their race. A carpenter at South Bay spent his days making caskets called "rough boxes" from the planks of what used to be the homes of the region. As the news of the tragedy finally reached the coast, truckloads of cheap pine boxes were soon de-

The hurricane of September 1928 remains Florida's single greatest tragedy, with a death toll that exceeds 2,000. The removal of bodies from the shores of Lake Okeechobee was a repulsive task that took weeks to accomplish. (Photo courtesy of the Florida State Archives)

livered. The stench was overwhelming, not only from the decay of human flesh but also from the scattered carcasses of fish, alligators, and other animals.

In the first few days, the cleanup progressed very slowly due to the lack of boats and the scarcity of workers. Finally, groups of Legionnaires and black workers were brought in to assist in the effort. Workers wore cotton gloves that were regularly doused with disinfectant. Even though Prohibition was in force at the time, law enforcement officials overlooked the fact that bootleg whiskey was regularly given to the workers. Will noted the importance of this supply:

> It would be impossible for anyone who has never been so engaged, to realize the utter repulsiveness of the task of searching for and recovering those reeking corpses in all stages of decomposition. Add to this the heartbreak experienced by those who identified and brought in remains of their own wives, children and friends. Without the stimulating effect of the whiskey ration it is doubtful if many would have had the stamina to continue. It was customary when a boat returned with its string of bodies for the crew to be given a stiff drink. The negroes, also, who loaded them on trucks were given periodic doses. Nobody got drunk (with the possible exception of sightseers), but all could look forward to their bit of refreshment.

Every town had its own outdoor morgue. Soon the stacks of bodies grew so large that the corpses could no longer be put into boxes; instead, they were "loaded like cordwood" into trucks and taken away. Most were apparently buried at the new Port Mayaca Cemetery, where a stone was later placed that reads: "In Memoriam: To the 1600 pioneers in this mass burial who gave their lives in the 1928 hurricane so that the Glades might be as we know it today." Some were buried at Ortona Cemetery, where the dead from the 1926 storm at Moore Haven were buried, and some were even shipped for burial in other states. Steam shovels dug trenches for mass graves in two locations in West Palm Beach, one for blacks and one for whites. In the common grave dug between Twenty-third and Twenty-fifth Streets and Tamarind Avenue, at least 300 black laborers were buried. Recent efforts have brought recognition to the site, and in 1991 a formal funeral service was held, at which descendants of the dead were in attendance.

The search for corpses continued through October, until finally on November 1 it was called off due to the lack of funding. Most of the dead had been found. Many of the bodies were never buried but were torched in makeshift funeral pyres. Some of the dead were reportedly eaten by the alligators that infested the canals. Since not all of the bodies were recovered, farmers through the years have often reported digging up the bones of storm victims in the fields that surround the lake region.

Several unusual events were reported in the aftermath of the storm. Arthur Stokes, a black worker arrested for murder before the hurricane, had to be released at his trial because the only witnesses had drowned in the storm. Similarly, the storm clarified the whereabouts of Deputy State Hotel Commissioner Pat Houston, who was believed to have absconded with a considerable sum of the state's money because of his long absence. It was reported that Houston's good name was returned when his body was found near Pahokee. Governor Martin said that the body of one of the storm victims, C. L. Reddick, was found five days after the flood, still guarded by the man's trusted dog. One local man, emotionally numbed by the calamity, worked long hours in search of bodies, even though he himself had twice been bitten by a water moccasin. Perhaps most amazing of all, an eighty-three-year-old woman from Belle Glade was found alive in a steel washtub on September 20, four days after the storm.

Unfortunately, because of the bad publicity Florida had received after the 1926 storm and the economic bust that followed, some officials at first downplayed the disaster at Okeechobee. But word of the tragedy soon spread, and more relief poured in. The Red Cross was well prepared for the storm's aftermath, having gained valuable experience during the Miami hurricane and the flood at Moore Haven. Local volunteer chapters went to work as soon as news of the storm's impact in Puerto Rico was known. Well before the hurricane struck Florida, the Red Cross had dispatched six experienced relief workers to the state. After the storm hit, while the American Legion was busy with rescue efforts and the search for bodies, the Red Cross set up twenty-two emergency feeding centers. Soon thousands of refugees had access to food, clothing, and shelter. The people of the glades were in particular need of clothing, as the swirling floodwaters had left many of the survivors nearly naked.

By early October, basic needs were being met, and the Red Cross announced that its part in the recovery would soon end since rebuilding the devastated

Two weeks after the September 1928 hurricane, general funeral services were held at Woodlawn Cemetery in West Palm Beach. Thousands heard the services, conducted by various clergy from the stricken area. (Photo courtesy of Noel Risnychok)

Seventeen bodies were doused with diesel fuel and burned at South Bay on September 25, 1928, more than a week after the storm. This was just one of many pyres set in the region. The burning was made difficult by heavy rains that fell during this period. (Photo courtesy of the University of Florida Archives)

towns was "not the job of the Red Cross." Controversy erupted as a result of this announcement, and the organization was denounced as a fraud. The little money and materials the Red Cross had for rebuilding were cautiously rationed to the people of Belle Glade and the surrounding community. But within a matter of weeks, the Red Cross's policies were dramatically changed. By mid-November, with the help of the Red Cross, many new homes were under way, most of which were built to much higher standards than they had been before. Soon the Red Cross was even supplying seed, fertilizer, and fuel for the replanting that was destined to rebuild the economy of the Okeechobee region. When all was said and done, the hurricane victims expressed their deep gratitude to the Red Cross and the many other relief organizations that had eased their burden.

After President Herbert Hoover's tour of the Lake Okeechobee region in February of the following year, a plan was developed to rebuild the failed dikes on the lake's southern shores. In 1929 the state legislature created the Okeechobee Flood Control District, and soon a $5 million bond issue was approved to fund the necessary engineering. A giant rock levee, eighty-five miles long and thirty-six feet high, was built along the lake's southeast, south, and southwest banks. This new dike was built eighteen to twenty feet higher than the lake's normal level. The Hoover Dike was later put to the test during hurricanes in 1947 and

1949, with only minor erosion as the result. The U.S. Corps of Engineers reported that the latter storm had "operated against the $24,000,000 levees for a period three times as long as any previous storm and with greater intensities."

SEPTEMBER 28–30, 1929

The 1929 Atlantic tropical season was exceptionally quiet. Only three well-defined storms were recorded, one of which drifted harmlessly into the central Atlantic. A powerful late-September storm, however, threatened South Florida and had the potential to deliver another disaster to the region. Fortunately its path was more southerly than the monster storms of the previous few years, and its overall impact was not significant.

The hurricane may have originated farther to the east, but it was first spotted as an organized storm on September 22 some 400 miles north of Puerto Rico. By the twenty-fifth, it had built up steam on its approach to the Bahama Islands. When its eye was fifteen miles west of Great Abaco Island, one vessel reported an uncorrected barometer reading of just 27.30 inches, suggesting that it was a storm of unusual intensity. At Nassau the pressure was 27.64 inches. According to Tannehill in *Hurricanes: Their Nature and History*, "There was enormous damage at Nassau and many lives were lost there." It was about this time that the hurricane took a turn toward the southwest and slowed down considerably. For the next three and a half days, it drifted toward the Straits of Florida at a forward speed of only 4 mph.

Warnings along the South Florida coast were ample. The slow movement of the hurricane gave residents time to prepare their homes and businesses for the worst. But because of the storm's movement farther south, residents of Miami and other cities along the southeast coast were spared another disaster. Finally, on the morning of September 28, the drifting storm passed over Key Largo on a course toward the west-northwest. According to Tannehill, it passed through with "barometer about 28 inches and wind estimated at 150 mph." Observers reported that there was about a ten-minute lull as the eye passed. The barometer at Long Key measured a low of 28.18 inches at 9:30 A.M. According to Weather Bureau records, the lowest recorded pressure in the Keys was 27.99 inches.

Partly due to the storm's slow forward speed, extremely heavy rains fell throughout South Florida. Miami recorded 10.63 inches on the twenty-eighth. Most notable in that region, however, was the occurrence of at least five tornadoes between Miami and Stuart. All of these twisters were spawned on the northern edge of the hurricane as it passed over the upper Keys. According to Gordon Dunn's technical memorandum, *Florida Hurricanes*, "The tornadoes moved from southeast to northwest with the wind on the edge of the hurricane circulation, possibly forming as waterspouts at sea. Their paths were short and did not extend far inland." None of the twisters were particularly destructive, although one caused some damages in Fort Lauderdale. Along with reports of the tornado at Goulds in 1919, reports of these tornadoes were among the first authenticated accounts of tornado activity within a hurricane.

Damages in southern Florida were confined to the locations nearest the storm's center. According to Weather Bureau reports, only $676,000 in losses were reported in Florida, although other accounts placed the figure at $821,000. The damages were significantly less than those of the more infamous hurricanes of previous years largely because the 1929 storm affected a less-populated area. The Weather Bureau noted that "property damage was remarkably small for a storm of this character." Damages were not severe but certainly typical. The *Monthly Weather Review* gave this rather generic summary of the toll: "Heavy damage to fruit and truck, highways, telephone and telegraph lines, small boats and equipment, timber, buildings, power plants, and shops." Three Floridians died in the hurricane, one of whom had been urged to leave an unsafe shelter but refused to go.

The small town of Everglades City north of the center of the hurricane caught a good bit of the storm. According to the *Collier County News*, winds were 90–100 mph, and rainfall measured over nine inches. The pressure there was recorded at 28.95 inches. Residents left their homes for the shelter of the Everglades Inn, a substantial structure. During the peak of the storm, floodwaters covered the inn's first floor, forcing the crowd of refugees up to the second floor. Residents of Dupont sought safety in a local pool hall. Newspaper reports indicated that sixty to sixty-five homes in Everglades City and Dupont had damaged roofs, but within ten days, all of them had been repaired.

As the hurricane left the southern edge of the Everglades, it continued into the eastern Gulf of Mexico on a slow and erratic course. After making a bizarre horseshoe turn southwest of Apalachicola, it entered the coast for the second time near Panama City on September 30. Here, the barometer dropped to 28.80 inches, and 100 mph gusts battered the coast. Winds were near hurricane force as far west as Pensacola. Trees and telegraph lines were downed, and considerable damages were reported to docks and small craft. The Weather Bureau later summarized the storm as "the most erratic and abnormal in fifty years prior."

SEPTEMBER 3–4, 1933

The Tropics exploded with activity during the summer of 1933, establishing a record for storm production that held for seventy-two years. Not only were there more storms during that year (21) than during any other Atlantic hurricane season to that date, but the tracks of most were predominantly westward, which brought many into populated regions of the United States, Mexico, and the Caribbean. Five hurricanes made landfall in the United States, including two in Florida—one in July and one in September. The July hurricane came ashore near Fort Pierce on the thirtieth, but it was barely of hurricane force as it moved inland. The September hurricane was somewhat more powerful and struck very near the same location a little more than thirty days later.

During this incredibly active season, tropical systems followed each other across the eastern Caribbean. Around the end of August, a storm developed east of Puerto Rico and slowly progressed westward toward the Turks Islands. It was at full hurricane intensity when it passed over Harbour Island, Bahamas, on September 3. Winds there were estimated at 140 mph, and the eye was reported to have lingered for only thirty minutes. Hurricane warnings were issued for Florida's east coast, and residents went through the well-established ritual of preparing their homes and watercraft.

Late that evening, winds and tides increased rapidly along the southeastern beaches, and those who remained along the shore waited anxiously for the hurricane's arrival. Damaging winds arose quickly, and within a matter of minutes, eyewitnesses reported seeing trees and utility poles snap. Just before midnight, the storm's calm eye passed over Jupiter Inlet and provided a brief respite of about forty minutes. Just afterward, the storm's highest winds were estimated at 125 mph. The local Weather Bureau observer recorded a barometric low of 27.98 inches. Once the storm had moved fully inland through Okeechobee County, its intensity dropped rapidly. For the next two days, the decaying tropical storm recurved northward through the Big Bend region and into Georgia, where it finally dissipated. Heavy rains were responsible for localized flooding throughout several counties in Florida. In Tampa over seven inches of rain fell, which caused the Tampa Electric dam on the Hillsborough River to collapse on the evening of September 7.

Damages were widespread along the coast, especially between Fort Pierce and Stuart. According to the *Monthly Weather Review*, the storm inflicted heavy damages to telegraph and electrical lines throughout the area. It was also reported that "at Stuart there was serious damage from both wind and water. The most extensive damage in the entire storm area was at Olympia Beach, north of Jupiter Inlet, where there was widespread destruction of trees and shrubbery and serious damage to houses. The greatest loss was to the citrus crop in the Indian River section from Jupiter to Fort Pierce. In the vicinity of Stuart there are several groves that sustained a 100 percent loss of fruit and the uprooting of many trees. The estimated loss of citrus fruit for the State is 16 percent, or 4,000,000 boxes."

In Stuart it was reported that 75 percent of the roofs in town were either blown away or seriously damaged. According to the *Stuart News*, some eighty truckloads of debris were hauled away from the rear of the newspaper's office building after the entire third floor was "blown off" in the storm. The same paper also reported that "chicken coops all over Stuart were smashed and the chicken population was generally blown to Indiantown." The National Guard later provided shelter to at least 400 homeless people in a town with a population at the time of only 5,100. Two deaths were reported: a farm worker was crushed by his home when hurricane winds caused its collapse, and a child was struck on the head by an airborne tree limb at Tropical Farms.

Although memories of the 1933 storm have been eclipsed by recollections of the greater hurricane disasters that occurred before and after it, locals in St. Lucie and Martin Counties still remember the fury of the storm. One story that has often been repeated is that of a gallant rescue by Joe Anderson, a barrel-chested commercial fisherman who was enduring the storm with his fellow crew in a Stuart pub. According to Ernest Lyons's column in the *Stuart News*, "There they and a few other hardy citizens of the community partook of pain killer, attempting to drown out the noise of the shrieking wind, the pounding gusts of rain, and the occasional clatter of bits of roof being torn off."

After numerous drinks, the men left the bar and staggered against the wind to the sheltered doorway of the old Peacock Arcade. Through the driving rain, they spotted a collapsed figure in the street amid a pile of storm debris. They could hear, over the roar of the wind, the moans of what sounded like an injured woman. Several of the men launched into the street in an attempt to rescue her but were blown back before they could make any progress. Anderson, who was described by Lyons as "about a yard and a half tall and two yards wide," asked the others to step aside and then proceeded to plunge into the gale toward the victim. While his buddies watched from the doorway, he wrapped his huge arms around the figure's waist, lifted it off the street, and carried it across Flagler Avenue to the safety of the arcade. Upon his return, Anderson's friends could only howl with laughter—mighty Joe had rescued a 250 pound hog that had been washed into the street after floodwaters invaded its riverbank sty.

On Hutchinsons Island the 328-foot American steamer *Elizabeth* was grounded in the early-morning hours about one-half mile south of the House of Refuge. The ship had foundered for hours in high swells that had kept its propeller out of the water for much of the time. The captain and crew of twenty-nine all survived, but the massive vessel remained high on the beach for more than a week. Once again, Ernest Lyons covered the story for the *Stuart News* and described his attempts to interview the ship's captain: "He wouldn't let me come aboard when I said I was from The Stuart News. Yelling that 'I represent the Associated Press' brought a scathing 'To H— with the Associated Press!' from the deck far above me. Then I noticed that the ship bore as home port New Orleans and shouted against the roar of the breakers: 'Ahh'm from the New Orleans Times Picayune.' He threw down a rope ladder and I quickly climbed up and got my story."

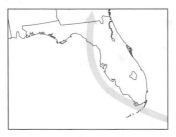

SEPTEMBER 2–4, 1935

During the summer of 1935, Florida was gripped by the Great Depression, along with the rest of the nation. Tourism was down, and the boom years of the previous decade were long gone. Jobs were hard to come by, although many Florida residents got along well by living off the land and the sea. In an effort to create jobs, the federal government employed laborers for construction projects throughout the country, including many in Florida. During that summer, hundreds of World War I veterans were sent to the Keys to work on several large projects. These vets were among the thousands of unemployed "Bonus Marchers" who had gathered in Washington, D.C., three years earlier demanding payment of the "adjusted compensation" bonuses Congress had promised them. President Hoover had dealt with them harshly by ordering troops with bayonets and tear gas to break up their camps around the Capitol. Three years later, President Franklin Roosevelt offered atonement for that episode by giving some of them jobs repairing Fort Jefferson in the Dry Tortugas and constructing a massive project—the new Overseas Highway to Key West.

Their work camps on Lower and Upper Matecumbe Keys, operated by the Federal Emergency Relief Administration (FERA), were little more than tents and small shacks that lined the crushed coral roadbed they were constructing. The 684 men labored each day under a baking sun, with little relief from their task. During the Labor Day weekend of 1935, nearly 300 who could afford to leave the hellish conditions of the camps went to Miami for a few days. But the laborers left behind soon faced disaster.

It was a small hurricane, with an eye only eight miles wide. Its movements toward the Straits of Florida were almost stealthlike. On the day before its arrival in the Keys, Weather Bureau warnings described it as a tropical disturbance with "shifting gales and probably winds of hurricane force." The *Miami Herald* of Sunday, September 1, paid little attention to the storm, but wise residents of the Keys began boarding up anyway. The Coast Guard hustled ships into port and used airplanes to drop warnings in pasteboard ice cream boxes on fishing fleets along the Keys. Cuban weather officials notified Miami that the storm was getting stronger, but no one knew it would intensify so quickly. It was later reported that just thirty hours before landfall it was barely of hurricane strength. By Labor Day, September 2, when it finally struck the Keys, it had become one of the most powerful cyclones in recorded history.

The eye of the compact storm passed over Long Key and Lower Matecumbe Key during the evening of September 2 and was accompanied by the most awesome storm effects imaginable. The eye lasted about fifty-five minutes at Long Key and about forty minutes at Lower Matecumbe. The storm's forward speed was only about 10 mph, but its comparatively small eye was wrapped with superdestructive winds. These winds were of unbelievable force, higher than survivors could begin to describe. All wind instruments were destroyed, but according to David Ludlum's *American Weather Book*, engineering analysis of the damage indicated that gusts were in the range of 150–200 mph over a fifteen-mile radius on the eastern side of the storm center. Some estimates suggest that winds could have approached 250 mph. Unquestionably, this hurricane's winds were far greater than those in any other hurricane in Weather Bureau history. Eyewitness reports and the observations of relief crews provided evidence to support the estimates.

Equally remarkable but more accurately recorded, this hurricane's intensity was indicated by extremely low measurements in barometric pressure. Aneroid barometers throughout the Keys recorded astonishing readings below 27.00 inches, which at first brought skepticism from seasoned weather observers in other parts of the country. At Upper Matecumbe Key the lowest pressure was 26.55 inches, and at Long Key a reading of 26.98 inches was recorded at 10:20 P.M., just before the barometer was washed away. Because of the hurricane's small diameter and extreme low pressure, it was estimated that while it was over the Keys, there was a pressure difference of one inch in only six miles. Grady Norton in *Florida Hurricanes* noted that "pressure gradients of this magnitude are exceeded only in tornadoes."

The lowest official recording in the area was made at Craig between 8:20 and 9:25 P.M., when a mark was made on a barometer case at 26.40 inches. This barometer was later sent to the Miami Weather Bureau office for calibration, where it was corrected downward to 26.38 inches. It was then sent to Washington, where further testing resulted in a correction to 26.35 inches. This adjusted reading set a new record as the lowest pressure ever measured in the Western Hemisphere, a record that stood until 1988 when a reading of 26.13 inches was measured in Hurricane Gilbert. According to a Weather Bureau report that was filed after the 1935 storm, "It may be said, in general, of these observers, that they are men who follow the sea, are familiar with the barometer, how to read it and apply the readings in following the course of a storm."

The Labor Day storm's winds were remarkable, but as often happens with powerful hurricanes, it was a massive storm tide that drowned hundreds of victims and completed the devastation of the middle Keys. Best estimates suggest that the tide was eighteen to twenty feet above normal, and little on these low islands of coral could withstand this deadly wall of water. A description of the tide's effects on the Florida East Coast Railway was included in the September 1935 issue of the *Monthly Weather Review*:

> As is usually the case, the destructive effects extended considerably farther to the right than to the left of the path of the center. Had there been no accompanying tide, the damage no doubt would have been severe but by no means so complete as that resulting from the tidal inundation. The track and crossties of the railroad were in one stretch washed off a concrete viaduct 30 feet above ordinary water level, but wave action superimposed on the tide no doubt played a part in this destruction. Reports agreed in the description of the great rapidity with which the rise of the sea came in from the southern side of the Keys as a "wall of water" or a "high wave."

It was this "wall of water" that was responsible for most of the deaths in the hurricane, including those of the laboring vets in the Matecumbe Keys. All day prior to the storm's arrival, the chief of the FERA veterans' camp at Upper Matecumbe Key made anxious calls to the Miami Weather Bureau for updates on the storm. At noon, as the pressure began to drop and the hurricane drew nearer, he wired the East Coast Railway office in Miami to request the train that had been promised to evacuate workers from the Keys. Whereas some local residents on Windley, Indian, and the Matecumbe Keys gathered their belongings and fled, others decided to wait for the train, including the government-sponsored vets. They left their barracks and waited for hours by the tracks; some played poker in the stinging rain, others drank, and a few eventually returned to their quarters. But unfortunately for those who waited, bureaucratic red tape and an apparent lack of concern delayed the train's departure. The train was supposed to have been standing by in Homestead, but it wasn't. After communication delays with Washington, and resistance from railroad crews because of the holiday, a group of volunteers finally put together a train in Miami.

In *The Railroad That Died at Sea*, Pat Parks wrote of the ill-fated rescue mission. After the order was given to send the train, it took two hours for the Florida East Coast to build up steam and assemble the lineup, which included six passenger cars, two baggage cars, three boxcars, and a locomotive. One car loaded with ninety tons of shell was to act as a ballast against the strong hurricane winds. Finally, at about 4:45 P.M. on September 2, the train left Miami, only to be delayed at the Miami River bridge. It arrived after five o'clock in Homestead, where the engineer moved the engine from the front to the rear of the train in order to provide more speed for the return trip from Islamorada.

By the time the rescue train made it to the Keys, the skies had darkened with rain, and winds began to whip the surface of Florida Bay. On several occasions, the train crew had to stop to clear the tracks of debris that was already blowing about in the storm. Some residents were picked up at Snake Creek, and the train continued slowly southward into ever-increasing wind as waves broke over the railway embankments. By this time, the veterans waiting by the tracks were drenched with rain; their faces bled from the assault of airborne sand. When the train finally reached Islamorada at 8:20 P.M., the engineer could not even see the station and passed it. As waves washed over the island, the train pulled back to Islamorada and finally stopped. For fifteen minutes, the crew struggled to gather men, women, and children into the cars and out of the storm. Suddenly, the massive storm surge arrived, and a wall of water at least seventeen feet high swept over the island, carrying with it houses, trees, construction vehicles, and most of the rescue train. The track was "turned on its side like a fence," and ten train cars were swept sideways almost 100 feet.

The storm wave that washed the train off its tracks overcame virtually every structure in Islamorada. Remarkably, a few of the railway crew survived by holding tight to the locomotive engine, which was too heavy to be carried off the tracks. One measure of the height of the storm was that seawater rose high enough to put out the fire in the engine's boiler. Thirteen people in the cars struggled to keep their heads and the heads of their children above water. It was later reported that after the storm, about twenty-five clocks were found around Upper Matecumbe Key, all of which had stopped between 8:25 and 8:35 P.M.—the time of the storm wave's arrival. Most of the vets in the labor camps were drowned in the tide. Most other visitors and many residents also perished.

Those who lived near the shore along the Keys considered themselves experienced with hurricanes. Most maintained "hurricane houses," which were small but sturdily built shelters on high ground that served as safe havens during the storm season. As hurricanes approached, families gathered their

most important belongings, their pets, and a couple of days' rations and left their homes for the safety of these shelters. After a hurricane passed, they returned to their homes to survey the damage. But the 1935 storm was like no hurricane they had ever experienced, and unfortunately their hurricane houses were no match for the winds and tides it delivered. Many families, some among the original settlers of the Keys, were tossed into the raging

The wreckage at Islamorada after the 1935 Labor Day storm. Ernest Hemingway was among those who first entered the damaged areas; he later expressed public outrage at the failed rescue of the laboring veterans at Islamorada. (Photo courtesy of the American Red Cross)

The gruesome scene of hurricane victims on Lower Matecumbe Key after the 1935 Labor Day storm. (Photo courtesy of Jerry Wilkinson)

flood when their hurricane shelters buckled under the pressure of 200 mph winds and high water. Their ordeal was made more horrific by the deafening roar of the wind and the frightening blackness of the night. The darkness was said to have been occasionally disrupted by an eerie illumination—high winds lifted sand granules into the air, generating static electricity that caused flashes in the sky "like millions of fireflies."

The storm's incredible winds and tide left corpses throughout its path in the Keys. In his article "Surviving the Horrific Hurricane of 1935" in *Florida Trend*, Gene Burnett vividly described the calamity:

> Objects careened through the air with deadly speed. Sheet metal roofs became "flying guillotines," decapitating several victims, amputating the limbs of others. Whirling lumber became lethal javelins, impaling victims or knocking them loose from precarious grips on poles and trees. Like exploding atoms, pounding sheets of sand sheared clothes and even the skin off victims, leaving them clad only in belts and shoes, often with their faces literally sandblasted beyond identification. And then came the rushing force of tons of water in an 18-foot tidal wave that smashed homes to splinters, crushing or drowning occupants and sweeping bodies pell-mell into tangled mangrove thickets or out to sea.

One helpless victim was discovered the day after the storm, impaled by a two-by-four piece of wood but still alive. He was found sitting calmly with the timber passing completely through him, in under his ribs and out over his kidneys. As a doctor prepared to remove the two-by-four, the man announced that he was going to die and refused the shot of morphine that was offered to him. Instead, he requested two beers, which he drank, and then he said, "Now pull." The doctor pulled out the board, and the man died.

One witness reported that a six-by-eight-inch wooden beam eighteen feet long was hurled through the air over 300 yards into his house. The home was almost completely destroyed by this and other flying missiles. The beam battered the house nearly three hours before the arrival of the hurricane's eye, but all accounts placed the highest winds after the passage of the eye. At the Alligator Reef Lighthouse, keeper J. A. Duncan and his men clung to the light's ladder as the twenty-foot tide crashed over them. They were said to have spent the entire night hanging halfway up the light. Eventually, powerful gusts broke the protective glass around the light and destroyed or swept away the lenses themselves, which were 135 feet above sea level. One of the lenses was said to have been later found unbroken on a beach almost eight miles away.

Another remarkable account of survival came from Long Key, where J. E. Duane was the cooperative observer for the Weather Bureau and ran a local fishing camp. His report later appeared in the *Monthly Weather Review*:

9:20 P.M.—Barometer 27.22 inches; wind abated. We now heard other noises than the wind and knew center of the storm was over us. We now head for the last and only cottage that I think can or will stand the blow due to arrive shortly. All hands, 20 in number gather in this cottage. During this lull, the sky is clear to northward, stars shining brightly and a very light breeze continued; no flat calm. About the middle of the lull, which lasted a timed 55 minutes, the sea began to lift up, it seemed, and rise very fast; this from ocean side of camp. I put my flashlight out on sea and could see walls of water which seemed many feet high. I had to race to regain entrance of cottage, but water caught me waist deep, although writer was only about 60 feet from doorway of cottage. Water lifted cottage from its foundations, and it floated.

10:15 P.M.—The first blast from SSW., full force. House now breaking up—wind seemed stronger than any time during storm. I glanced at barometer which read 26.98 inches, dropped it in water, and was blown outside into sea; got hung up in broken fronds of coconut tree and hung on for dear life. I was then struck by some object and knocked unconscious.

September 3: 2:25 A.M.—I became conscious in tree and found I was lodged about 20 feet above ground. All water had disappeared from island; the cottage had been blown back on the island, from whence the sea receded and left it with all people safe. Hurricane winds continued until 5 A.M. and during this period terrific lightning flashes were seen. After 5 A.M. strong gales continued throughout day with very heavy rain.

After the storm swept over the Keys, it continued on a broad recurve up the Florida Gulf coast, passing just west of Tampa on the evening of September 3 and striking near Cedar Key on the morning of the next day. It dropped to tropical storm strength soon after landfall and continued tracking to the northeast over Georgia and the Carolinas. It finally reentered the Atlantic at Cape Henry and then quickly regained hurricane strength and sped out to sea.

Tides ran well above normal all along Florida's west coast, especially near the point of landfall. At Cedar Key three lives were lost, and considerable damages were reported to docks, fishing vessels, and structures near the shore. The flooding was the worst there since 1896. At Tampa winds were clocked at 75 mph, the barometer dropped to 29.31 inches, tides were 5.3 feet above normal, and over 7.3 inches of rain fell. Tampa was at the time suffering through political turmoil, with a corrupt city government and threats of violence between rival parties. This all came to a head when a contentious municipal election was held on September 3, 1935, the same day as the hurricane. The National Guard was called in to prevent riots, and many people stayed away from the polls because of political threats and the raging storm. In the end, incumbent mayor Robert E. Lee Chancey was reelected, and election reforms were adopted.

Several ships in the vicinity of the Keys were caught in the hurricane's fury and tossed about. The Danish cruiser *Leise Maersk* was lifted over Alligator Reef, carried inland for almost four miles, and grounded. None of the crew were lost, but the ship was badly battered and was salvaged on September 20. The American steamship *Dixie* was also carried aground on French Reef, and all of its passengers were rescued. Those who survived the ordeal were reported to have cried for hours on their return trip to New York. The American tanker *Pueblo* lost power and drifted helplessly in the storm. Over a period of eight hours, the ship was carried completely around the center of the hurricane and wound up just twenty-five miles away from its original position near Molasses Reef.

On the morning after the storm, those who survived the night on Upper Matecumbe Key faced the torment of discovering the bodies of their friends and loved ones scattered among the mangroves. Clifton Russell, one of the original Russell clan that had settled at Matecumbe in the 1850s, survived, but his wife and four of his five children were gone. They had tried to ride out the storm in their hurricane house on the highest part of the island, about twelve feet above sea level. The storm wave shattered their shelter, and each family member was left to struggle alone in the darkness. In a tragic coincidence, Russell's brother John also survived but lost his wife and four children. The hur-

Relief workers dipped their hands in buckets of Mercuro-chrome to sanitize them after handling corpses at Matecumbe Key following the Labor Day hurricane of 1935. (Photo courtesy of Jerry Wilkinson)

ricane hit the Russell family hard; of the seventy-some family members living on Upper Matecumbe Key, only eleven survived.

It was a ghastly scene the following day. Some men in boats managed to make their way to Homestead to seek help, and relief crews were organized. Because the bridge at Snake Creek was washed away, the Keys were completely cut off from the mainland. Communications were out, and no one in Miami knew of the disaster. Meanwhile, injured survivors lodged in trees were thirsting to death. It rained hard all day on Tuesday, and some storm victims were able to collect enough rainwater to survive. By Wednesday rescue crews were working under the hot sun to transport the injured to mainland hospitals and retrieve the bodies of the dead. Survivors searched through the debris for canned goods and other sources of food. Almost all survivors had some form of injury and were dressed in cotton bandages.

The first doctor to make his way down to the labor camps was G. C. Franklin of Coconut Grove. Upon his arrival, he immediately discovered the bodies of thirty-nine men left by the waves amid a windrow of debris. For the next few days, bodies were pulled out of trees, from under mounds of sand, and from the wreckage of crushed houses. Just as in the tragedies at Moore Haven in 1926 and Pelican Bay in 1928, another great Florida hurricane had left strings of corpses in the sun.

Among the first to enter the devastated area was Ernest Hemingway, who was a member of a rescue team that traveled up the Keys the morning after the hurricane. During the storm, Hemingway had been at his home in Key West, where strong winds had been felt but relatively light damages were reported. The appalling scene enraged the well-known author, who lashed out at officials in Washington for sending the vets to labor in the Keys during "the hurricane months" with an ill-conceived plan of rescue. In an article entitled "Who Murdered the Vets?" that appeared in *New Masses* on September 17, he wrote:

Who sent nearly a thousand war veterans, many of them husky, hard-working and simply out of luck, but many of them close to the border of pathological cases, to live in frame shacks in the Florida Keys in hurricane months? Why were the men not evacuated on Sunday, or at latest, Monday morning when it was known there was a possibility of a hurricane striking the Keys *and evacuation was their only possible protection?* Who advised against sending the train from Miami to evacuate the veterans until four thirty o'clock on Monday so that it was blown off the tracks before it ever reached the lower camps? These are questions that someone will have to answer, and answer satisfactorily, unless the clearing of Anacostia Flats [the Washington, D.C., site of the Bonus Marcher clash] is going to seem an act of kindness compared to the clearing of Upper and Lower Matecumbe.

Hemingway later described the gruesomeness of what he had witnessed in a letter to his publisher, Maxwell Perkins. The letter was later published in *Ernest Hemingway: Selected Letters, 1917–1961.* He wrote: "Max, you can't imagine it, two women, naked, tossed up into the trees by the water, swollen and stinking, their breasts as big as balloons, flies between their legs. Then, by figuring, you

locate where it is and recognize them as the two very nice girls who ran a sandwich place and filling-station three miles from the ferry. We located sixty-nine bodies where no one had been able to get in. Indian Key absolutely swept clean, not a blade of grass, and over the high center of it were scattered live conchs that came in with the sea, craw fish, and dead morays. The whole bottom of the sea blew over it."

Hemingway's angry discourse fueled the controversy over the treatment of the vets and the poorly executed rescue attempt. A congressional investigation was launched into the actions of the Weather Bureau and FERA, which had coordinated the work project. Over the next few months, politicians took sides on the issue—some saw the disaster as an "unforeseeable act of God," and others viewed the inquiry and subsequent compensation legislation as a "whitewash." Among those who testified before Congress in the spring of 1936 was Ivan R. Tannehill, chief of the Weather Bureau's Marine Division and author of *Hurricanes: Their Nature and History* two years later. The final report from the House committee concluded: "The evidence clearly shows, that the tidal wave was entirely unexpected and that it was impossible to even anticipate the hurricane within sufficient time to ensure safety for those concerned."

The task of counting, identifying, and removing the dead from the Keys went on for days after the storm. The Coast Guard sent supplies on five seaplanes and several cutters. The National Guard was brought in to maintain order. Young men, some much too young, were sent from government work camps in Miami to remove the dead. At first, orders were given that all of the dead veterans were to be transported to Washington for burial at Arlington Cemetery.

Then it was determined that they should be sent to Miami instead. It quickly became clear, however, that transporting all of the rapidly decomposing bodies was not feasible. State health officials, fearing an epidemic, ordered the mounting corpses cremated at the site. Tensions flared when National Guard officers tried to stop local residents from taking the bodies of their family members away for private ceremonies. The first funeral pyre was on the north bank of Snake Creek, where scores of wooden caskets were doused with diesel fuel and burned. Soldiers standing nearby offered a final salute by firing their rifles, and a young Salvation Army worker sounded out taps on his bugle.

As in other great hurricane disasters, the exact number of victims claimed by the Labor Day hurricane will never be known. The Red Cross initially placed the figure at 252 veterans dead or presumed dead, another 106 injured, and 164 civilians dead or missing. Some reports indicated that the actual figure was much higher—over 500 dead. The coroner's report from Islamorada on September 7 gave the total number of dead and missing as 423. Later reports by the Red Cross and others indicated a final death toll of 408, which is generally recognized as the best estimate. Accurate death counts were made difficult because of the large number of bodies that were never found and the fact that the exact number of veteran laborers who had spent the holiday weekend in Miami was never known. After learning that the work camp had been destroyed, many of these vets moved on.

After the storm, cleanup in the Keys took weeks, and rebuilding efforts continued for many months. The ill-fated rescue train's engine was placed on a barge and floated back to Miami. Flagler's famous railway through the Keys was virtually destroyed. Thirty-five miles of tracks and embankments were washed away, and many rails were twisted into peculiar shapes of rusted steel. Already bankrupt and in receivership, the Florida East Coast Railway was in no position to rebuild after the disaster. Ironically, many of the railway trestles and bridge structures that survived were later used in the completion of the Overseas Highway, which finally opened in 1938. Overall, the total damage estimate for the storm was in excess of $6 million.

During the following year, the Great Depression deepened in the Keys, as the island chain's one connection with the mainland had been severed. Jobs were as scarce as food; it was said that even the fishing was poor. In *The Day of the Seventh Fire*, James Leo Herlihy wrote of the lunacy that gripped the people of Key West: "Many people had taken to eating grass and weeds, boiling the stuff with nothing to flavor it but a bird shot out of a tree with a BB gun. . . . One old man took off all his clothes, ran into the swamps and died there a week later, stark-naked and alone; a middle-aged teacher surprised her students and colleagues one Monday morning by walking into the grade school dead-drunk, her hair freshly dyed in the color of ripe tomatoes and twirling a loaded pistol around her forefinger; and so on. Nothing made sense anymore."

The bodies of 116 of the veterans were brought to Miami in pine boxes for a funeral with full military honors after the 1935 Labor Day storm. (Photo courtesy of the Florida State Archives)

A funeral pyre is readied for burning bodies of victims of the 1935 Labor Day storm at Matecumbe Key. Witnessing the cremation are a Jewish rabbi, a Catholic priest, a Protestant pastor, a FERA representative, and an officer of the National Guard. (Photo courtesy of Jerry Wilkinson)

An eighteen-foot coral monument in Islamorada was dedicated to the victims of the 1935 Labor Day hurricane. Buried beneath the monument are the ashes and remains of some of the storm victims. (Photo courtesy of the Florida State Archives)

Headlines from the Miami Beach Sunday Tribune *on September 8, 1935, announcing the cremation of bodies of storm victims. (Photo courtesy of Noel Risnychok)*

Today visitors to the Keys can pause on their journey southward to visit the final resting place of many of the hurricane's victims. The 1935 Hurricane Monument, located just off U.S. 1 in Islamorada, was designed by the Florida Division of the Federal Art Project and constructed by the Works Progress Administration. The eighteen-foot memorial, made of coral from a nearby quarry, was built on top of a crypt that contains the bones and cremated remains of many of those who died on the Matecumbe Keys. A bronze plaque on the monument is inscribed: "Dedicated to the memory of the civilians and war veterans whose lives were lost in the hurricane of September second, 1935." It was unveiled before a crowd of 5,000 by nine-year-old survivor Fay Marie Parker on Sunday, November 14, 1937.

NOVEMBER 4, 1935

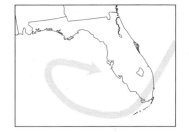

Two months after the Keys were rocked by the most powerful hurricane ever known, residents of South Florida were tested by another storm. This time, however, the Weather Bureau's warnings came when the storm was far away at sea. Residents from St. Augustine to Key West listened intently for updated bulletins. Their anxiousness was fed by the recent horrors at Matecumbe, as well as by the peculiar approach of the storm. It was well known that hurricanes generally moved northwestward toward Florida's east coast, but for some unknown reason, this late-season storm carved an erratic path down from the north. For this reason, it would later become known in Miami as the "Yankee Hurricane."

Its origins as a weak disturbance east of Bermuda on October 30 were probably of an extratropical nature. For more than two days, it slowly drifted toward the west-northwest until it grew to hurricane strength and threatened the North Carolina coast on the morning of November 1. The following day, it took a sharp turn southward and moved over the warmer waters of the Bahamas. Then, around midnight on November 3, the well-formed hurricane changed course again and turned toward Miami. The eye of the storm passed over the city at about noon on the fourth before tracking across the Everglades and into the Gulf of Mexico. Over the next four days, it spun in a broad clockwise loop and eventually dissipated before drifting back over land near Tampa.

The storm's bizarre path and other oddities provided hurricane meteorologists with a great deal to study and attempt to understand. Weather Bureau forecaster Gordon Dunn wrote about the storm in the *Monthly Weather Review*: "Many peculiarities attended this storm aside from its most unusual path. About 0.24 inch of rain fell at Miami before the arrival of the lull and about 3.80 inches after the passage of the center. I have no recollection of any such rainfall distribution at any place over which the center of a tropical storm has passed. Indeed, the heaviest rainfall usually occurs in the front quadrants and least in the rear. Reports from cooperative stations indicated that decidedly heavier precipitation occurred in the left hand quadrant than in the right, also unusual."

Damages were heavy in the Bahamas. The storm's lowest recorded pressure of 28.46 inches was measured on board the *Queen of Bermuda* just north of the islands on November 3. Five sponge-fishing vessels were lost at sea. A total of fourteen people were killed on Great Abaco Island, including Commissioner John Eldridge Russell, who was drowned after being knocked overboard by the swing of a ship's boom. He had been distributing relief supplies to islanders who had suffered through a previous hurricane on September 28.

In Miami, where the eye lasted sixty-five minutes, the pressure was measured at 28.73 inches. Sustained winds were just above hurricane force—75 mph, with one gust reported at 94 mph. Along the waterfront, storm tides caused damage to docks, marinas, and low-lying structures. At Miami Beach tides were more than six feet above normal; at Fort Lauderdale they measured about eight feet above normal high water. Damages were confined to the coast within this area because of the relatively small diameter of the storm.

Even though warnings were issued well in advance and precautions were taken, Miami was still hit hard by the hurricane. Damages were heavy in the city and on Miami Beach. Gusting winds downed utility lines and shattered storefront windows in many locations. Local reports indicated that 117 persons were injured, most of whom were either cut by glass or wounded by falling objects. Two yachts broke from their moorings and were dashed into a causeway and wrecked. Fortunately, even though there were many injuries, only five deaths were reported in Florida. Damages to public utilities totaled $750,000; small craft, $120,000; and trees and shrubbery, $150,000. After all of the effects of the storm had been assessed, damage estimates in Florida were placed at $5.5 million, and the combined death toll in Florida and the Bahamas was nineteen.

JULY 31, 1936

In July 1936, while dust storms plagued portions of the Great Plains, Florida experienced a midsummer storm that struck the state twice. It was first seen north of the Turks Islands on July 26, and over the next two days, it steadily progressed toward southern Florida. Its center moved inland just thirty miles south of Miami during the early evening of July 28. At this time, it was only a tropical storm, with winds of about 60 mph. At the Miami airport, sustained winds measured 49 mph with gusts to 65 mph. It moved south of Homestead with a forward speed of about 12 mph and passed near Everglades City at 2:00 A.M. At that location, the barometer dipped to nearly 29.00 inches, and winds were from the northeast at 55 mph. Just after the storm center passed, an "abnormally high tide" occurred, which measured 5.5 feet above normal and left water 18 inches deep in the streets of Everglades City. Around noon, winds were about 60 mph at Boca Grande—not severe enough to bring about significant damage. Weather Bureau reports indicated that damages were "slight" in South Florida.

As the tropical storm pulled away from the coast and out into the Gulf of Mexico, warnings were issued from Cedar Key to Apalachicola and then later extended westward. But before the storm approached the upper Gulf coast, its forward speed slowed considerably, and according to Gordon Dunn's report for the Weather Bureau, "abnormally high tides were produced considering the size and intensity of the disturbance."

The storm intensified to hurricane strength just twenty-four hours before moving ashore near Fort Walton Beach on the morning of July 31. At 11:00 A.M., the barometer at nearby Valparaiso recorded a low of 28.73 inches, with winds estimated at 90–100 mph. Gusts at Fort Walton Beach were reported to 125 mph, and tides ran about six feet above normal. Residents experienced the calm eye of the hurricane for eighty minutes. Hurricane winds were reported along a seventy-mile stretch of coastline. Soon after landfall, the storm weakened considerably and tracked just north of Pensacola and into southwestern Alabama.

This short-lived hurricane was not particularly destructive, although moderate wind and tidal surge damages were reported around Valparaiso. The total dollar estimate for that region was placed at $123,000, and total damages for all of Florida were $200,000. All areas affected by the storm had the benefit of at least a twenty-four-hour warning, and most residents were well prepared. Most of the sponge fleet remained in port because of the storm, and the Coast Guard dispatched airplanes to warn eleven vessels in the hurricane's path to return to safe harbor. One fishing boat, the *Ketchum*, was lost in the Gulf, however, with four persons aboard. It left port on the twenty-third, before the first advisory was issued, and was not heard from again.

OCTOBER 5–7, 1941

During the 1940s, Florida residents felt the wrath of an extended period of severe tropical weather. According to Weather Bureau records, only once before, during the late 1880s, had so many hurricanes struck in such a brief period. From 1941 to 1950, Florida was hit by a steady barrage of hurricanes—twelve storms in ten years. The first occurred in the fall of 1941, yet another hurricane to make a double hit on the Florida coast. And once again it was the storm-prone glades south of Miami and the shores of the Panhandle that took the blow.

The 1941 hurricane was first spotted several hundred miles north of Puerto

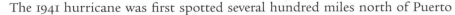

Rico on October 4. The following day, it passed near Nassau with winds of 102 mph on a steady west-northwest course toward South Florida. For two days prior to its arrival, the Weather Bureau distributed frequent bulletins on its progress to residents along the Florida coast. A total of forty advisories were issued, which led to widespread preparations.

At 5:30 A.M. on October 6, the eye of the hurricane made landfall thirteen miles south of Miami. At Fowey Rock Lighthouse winds were less than hurricane force, and the barometer only reached a low of 29.28 inches. At the Pan American Airways base at Dinner Key, however, a peak gust of 123 mph was recorded, with sustained winds of 90 mph. Little rainfall was measured with the passage of the storm, which was noted by the Weather Bureau as very unusual. Only 0.35 inch fell in Miami, and other locations near the center of the hurricane reported accumulations of less than 1 inch. Significant damage to crops, trees, and shrubbery was caused by the burning effects of salt spray that was blown several miles inland by strong winds. With so little rain to wash away the salt, vegetation throughout the region was left blistered after the storm. The primary damages reported in Dade County resulted from fallen trees and utility poles and shattered windows.

The relatively small hurricane passed over the Everglades and tracked between Everglades City and Fort Myers later that morning. Winds at Everglades City were clocked at 65 mph, and the accompanying storm tide flooded the town's streets to a depth of one foot. Fishing vessels were washed about, and extensive damages were reported to docks, packinghouses, and fishing gear.

Like so many other hurricanes that spin across South Florida, this storm moved into the Gulf on a broad curve that carried it just offshore along the west coast. On the afternoon of October 6, winds at Egmont Key at the mouth of Tampa Bay were estimated at 60 mph. The storm remained offshore until the early-morning hours of October 7, when it struck Carrabelle. Just after the eye moved inland, winds were estimated at 75 mph, and the barometer read 29.00 inches. Its path then turned toward the northeast, and the storm moved beyond Tallahassee and into Georgia, with winds that still gusted to 75 mph. It continued to diminish in strength into South Carolina and finally returned to the Atlantic at Charleston. From there, it was tracked for four more days, first turning toward the southeast, then making a small loop, and finally passing harmlessly out to sea.

The Big Bend region was also well warned, and relatively few casualties resulted. Seven people were reported injured in the area, and five men working at a fishing net drying yard near Panacea were drowned when the storm tide arrived. Tides in the area were estimated at close to eight feet above normal. At Tallahassee high winds knocked down countless trees and power lines, plunging the city into darkness. Roadways were impassible because of the fallen trees and scattered wreckage. Fears quickly arose that heavy losses had resulted at the coast, and rescue crews led by Governor Spessard Holland pushed their way through the debris-choked roads toward St. Marks. Once they arrived, they were met by a group of local people who convinced the rescuers that help was not needed.

The *Tallahassee Democrat*, handicapped by a lack of electricity, managed to put out 6,000 copies of a special eight-page storm edition that was written on a typewriter, mimeographed, and stapled together. The paper reported on the adventures of the U.S. Army's Thirty-first Dixie Division of some 6,000 troops, which had camped overnight in the city on Magnolia Drive while en route to a camp in Georgia. The hurricane apparently surprised the soldiers, blowing down many of their tents. At the height of the storm, the army commander gave orders to move out, and the entire division slowly pulled away in the howling wind. Many of its 700 vehicles had to be hauled out from under fallen trees or towed out of deep mud.

The *Democrat* also reported that "at the height of the wind several hundred Tallahasseeans were seen rushing into their yards to gather pecans which were knocked down by the swaying trees." It also noted that "the greatest disaster of the storm in Tallahassee was the loss of automobiles." Countless cars around the city were smashed by large hardwoods. Even though the Japanese would not attack Pearl Harbor for another two months, new cars were very difficult to come by because assembly plants were busy producing vehicles for the army. Once the country became involved in World War II, new cars were unavailable, and many in the hurricane-affected area returned to an earlier form of transportation—the horse and carriage.

Total damages for the storm were estimated at $675,000, "about equally divided between the northern and southern portions of the State," according to the *Monthly Weather Review*.

OCTOBER 18–19, 1944

In 1943 the Weather Bureau moved its primary hurricane forecast office for the Atlantic basin from Jacksonville to Miami, where it was teamed with forecasters from the navy and the air force. This new forecast office served the region throughout World War II and established the presence of what would later become the National Hurricane Center. The new office was created with the intention of providing the best equipment and personnel to warn citizens and the Allied forces of approaching tropical storms. New technologies like radar were employed, and communication systems were improved. During the same year, the first reconnaissance flight was made into a hurricane to gather data, and a new age of hurricane meteorology was born.

During the next year, two major hurricanes struck the United States, testing the abilities of the Weather Bureau's new station. The first of these was the

Great Atlantic Hurricane of 1944, a mighty September storm that forecasters at one time believed to be almost as powerful as the awesome Labor Day hurricane of 1935 but much larger in diameter. It grazed the North Carolina coast near Cape Hatteras and then raced into New England, where it shattered wind records and was compared to the devastating hurricane of 1938. Loss of life was heavy, especially at sea, where wartime patrols tried to ride out the storm. Among the losses were a destroyer, two Coast Guard cutters, a minesweeper, and other craft. A total of 390 deaths were recorded, many of whom were sailors aboard vessels sunk in the storm.

Reconnaissance flights helped the Weather Bureau keep up with the progress of the hurricane. They not only provided new and crucial information to hurricane forecasters but in many cases replaced ship reports that were unavailable due to wartime radio blackouts. In Tannehill's *Hurricanes: Their Nature and History*, an official report on the Great Atlantic Hurricane of 1944 by H. C. Sumner described one of the earliest reconnaissance flights ever sent into a major hurricane: "The weather officer (Lt. Victor Klobucher) aboard an army reconnaissance plane which became involved in the storm estimated the wind at about 140 mph. He reported turbulence so great that with the pilot and copilot both at the controls the plane could not be kept under control, and several times it was feared it would be torn apart or crash out of control. When they returned to base it was found that 150 rivets had been sheared off one wing alone."

The second big storm of the season formed in October and would later become known as the Havana-Florida hurricane. First reports of the storm came from the Swan Islands in the western Caribbean on October 13. It meandered through the warm waters around Grand Cayman for several days before finally tracking northward into Cuba on the morning of October 18. The storm was of incredible intensity during its course through the upper Caribbean. At Grand Cayman 31.29 inches of rain fell with its passage. As it struck Cuba, a massive storm surge flooded coastal communities of Havana Province, killing dozens of residents and destroying entire villages. According to Tannehill, the strength of the storm can be gauged by a report that a Standard Oil barge was carried ten miles inland by the tidal flood. The eye passed some ten to fifteen miles west of Havana, where an extreme wind gust was clocked at 163 mph.

The Weather Bureau followed the storm closely as it pounded Cuba. Communications with Havana were severed, and the extent of damages there was not immediately known. Forecasters in Miami continued to issue warnings that the powerful storm was moving generally northward and would affect the Keys and southern Florida within hours. Official reports later stated that "systematic evacuation of all dangerously exposed beaches doubtless saved many lives."

On the afternoon of October 18, the hurricane tracked over the Dry Tortugas, where the calm eye was observed from 3:00 to 5:00 P.M. The barometer there recorded a low of 28.02 inches, and winds were in excess of 120 mph. The storm was very large and was moving at a forward speed of about 20 mph. Reports from the Dry Tortugas indicated that winds there were above gale force (over 38 mph) for more than seventy-two hours and 120 mph or more for two hours.

At the same time that the hurricane's eye was over the Dry Tortugas, broad, spiraling rainbands on its leading edge were working their way up through central Florida. During the afternoon, several tornadoes touched down in Arcadia, Wauchula, and southern Polk County, some of which caused extensive damage. As the storm tracked up the Gulf coast and inland near Sarasota, its effects were already being felt over much of the state. Its large size was later illustrated by wind-field maps that showed damaging winds of 50 mph or more extending 200 miles east and 100 miles west of the center of the storm. Gusts of 100 mph were reported at Tampa and Orlando, and Miami experienced winds of 65 mph.

As it tracked northward through the heart of the Florida Peninsula, its unusually large and distorted eye became apparent. Its eye was shaped more like a stretched-out oval than a tight circle, and its primary axis was along its line of advance. At one time, the eye reached from Jacksonville to Ocala, a distance of almost seventy miles. Even though the storm was moving about 20 mph when it passed through Jacksonville, the "calm" was reported to have lasted more than five hours. After traveling briefly over the Atlantic along the Georgia coast, the storm passed inland again just north of Savannah. It continued through the eastern portions of the Carolinas and Virginia with diminished strength and finally returned to sea off Maryland's Eastern Shore.

In Florida damages were scattered from one end of the state to the other, and serious flooding plagued both coasts. High tides struck upon the storm's landfall, and heavy losses were reported in the vicinity of Fort Myers. Tides at Naples were up to twelve feet above normal. Low-lying areas between Sarasota and Everglades City were inundated. At Everglades City heavy rains dumped at the time of normal high tide were blamed for much of the flooding, which once again filled the town's streets. The Coast Guard took a break from its wartime duties to assist residents of the submerged town.

Along the Gulf coast north of Sarasota, including Tampa Bay, offshore winds of over 50 mph prevented flooding problems. The storm center passed just east of Tampa, where a new record low pressure was set for that location—28.55 inches. It is interesting to note that the hurricane's highest tides in Florida were not on the southwest coast near the place of landfall but on the northeastern beaches where the storm made its exit from the state. Gale-force winds from the Atlantic piled water along the shore from Cocoa Beach, where a causeway was washed out, to Savannah. The storm's highest tide was recorded at Jacksonville Beach—12.28 feet above mean low water. In some areas, beach erosion exceeded 150 feet.

The large size of the hurricane was the primary reason damages were so extensive in Florida. Orlando was among the hardest hit of all inland cities, receiving damages estimated at over $1 million. A Weather Bureau summary reported that "throughout the state there was extensive damage to telephone, telegraph, and power lines, trees, roofs, chimneys, signs, and radio towers." A total of about $13 million in property losses was reported around the state, and the Florida Marketing Bureau placed the damages to the citrus crop and truck farms at $50 million. Over 25 million boxes of fruit were blown down by the winds, very little of which could be salvaged. Including the losses in Cuba and other parts of the Caribbean, the total cost of the hurricane exceeded $100 million.

The October hurricane was almost as deadly as the one that preceded it in September. There were eighteen deaths in Florida and twenty-four serious injuries. In Cuba the death toll was much greater. Tannehill noted that the total count of 319 deaths in the storm is incomplete since many deaths in rural areas of Cuba were never reported.

SEPTEMBER 15–16, 1945

Just eleven days after a tropical storm struck Miami with 50 mph winds, one of the fiercest hurricanes to ever visit Dade County roared ashore near Homestead in mid-September 1945. It most likely began as a classic Cape Verde–type storm, building to hurricane strength hundreds of miles east of the West Indies. Its steady westward course was well north of the Leeward Islands and Puerto Rico, and on September 13, its weaker southern side brushed the coast near San Juan. On the morning of the fourteenth, its eye passed near the Turks Islands, where high winds disabled wind instruments and tore away the roofs of many homes. Its passage through the Bahama Islands was similarly destructive, killing twenty-two people in thirty hours.

The Weather Bureau office in Miami issued ample warnings concerning the fast-approaching hurricane, and oceanfront communities like Miami Beach were well evacuated. Initially, the storm's course appeared to be directed toward the Florida Keys. But in the hours just before landfall, its westward trajectory began to arc more toward the northwest, edging the center of the storm toward the mainland. Fortunately for the population of Greater Miami, this change of course did not occur rapidly, and the storm finally came ashore just below Homestead on the afternoon of September 15. Its destructive path was relatively narrow, but it was still described by the press as "Miami's worst hurricane since 1926."

The most severe damages occurred along a path about forty miles wide through the towns of Florida City, Homestead, Redlands, Princeton, Goulds, Perrine, Richmond Heights, Kendall, and South Miami. Winds were measured

Grapefruits cover the ground near Lakeland after being blown down by strong winds in the October 1944 hurricane. (Photo courtesy of Noel Risnychok)

at 138 mph at Carysfort Reef Lighthouse and 107 mph in Miami. Extremely high winds were clocked nearer the storm's dangerous eyewall; according to Tannehill in *Hurricanes: Their Nature and History*, "Records obtained at the Richmond Base, after correction for instrument error, indicated an average two-minute maximum wind velocity of 170 miles per hour. It was estimated that the wind reached 196 miles per hour for a few seconds. An investigating group found deformation of steel framed doors which could not have occurred without winds in excess of 161 miles per hour. The lowest pressure recorded in this hurricane was 28.09 inches at the Army Air Base in Homestead, Florida."

High tides also battered the area, and large waves rolled over the local beaches. Tides at Miami Beach were 4.5 feet above mean low water; portions of Miami saw flooding up to 10.7 feet; and at Cutler Ridge, about fifteen miles south of Miami, the storm surge rose 14 feet above mean low water. Waterfront damages to small craft, docks, and marinas were somewhat typical. Collins Avenue on Miami Beach was under water and was said to have been filled with the roofs of cabanas from nearby homes and hotels. One of the major losses was that of the 70-ton Honduran schooner *Acares*, which was pounded to splinters near Miami Beach, with the loss of one member of the crew. Boats of all kinds were tossed out of Biscayne Bay across South Bayshore Drive and ended up in piles of rubble near Mary Street. Longtime Miami residents could not resist comparing the storm with the disaster of 1926, even though the destruction was not as severe.

Although significant damages were spread among numerous Dade communities, the hurricane's greatest disaster occurred at the U.S. Naval Air Station

Richmond Naval Air Base suffered a double tragedy on September 15, 1945, as powerful hurricane winds fanned the flames of a fire that destroyed most of the base's aircraft. (Photo courtesy of the Florida State Archives)

The hurricane of September 1945 flooded the banks of Biscayne Bay south of Miami. (Photo courtesy of Noel Risnychok)

at Richmond Heights. Three enormous hangars, designed to house the navy's large blimps and warplanes, were blown down by the storm's peak winds. This was the site where the 170 mph extremes were measured, and it was the 196 mph gust that was believed to have brought the hangars down. As they collapsed at the climax of the storm, their contents were scattered, and the disaster escalated as enormous fires erupted, fed by high-octane fuel and fanned by the incredible gusts. Destroyed in the hangars were 25 blimps, 183 military planes, 153 civilian planes, and 150 automobiles. Over 200 people were injured in the blaze, many of whom were hurt while attempting to fight the fire at the height of the storm. Others on the base were at first relieved that they had not stored their own cars in the hangars but instead had parked them in an open field nearby. They discovered, however, that the storm's incredible winds had blown sand across the runways and sandblasted the paint off one side of their cars, turning them from shiny colors to a dull silver. The total estimate of losses at the base was placed at $35 million.

Soon after landfall, the hurricane turned almost due north and sped up the Florida Peninsula with diminished fury. It eventually curved back out to sea near the Georgia line and followed a path similar to that of the October storm of the previous year along the Georgia coast and into the heart of the Carolinas. It continued through the Northeast as an extratropical storm and eventually pulled out to sea again near Newfoundland on September 20.

In addition to property damages in Dade County, agricultural losses were

significant. According to the *Monthly Weather Review*, losses were heavy to the
avocado and lime crops in southern Florida and to the citrus crops in Highlands and Polk Counties. The total loss to the state's citrus crop was estimated
at 5 percent. Heavy rains flooded the truck farms that bordered the Everglades,
ruining a large percentage of crops. Pastures along the Kissimmee and St. Johns
River valleys were flooded. The storm caused four deaths in Florida and losses
that approached $60 million.

OCTOBER 7, 1946

The October hurricane of 1946 was not severe, and its impact on Florida was
less than remarkable. It originated on October 6 in the western Caribbean, a familiar breeding ground for hurricanes during this part of the season. It crossed
the western tip of Cuba later the same day and advanced toward Tampa the
following morning. It made landfall at about 7:00 P.M. near Bradenton, with
80 mph winds and a pressure of 28.95 inches. It immediately lost hurricane
strength and moved rapidly toward the north as a small tropical storm. Eventually, it tracked into southeastern Georgia and the Carolinas before returning
to sea near Nags Head, North Carolina.

Even though winds in the hurricane were clocked by reconnaissance aircraft
at 132 mph near Cuba, along the Florida Gulf coast, they were barely of hurricane force. Tides were several feet above normal, and some piers, wharves,
and warehouses were damaged. Trees were downed, and brief power outages
occurred, but this storm's impact was not nearly as great as that of other recent

hurricanes. No storm-related deaths were reported. Florida's citrus farmers suffered the only major damages, with total crop losses of about $5 million.

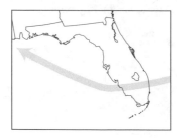

SEPTEMBER 17, 1947

Florida was battered by two hurricanes in 1947, both of which approached the state in classic form: a Cape Verde–type powerhouse in September and a blast from the deep Caribbean in October. The September hurricane was particularly potent in South Florida and later in New Orleans. High winds once again whistled through the streets of Miami, although Fort Lauderdale took the brunt of the storm. Storm tides swept the beaches, wind-speed records were broken, and the people of Dade, Broward, and Palm Beach Counties were left once again with a mountain of hurricane debris.

The September storm formed far across the Atlantic in Africa as a strong low-pressure area in Dakar, Senegal, before it ever moved out over water. It was believed to have reached hurricane strength near 25 degrees longitude, just off the African coast below the Cape Verde Islands. It became a hurricane on September 4 and remained at hurricane strength until it dissipated over central Louisiana on the nineteenth—a total of fifteen days. Its course through the Atlantic was fierce, and few ships were close enough to its path to file reports. It moved well above the West Indies, skipping past Puerto Rico and Haiti with little effect. On September 15, however, the large and powerful storm hesitated, and its forward movement stalled for almost twenty-four hours. Then its gentle northwesterly track shifted to just south of due west. The Weather Bureau changed its bulletins from storm warnings to hurricane warnings for the lower Florida coast. Early the next day, the northern Bahama Islands were hammered by tremendous winds and floods that brought heavy damages. Winds at Great Abaco Island were clocked at 160 mph, the highest ever recorded at that location. Within hours, it became apparent that this monster storm was indeed on its way to the Florida coast.

The Weather Bureau's forecast office in Miami, still operating in conjunction with the military, gave the storm a name, referring to it as "George." Meteorologists with the Pacific fleet during World War II had begun the practice of issuing names to tropical storms as a means of discerning one from another. After the conclusion of the war, this system continued unofficially but was not widely publicized by the Weather Bureau.

On the morning of September 17, Hurricane "George" swept ashore near Fort Lauderdale with category 4 intensity. Hurricane-force winds blasted the shoreline from the Carysfort Reef Lighthouse, south of Miami, to Cape Canaveral. The hurricane's highest winds were recorded at Hillsboro Lighthouse, where a one-minute maximum of 155 mph was observed. At that same location, winds of 121 mph were sustained for five minutes, and a barometric low of

27.97 inches was measured at 11:25 A.M. According to NOAA's *Deadliest, Costliest, and Most Intense United States Hurricanes of This Century* by Hebert, Jarrell, and Mayfield, the storm's lowest recorded pressure was 27.76 inches. In Fort Lauderdale gusts were measured up to 127 mph. Even though the Labor Day hurricane of 1935 and Hurricane Andrew undoubtedly had stronger winds, the 155 mph winds recorded at Hillsboro Lighthouse remain the highest sustained winds ever officially observed in Florida.

The storm was not only powerful but also large and slow moving. Its forward speed as it churned over the Florida coast was less than 10 mph, which meant that residents were pounded for many hours after landfall. Its size was equally impressive. In a 1955 article in *Weatherwise* entitled "A Comparison of Six Great Florida Hurricanes," Donald C. Bunting wrote that "it was reported in the 1947 storm that winds of 100 mph or over extended along the Florida east coast for a distance of 70 miles and hurricane force winds along the same area for 240 miles." Another account from the Weather Bureau estimated the width of the storm's path in which winds over 50 mph were observed at close to 300 miles—virtually all of the Florida Peninsula south of Brevard County.

Considering the storm's size and power, it is not surprising that it crossed Florida with little loss of strength. Its eye churned slowly across the Everglades, over the sparsely populated inland sections of Broward and Collier Counties, before exiting the state near Naples. Heavy rainfall was distributed over a wide

The Seacrest Hotel at Delray Beach was among the oceanfront structures affected by the September 1947 storm. (Photo courtesy of the Florida State Archives)

area; 7.36 inches were recorded at Bonita Springs, 8.72 inches at Fort Myers, and 10.12 inches at St. Lucie Lock. Winds over 100 mph buffeted the west coast from Everglades City to Punta Gorda. Wind-driven water once again flooded much of the southwestern Gulf coast. Tides at Everglades City were 5.5 feet above mean low tide, filling the town's streets and driving residents into their attics. Flooding also affected areas other than the Florida coastline. Even though the dikes on Lake Okeechobee held, tides measured 21 feet at Clewiston and Moore Haven.

Serious flooding also plagued the cities on the east coast that caught the brunt of the storm. Weather Bureau records indicate that a maximum tide at Hillsboro Lighthouse of 11 feet above mean low tide was maintained for thirty minutes. Tides of 11 feet were also reported along the coast from Fort Lauderdale to Palm Beach. In Miami, City Manager Richard Danner reported that 200 miles of streets were a total loss. Flooding was reported in every home from Miami Avenue to Northwest Second Avenue between Seventy-first and Seventy-ninth Streets. Winds gusting up to 110 mph tore down signs, awnings, trees, and power lines, making streets impassable. At the Miami airport hangars were damaged, and numerous planes were overturned and destroyed. More than half of the homes in Miami Springs were under water, and the *Miami Herald* stated that Homestead "resembled Venice, Italy." After the storm, floodwaters had little chance to retreat, as another tropical storm arrived in Miami just six days later with winds of 60 mph and more torrential rains.

Miami Beach was also severely flooded in the hurricane, although the surge

there was not as great as on many of the region's other beaches. The tide did not exceed seven feet above mean low water. The state highway between Baker's Haulover and Sunny Isles was washed out, and the destruction worsened farther north.

Hollywood and Fort Lauderdale suffered the greatest wind damages, with virtually every structure affected to some degree. Many homes and apartments lost their roofs, and few utility poles were left standing, many having been snapped like toothpicks by the 150 mph gusts. Tornadoes were reported in several locations across the state. Most occurred in the hours preceding the arrival of the storm's strongest winds. After hearing reports of the damages at Fort Lauderdale, President Harry Truman declared a state of emergency along the entire southeast coast of Florida. A total of seventeen deaths were reported in the state, and damage estimates totaled almost $32 million, about a third of which was attributed to agricultural losses.

When Hurricane "George" passed over Florida and entered the Gulf of Mexico around midnight on September 17, it was still fairly well organized. Early the next day, it began to regain strength and turn toward the northwest, crossing the Gulf on a collision course with the Louisiana coast. As it moved across the warm Gulf waters, its forward speed accelerated, and by dawn of September 19, it was positioned just beyond the Mississippi River Delta. The eye passed directly over New Orleans later that morning, where a barometric low of 28.61 inches was recorded just before 11:00 A.M. Winds were clocked at 90 mph, with a one-minute maximum of 110 mph. The Weather Bureau later calculated that the eye was twenty-five miles in diameter as it moved over the city's business district. The storm remained strong as it passed into central Louisiana, with sustained winds of 96 mph reported at Baton Rouge and estimated gusts to 120 mph.

Because the storm was still large, hurricane effects were spread all along the Louisiana and Mississippi coastlines. Destructive tides hammered waterfront properties, demolishing 1,642 homes and damaging another 25,000. Tides rose twelve feet above normal at Biloxi, Bay St. Louis, and Gulfport, Mississippi. Twenty-two people died in these coastal areas, and another twelve were killed in Louisiana. The total death count for this storm in the United States reached fifty-one. Total financial losses were placed at $110 million.

Considering the large size of this September hurricane, its incredible wind strength, and the fact that it struck the United States twice, the total number of deaths that resulted was thought to be remarkably low. After witnessing the horrible loss of life in storms of the past decades, the Florida press acknowledged that the Weather Bureau's timely warnings were now effectively saving lives. Although this storm was one of the most awesome hurricanes in Florida history, evacuations and preparations in advance of its arrival had lessened the blow. Florida residents had, to some degree, become wise to the ways of tropical cyclones, and this 1947 powerhouse gave them an opportunity to prove it.

OCTOBER 11–12, 1947

The second hurricane to strike Florida in 1947 was not exceptionally powerful, and its effects on the state were not as widespread as those of the September storm. The Weather Bureau office in Miami unofficially labeled it "King"; it was the eleventh storm to develop that season. It was first spotted as a tropical low deep in the Caribbean off the coast of Nicaragua on October 8. It slowly drifted northward with little increase in strength until the morning of the eleventh, when it passed over western Cuba. At that point, it turned toward the northeast and intensified rapidly, growing from tropical storm to hurricane strength in the few hours prior to its landfall in Florida. Weather Bureau reports indicated that the anemometer at the Dry Tortugas "froze at 84 mph due to friction from lack of oil." Observers at that station watched the wind increase until it reached an estimated 150 mph. The storm center apparently turned just after passing the Dry Tortugas and struck the Florida coast near Cape Sable. The Weather Bureau reported that "as the storm passed over Florida it was preceded by spectacular thunderstorm activity and heavy rainfall. Baragrams show a double minimum, a weak one at the time of the thunderstorm with a short recovering before the minimum of the storm center itself." Witnesses reported seeing an almost continuous display of lightning around the eye, which some local meteorologists noted was among the most vivid they had ever seen.

Winds of 95 mph buffeted the area around Cape Sable, where the hurricane came ashore. At the Miami airport, winds were sustained at 80 mph, and the Hillsboro Lighthouse recorded maximum winds of 92 mph. This storm's most damaging effects were not caused by high winds, however, but resulted from very heavy rains. In Hialeah the storm dumped water quickly: 1.32 inches fell in ten minutes, 3.62 inches came in one hour, and at the U.S. Geological Survey gauge, 6 inches fell in seventy-five minutes. The rapid accumulation of water was more than the streets of South Florida could handle, and severe flooding resulted. Water was waist deep in Hialeah, Miami Springs, and Opa-Locka. In some portions of Hialeah, standing water was more than six feet deep. Mayor Henry Milander declared a state of emergency and restricted access to the city.

Flooded neighborhoods throughout the area left more than 2,000 Dade County families homeless. U.S. 1 was under water from Miami to Fort Lauderdale, as was much of the Tamiami Trail all the way to Everglades City. Miami was also submerged; most streets became flowing streams, and cars stalled when water rose over their engines. The Miami River overflowed near the Northwest Twelfth Avenue bridge, and Little River and the Seybold Canal also spilled over

Although the hurricane of October 1947 was not as powerful as its predecessor, it still caused extensive flooding over a broad portion of South Florida. (Photo courtesy of Noel Risnychok)

Floridians made the most of the numerous hurricanes they experienced during the 1940s, as evidenced by these Miami area residents after the October 1947 storm. Because of the mostly flat terrain, floodwaters are slow to recede in many parts of South Florida. (Photo courtesy of Noel Risnychok)

This residential section of Hialeah was flooded after the hurricane of October 1947. (Photo courtesy of Noel Risnychok)

their banks. Miami Beach was also affected; North Bay Road was inundated, as were many sidewalks along Collins Avenue from South Beach through Surfside. Store owners were helpless to prevent the destructive flood from saturating their goods and furnishings.

At least two tornadoes were documented during the hurricane's approach

Portions of Fort Lauderdale remained knee deep in rainwater after the October 1947 hurricane. (Photo courtesy of Noel Risnychok)

—one that ripped through portions of Coral Gables and Miami and another that struck Miami Beach. The Miami Beach twister was short-lived, but it touched down on Lenox Avenue just long enough to destroy three large construction warehouses.

In the aftermath of the storm, residents of the Miami area could travel only by small boat. Skiffs and rafts of all kinds were employed to seek help, check on friends, and tour the flooded city. The floodwaters did not quickly recede, partly because the region had recently experienced a very wet period and water levels were high before the storm. Even the great hurricane of 1926 had not left this much water behind. According to the *Miami Herald*, Red Cross rescue chief

Many residents motored through the streets of Dade County in skiffs after the October 1947 storm, including city workers in Miami Springs. (Photo courtesy of Noel Risnychok)

E. W. Deering said: "We have never had a water situation like this before." Ultimately, the flooding experienced during this storm prompted the construction of long levees to protect the region and the later development of the South Florida Water Management District. Fortunately no lives were lost in Florida.

The October hurricane of 1947 is remembered for another distinction: it was the first hurricane ever to be "seeded"—an experimental process in which chemical compounds are dispersed within a storm in an attempt to weaken it. Scientists had speculated in the laboratory that adding dry ice to clouds near the eye might reduce a hurricane's strength by forcing its clouds to "rain them-

selves out." Others had even suggested that hurricanes could be stopped by destroying their structure with an atomic blast—an idea that fortunately never got very far. Early in 1947, scientists from General Electric and teams from the U.S. Army, the Office of Naval Research, and the U.S. Weather Bureau formed Project Cirrus, which set out to test the dry ice theory on a real storm.

After soaking much of South Florida on the night of October 11, the second hurricane of 1947 skipped out to sea near Pompano Beach just after dawn the following day. Once it was safely offshore, the Project Cirrus team selected this hurricane for its experiment. By this time, it was some 350 miles off the coast of Jacksonville and headed on a northeasterly track that should have carried it far out into the open Atlantic. On the morning of October 13, a plane carrying eighty pounds of dry ice flew into the storm and dispensed the substance over a course of 100 miles. The scientists hoped that the seeding would have some measurable effect so further adjustments could be made in future hurricane experiments. But the Project Cirrus team got results it never expected. Shortly after the seeding, the hurricane abruptly stalled and then turned back toward the U.S. coast—a most unwelcome development. It moved due west with little drop in intensity and struck the Georgia coastline below Savannah. High tides flooded the barrier islands as far north as Charleston, and heavy damages were reported to fishing fleets, wharves, and warehouses. Winds at Savannah were clocked at 85 mph, with gusts to 95 mph. One Savannah resident was killed, and many people were injured. Including the property losses in Florida, the total damage estimate for the storm topped $20 million.

The Project Cirrus team was stunned. Could its seeding experiment have been responsible for the hurricane's dramatic turn? The Weather Bureau staff quickly searched through their records for similar occurrences and found a few, including one storm forty-one years earlier that had also turned toward the west and struck the coast. But many people, including Irving Langmuir, one of the scientists involved in early research on the project, remained convinced that the dry ice experiment had brought about the change of course. As a result of the disaster at Savannah, scientists were reluctant to pursue further experimentation. It wasn't until the early 1960s that the concept of hurricane seeding was once again tested.

SEPTEMBER 21–22, 1948

The two hurricanes that struck South Florida in 1947 were followed by two more the next year. The two storms in 1948 took similar paths—they both originated in the Caribbean, crossed western Cuba, swept over the Keys, and entered the southern end of the Florida Peninsula on a northeasterly track. The first was a category 3 storm that arrived in September. It was during this part of the hurricane season that South Florida always took a beating, and newspapers announced the storm's approach as "right on schedule."

It formed over Jamaica as a tropical low that rapidly blossomed into a storm, then a hurricane. On September 18, it became well organized and turned northward, passed over the Cayman Islands, and bore down on the southwestern coast of Cuba. Its forward speed was less than 8 mph as it drifted over the Cuban countryside on the night of September 20. Winds of 100 mph caused widespread but moderate damages just east of Havana. Over the next few hours, it made the short journey to Key West, where its ten-mile-wide eye passed over the Boca Chica airport. The pressure there dropped to 28.45 inches, and sustained winds of 122 mph were recorded before the airport's anemometer was blown away. Gusts were said to have reached 160 mph. Even though the wind howled, tides at Key West only reached six feet above mean low water.

Hours after its arrival in Key West, the storm struck the mainland near Everglades City. It passed inland through sparsely populated portions of Collier County, moved just below Belle Glade, and eventually emerged over the Atlantic near Jupiter on the morning of September 22. One notable feature of this storm was the distorted shape of its central core, which caused observers throughout South Florida to report numerous calms and lulls. Some meteorologists at the time suggested that the storm had several distinct centers; others theorized that the lulls were pockets of dry air between approaching rainbands. Near Lake Okeechobee, reliable witnesses reported two distinct lulls several hours apart.

In Miami winds reached 90 mph, and almost 4.5 inches of rain fell. High tides covered portions of the bayfront, and large breakers pounded the shore. The tide was 4.5 feet above mean low water. Boats and small craft were battered by waves; some broke their moorings and were bashed against their docks. Docking facilities at Coconut Grove were badly damaged, and piers and boat houses around the bay suffered from the rising tide. At Miami Beach the ocean road approach to Haulover Bridge was washed away. Palm trees littered the area around Lummus Park, and homes and businesses had shattered windows and torn awnings. A tornado was reported in Homestead on the afternoon of September 21, just before the storm moved into the state. In all, three deaths were blamed on the hurricane in Florida, and damages topped $12 million.

OCTOBER 5, 1948

The second of the two hurricanes to strike Florida in 1948 also developed deep in the Caribbean, just two weeks after the first. On October 4, it gained hurricane strength just below Cuba and tracked over Havana on the morning of the fifth. Winds there were measured at 132 mph, and heavy rains caused flash floods that swept away homes and cattle. Eleven Cubans were killed, 300 were injured, and damages were estimated at $6 million.

On the afternoon of October 5, the hurricane moved up the Keys, where winds were estimated at around 100 mph. This storm passed through more quickly than its predecessor, and by 7:00 P.M., its eye was centered over Miami. Sustained winds of 90 mph were recorded at the Weather Bureau station, and the barometer reached a low of 28.92 inches. The storm surge in Biscayne Bay matched that of the September storm—about 4.5 feet above mean low tide. Rainfall at the Miami airport exceeded 9.5 inches, and once again streets and alleyways around Miami were submerged under deep standing water. Streets in Homestead, Miami Springs, Hialeah, and portions of Miami Beach were turned into flowing streams. In Hialeah, so troubled by floods in recent years, Mayor Henry Milander reported that the depth of standing water in many streets surpassed 3.5 feet. In Miami the Southeast Second Avenue bridge, near the mouth of the Miami River, was damaged when it was rammed by a banana boat during the height of the storm. Numerous airplanes were flipped over and damaged by high winds at the Tamiami airport. And two tornadoes were reported—one at Fort Lauderdale and another near Opa-Locka, where numerous cars were overturned and considerable damages were inflicted at the Royal Palm dairy farm.

Amazingly, no deaths were directly associated with the hurricane in Florida. Damages in the state were placed at about $5.5 million—less than would have been expected. This was partly because the same region had been struck just two weeks before, and many crops had not been replaced and repairs had not been made. Still, the people of South Florida were seemingly overrun with hurricanes, and anxiety over the situation prevailed. Special prayer meetings were held in local churches to attempt to end the long spell of stormy weather. Some believed that Florida, and particularly Miami, was being punished for its rampant vices.

Once the storm left the Florida coast, it steered out to sea, but not before raking over Grand Bahama Island with gusts estimated near 110 mph. From there, it tracked toward Bermuda, which would become its last victim. On October 7, it raced over the island with winds that topped 100 mph and a forward speed that approached 30 mph. It then went on for over a week, carving a large clockwise loop in the open Atlantic before finally dissipating over cooler waters.

AUGUST 26–27, 1949

Only one hurricane struck Florida in 1949, but it was one for the record books; according to the Weather Bureau's chief forecaster Grady Norton in *Florida Hurricanes*, it was "in a category just under the great hurricanes in Florida history." It arrived at the end of August, swept inland at Delray Beach, and turned northward to blast through at least seventeen Florida counties on its way to Georgia. The Weather Bureau's forecasts and warnings were timely, and most of the state was well prepared. But as one Martin County resident put it, "There's only so much you can do to prepare for a 150-mph blow!"

The Delray Beach hurricane, as weather observers would later call it, most likely began as a tropical wave from the Cape Verde region. It was first detected in its formative stage about 125 miles northeast of St. Martin on August 23. It moved rapidly toward the northwest but did not reach hurricane strength until the twenty-fifth, when it entered the Bahama Islands. It stayed on course with a steady forward speed of almost 20 mph and threatened the Florida coast on the morning of the following day. It crossed the coastline near Delray Beach at 6:00 P.M. on August 26 and delivered vicious winds and tides to much of the coast from Miami to the Georgia line.

It was the worst hurricane to strike the Palm Beach area since the great disaster of 1928, and its general path was almost the same. As the storm carved northward through the peninsula, its wide swath spread winds of at least 50 mph over much of the state. Extreme winds of hurricane force were felt as far south as Miami Beach and as far north as St. Augustine. At the West Palm Beach airport the calm eye was observed from 7:20 to 7:42 P.M., at which time the storm's lowest pressure was observed: 28.17 inches. Prior to the arrival of the eye at the airport, northeasterly gusts of 125 mph destroyed the tower's anemometer, so the highest winds at that location were never recorded. Several higher readings were reported, including a one-minute maximum of 153 mph measured at the Jupiter Lighthouse just before that wind instrument was also carried away. Earlier, the same instrument had recorded a five-minute maximum of 132 mph. Unofficial reports included a gust of 155 mph at a residence in Palm Beach and a reading of 160 mph at a fire station in downtown Stuart. Neither of these instruments survived the storm either.

After the eye of the hurricane barreled inland, it passed directly over the northern end of Lake Okeechobee, setting the stage for another potential catastrophe. This time, though, the Okeechobee's wind-driven waters were held back from the towns along the southern shore by the protective dike built in the 1930s. The tides at Clewiston and Belle Glade reached twelve feet but did not top the levee. Minor erosion was reported in some locations, but the massive dike did its job and the only flooding in the region resulted from heavy rains. The deluge at Belle Glade measured 8.18 inches, Okeechobee City recorded 7.10 inches, and 9.51 inches fell at St. Lucie Lock near Stuart.

The storm remained powerful as it turned across the central portion of the state and curved northward above Tampa Bay. Pressure readings on the eastern side of the storm remained below 29.00 inches as far north as Levy County, above Cedar Key. Winds gusted to 75 mph in Clermont, and other communities in central Florida experienced significant wind damage. The storm's forward speed slowed as it churned through the state. It finally passed into Georgia as a strong tropical storm around 8:00 P.M. on August 27, just over twenty-four hours after it had made landfall. It continued to cause headaches through Georgia and the Carolinas, where heavy rains overfilled rivers and caused widespread flooding. At least four tornadoes touched down in central North Carolina, causing millions of dollars in damages. Another twister was spawned in the Tidewater region of Virginia. The decaying storm tracked through Maryland, Pennsylvania, New York, and New England, where damaging floods ended an extended drought.

The greatest damages left by the hurricane were, predictably, in the coastal communities near the point of landfall. At Palm Beach, Jupiter, and Stuart, high winds and high waters tested every structure. In some areas, the trunks of palm trees were snapped off just a few feet above the ground, leaving boulevards lined with sticks and stumps. Hundreds of apartments, homes, stores, and warehouses lost their roofs, their windows, and in some cases their furnishings, which were sucked out into the street by the force of the winds. In Stuart, for example, officials estimated that 40 percent of the residential and commercial buildings were severely damaged and 90 percent were in need of at least some repair. The city's black neighborhoods were especially devastated, with many homes leveled by the ferocious winds. Among the landmarks that were totally destroyed were the Macedonia Baptist Church, the Little Dixie baseball park, and the Olympia Ice Company. Frightened residents took refuge in any sturdy building they could find. Stories abounded of families and friends who were huddled together to pray when the roof over their heads lifted away, exposing them to strong blasts of drenching rain.

The storm's incredible winds carried large timbers through the air like missiles. At a car dealership near West Palm Beach, automobiles were overturned *inside* the showroom after winds smashed the building's plate glass windows. Large airplanes were toppled at the nearby airport, and in some locations, utility poles were carried upward onto second-story balconies. The roof of the Stuart City Hall was peeled away by the wind and scattered in the streets across town. According to the *Martin County News*, Bernard Hodapp and Police Chief Roy Baker, who were out patrolling during the storm, stepped out of Hodapp's car just before the City Hall's roof exploded into the streets. Two of the structure's rafters sailed through the air and pierced the car—one went straight through the engine and plunged into the pavement, and the other punctured the roof on the driver's side and came out through the passenger door. Neither of the men was injured.

High tides lifted piers and fish houses off their pilings and tossed them onto the shore. At Palm Beach the storm surge carried sand into the streets and left wreckage piled high. Heavy rains across the region added to the flooding problems, and many portions of Palm Beach and Martin Counties were under water following the storm. Days afterward, residents reported finding snakes in their homes, and the plague of mosquitoes that swarmed over the area was said to have been "the worst infestation ever witnessed."

Heavy damages were reported to citrus crops, and in many groves, up to a third of the trees were uprooted. Total agricultural losses in Florida were estimated at $20 million, which included the estimated loss of 14 million boxes of fruit. Property damages were placed at $25 million, most of which occurred within a few hours of landfall. Damages totaling another $7 million were reported in states that endured the remnants of the storm, placing the total cost of the disaster at $52 million. Even though dozens of injuries were reported, only two deaths resulted, both of which occurred in Florida. This astonishingly low figure was due, at least in part, to the early warnings provided by the Weather Bureau.

In Miami damages were limited to downed trees and power lines. As the storm made landfall, Weather Bureau chief forecaster Grady Norton issued a radio broadcast to Miami residents that was characteristic of his homespun style: "I think that Miami should be very thankful that we are not getting any worse than this. When you hear what is going on up the road a bit you will all be glad that we missed this big one. Brother, that thing has really wound up; its a real pumpernickel. There are enough hurricane effects in the area to put on a palm-shaking, wave-tossing good show, but not enough to be dangerous."

THE MODERN ERA,
1950–1999

BAKER (AUGUST 30–31, 1950)

After suffering through so many hurricanes during the 1940s, Florida received a break in the following decade when only a handful of tropical cyclones made landfall. But the lull was preceded by one last blast of activity in 1950, when a trio of hurricanes affected the state. Across the Atlantic basin, the 1950 season was remarkable not for the total number of tropical storms but for the number of storms that reached full hurricane intensity. Eleven hurricanes developed during the year, one more than during the record-breaking season of 1933. The Tropics remained unusually quiet until mid-August, when the first of the storms took shape. For the next seven weeks, a new hurricane was born every week in the Atlantic or Caribbean. Although most of the season's cyclones spun harmlessly out to sea, three left their mark on Florida and culminated one of the most active ten-year periods in Florida's hurricane history.

The Weather Bureau, in concert with forecasters at the Joint Hurricane Center and the Air Force Hurricane Office, officially began using military code names for storms during the 1950 season. The first was Hurricane Able, which formed east of Puerto Rico and passed well off the coast of Cape Hatteras in mid-August. Hurricane Baker, the season's second storm, was first spotted east of Antigua on August 21. It crossed the Lesser Antilles with considerable force and then lost strength on its westward course through the Caribbean. It reorganized just below western Cuba on August 26 and then pounded the tip of that island the following day. As it churned into the Gulf of Mexico over the next few days, it gained strength and curved northward, threatening the Louisiana coast on the morning of August 30. In the hours prior to landfall, Hurricane Baker curved more toward the northeast and finally struck the coast between Mobile and Pensacola around eleven o'clock that evening.

Winds along the Alabama coast were reported at 115 mph. The highest winds in Florida were measured at Santa Rosa Island, where gusts topped 100 mph. Heavy damages were reported at Panama City, where high tides and heavy rains inundated homes and businesses. Rainfall at that location measured 14.96 inches. Two tornadoes were spawned as the hurricane approached the coast—one destroyed a home in Jackson County, Florida, and the other ripped through a residential section of Apalachicola, demolishing four dwellings and a store. The hurricane remained vicious through inland portions of Alabama, where hundreds of trees were downed as far north as Birmingham. The damages to property and crops totaled over $2.5 million, and one person was killed.

EASY (SEPTEMBER 3–7, 1950)

In many ways, Hurricane Easy was one of the most bizarre storms to ever strike Florida. Not only did it have an odd name, but its peculiar, almost lethargic movements puzzled the forecasters who tracked it. While it seemed to almost "park" itself over Florida's upper west coast, it drenched residents with record-breaking rains. Its remarkable double-loop track caused it to strike the same region of the Florida coast twice in the same day!

Easy began as a tropical low in the western Caribbean on September 1 and remained almost motionless for two days before crossing Cuba as a minimal hurricane. The center of the storm passed just east of Havana at 6:00 A.M. on September 3. Naval reconnaissance aircraft, by now a routine component of hurricane investigation, were dispatched into the emerging storm while it was still south of Cuba. According to navy records, status reports were then issued with such regularity that "it was possible to nearly pinpoint the position of the center at any time." Throughout the hurricane's seven-day life, navy planes penetrated the storm center seven times, and additional flights obtained a total of fifty-one radar fixes. Once the storm's eye moved inland, another twenty-two radar fixes were recorded by a recently installed land radar station at the University of Florida at Gainesville. This combination of reconnaissance flights and radar imaging provided forecasters with up-to-the-minute information that had not been available in previous years.

On the morning of September 3, Hurricane Easy moved into the Gulf of Mexico, and storm warnings were issued from Key West to Pensacola. The storm swept just to the west of Key West around noon, where maximum winds of 72 mph "shredded shrubbery and toppled trees." The Associated Press labeled it the "Baby Hurricane" and described it as "acting more like a spoiled brat than a storm." Its movements northward were erratic and slow, but high waters piled onshore as it paralleled Florida's west coast. The tide in Tampa Bay rose 6.5 feet, the highest at that location since 1921. A twenty-foot section of flashboards atop the waterworks dam on the Hillsborough River was washed away, flooding the north Tampa community of Sulphur Springs with two feet of water. About forty homes were destroyed and valuable beachfront property was damaged in the St. Petersburg–Clearwater area. According to another Associated Press report, "Tides from six and a half to eight feet above normal swept the pretty resort area from Clearwater to Sarasota, washing out roads, toppling beachfront houses, sinking a few small boats, putting a tug into distress and piling sea water like lakes around homes and hotels." The tug *Cherokee* lost its rudder and was forced to cut its barge free. The tug was aided by the Coast Guard cutter *Nemesis*.

Once the storm passed Tampa on September 4, its forward motion slowed to a crawl. It finally came to a standstill about fifty miles west of Tarpon Springs, where it apparently became "wound like a spring" and intensified dramatically. Reconnaissance aircraft estimated the highest winds to be over 125 mph. It sat spinning like a top over warm Gulf waters and remained almost stationary for six hours. During this time, it actually tracked in a tight counterclockwise loop. Then it made its move, drifting toward the east-northeast at a rate of 5 mph and coming ashore some twenty miles south of Cedar Key at around daybreak on the fifth.

No sooner had the erratic storm moved inland than it again turned sharply toward the north and carved another loop, circling around Cedar Key, reentering the Gulf, and striking the coast a second time near Homosassa Springs, just below the first landfall. This drifting storm track was hardly perceivable to the people of Cedar Key, who were pounded for hours by fierce winds, dangerous tides, and incredible amounts of rain. To them, it was as if the storm had sat down and refused to leave. One report indicated that hurricane winds at Cedar Key blew steadily for more than eighteen hours. Eventually the storm's definition weakened, however, and it moved in yet another broad curve through central Florida as a drenching tropical storm. It then passed west of Jacksonville and into southern Georgia and eventually died over northern Alabama on September 8.

Radar images of the storm showed that while it was drifting in a loop offshore, its eye shrank from twenty-six miles in diameter to only twelve miles at the time of landfall. The intensification that occurred during this period was not good news to the people of Cedar Key, who endured the worst storm in the town's history. Winds howled for a full day, and the destruction was heavy. The pressure dropped to a low of 28.30 inches. An anemometer recorded winds of 125 mph before it was knocked down by a falling tree. A twenty-four-inch Weather Bureau standard rain gauge overflowed, and later squalls added at least another 1.20 inches, bringing the hurricane's total rainfall at that location to more than 25.20 inches. The drenching was spread throughout the area, with several locations reporting more than 30 inches. The deluge peaked at Yankeetown, where a new twenty-four-hour rainfall record of 38.70 inches was established on September 5!

Even though the rain seemed unending, it was the combination of high tides and battering winds that caused the most destruction at Cedar Key. Few people of the town of 900 had fled after receiving the hurricane warnings. Most of the remaining residents, about 500 people, jammed into the community's two most substantial structures—the grammar school and the high school. Crowded into the small classrooms were men, women, and children who had been forced to leave their homes in the terrifying gusts. Electricity and water were cut off, and many caught rainwater in buckets for drinking and bathing. Trees and telephone poles were downed everywhere, and wires were tangled across virtually every street. At least eight people had to abandon their cars during the storm when floodwaters drowned out their engines.

The storm's winds unroofed about three-fourths of Cedar Key's 200 buildings and left the others with various damages. Newspaper reports from the Associated Press said that "winds had ripped them apart and wrapped the pieces around trees." Among the buildings torn apart were a hardware store and the town's bank. Roads throughout the area were under eighteen inches to two feet of water. Bridges and causeways were covered with seaweed and timbers, and most were impassable. A highway patrolman reported that his car was nearly bashed by debris from a home that collapsed near Bronson, about thirty miles inland from Cedar Key.

The hurricane dealt a crippling blow to Cedar Key's economy. The town's two primary industries were wrecked—the fishing fleet and the fiber factory. The factory, where Dan Andrews had employed thirty-five people to make brooms and brushes from palm fiber, was badly damaged. Andrews had only recently reopened the plant after a two-year shutdown. The town's fishing fleet of 100 boats was also ruined, and another 50–100 pleasure craft were wrecked. Virtually all of the town's fish houses and docks were washed away, many of which had just been rebuilt after a major fire in April. The Red Cross announced it would replace lost boats and nets "where they were necessary to support a family." Rebuilding would be a challenge, especially since there were reportedly only two carpenters in the town. Governor Fuller Warren, who visited the area in the days following the storm, dispatched the chairman of the State Industrial Commission to Cedar Key to establish an office for those making unemployment claims. Most, however, soon found work in the cleanup and rebuilding effort that took place after the hurricane.

As the storm slowly turned northward through upper Florida and entered Georgia, its winds diminished to less than gale strength. Heavy rains continued to pour, and some localized crop flooding was reported. Most citrus producers were happy to see the rain, however, after having endured an extended dry spell prior to the storm. Unusually heavy rains extended in a strip from Tampa Bay all the way to southeastern South Carolina. Jacksonville recorded over 12 inches, and Savannah received 16.21 inches in about seventy-five hours. The incredible rains dumped by Hurricane Easy caused some to make unfounded accusations that the Weather Bureau had again experimented with storm "seeding."

The majority of the hurricane's damages occurred along a sixty-mile stretch of the Gulf coast from Cedar Key to St. Petersburg. The losses in Florida totaled $3.3 million, and three deaths were reported. Ned Cosgrove, an oil company official from Tampa, was electrocuted while trying to remove a fallen wire from his backyard fence; Hattie Kersey touched a live wire while trying to anchor her mobile home in Jacksonville; and a third victim was electrocuted by a fallen wire in St. Petersburg. In addition to these misfortunes, twenty-seven people were injured. According to Weather Bureau records, Hurricane Easy destroyed a total of 57 homes in Florida and damaged another 1,001. Over 2,800 families were left in need of food and shelter after the storm.

One unusual story reported in newspapers across Florida concerned automobiles that developed a mysterious case of the "measles" after the hurricane passed. Hundreds of car owners in Clearwater, Lakeland, Orlando, Jacksonville, and other cities reported that blisters filled with water had formed under the surface of the paint on their autos shortly after the hurricane had passed. The blisters, numbering in the thousands, gave the cars the appearance of having the spotted disease. When the sun returned the following day, the blisters disappeared just as mysteriously as they had formed. Researchers at the University of Florida studied the automobile "disease" and developed several theories about its cause. They concluded that air pockets under the surface of the paint had expanded because of the lowered barometric pressure, causing the paint to blister.

KING (OCTOBER 17–18, 1950)

King, the tenth hurricane of the unusually active 1950 season, was a small but powerful storm that moved lengthwise up the Florida Peninsula. Although it began deep in the Caribbean as October storms often do, it ended up striking Florida's east coast, a rare trajectory for late-season hurricanes. Its ferocious inner core was quite small, but it blasted Miami, delivering the worst blow to that city since the great hurricane of 1926.

It was first detected on October 15, some 300 miles southwest of Jamaica, in a prime breeding area for October hurricanes. Over a two-day period, twenty-five inches of rain fell on Jamaica, and crops, highways, and communications were heavily damaged. It crossed over central Cuba on the night of the sixteenth, passing just west of Camagüey with hurricane-force winds and drenching rains. On the morning of October 17, hurricane warnings were issued for southern Florida as the storm regained strength over the warm waters of the Straits of Florida. It shifted course toward the west-northwest and then zigged and zagged toward the mainland. In Miami forecasters with the Weather Bureau and the Air Force Hurricane Office struggled to keep up with the small storm. A reconnaissance flight during the early morning indicated that winds were gusting over 100 mph near the center. But other sources failed to confirm its severity. According to a U.S. Air Force report, "Due to the small size of the storm the automatic weather station in the Florida Straits and the Coast Guard stations along the Keys gave little indication of a severe storm. Before the storm center reached Miami, forecasters in all three hurricane offices were ready to admit that the storm had weakened or had been overestimated by reconnaissance. As the center reached Miami, however, it became apparent that despite its minute size, king packed a terrific punch."

Just before midnight on the seventeenth, the small hurricane crossed the Florida coast slightly below Miami Beach. The eye of the storm was only about six miles wide, and it passed directly over Miami, where witnesses reported a lull that lasted about twenty-five to thirty minutes. The Weather Bureau's downtown office was on the eastern rim of the eyewall and experienced the most severe portion of the storm. Winds of 97 mph were sustained for five minutes, and a one-minute reading of 122 mph was recorded at 12:30 A.M. Gusts during this period reached 150 mph, and the barometer recorded a minimum pressure of 28.25 inches. A lower reading of 28.20 inches was recorded on a standard microbarograph by a Weather Bureau employee at his home near the center of the path. Records showed that the pressure remained below 29.00 inches for one hour and thirty minutes. At the airport station, six miles west of the downtown office, observers experienced the western rim of the vortex, and winds were less severe. Gusts there reached 125 mph, and the minimum pressure dropped to 28.34 inches. Witnesses reported seeing lightning and hearing thunder during the storm's passage, a rather uncommon occurrence in hurricanes.

In the hours prior to its landfall, Hurricane King apparently decreased in size—or least its eye seemed to. Less than eighteen hours before the storm struck Miami, radar indicated that the eye was thirty miles in diameter, yet estimates made when it was over land placed its size at only five or six miles. The path of primary destruction was also exceptionally narrow. The Weather Bureau's chief forecaster, Grady Norton, inspected the damage area and reported that the destruction was limited to a very narrow path. In his report, he found that "the path of extensive damage was about 7 to 10 miles in width and extended from Miami and Miami Beach north-northwestward through the suburban towns of Opa-Locka, Davie, West Hollywood, and West Fort Lauderdale. So sharp was the line of demarcation marking the area of extensive damage from the minor damage that you passed from one to the other within a quarter of a mile. It was almost like a large tornado. The calm center was about six miles in diameter. In the heavy damage zone, there was extensive structural damage, much loss of glass, and hardly a roof in the area escaped being badly damaged or stripped entirely."

The tornadolike hurricane continued up the peninsula, delivering hurricane-force winds to much of the Florida east coast. It passed directly over the eastern portions of Lake Okeechobee, where hurricane-force winds were reported from all stations. High winds drove the waters of the lake toward Clewiston, where a tide of 19.3 feet was recorded. As it tracked northward, it remained about forty miles inland, passing near Orlando on its way toward southern Georgia. Winds of hurricane speed were recorded at Jupiter, Melbourne, and

Cape Canaveral. Even Jacksonville, so often spared ferocious hurricane gusts, experienced some of its highest winds of record. A one-minute maximum of 72 mph was measured, and gusts were estimated at 82 mph. Heavy rains also accompanied the storm; many locations along Florida's eastern shore received over 10 inches. Jacksonville recorded a storm total of 11.73 inches.

Although the storm brought damages to much of the Florida Peninsula, the Greater Miami area suffered the most losses. Miami residents were well warned, however, as the Weather Bureau had issued thirty-three advisories and bulletins, starting more than twenty-four hours before the storm's landfall. Norton maintained a soothing presence on the radio as the storm struck, reducing the panic and anxiety experienced in previous storms. Few deaths occurred, but property damages were high. The storm's gusting winds were responsible for most of the destruction. Snapped palm trees and toppled telephone poles blocked many city streets. Coconuts and palm fronds littered nearly every yard and roadway. Newspaper accounts reported that Flagler Street was "paved with broken glass." High winds downed eleven local radio towers, overturned a half dozen airplanes at the Miami airport, and unroofed hundreds of homes and apartments. Dozens of empty freight cars were tossed on their sides at the Seaboard Railroad yard. Winds and waves bashed the Quarterdeck Club on Biscayne Bay until it was nearly destroyed.

In Miami Beach many streets were buried deep in sand, especially along Ocean Drive and Lummus Park. Flooding was more than two feet deep in some locations. The lobbies and oceanfront rooms of dozens of hotels were filled with deep sand. At the Macfadden-Deauville Hotel, water was more than six inches deep in the lobby. Storefront windows were smashed, and parked cars were blown over. There were scattered reports of looting along Lincoln Road, but no arrests were made. South Beach was hit hard as well, as dozens of shops and businesses were demolished. Telephones and electricity were out over much of Dade County, and it took several days for services to be restored.

Three people died in Florida during the storm, including a West Hollywood woman whose mobile home collapsed, seriously injuring her husband and four children. One man was found dead in the wreckage of his home in West Hallandale, and another reportedly drowned when he jumped from a small boat near Bunnell. Although the death toll was small, almost 200 injuries were reported throughout South Florida. At least 25 people were hospitalized in West Hollywood, where 125 homes were severely damaged and 25 were completely destroyed.

Fifty-five buildings were damaged and one airplane destroyed at the Broward County airport. Gusting winds ripped the doors off one hangar and wrecked the plane inside. In some cases, buildings were completely blown away, leaving only their foundations behind. After the storm in Miami, a roofing company executive died when he fell from the roof of a hangar at the Twentieth Street airport. Another death occurred in Miami after the storm when a power company lineman was electrocuted while working on a damaged utility pole. Moments later, a fireman was seriously injured when he fell from a ladder truck while attempting to rescue the lineman.

The hurricane's lashing tides eroded seawalls and battered oceanfront properties all along Florida's eastern shore. Navy personnel and civilians from all walks of life worked through the night to sandbag oceanfront properties north of Miami. Angry tides ripped away city docks and fish houses at Indian River and Titusville, and seawalls at Cocoa Beach collapsed. Causeways and bridges were washed out in at least four counties, and small craft were scattered and sunk. Daytona Beach and Deland in Volusia County were among the cities reporting their worst damage in many years. A large hangar at the Orlando airport was demolished by the wind. Losses were high to citrus crops throughout the region, including more than 30 percent of the grapefruit from Indian River. Almost 15,000 acres of early fall vegetables were destroyed, with a value of more than $2 million.

The totals for the storm were staggering—$28 million in damages in Florida and Georgia, 6 dead, 128 homes completely destroyed, and another 13,464 residences damaged. Damages in Miami alone totaled $15 million. Almost 29,000 families were impacted in some way by Hurricane King's destruction, either by damaged property or by lost livelihoods. In the storm's aftermath, there was much discussion about the quality of home construction in the Miami area, and building codes were scrutinized. In fact, the storm touched off a Veteran's Administration housing scandal because the roofs of countless homes constructed for GIs were blown away due to inferior construction. As a result, building practices improved, stiffer building requirements for government-mortgaged properties were implemented, and the Miami building code was toughened.

FLORENCE (SEPTEMBER 26, 1953)

Whereas the Carolinas were pounded by hurricanes during the mid-1950s, Florida suffered few direct hits. Only two hurricanes struck the Sunshine State after King in 1950 and before Donna in 1960. Florence in 1953 and Flossy in 1956 were both category 1 storms, and neither had the impact of the hurricanes of the previous years. This respite from severe tropical weather was surely welcomed by Florida residents and hurricane forecasters.

The first year that the Weather Bureau widely publicized its system for naming hurricanes was 1953, even though the practice had been in use for the past few years. It was determined that women's names would be used instead of the old military codes. Hurricane Florence, which made landfall between Valparaiso and Panama City, was actually the eighth storm of the season and the third hurricane to affect the United States during the year.

Florence first developed in the Caribbean, south of Jamaica, on September 23. Its course took it westward through the Yucatán Channel and into the Gulf of Mexico the following night. On September 25, it reached its greatest force while in the central Gulf, where reconnaissance aircraft reported winds of up to 138 mph. Over the next few hours, its course edged toward the north and then northeast, bringing it ever closer to the northwest Florida shore. The next morning, just before making landfall, Hurricane Florence shifted abruptly toward the east-northeast and missed Pensacola, turning instead toward a more sparsely populated stretch of coast near Seagrove Beach.

Sustained winds of 87 mph were recorded at Panama City, where the barometer measured 29.35 inches. The lowest observed pressure was 29.26 inches at De Funiak Springs. Niceville received the storm's heaviest rains, which totaled 11.85 inches. Tides were five feet above normal at Apalachicola and Carrabelle and "six or seven feet" at Panacea. Pensacola only received wind gusts of 75 mph and a tide of three feet.

The hurricane's gusting winds tore down utility poles and trees and unroofed several houses. Flooding near Carrabelle destroyed numerous homes, and fishing boats and docks were damaged. According to the Red Cross's review of the storm's damages, Franklin and Okaloosa Counties were the hardest hit areas. It was estimated that in those two counties alone, 273 homes were destroyed, and another 145 buildings were damaged. Damage estimates in extreme northwestern Florida topped $200,000, and crop losses in southeastern Alabama were over $3 million. Lost at sea was the fishing trawler *Miss Tampa*, which was last heard from on the twenty-fifth. At least two deaths resulted from the storm.

Four other tropical storms passed over Florida during the 1953 season, including Hazel, which came inland just above Fort Myers on October 9. Although Hazel's winds were below hurricane force, heavy rains caused widespread flooding that resulted in crop losses in Florida of $10 million. This storm should not be confused with Hurricane Hazel, which caused great destruction in Haiti, the Carolinas, and the Northeast during the 1954 season.

FLOSSY (SEPTEMBER 24, 1956)

Hurricane Flossy is thought to have originated as a depression over the Yucatán Peninsula but may have actually developed from squalls that were first spotted in the Pacific Ocean, south of Guatemala. On September 21, the depression first showed signs of circulation and moved out into the warm waters of the Gulf of Mexico as a tropical storm. It slowly tracked northward toward the Louisiana coast, steadily gaining intensity and rapidly growing in size.

Once the storm was 125 miles off the Louisiana coast, it reached hurricane strength and turned sharply toward the east-northeast. At six o'clock on the morning of September 24, it made landfall on the Mississippi Delta just north of Burrwood, Louisiana. At this time, the storm was reaching its peak, with winds of 84 mph, gusts estimated at 110 mph, and a pressure of 29.03 inches. An oil rig off the Louisiana coast recorded gusts up to 95 mph. Heavy rains (totaling 16.70 inches at Golden Meadow) combined with wind-driven waters to cause severe flooding in Louisiana, especially around the levees near New Orleans.

By noon Flossy's eye was brushing the Alabama coast at Gulf Shores, where 16.30 inches of rain fell. The storm tracked just south of Pensacola and made landfall for the second time at Fort Walton Beach. Winds were near hurricane force along much of the coastal area as far east as Panama City. Observers at the Pensacola Naval Station recorded sustained winds of 64 mph, gusts to 88 mph, and a barometric low of 28.93 inches.

After passing inland, Flossy quickly became extratropical but maintained significant energy through Georgia and the coastal sections of the Carolinas. Heavy rains poured all along its course, from more than sixteen inches on the Alabama coast to about three inches in Virginia. Some streets in Norfolk were flooded with up to 2.5 feet of water. The storm finally exited the coast of Virginia on the afternoon of September 27.

At least three tornadoes touched down in northwestern Florida, including one that arrived in advance of the storm and destroyed numerous buildings near Wewahitchka in Gulf County. Other twisters occurred in Jefferson and Suwannee Counties, although no damages were reported. Flossy's highest tides in Florida ranged from five to six feet and caused minor damages to piers and small craft. Beachfront erosion was severe, and several homes were destroyed.

Damage estimates for Louisiana, Alabama, and Florida totaled $24.8 million, of which over $15 million were in agricultural losses. Damages in Georgia, the Carolinas, and Virginia were minor and were outweighed by the beneficial effects of the rains, which brought relief to drought-stricken farmlands. Fifteen deaths were directly or indirectly blamed on the hurricane, including four drownings in Louisiana, four deaths in Alabama, and several deaths that resulted from accidents involving automobiles and airplanes.

DONNA (SEPTEMBER 9–11, 1960)

Donna was a husky lass,
A lusty dame was she,
She kicked her heels and swirled her skirts,
And shrieked in fiendish glee.

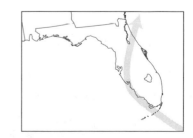

She ripped at all our buildings,
Uprooted trees galore.
She took the Gulf of Mexico,
And flung it on the shore.
She blew her breath from North and East,
And then gave us the eye.
And when she found we still were here,
She made another try.
From South and West she did her best,
A thorough job to make.
She passed with great reluctance,
Leaving havoc in her wake.
—"Donna," by W. R. "Plumb Bob" Wilson;
    courtesy of the Collier County Museum

On August 29, 1960, a large squall of heavy rains and high winds wrapped around Dakar, Senegal, on the westernmost tip of the African continent. This was more than the usual summer thunderstorm; it was blamed for the crash of an airliner and the deaths of its sixty-three passengers. The following day, heavy rains were reported near the Cape Verde Islands. No further reports of the disturbance were received until September 2, when the origins of what would become Hurricane Donna were identified. Donna then went on to travel thousands of miles and claim hundreds of lives, blasting Puerto Rico, the Bahamas, Florida, and the U.S. east coast as one of the greatest storms in history.

Donna strengthened as it crossed the Atlantic and arrived in the northern Leeward Islands on the night of September 4. Packing sustained winds of 125 mph, its eye passed directly over Barbuda, St. Barthélemy, St. Martin, Anguilla, and just south of Anegada. Damages were heavy throughout this section of the Leewards. A large percentage of homes on St. Martin, Barbuda, and Anguilla were destroyed or severely damaged. Many interisland schooners were wrecked, and at least seven fatalities were reported.

The next day, the center of Donna passed just to the north of St. Thomas and then about eighty-five miles north of San Juan, Puerto Rico. Because these locations were on the southern side of the storm as it tracked westward, winds and tides were not significant. Instead, a massive rainfall event triggered chaos in portions of the Virgin Islands and the eastern half of Puerto Rico. Up to twelve inches fell within three to four hours, and some stations at higher elevations recorded over fifteen inches. This incredible deluge turned small streams into raging rivers. Some rivers rose as much as twelve to fifteen feet in one hour and crested at up to twenty-nine feet. According to Weather Bureau reports, "At Humacao, where residents had returned to their homes in the river bed or on the flood plain despite issued flood warnings, 90 persons were drowned or unaccounted for. A landslide buried 8 persons near Patillas. Total fatalities were 108, and damage to property and crops nearly $8 million."

As the storm approached the southeastern Bahamas, it slowed in forward speed, turned somewhat more to the west, and intensified dramatically. The Turks Islands escaped the hurricane's full force, although twenty inches of rain fell there within twenty-four hours. The eye passed over Mayaguana, where hurricane winds were observed for thirteen hours. After winds blew away the anemometer at Fortune Island, observers there estimated the maximum winds at nearly 170 mph. Miraculously, no lives were lost in the Bahamas.

After buffeting the northern coast of Cuba with strong winds and high surf, the storm labeled by the press as the "Killer Hurricane" turned toward the northwest and headed for the Florida Keys. On September 7, the same newspapers that had carried stories of the devastation Donna left in the Caribbean ran headlines that all of South Florida was on alert. At 11:00 A.M. the following day, the dreaded warning flags—red with black squares—were hoisted throughout the Keys. Weather Bureau bulletins placed the hurricane in frightening perspective by stating that it packed the same energy as a hydrogen bomb exploding every eight minutes. Many Keys residents, reminded of the awesome Labor Day storm of a generation before, packed their bags and left for Homestead and Miami. The population of the upper Keys was only 3,126 in 1960 (compared with over 26,000 in 2000), and about half of the residents from Marathon to Tavernier chose to not take any chances and fled the approaching hurricane.

Gale-force winds were first felt in the early evening of September 9, and conditions worsened toward midnight. Winds picked up dramatically early on the tenth, just before the storm's twenty-one-mile-wide eye swept over the middle Keys at about 2:30 A.M. Winds howled at over 150 mph, and a storm tide of thirteen feet pounded the narrow string of islands. Keys residents were under siege by the worst storm to strike the region since 1935. Donna's forward speed slowed as it raked the Keys, which would amplify its effects over its next target—the southwestern corner of mainland Florida.

The mighty storm began to recurve toward the northwest over Florida Bay and paralleled the coastline while passing over Cape Romano, Naples, and Fort Myers. Its turn to the north sharpened and its forward speed increased as it passed through central Florida on the afternoon of September 10. It maintained vigor on its course across the state, with winds over 100 mph reported from numerous inland locations. It continued on a northeasterly track until it returned to the Atlantic just north of Ormond Beach at about 4:00 A.M. on September 11. Even as it returned to sea, wind gusts of 99 mph were measured at the Federal Aviation Administration tower at Daytona Beach.

Like many other great hurricanes in Florida's history, Donna's visit to the

United States wasn't over when it pulled away from the Sunshine State. Rapid reintensification and forward acceleration occurred once it reached the warm Gulf Stream waters off the Georgia and South Carolina coasts. By the time the storm reached the beaches of North Carolina on the evening of the eleventh, it was racing toward the northeast at over 30 mph, and maximum sustained winds were up to 115 mph. During the afternoon, several small tornadoes touched down in coastal South Carolina, causing much damage and several injuries. Even though the hurricane regained intensity before it struck the North Carolina coast, its eye had expanded to become a broad, diffuse area of calm, ranging from fifty to eighty miles in diameter. It made landfall around 10:00 P.M., inflicting extensive damages from Topsail Beach to the Virginia line. Donna was particularly destructive from Morehead City to the Outer Banks, where it was considered worse than any of the severe storms of the past decade.

After passing into the Atlantic off the Virginia capes, Donna paralleled the mid-Atlantic states and sped toward New England. The western edge of its eye brushed the coast from Virginia to New York, with many coastal areas reporting periods of intermittent calm. At Ocean City, Maryland, where winds of 83 mph were recorded before the anemometer was disabled, it was described as the worst storm in the city's history. The eye apparently was further enlarged to almost 100 miles in width as it approached the New York coast. High winds and record tides pushed onto the waterfront at Atlantic City, New Jersey, and the Battery in New York City. Finally, the indomitable hurricane made landfall again on Long Island at about 2:00 P.M. on September 12. Several stations on Long Island reported sustained winds over 100 mph, and gusts of

125–30 mph were recorded at the eastern end of the island. It then passed into eastern Connecticut, through southeastern New Hampshire, and diagonally across Maine. As it tracked over New England, cooler air was entrained in the storm's circulation, and it began to weaken. By the time it raced into Newfoundland and over the Davis Strait, the once mighty storm was reduced to a broad frontal low.

The ferocity of the hurricane was evident by the pounding it delivered to the middle and upper Keys. A lull was observed from Marathon to Lower Matecumbe and was preceded by some of the fiercest winds ever witnessed in Florida. Measured wind gusts near the center were 135–50 mph, and reliable estimates from some locations put sustained winds at 140 mph, with momentary gusts to 180 mph. At Tavernier, where the anemometer would not register above 120 mph, observers noted that the "needle was solid against the pin for 45 minutes." A gust of 150 mph was recorded at Sombrero Lighthouse, and a gust of 155 mph was measured on Lignum Vitae Key, where the lull lasted only twenty minutes.

At Conch Key a barometric-pressure reading of 27.55 inches was recorded, and at Craig three private barometers recorded a range between 27.40 and 27.50 inches. According to NOAA's *Deadliest, Costliest, and Most Intense United States Hurricanes of This Century* by Paul J. Hebert, Jerry D. Jarrell, and Max

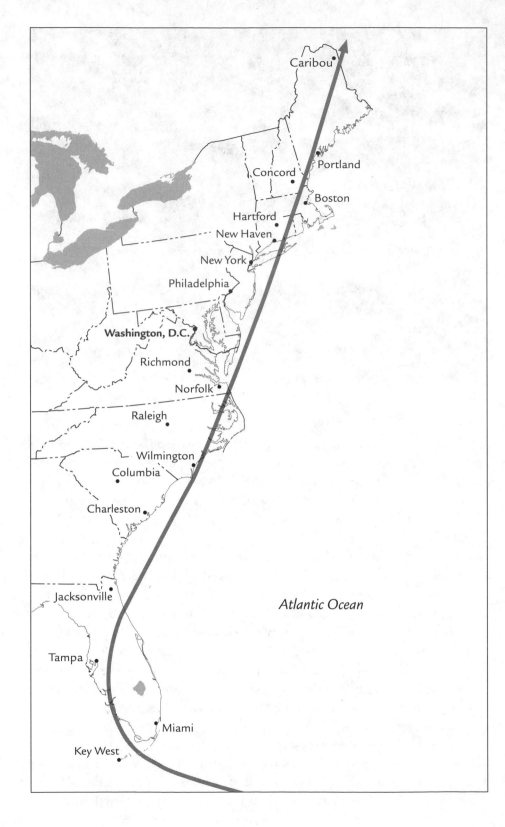

Donna's destructive course brought hurricane effects to Florida, North Carolina, New York, and New England.

Caribou

Portland

Concord

Boston

Hartford

New Haven

New York

Philadelphia

Washington, D.C.

Richmond

Norfolk

Raleigh

Wilmington

Columbia

Charleston

Atlantic Ocean

Jacksonville

Tampa

Miami

Key West

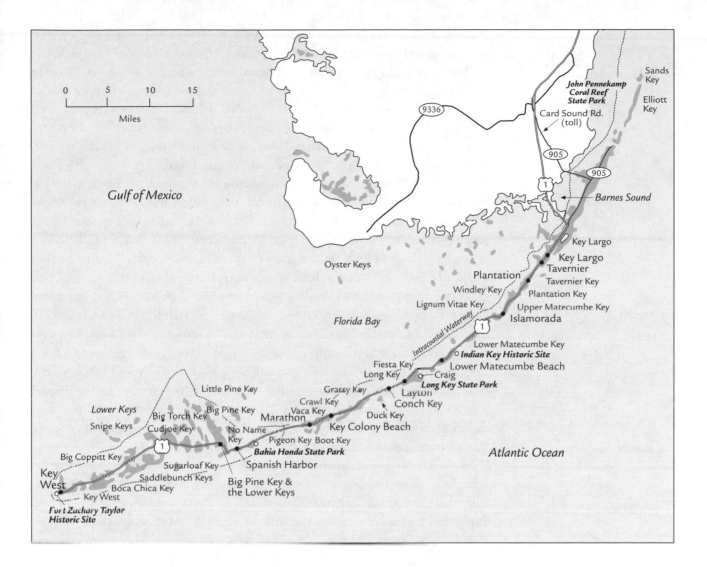

The Florida Keys.

Mayfield, Hurricane Donna's lowest official pressure was 27.46 inches, making it the sixth most intense hurricane to strike the United States in the twentieth century. Not only was Donna's intensity extreme at the point of its landfall in the Keys, but it went on to shatter barometric-pressure records across Florida and throughout its journey northward.

Not surprisingly, the middle and upper Keys were pounded by large waves and a massive storm surge as Donna passed. The highest tides in the Keys occurred just north of the center of the storm. Tides in Marathon were 8–9.5 feet, and tides at Upper Matecumbe Key were 9–13.5 feet. At Tavernier the water reportedly rose to within 18 inches of the record mark established in the 1935 Labor Day storm. Beyond the center of the storm, tides were about 6 feet at Long Key and 6 feet at Key Largo. According to a Weather Bureau summary of the storm, "Destruction was almost complete from wind and water over an area 40 miles to the northeast and 20 miles to the southwest of the track."

Heavy rains fell throughout the region, with most stations on the Florida Peninsula receiving 3–8 inches. The largest recorded accumulation was at Homestead Air Force Base, where 12.17 inches fell; 12.10 inches were measured at Marathon. Greater amounts may have fallen in other areas near the center of the storm, but unfortunately many weather instruments, including rain gauges, were destroyed by high winds and raging tides.

The destruction throughout the middle Keys was awesome. The high storm tide battered virtually every structure for forty miles, and the Overseas Highway was washed out in several places. The Tea Table Bridge between Upper and Lower Matecumbe was exposed to the worst of the surge, and boiling seas washed away a 1,000-foot section of the concrete span. The pipeline that supplied fresh water to the Keys was broken in six places, and as would be expected, telephone and electrical services were also destroyed. Automobiles, yachts, furnishings, and appliances were scattered with the tides and tumbled and tossed into mangrove thickets and streets. A report in the *Florida Keys Keynoter* described the scene at Islamorada: "Nearly every home, resort and business building fronting the ocean was either gutted or destroyed. Many of the older wooden buildings, some dating back to the '35 hurricane, were floated two and three blocks away. Some ended up on the Overseas Highway, and others traveled even farther toward the Gulf. Even well constructed concrete block houses could not withstand the force."

Homes, resorts, and businesses of every kind suffered almost complete destruction. The Chesapeake Seafood House, which had only recently opened, was blasted by wind and tides. Thousands of dollars worth of antiques and furnishings were carried into the Gulf as waves rolled through the structure. Poucher's Supermarket was gutted by the storm after a large palm tree was hurled through a rear wall. Heavy rains and rising tides damaged most of its goods, but its total destruction did not occur until two days after Donna. Health officers ordered it burned to the ground because of the risk of disease from its scattered stocks of contaminated food.

At Marathon the destruction was described as "appalling." Winds of unimaginable force snapped large creosoted utility poles in half—poles that had recently been installed and were supposed to withstand winds of 150 mph. Homes, office buildings, and stores were unroofed and ripped apart. House trailers appeared to have exploded, and one mobile home park was left devastated, with not one home left standing. Bayles's Boatyard, where scores of boats had been moored to escape the storm, was totally wrecked. The *Keynoter* described it as "a scene of destruction almost beyond belief. Sleek cabin cruisers, luxury yachts, and smart charter boats were jumbled together in a mass of splintered hulls, shorn super-structures, smashed cabins and twisted shafts

and propellers." The landmark Davis Docks Lighthouse survived the storm, but a 70-foot yacht and two charter boats foundered and sank in a nearby basin.

Amazingly, and in stark contrast to the disastrous Labor Day hurricane of 1935, only four lives were lost in the Keys during Donna. The bodies of two men were found in waters off Key Largo, and a third victim was a woman who was a resident of "the rock" at Marathon. The fourth, who was lost and presumed dead, was the wife of Islamorada realtor Buck Grundy. After Grundy was taken to Monroe General Hospital in Key West with injuries suffered in the storm, he told the *Keynoter* that his wife had been swept away in the darkness as they tried to reach higher ground during the peak of the storm. The Grundys, along with some friends, had formed a "human chain" and tried to wade through the tide, but the swirling waters carried her away.

Most of those who chose to ride out the storm on the upper Keys gathered in the few buildings known to be substantial enough to withstand the blow. About 80 were sheltered in the Key Largo firehouse, and at Tavernier another 300 or so took refuge in the Florida Keys Clinic and the Florida Keys Electric Cooperative warehouse. Dozens more gathered at the old county building and the Methodist church in Islamorada. Others remained in their homes, in motels, or in businesses they considered safe. Several journalists, including two reporters from the *Miami Herald*, rode out the hurricane in the *Florida Keys Keynoter* office in downtown Marathon. They huddled together as Donna's gusts shattered six of the building's ten large plate glass windows, which had been

carefully boarded up. Driving rain blew through the office for hours, ruining furnishings and expensive equipment and turning stocks of paper into soggy waste. Just after dawn, the reporters coaxed two cars to start and drove off to survey the damage. One headed west on U.S. 1, and the other headed east.

Even though clouds still hung low over portions of the Keys through the early morning, bewildered residents slowly emerged from their homes and shelters. They encountered mounds of debris in every street and houses that had been swept to new locations. Most of those in the shelters were shocked at the amount of destruction that surrounded them. Upon returning to their neighborhoods, many became lost because familiar surroundings like trees, signs, and buildings had been blown down or washed away. Many lost all of their possessions. Physicians in Miami would later refer to the shock experienced in the storm's aftermath as "hurricanitis." The *Keynoter* later commented on the loss: "An old man sat crying on a smashed fence. A pelican with a broken leg whimpered in the littered streets. This was the thing that always happens to the other fellow—only the tables were turned. . . . For in a matter of minutes the banker, the shrimper, the waiter, the lawyer and the clergy were of the same circumstances. Two hours had completely destroyed the system of various social levels."

In the afternoon, navy crews from Key West moved into the stricken area and set up a relief canteen at the Marathon firehouse. The Red Cross served hot meals at the American Legion building, and at one time, the two stations were serving 5,000 meals a day. Other navy units moved on to the washed-out Tea Table Bridge and began the monumental task of building an emergency bridge and repairing the water pipeline. Marines were also brought in to patrol the streets and guard against pilfering. Over the next few days, more assistance arrived, and evacuees returned to their homes. Residents hauled saltwater into their homes to flush toilets. An 8:30 P.M. curfew was established, and sales of hard liquor were banned; beer could still be purchased from noon until 6:00 P.M. Governor LeRoy Collins visited the area, and the Keys were officially designated a disaster area by President Dwight Eisenhower. Soon roofers, carpenters, masons, and insurance adjusters filled what few motel rooms were left in the mighty storm's wake.

Within hours after crossing the Keys, Donna blasted the coastal fringes of the Everglades with punishing winds and tides. At the Flamingo observation station, a pressure reading of 27.90 was recorded, and all wind instruments were blown away. Park officials reported that during the peak of the storm, the station was submerged under more than twelve feet of water. Winds approaching 150 mph battered Everglades National Park, destroying about 50 percent of the "largest stand of big mangrove trees in the world." In some areas, investigators later found massive losses of mangrove and mahogany trees. Almost all of the large mangroves that survived the 1935 storm were killed by Donna. Wildlife suffered as well. The park's endangered population of great white herons, found in the United States only in extreme southern Florida, was battered by deadly winds. It was later estimated that 35–40 percent of the majestic birds were killed, leaving only about 600. The park also had contained one of the nation's largest concentrations of nesting American bald eagles, and virtually all of the eagle nests were destroyed. Four months after the storm, some twelve had been rebuilt.

As Donna rolled up the coast and into Collier County, Everglades City was the next populated area to experience the blow. The center passed nearby around 9:30 A.M. on September 10, during which time winds diminished, although no true calm was reported. The barometer read 28.13 as the eye approached, and the tide was reported to have been about one foot below normal. All wind instruments were blown away, but official estimates placed the top winds at 150 mph, with one easterly gust at 175 mph. In all, winds of gale force or greater lasted thirteen hours.

It wasn't until after the eye passed Everglades City that the tide rebounded and swept into town. Many residents had wisely evacuated to higher ground inland. Those who remained were forced to flee their homes and retreat to the only two buildings high enough to escape the flood—the Collier Company offices and the Collier County courthouse. About 200 people crowded into the upper floor of the courthouse and watched as gushing rains added to the rising flood of seawater below. At the peak of the flood at 2:30 P.M., water

In the wake of Donna, Florida residents were forced to dig themselves out just as they had so many times before. (Photo courtesy of Noel Risnychok)

was seven to eight feet deep in the streets and waist deep on the first floor of the courthouse. Many of the county's files and records were destroyed, even though they had been placed high above the floor. The high waters lingered, many homes remaining under seven feet of water for up to ten hours. According to reports in the *Naples Daily News*, the storm tide crested four miles inland beyond the Tamiami Trail.

After the storm finally passed and the waters began to recede, Everglades City was left a damp and muddy mess. According to a report from the Florida state climatologist in *Weatherwise*, half of the town's buildings were destroyed by high winds and the subsequent flood. Piles of lumber and debris filled every street, and some homes were knee deep in seaweed, fish, and filth. Older structures were twisted off their foundations by the winds and carried for blocks. Many of those still standing were later torn down because they were condemned as structurally unsafe.

The Everglades City supermarket was completely wrecked, its shelves of canned and packaged foods mixed with piles of soggy rubble. The store's large walk-in freezer was knocked over onto its heavy doors, and its contents—tons of meat, poultry, and seafood—could not be removed. The *Naples Daily News* reported that "the electric power was off so the perishable meats and fish rotted into a stinking, explosive mass of garbage. . . . A powerful bulldozer dredged the corruption out of the supermarket and broke open the freezer before it could explode from the pressure of noxious rot."

The ordeal was almost more than Everglades City could withstand. Over the following years, the Collier Company moved its headquarters to Naples, the Bank of Everglades relocated to Immokalee, and the Collier County seat was moved, under some citizens' protest, to East Naples. But many residents rebuilt their homes and renewed the charm of the "little city in the heart of the Everglades National Park."

Donna's next victims were Goodland and Marco Island. Eight feet of water filled several village streets, leaving behind a scene similar to that in Everglades City. Several people endured the storm in a house atop Indian Hill, some fifty-eight feet above sea level—the only structure that remained above the flood. As the eye approached the area, it pulled waters toward it from the Gordon River and Naples Bay, which went dry. The waters rebounded once the storm passed and roared into the streets of Naples in a tidal surge that crested at 10.2 feet above mean low water. The tide swept into the center of the city and damaged buildings and docks along a ten-block strip. It left three to four feet of water in most streets and carried with it trees, lumber, appliances, cars, houses, and boats. The famous Naples Fishing Pier, which had withstood many hurricanes since it was built in 1888, was reduced to a ragged row of twisted pilings. The Naples weather station was abandoned after gusts reached 100 mph, and a barometer reading of 27.97 inches was recorded. Observers also noted that the eye lasted about an hour.

Dan Paquette of East Naples had firsthand experience with the storm surge that rolled into town. According to a report in the *Collier County News*, Paquette was with his family at their shop when he saw the cresting wave plow down the street toward him: "To him it appeared like a great wall of sand pushing and gurgling its way up the narrow spaces of Jackson Avenue." He quickly gathered his family and fled to higher ground a block away. At first the water was only knee deep, but within moments it had reached Paquette's chest. The *News* account described what they encountered next: "When the family arrived on the high ground of the Trail, they found a collection of wildlife who were also seeking refuge from Donna's big torrent. There were snakes, pigs, rabbits and rats sitting on boards or swimming feverishly across the swiftly moving current. Paquette said the rats were constantly seeking higher ground and when he and his family waded by, they jumped at them to get away from the water. Dan and his family made it to the Old Barn on the Trail where they waited out the storm."

Alligators, snakes, and rats were a menace in the weeks after the storm. Numerous snakebites were reported, mostly from the reptiles that had taken up residence in homes and furnishings. One truck driver had operated his vehicle for three days before discovering a rattlesnake coiled under the seat. The proliferation of rats was a health concern and prompted the state to implement a rodent control program. Five thousand pieces of poisoned meat were distributed over South Florida by boat and helicopter in an effort to exterminate the vermin. Leaflets were dropped from airplanes over Goodland and Marco advising residents to boil all drinking water, get immunizations, and keep children from playing in contaminated streams and lakes. Amazingly, no lives were lost in Collier County, and not a single case of a communicable disease was reported in the entire state following Donna's visit.

On Tuesday night after the storm, a Naples radio station went back on the air and announced that a shipment of typhoid serum was to be flown in to prevent the outbreak of an epidemic. Since the airport still had no electrical power, the town curfew would be lifted so that twelve volunteers could use their car headlights to illuminate the runway. Twenty minutes later, the radio appeal was halted when over 300 cars showed up, jamming the muddy road to the airport. Within a few days, power was restored to most of Collier County.

Lee County also caught the brunt of the storm. Three deaths were reported in the vicinity of Bonita Springs. At Fort Myers the eye passed around 2:30 P.M. on September 10. Winds gusted to over 120 mph, and tides ran up to seven feet above normal. Farther up the coast, the tides diminished, and the wind extremes lessened. Donna made its turn in the vicinity of Fort Myers and began its course inland through the heart of the citrus belt. A large portion of the central peninsula was hit by the stronger right side of the hurricane. High winds were recorded throughout the storm's march across the state. Gusts were clocked at 120 mph at Parrish, in Manatee County; 140 mph at Wauchula, in Hardee County; and 150 mph at Fort Meade, in Polk County. New record lows for atmospheric pressure were set at Fort Myers on the Gulf coast (28.08 inches) and at Daytona Beach on the Atlantic coast (28.73 inches).

All along Donna's course, windows were shattered, houses unroofed, and utility poles prostrated. Strong winds uprooted or splintered trees in unprotected locations and stripped other trees of their leaves and fruit. The U.S. Department of Agriculture estimated that Florida lost 25 to 35 percent of its grapefruit crop and 5–10 percent of its oranges and tangerines. All of the fruit was immature, and none could be salvaged. Avocado trees and truck crops were also badly damaged. Crops were flooded by the heavy rains that followed the storm. Several inches of rain fell across the counties in its path, but the six to ten inches that had fallen in the previous weeks had saturated the ground, setting the stage for Donna's inland flooding.

After Donna exited Florida, its rampage continued in the Carolinas, the mid-Atlantic states, and New England, where records continued to be set for low pressures and high tides. According to NOAA's *Deadliest, Costliest, and Most Intense United States Hurricanes of This Century* by Hebert, Jarrell, and Mayfield, Donna's total death toll in the United States was 50, although a Weather Bureau summary, counting both direct and indirect fatalities, placed the total slightly higher. The geographical distribution of the deaths is a testament to

the remarkable endurance of the storm. In addition to 13 deaths in Florida, there were 11 in North Carolina, 3 in Virginia, 2 in Maryland, 1 in Pennsylvania, 9 in New Jersey, 3 in New York, 9 in Massachusetts, 1 in New Hampshire, and 1 in Vermont. Including the deaths in the Caribbean, Donna killed more that 320 people.

In Florida 122 people were hospitalized with injuries. A Florida Civil Defense Agency survey after the storm concluded that 1,844 homes were destroyed, 3,253 suffered major damage, and 31,000 received minor damage. Over 700 farm buildings were demolished, and 1,450 were severely damaged. Agricultural losses in the state topped $50 million, and the total damage estimate for Florida reached $300 million.

Hurricane Donna was widely regarded as the most destructive hurricane in Florida's history. Its south-to-north journey through the eastern United States was unprecedented, and a new generation of coastal residents witnessed the power of a great storm. A 1961 summary published in the *Monthly Weather Review* defined Donna's place in history: "Donna was unique in that it gave hurricane force winds to Florida, the Middle Atlantic States, and New England. However, although it was one of the most destructive hurricanes of all time, loss of life was remarkably low. This can be attributed to three factors—timely and accurate warnings, effective dissemination by news media and other agencies, and the taking of proper precautions by the public. The accuracy of the

warnings is in large part a reflection of the continuous tracking by aircraft reconnaissance and land-based radar, which was probably the most complete of any hurricane in history."

CLEO (AUGUST 27–29, 1964)

With the exception of the infamous Hurricane Donna in 1960, most of Florida experienced a lull in tropical cyclone activity from 1950 through the 1963 season. But in 1964, the lull turned into a roar as three hurricanes and the remnants of a fourth spun across the state within eight weeks. Hurricanes Cleo, Dora, and Isbell were not as vicious as Donna when they tracked over the peninsula, but the accumulated damages they left behind totaled almost $350 million, making the 1964 hurricane season the most expensive in Florida's history up to that time. Prior to this trio of storms, the last time three hurricanes struck the state in a single year was almost seventy years earlier, back in 1896 when Florida was sparsely developed. In addition, the extratropical remains of Hurricane Hilda affected the Panhandle in early October.

Hurricane Cleo was the first of the three 1964 storms and the first hurricane to strike Dade County in fourteen years. Its origins were spied by a new tool put into use by forecasters during the early 1960s: the *Tiros VIII* satellite. For the first time, photographs of cloud formations taken from space augmented aircraft reconnaissance of developing storms. These satellite pictures, images we now take for granted as part of our daily weather forecasts, were an exciting new resource for those responsible for forecasting tropical cyclones in the early 1960s.

The first pictures of the disturbance that would later become Cleo were taken several hundred miles southwest of the Cape Verde Islands on August 18. Navy planes encountered the growing storm on the twentieth, and by the afternoon of August 22, it was crossing the island of Guadeloupe. Wind gusts were only measured to about 80 mph, but over 1,000 homes were destroyed, 40 people were injured, and 14 were killed.

By the time the small but powerful storm was south of Puerto Rico on August 23, it reached its peak intensity with winds of 140 mph and a pressure of 28.05 inches. It was at this time that a U.S. Navy *WC-121* reconnaissance airplane suffered considerable structural damage as it passed through Cleo's eyewall. According to Gordon Dunn's report in the *Monthly Weather Review*, the plane was rocked when it left the eye and penetrated the wall cloud, where the wind increased by 90 mph within a distance of one mile. Both of the plane's wing fuel tanks were stripped off, and the radome was cracked open. Seven crew members suffered injuries, although none were serious. No flights were scheduled into the storm the following day, and no information on the storm's intensity was obtained.

Cleo's westward course brought it just south of the Dominican Republic early on August 24; seven lives were lost there. A slight turn toward the northwest carried it across the Haitian peninsula, where significant destruction occurred from the coastal sections to the mountains. Aerial surveys determined that the path of severe damage measured only eighteen miles in width, a reflection of the small size of the storm's destructive core. High winds and flash flooding across the peninsula claimed 192 lives.

The mountainous Haitian terrain may have temporarily disrupted Cleo's circulation because after leaving Haiti, it never regained its former intensity. It meandered across Cuba as a minimal hurricane on the morning of August 26 and then turned northward toward Florida's lower east coast. As it zigzagged over the Straits of Florida throughout the day, reconnaissance aircraft flew through the storm and reported on conditions. At the same time, radar stations in Miami and Key West kept it under constant surveillance. By midday Cleo had intensified somewhat, and maximum winds were around 85 mph. Forecasters believed its wobbling track would bring it near or just east of the coast. Throughout the afternoon, aircraft reports "found no winds of hurricane force in the western semicircle" and central pressures that were "stable."

Based on the best available information, Weather Bureau forecasters in Miami suggested that afternoon that Cleo would likely pass twenty miles offshore with maximum winds in Miami of about 45 mph. Unfortunately, throughout the evening hours, the fickle hurricane did the two things forecasters fear most—it intensified rapidly and turned toward the coast. The eye of the storm passed over Key Biscayne at about 2:00 A.M. on August 27. It was reported that during the passage of the ten-mile-wide eye, the moon was clearly visible. Within minutes, winds in downtown Miami rose, and many Dade County residents were awakened by the roar of the blow and the sound of shattering glass. Because forecasters had seemingly missed the mark in predicting the strike, Florida senator George Smathers later called for an investigation into the "reported misinformation" distributed by the Weather Bureau. The response from forecasters was consistent with statements from the past: tropical cyclones are sometimes unpredictable!

At the time of Cleo's landfall in Miami, Weather Bureau reports indicated that its maximum sustained winds were in the 100–110 mph range, with gusts to 135 mph. The storm's lowest recorded pressure over Florida was 28.57 inches, which was measured in North Miami. This was more than one-half inch lower than reconnaissance aircraft had reported just a few hours earlier. Rainfall was moderate, ranging from 3 to 6 inches in most areas near the storm's path. The Miami Weather Bureau office recorded 6.80 inches, which was one of the greatest accumulations.

Cleo moved north-northwest during the morning hours, paralleling the coastline with its center just ten to twenty miles inland. It gradually began to

decrease in intensity, and winds diminished as it passed up the coast toward Jacksonville. The center of the storm returned to sea during the afternoon of August 28 somewhere between St. Augustine and the Jacksonville beaches. Within a few hours, Cleo was back over land again, entering the coast near Savannah as a weak tropical storm. Its movement slowed, its course turned inland, and its winds dissipated, but the decaying storm unleashed heavy rains throughout eastern Georgia, western South Carolina, and much of central North Carolina and eastern Virginia. On September 1, the remnants of the storm passed out to sea between North Carolina's Outer Banks and Norfolk, Virginia. Within hours, it became better organized, its winds increased, and it regained tropical storm status. The following day, Cleo became a hurricane for the second time, but this time its course carried it harmlessly away from land. It finally passed east of Newfoundland and acquired extratropical features on September 4. In its final breath, it rocked the British liner *Queen Mary* and forced it into port at Southampton, England, with thirteen injured passengers.

In Florida the most notable damage occurred within a relatively narrow strip twenty to thirty-five miles wide along the southeastern coast, from Miami to about Melbourne. In the *Monthly Weather Review*, Gordon Dunn reported that "although the geometric center of the eye apparently passed over Virginia Key and reached the west side of Biscayne Bay at about the 36th Street Causeway, damage was minor at nearby Perrine and Homestead and west of Bird Road and 90th Avenue. Storm intensity north of Melbourne was such that only minor damage resulted."

Tides were less than four feet above normal in the Miami area, about five feet at Fort Lauderdale, and five to six feet at Pompano Beach. No serious tidal damage was reported anywhere in Florida. Also, amazingly little structural damage was discovered. In Dade and Broward Counties, where Cleo's winds were strongest, most of the destruction occurred when shattered windows allowed rainwater to saturate the interiors of homes, shops, and businesses. Power failures and disrupted communications were widespread, trees and utility poles were toppled, and signs, awnings, and stoplights were thrown to the ground. But largely because of tougher building codes and the relatively narrow field and short duration of the destructive winds, fewer than a dozen Dade County homes had seriously damaged roofs.

Other kinds of destruction were tallied along the hurricane's northward trek up the coast. Over 100 parked aircraft were overturned at airports in Florida, mostly in the Miami–Fort Lauderdale area. Once the storm reached the Indian River citrus area, 10 percent of the oranges and up to 30 percent of the grapefruit were blown down. Truck crops suffered as well, and virtually all of the sugarcane east of Lake Okeechobee was flattened. No deaths were reported in Florida from the storm, but 175 people were injured in the Miami area, many of whom were slashed by falling shards of broken glass. An employee at the Fontainebleau Hotel was critically injured when a large plate glass window in the hotel lobby burst. Looting in Miami was a concern after the storm because so many storefronts were shattered. Police shot and seriously injured one looter, who was caught taking advantage of the storm by raiding a Northwest Second Avenue pawnshop.

Several observers in the Miami area reported seeing lightning during the passing of the storm. Gordon Dunn described the phenomenon in the *Monthly Weather Review*: "It has now become well established that lightning is rather common in the hurricane eyewall cloud whenever this is present. During daylight hours lightning is usually not noticed by observers because flashes are cloud to cloud rather than cloud to ground and thunder is not audible over the high noise level of the wind. In Cleo lightning was noted in the wall cloud by numerous observers. There were some reports of 'greenish' and 'pink' lightning. Whether these were actual lightning or discharges from high tension lines or transformers is not known."

The same report also included this record made by an experienced meteorologist at his home in northern Dade County: "0250 EST—St. Elmo's fire was apparently observed and thunder heard. Some evidence of ball lightning seen. Looking south-southeastward from my house the sequence of events would be: St. Elmo's fire, then ball of light, then discharge, then thunder. This was observed about four times. In addition, frequent lightning was observed. Occasional thunder was heard—at least 10 peals."

As Cleo left Florida and drifted northward, widespread damages resulted from heavy rainfall and scattered twisters. In Georgia up to nine inches of rain fell in the east, flooding some homes in Savannah and Augusta. At Brunswick one man drowned while attempting to secure his boat. Scattered damages were seen in the Carolinas as a result of the rains, but most of the losses occurred during an outbreak of tornadoes that came as the hurricane's remnants crossed the region. At least eight touched down in South Carolina, and two more hit North Carolina, including a twister near Laurinburg that injured fifteen and caused $250,000 in damages. Three tornadoes had also been spotted in Florida—at Titusville, New Smyrna Beach, and Davie.

Finally, as Cleo passed eastward toward the Atlantic, it met a cold front from the north and dumped record rainfall on the Norfolk area. Some local records for rain were almost doubled. Norfolk received over 10 inches, and 14.09 inches were measured at Back Bay Wildlife Refuge. Many streets and bridges were washed out, and two people succumbed to carbon monoxide poisoning when their vehicle became stranded by high waters. Flood damages in Virginia topped $3 million.

In Florida, where the damages racked up by the hurricane totaled $125 million, President Lyndon Johnson declared nine counties disaster areas. Cleo's toll in the Caribbean was much heavier—not in dollar losses but in lives. The hurricane killed a total of 217, almost all of whom were from Haiti, the Dominican Republic, and the French West Indies. Florida and the United States were spared a great tragedy, although many in the Miami area saw the storm as a wake-up call. In a 1965 article in *Weatherwise*, Neil Frank commented on the storm's arrival: "Cleo was the first hurricane for many residents of Florida's gold coast, the last hurricane to strike this area having occurred in 1950. Since that time thousands of people have moved to southern Florida. In a way, it was fortunate that their first encounter was with a rather weak storm. It is difficult for an inexperienced person to comprehend the destructive power of a hurricane. These people are certainly better prepared to take proper precautions in the future."

DORA (SEPTEMBER 9–11, 1964)

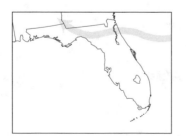

About the same time that Cleo was drifting out to sea off the North Carolina coast, the season's next tropical storm was brewing east of the Windwards. Its name was Dora, and its course was far to the north of its predecessor. By September 5, Dora was a full-fledged hurricane and was still some 1,000 miles from Florida. At this time, its latitude was already near 25 degrees, and its track was to the northwest. All indications suggested that it would curve out to sea and miss the United States or perhaps threaten Bermuda, which was a few hundred miles away. But Dora's course gradually turned toward the west, and as the days passed, it became apparent that this storm would be the second hurricane to strike the Florida coast in two weeks.

As Dora moved closer to the northeastern coast of the state, reconnaissance reports showed that it was an exceptionally large and powerful storm. Winds reached 150 mph near the storm center, and aircraft flying into the hurricane recorded a pressure reading of 27.82 inches. Col. Eugene Wernette, commander of an air force hurricane-hunter plane that flew into Dora's eye, said upon his return to Savannah that the storm was "well-organized and dangerous" and that it was "a very impressive hurricane that more nearly resembles a typhoon." Weather Bureau bulletins warned Florida residents that even though the hurricane was over 700 miles away, large and dangerous swells were beginning to pound coastal beaches. By the time the mighty storm slowed off the Daytona and Jacksonville coasts on September 9, it spread its hurricane- and gale-force winds over a 200,000-square-mile area. Bulletins warned that destructive winds were expected over a 450-mile section of coastline, an area said to be "larger than New England."

The fact that the massive hurricane slowed as it neared the continent was a blessing for coastal residents from Daytona Beach to the Georgia line. So few hurricanes had threatened this stretch of the coast that many residents were reluctant to pack their belongings and leave. As the storm drew nearer, many did decide to make last-minute evacuations and fortunately had adequate time to escape. The center of Dora eventually made landfall near St. Augustine in the early hours of September 10.

Fortunately, too, the storm had weakened somewhat as it approached land. It remained a formidable hurricane, however, with sustained winds of 125 mph at St. Augustine just after the passage of the eye. The lowest pressure recorded on land was 28.52 inches at that same location. Winds were greater than 100 mph from St. Augustine northward through the Jacksonville beaches and were said to have exceeded hurricane force from Flagler County to southeastern Georgia. In Jacksonville, several miles inland, a sustained wind speed of 82 mph was recorded, which was the first occurrence of sustained hurricane-force winds at that location in Weather Bureau history, dating back some eighty years. Dora was in fact the first Florida hurricane to make a direct hit on the east coast above Fort Pierce since the great storm of August 1880.

After passing inland, Dora moved slowly on an unusual path slightly north of westward. It gradually weakened and passed over Tallahassee and into eastern Alabama on the evening of September 11, by this time having lost its more destructive winds. At Tallahassee wind gusts were clocked at only 44 mph, but the capital city established a new record for low pressure—29.29 inches. Once it reached the Alabama border, the storm recurved toward the east-

A Jacksonville Beach man
watches helplessly as Hurricane
Dora's storm surge batters his
beachfront home and bathes
his car in foam in September
1964. The front wall of his home
collapsed just moments after
this picture was taken. (Photo
courtesy of UPI/Bettmann)

northeast and sped up slightly as it tracked through southern Georgia on
September 12. The following day, it moved through the Carolinas and exited
the coast near Cape Lookout, North Carolina. By the time the remnants of
Dora were out to sea again, cold air had weakened the storm considerably. It
continued on its northeasterly track for two days, racing over Newfoundland
on the fifteenth.

Dora was somewhat of a surprise to those who lived on Florida's northeastern coast. Although the Weather Bureau's warnings had been accurate, many
residents in the affected area had become complacent through the years because so few hurricanes from the Atlantic had struck that portion of the state.
Jacksonville had caught the backside of hurricanes before—storms like King
and Donna that made landfall elsewhere, crossed the peninsula, and passed
nearby. But for whatever reason, not many hurricanes had made landfall on
that part of the coast, and for most residents, Dora was their first true hurricane experience.

Damages were heavy throughout northern Florida and southern Georgia.

Areas near the coast suffered extensive wind damage from Daytona Beach northward, although the greatest property losses were from St. Augustine to the Georgia line. High winds in the Jacksonville area ripped down utility poles and trees, leaving telephone and electric lines tangled and severed. Major structural damages caused by winds were limited to areas within a few miles of the coast, and older structures seemed to suffer the greatest losses. At St. Augustine large oaks, cedars, palms, and other trees were uprooted and tossed into buildings and cars throughout the city. The storm was said to have battered the area with hurricane-force winds for fifteen hours. The winds left behind a mess, but it was the severe flooding that was most shocking to many of the town's residents.

Dora's head-on assault brought a major storm surge to the beaches and low-lying areas in its path. Because of the long duration of Dora's hefty on-shore winds, tides five to eight feet above normal flooded the coast north of Daytona Beach. Tides estimated at twelve feet—four feet higher than had ever been recorded—swept across Anastasia Island near St. Augustine. At Mayport floodwaters were ten feet above normal. These massive surge levels caused tremendous beach erosion, washed away many beach roads and causeways, and swept several dwellings and structures into the sea. In addition to the high surge, giant waves crashed onto the shore and battered seawalls, piers, and other man-made structures. Major damage was inflicted to the boardwalk and pier at St. Augustine Beach and to nearby S.R. A1A, which was closed to traffic. In St. Augustine heavy damages occurred along the bayfront, in Davis Shores, and in the vicinity of the San Sebastian River. Water was said to have "flowed hip deep" in the ancient Slave Market Square. Reports from the submerged offices of the *St. Augustine Record* noted that after the storm, outboard motorboats cruised Cordova and Bridge Streets.

At New Smyrna Beach two concrete approaches to the beach were washed out, and the Coast Guard station lost over 200 feet of beach. At Daytona Beach some 5,000 oceanfront residents ignored evacuation warnings from civil defense workers and remained in their homes. Fortunately damages were less severe on the southern side of the hurricane. Sixty-three homeowners reported damages, and a nearby airport building lost over 1,000 square feet of its roof. Piers were destroyed at Flagler Beach and Atlantic Beach, and many other piers up the coast suffered major damage.

At Jacksonville Beach the oceanfront Sea Ranch Motel lost its roof during the peak of the storm. In a news report by the Associated Press, owner George Takach described the ordeal: "I thought all hell had broken loose. It sounded like a car with four flat tires scrambling across the planks right over my head." Takach and several members of his family were huddled in the motel office when the roof was peeled away. "One fellow from Tennessee checked in just 15 minutes before the roof blew off," added Takach, "but he didn't leave. There wasn't any place for him to go." At nearby Atlantic Beach a large section of a fifty-seven-year-old hotel collapsed, but the owner stated that he couldn't hear the crash over the roar of the wind and rain.

At Cape Kennedy (Cape Canaveral), where hurricanes had sometimes delayed rocket launches but had never caused major damage, emergency crews lowered five large rockets from their pads in preparation for the storm. A sixth rocket, the 190-foot *Saturn VII*, was left poised for flight in its supporting gantry. Engineers were confident that the rocket could endure Hurricane Dora, as it was designed to withstand wind speeds of 175 mph. NASA operations suffered no damages in Cleo or Dora, but Dora delayed the launching of *Saturn VII*.

In the hours Dora was stalled off the coast on September 9, thousands of Florida residents fled their oceanfront homes and businesses for the safety of inland shelters. All along the coast, it was estimated that about 50,000 people evacuated to escape the worst of the storm. About 200 shelters were opened throughout the region, and more than 11,000 evacuees were housed in churches, schools, and National Guard armories. At Jacksonville Beach some 1,200 refugees tried to sleep on the floor of the high school gym, but rain blasted in through broken windows and soaked their bedding. Outside, floodwaters raced through the streets like rivers, and sea foam "covered shrubbery like snow."

As Dora moved inland on a westward course, its winds gradually diminished. Extremely heavy rainfall then spread over the interior portions of northern Florida and southern Georgia. These rains fell steadily for three days during both the western and eastern movements of the storm. According to the *Monthly Weather Review*, "Storm totals in excess of 10 in. fell over an estimated 10,000-sq.-mi. area, and totals of more than 6 in. were general from near Brunswick and Waycross, Ga. to near Tallahassee and Orlando, Fla." The heaviest rains fell in Lafayette and Suwannee Counties on September 12, three days after the storm struck the coast. Over the three-day period, 23.73 inches of rain soaked Mayo, including 14.62 inches that fell during one twenty-four-hour period.

Live Oak, which was the scene of some of the storm's most severe flooding, received 18.62 inches during a four-day period. The town was almost completely isolated by floodwaters that were more than ten feet above floor level in portions of the downtown business district. In many homes, water rose several feet above second-story windows; other houses simply floated off their foundations. All highways into the town were closed, and the Red Cross was forced to deliver typhoid serum to isolated areas by helicopter. Dozens of residents became trapped on their rooftops and had to be evacuated by boat. In many neighborhoods, cars were completely submerged and only chimney tops were visible.

During the passage of Dora, over eighteen inches of rain fell in Live Oak, inundating the business district with up to five feet of water. (Photo courtesy of the Florida State Archives)

By the time President Lyndon Johnson flew to Florida to inspect the damages, Hurricane Dora had been reduced to a drenching tropical storm. From his window aboard *Air Force 1*, he saw the uprooted trees, debris-filled streets, and torn structures of the hard-hit coastal zone. The presidential plane circled twice over St. Augustine before landing at the Naval Air Station in Jacksonville, from which Johnson was driven to Jacksonville Beach. He soon left the comforts of his limousine to wade through the water and muck to visit with storm victims whose homes had been shattered. Although his visit wasn't required for a presidential declaration of federal aid, it was a much-appreciated gesture to the storm-ravaged people of Florida. His hurricane-inspection tour was born of sincere concern and political correctness, and such visits have been repeated by every U.S. president since that time.

Among those whose lives were disrupted by Dora were thousands of adoring Beatles fans in Jacksonville. The hurricane's arrival forced the postponement of a much-anticipated performance by the British group, which had only recently become an American sensation. The Beatles' flight into Jacksonville was detoured by the storm to Key West, where they spent the night. They arrived in Jacksonville the following day and took some time to explore the storm-battered streets of the city before their concert.

Dora caused considerable agricultural damages in Florida, including extensive flooding of unharvested corn, cotton, and peanuts. The state's citrus crop suffered little damage from wind, but growers saw significant losses from root rot caused by standing floodwaters. Property losses were staggering in the coastal counties and some inland areas that experienced the worst flooding in their histories. The total price tag for Dora was estimated at $250 million in Florida and another $9 million in Georgia. Fortunately loss of life was not great. Only one fatality was directly related to the hurricane—a drowning in the sunken community of Live Oak. Four other deaths were indirectly attributed to the storm: two navy airmen died when their plane crashed upon takeoff near Sanford, Florida, and two men drowned while attempting to secure boats—one near Brunswick, Georgia, and the other near Norfolk, Virginia.

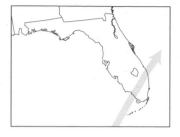

ISBELL (OCTOBER 14, 1964)

Isbell, the last of the trio of hurricanes to strike Florida during the 1964 season, was not nearly as destructive as the first two storms. Like many October hurricanes, it was slow to form over the western Caribbean but eventually built up steam and turned northward. It didn't reach hurricane strength until October 13, when it crossed western Cuba. In Havana winds gusted to 70 mph, and stronger winds were reported in the vicinity of Guane, where three people died and damages were described as "heavy." After entering the Gulf of Mexico on a northeasterly course, it accelerated toward the Florida coast. Its origin and path caused forecasters to label it a "typical mid-October hurricane."

The minimal hurricane picked up speed as it made its way toward southwest Florida. By the time it entered the coast near Everglades City at about 4:00 P.M. on October 14, top winds were around 90 mph. Its forward speed reached 20 mph, and its calm eye was observed for only about twenty minutes. Gusts of 76 mph reached Key West, and the Fort Lauderdale airport recorded a gust of 81 mph. The storm held its northeasterly course across the peninsula and exited the coast near Jupiter. Even as it entered the Atlantic, winds of almost 90 mph were still reported from locations near the storm center. Within the next day and a half, Isbell turned toward the coast again and came ashore in North Carolina. By this time, it was rapidly becoming extratropical, and it soon faded away over eastern Virginia.

Isbell's impact on Florida was not severe. As the storm approached the southern coast near Cape Romano, a weather system some 300 miles to the northwest apparently brought cooler and drier air into the hurricane's circulation. This caused Isbell to become somewhat lopsided. As a result, winds and rains were greatly reduced in the southern half of the storm. According to a report in the *Monthly Weather Review*, "No rain of consequence occurred in Everglades City after the center passed. Winds were considerably less in the rear portion than in the forward portion of the storm which in turn accounted for the small storm surge." Tides in the vicinity of landfall were only three to four feet above normal.

Although Isbell's winds, rains, and tides were not extreme, it did spawn at least eleven tornadoes across several coastal counties. Twisters were reported from Coral Gables to Eau Gallie, in Brevard County, and a total of fifty people were injured. One tornado lifted a tractor-trailer rig off a highway and deposited it in a ditch. Another was said to have "pulled pieces of fruit from trees and scattered them over a mile."

Palm Beach County suffered the greatest property damages in the hurricane—around $700,000, about half of which was attributed to tornado activity. Property damages in the lower Keys totaled about $175,000, most of which was in damage to telephone equipment. Vegetable crops in the Everglades region suffered heavy damages, and overall agricultural losses for the state exceeded $5 million. Isbell's total cost in the United States reached $10 million, most of which occurred in Florida.

Only a few lives were lost due to the storm—three in Cuba and three in Florida. Two fishermen drowned when their forty-two-foot shrimp boat was sunk off the lower Keys, and a Palm Beach resident died of a heart attack while installing storm shutters on his home. Isbell was not the killer other recent storms had been, such as its predecessor, Hurricane Hilda, which had killed thirty-eight in Louisiana the previous week.

BETSY (SEPTEMBER 7–8, 1965)

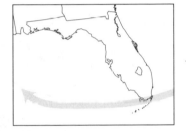

Only 6 tropical storms developed in the Atlantic basin during the 1965 season, well below the 9.5 that can be expected in an average year. Of these 6, only Betsy made landfall in the United States as a hurricane—but it struck twice. Betsy flirted with forecasters for days before sweeping over South Florida and then sailing across the Gulf to bash Louisiana. Its broad effects were felt in several states, and it left behind a tremendous toll in damages. When it was all over and the losses were totaled, Betsy was recognized by the Weather Bureau as the most destructive hurricane in history.

Like many storms of the satellite age, Betsy was first spotted as a small cluster of thunderstorms thousands of miles across the ocean. For several days, the clouds thickened, and on the morning of August 27, the *Tiros* weather satellite photographed it as a weak tropical depression in the Atlantic, some 350 miles east of Barbados. Navy reconnaissance aircraft confirmed the status of the storm, and by nightfall it was named Betsy. As Betsy moved through the Lesser Antilles, little intensification occurred, winds were of less than hurricane strength, and no damages were reported. Its northwestward path carried it east of Puerto Rico, and on August 29, it reached hurricane strength as it passed well north of the islands. By all appearances, it seemed Betsy would either move northward and pose a threat to the New England states or curve harmlessly out to sea.

Over the next two days, the hurricane weakened and slowed to a crawl, blocked by high pressure from the north. By August 31, its forward movement had shifted toward the west, and it once again began to spin toward the U.S. coast. On September 2, the erratic hurricane took a gentle turn toward the northwest, intensified dramatically, and continued for three days on what appeared to be a collision course with the Carolina coast. Here the storm reached its peak intensity, with a recorded pressure of 27.82 inches and winds of 150 mph. But once again changes in the surrounding atmosphere altered Betsy's path. An unexpected low-pressure trough developed over the continental United States that drew the Bermuda high toward the west, effectively blocking Betsy's northward progress. The hurricane again came to a standstill, then turned in a short loop on September 5 and headed south. At this time, it was about 400 miles due east of Jacksonville.

Forecasters in Miami paid close attention to Betsy's every move. Its unusual turn was of particular concern to residents in the Bahamas, who soon became the storm's first victims. On Labor Day, September 6, Betsy paralleled Great Abaco Island, where hurricane-force winds lasted twenty hours and a maximum wind of 147 mph was recorded. At Hope Town a gust of 178 mph was clocked. Damages in the Bahamas were estimated at $14 million, and one fatality was reported—a man died aboard a boat that wrecked in the Nassau harbor.

The following morning, the hurricane turned toward the west but became almost stationary just above Nassau. At 5:00 A.M. that day, all of South Florida was put under a hurricane watch; the watch was changed to a warning before noon. Miami's chief forecaster, Gordon Dunn, told the Associated Press: "Florida is in for a long siege. We must be reconciled to a prolonged period of warnings and threats. Betsy may be around for several days."

After Betsy left the Bahamas on the afternoon of the seventh, its due west track carried it directly into the "hot zone" of hurricane activity in South Florida—the upper Keys and southern portions of Dade County. Warnings had been issued well in advance, providing adequate time for residents to board up their properties and flee their homes. The Red Cross estimated that over 18,000 persons jammed into 143 shelters across South Florida on the night of the storm. In the early-morning hours of September 8, Betsy cut across the Keys with wind and tide extremes that approached those experienced during Hurricane Donna a few years before. The southern edge of the hurricane's eye passed over Marathon and the northern edge over the Flamingo ranger station, suggesting that the eye was forty miles in diameter as it crossed Florida Bay. Betsy's arrival in Florida was a topic of much discussion since it was only the second significant hurricane of record to approach the state from the northeast. The other was the "Yankee Hurricane" that moved inland over Miami in November 1935.

Betsy's highest winds blasted the upper Keys, and many wind instruments were either destroyed or reached the top of their range. According to Weather Bureau records, "Sustained winds of 100 mph or higher were recorded between

Big Pine Key and Homestead." Many of the highest wind speeds were esti-mates, including reports from Tavernier of sustained winds of 120 mph, with gusts to 140 mph. At Big Pine Key sustained winds were estimated at 125 mph, with gusts to 165 mph. Estimated gusts of 160 mph were reported at North Key Largo, Grassy Key, and the Flamingo ranger station. At Miami measured gusts topped 100 mph, and at Fort Lauderdale observers estimated gusts of 120 mph. The weather observer at Tavernier claimed that he was in the eye from 4:30 to 7:10 A.M. and that the barometer reached a low of 28.12 inches at 6:00 A.M., the lowest pressure recorded in Florida during the storm.

As in most hurricanes, the flooding experienced in South Florida dur-ing Betsy shifted as the storm swept through the region. Northerly winds in advance of the storm center pushed the waters of Florida Bay southward toward the Keys, flooding the northern sides of the islands and causing the most extensive damages. As the storm passed through, southerly winds fol-lowed, pushing waters from the Atlantic and the Straits of Florida northward. Tides ranged from five to seven feet above mean sea level in the western Keys to seven to nine feet in the eastern Keys. At North Key Largo tides were measured at nine feet above normal. Floodwaters covered many areas to a depth of several feet, closing highways and inundating the first floor of many buildings.

Farther northward at Miami Beach, the storm surge was the greatest since 1926, although it was not even close to the level in that storm. Tides at South Miami Beach measured 6.1 feet above mean low water. Seawater filled most of the streets facing the ocean and fronting Biscayne Bay. Resort hotels weath-ered the storm as they had in the past, some suffering more than others. The Roney Plaza lost seventy oceanfront cabanas and its restaurant. According to reports by the Associated Press, water was eighteen inches deep in the hotel's lobby, and "fish and eels were found in the basement lobby of the opulent Fon-tainblue." In spite of the howling storm, the hotels sent telegrams to sched-uled convention participants encouraging them to "come on down."

The Rickenbacker Causeway, Key Biscayne's connection to the mainland, was severed when three barges that had broken their moorings were dashed into a bridge. Hundreds of the island's residents were evacuated by boat and by amphibious vehicle. Many commented that officials had been right when they had advised them to leave the island prior to Betsy's arrival. One Key Biscayne resident was quoted by the *Tallahassee Democrat* as commenting: "The water came down this street like the Mississippi River on a rampage." A spe-cial weather summary prepared by the Weather Bureau further described the flooding: "Rising waters flooded extensive sections of Key Biscayne, covering virtually all of the island, reaching depths of a foot or more over many of the paved streets. In South Dade County, similar conditions were experienced in parts of the area east of the coastal ridge. Virtually all of the land south of

Homestead Air Force Base and east of highway U.S. #1 was covered with water. The area west of #1 was similarly flooded northward to within 3 miles of Florida City."

On the western reaches of Biscayne Bay, floodwaters invaded homes and businesses near Biscayne Boulevard and Bayshore Drive, and some portions of these streets were under three feet of water. Considerable damages were reported east of the ridge from Mercy Hospital southward to the Kings Bay area. High winds toppled billboards and crashed neon signs, and many of Miami's famed royal palms were said to have resembled "plucked ostriches." The Miami River overflowed its banks, and muddy water swept into the city's streets. But most buildings in the Miami area fared well in the storm, a fact that was later credited to the stiff building codes that had been employed in Dade County in recent years.

Criminals rarely seem to suspend their activities during hurricanes. During Betsy's visit, Miami Beach police arrested numerous looters who were taking advantage of shattered store windows along Collins Avenue. At the height of the storm in Miami, two masked gunmen broke into the home of Mr. and Mrs. Alan Murray, tortured them for three hours with lighted cigarettes, and eventually fled into the torrential rain with $5,000 worth of jewelry. Some storm victims reportedly were robbed of cash and personal belongings while they slept in hurricane shelters in the Miami area.

Farther up the coast, high tides, battering waves, and beach erosion were a concern. Tides five to seven feet above normal were reported in Broward and southern Palm Beach Counties, and even the Jacksonville area experienced tides almost two feet above normal. The outer fringes of the storm disrupted the High Mass being held on the old mission grounds in St. Augustine in celebration of that city's 400-year anniversary. Many of Florida's Atlantic coast beaches suffered significant erosion, and seawalls were tested by twelve-foot breakers. The Panamanian cargo ship *Amarylis* was driven aground near Palm Beach with a crew of twenty-eight aboard, but no one was injured and the ship was later refloated. At Hollywood much of the two-mile ocean boardwalk was undermined and destroyed. Piers and small craft suffered minor damages, but most of the damage from wind and water was found farther south, below Fort Lauderdale.

In the Keys, high tides washed out the Overseas Highway in at least one location, and fallen utility lines and other debris made passage along the road very difficult. On Upper Matecumbe Key, a 30-foot fishing boat washed onto the highway near the same location where the rescue train had stalled during the Labor Day storm of 1935. All electric and communication lines were downed, but fortunately the freshwater pipeline that supplied drinking water to the islands was not severed, as it had been during Hurricane Donna in 1960.

Flooding was severe at several locations, including Sugarloaf Key, where water was reported at rooftop level. All of Stock Island was said to have been under water at one point, and flooding was five feet deep at Big Coppitt Key and Key Haven. At Key West wind damages were minor, but two dozen mobile homes were destroyed, and several large shrimp boats and pleasure craft were sunk. Key Largo, which was hit hard by flooding from both sides, was the scene of major damages to structures, docks, boats, and mobile homes.

Two tornadoes were confirmed in the Keys during the passage of the storm—one at Big Pine Key and one near Marathon. The twister at Marathon ripped through the Gulf side of the island about midday, damaging several buildings and destroying a dozen mobile homes. Four other tornadoes were associated with Betsy in Alabama and Mississippi. According to a 1966 report by A. L. Sugg in the *Monthly Weather Review*, "The relatively low number of tornadoes that was spawned while Betsy was of hurricane force is not surprising. Fast-moving hurricanes and those with westward tracks (as opposed to northward tracks) usually have the least number of tornadoes."

Some of the storm's heaviest rainfall was recorded in the Keys—10.52 inches at Big Pine Key and 11.80 inches at Plantation Key. Even with these large amounts, meteorologists noted that Betsy was not a particularly wet hurricane. Rainfall over much of extreme southern Florida ranged between three and five inches. Naturalists at Everglades National Park were happy to see the rains, which helped to counter an extended drought that had left water levels low, threatening populations of fish, alligators, and other wildlife.

As Betsy moved into the Gulf of Mexico on September 8, its forward speed increased, its direction became north-northwest, and it once again strengthened. Within hours, reconnaissance aircraft reported that its winds were back up to 150 mph. Tides along Florida's Gulf coast had been abnormally low the previous day, but as the storm moved into the Gulf, local inundations were widespread. Over the next two days, considerable erosion and flooding occurred, particularly south of Clearwater. Between Clearwater and Pensacola, significant variations were noted in tidal extremes due to differences in coastal geography. Many areas along the Panhandle experienced tides of 4–5 feet, whereas St. Marks recorded an extreme of 11.57 feet above mean low water—just short of the record of 12 feet set back in 1877. Dozens of seawalls and piers were demolished along the Ochlockonee River, and houses were undermined on Alligator Point. All of this resulted from a hurricane that passed several hundred miles offshore.

By the morning of September 9, Betsy was once again a monster storm and was quickly bearing down on the Louisiana coast. Residents heeded warnings and took precautions, then faced the inevitable. Betsy made landfall just before midnight over the low, marshy expanses of the Mississippi River Delta.

Winds over southeastern Louisiana were as strong as those that had been observed over the Florida Keys. At Grand Isle gusts were estimated at 160 mph, and a barometric low of 28.00 inches was recorded. At Port Sulphur sustained winds of 136 mph were recorded, as well as gusts of 145 mph. Winds of hurricane force battered the state from Grand Isle up to Baton Rouge, where the Mississippi River crested at 15.5 feet above sea level and a barometer reading of 28.53 inches established a new record.

At New Orleans the Mississippi rose more than ten feet. Winds of 125 mph peeled back roofs and toppled billboards and utility poles. Canal Street was said to have looked "like the day after Mardi Gras, only much worse." In the Mississippi River from New Orleans to Baton Rouge, ships, tugs, and barges were torn loose from their moorings and tossed about. Hundreds of barges were either sunk or driven aground, including one containing 600 tons of chlorine gas that went down near the Louisiana State University campus. Although it could have caused an even greater disaster, the submerged barge was safely refloated a week after the storm.

Damages in Louisiana were immense, but no place suffered like Orleans Parish. New Orleans has an unusual topography; most of the city is below sea level and surrounded by an elaborate system of levees, canals, and pumping stations that keep it dry. As Hurricane Betsy swept through, the city's levees could not hold back the tremendous quantity of seawater that immersed the region. The massive pumping system, the largest in the world, was overloaded and failed when 90 percent of the city lost electrical power. One woman later reported that the rush of water was so great that it filled her home to the ceiling within thirty minutes, forcing her to quickly scramble onto her roof. Over 300 city blocks were submerged, and many residents waited on rooftops for up to twenty hours in driving rain for rescue teams to find them. In some areas, the flooding was delayed and did not peak until hours after the storm had passed. Since natural drainage is not possible in New Orleans, floodwaters remained for several days, which made evacuation and cleanup extremely difficult. Betsy was actually a harbinger of worse things to come, as forty years later Hurricane Katrina devastated the city in much the same way.

After hammering the Delta region on September 9, Betsy moved through central Louisiana and into eastern Arkansas on the tenth. Winds diminished, but heavy rains continued to fall as it drifted toward the Ohio Valley as a tropical storm. It took residents and local officials weeks to assess Betsy's impact on the region. Louisiana clearly suffered the greatest losses, with more than 27,000 homes destroyed or severely damaged and over 17,000 people injured, 679 hospitalized, and 58 dead. The destruction in Louisiana was tallied at over $1.2 billion, making Betsy by far the most expensive hurricane in U.S. history up to that time, without even factoring in the losses in Florida, Mississippi, Alabama, and Arkansas.

In Louisiana tragedies abounded in the storm. Many died as they fled the terrible flood. Some escaped in caravans of small skiffs pulled by small powerboats, but one such rescue ended horribly when one of the boats tipped over, drowning two children. One evacuee reported seeing an elderly couple in wheelchairs who were waiting to be rescued when floodwaters rose above their chins. Four young children apparently drowned when the pickup truck they were clinging to was overturned by the raging current of a flooded street. The total number of deaths caused by Betsy in the United States was 75, the most since Hurricane Audrey killed 390 in 1957.

In Florida damages totaled $139 million, far less than the awesome destruction across the Gulf. Most of the damage occurred along the coastal sections south of Palm Beach County and in the Keys. The major citrus-producing areas were spared the worst of the storm, although Dade County lime and avocado crops were severely beaten. Most of the wind damage was confined to utility equipment and windows. Saltwater inundation was responsible for the greatest portion of property losses.

Thirteen Floridians died in the storm. An elderly woman was killed in West Palm Beach as she attempted to close her garage doors, which were banging violently in the wind. An eighty-seven-year-old Miami man died after refusing to leave his flooded home, and another Miami resident, Helen Cooper, was electrocuted when she was hit by a falling power cable as she was walking into the fierce winds with her head lowered. Other deaths were reported in Homestead, Taylor County, Panama City, and Pensacola.

In the aftermath of the hurricane, a major controversy erupted regarding the U.S. government's possible involvement in "seeding" the storm. Some suspected that this experimental technique, which had been used on hurricanes in the past, was responsible for the unusually abrupt turn Betsy made while over the Atlantic. Project Stormfury, which involved dispersing silver iodide crystals into hurricanes in an effort to lessen their potential threat, had seen limited success, but government officials insisted that Betsy had not been a target of these experiments. Nevertheless, rumors persisted that Betsy's turn toward Florida had been brought about by scientists' failed attempt to quell the storm.

ALMA (JUNE 8–9, 1966)

The 1966 hurricane season featured several record-setting events, the first of which was the early arrival of Hurricane Alma. Alma was a rather typical hurricane, except for the fact that its June 9 landfall in the United States was the earliest in Weather Bureau history. Actually, however, at least one other hurricane is known to have hit the U.S. mainland on an earlier date. In *Early American Hurricanes, 1492–1870*, weather historian David M. Ludlum noted a hurricane that struck the coast near St. Augustine on June 2–3, 1825. More recently, Hurricane Allison invaded Florida on June 5, 1995, although it had diminished to tropical storm intensity prior to landfall.

Alma's beginnings can be traced to the steamy jungles of Nicaragua and Honduras, where a tropical depression developed on June 4. The following evening, nearly thirty inches of rain poured over the countryside near San Rafael, Honduras, turning once-timid rivers into relentless seas of mud. The town of San Rafael was virtually eliminated by the catastrophe, and seventy-three lives were lost. Over the next few days, Alma slowly drifted northward across the Gulf of Honduras and toward Cuba. It reached hurricane strength late on June 6 and eventually rolled over western Cuba on the morning of the eighth. The Institute of Meteorology in Havana reported maximum winds of 110 mph, and the destruction in Cuba was significant; over $200 million in damages and eleven deaths were reported.

The storm sped up considerably as it crossed Cuba and entered the Gulf of Mexico. A hurricane watch was issued for both Florida coasts, as far north as Daytona Beach on the east coast and Cedar Key on the west. Northbound traffic on U.S. 1 was heavy as Keys residents fled to the mainland. Ships from the naval base at Key West took to sea to ride out the storm, and the Sixth

Missile Battalion, stationed there since the Cuban Missile Crisis, moved its Hawk missiles to higher ground. In Greater Miami, according to the *Miami Herald*, residents were also making preparations. Before the winds picked up, sixteen-year-old Charlene Jensen brought her 1,500-pound quarter horse, Lady, into her family's home to escape the storm. "She'd never been in a hurricane," Charlene said. "When she walked into the living room, though, I thought the room was going to cave in." Charlene's parents soon arrived, however, and Lady was returned to the backyard, where she apparently endured the storm without incident.

Reconnaissance aircraft, which had been running regular missions into Hurricane Alma, reported that the storm's forward speed reached 25 mph as it neared the western Keys and southwestern Florida. On the afternoon of June 8, it passed very near the Dry Tortugas, some seventy miles west of Key West. It was at the Dry Tortugas weather station that Alma's greatest extremes were recorded. Sustained winds from the north of 125 mph were measured, along with a barometric low of 28.65 inches. A short distance away, Key West clocked top winds of only 60 mph, with gusts to 70 mph. Damages there mostly involved docks, piers, and seawalls on the south side, the cost of which totaled $350,000. Alma's near-visit marked the third year in a row Key West had experienced a hurricane or the fringes of one.

For a time, it appeared that Alma might veer toward the northeast, which would have carried it onto the coast near Sarasota, but it held its course and remained just offshore as it churned through the Gulf. As it passed by Florida's southernmost counties, tides were moderate, but up to eight inches of rain were recorded in portions of Dade, Broward, and Palm Beach Counties. Even though its path was more or less straight as it paralleled the coast, forecasters struggled to predict its next move. It didn't seem to be following the high-level steering currents over southern Florida, and its eye was "large, ragged, and ill-defined." Early on the morning of June 9, Alma turned more toward the north-northwest and passed just fifty miles west of Tampa. Tides in Tampa Bay were about three to five feet above normal, and moderate damage was reported. By afternoon it was clear that the storm was bound to strike somewhere farther up the coast, and the skies darkened all along the Big Bend.

Residents of Apalachicola were well prepared for the storm. They watched the ominously low tides throughout the day, knowing that an onrush of water would occur with the hurricane's arrival. The town's fishing fleet of over 400 boats was moved up the Apalachicola River to safety, and most people sought refuge in the public shelters established in Apalachicola, Eastpoint, and Carrabelle. Some residents refused to leave Dog Island and other vulnerable areas, and Governor William Burns broadcast an urgent television and radio plea, asking them to seek higher ground. But by the time Alma made landfall just east of Apalachicola, its forward speed had slowed, its strength had diminished, and it had begun a sharp turn toward the northeast. As a result, the impact on the region was less destructive than had been feared.

At Crawfordville and Alligator Point, winds were estimated at about 75–100 mph. Because of the concave shape of the coastline from Clearwater to Apalachee Bay, tides throughout this region ranged from four to ten feet above normal. Gale-force winds extended across northern Florida and into southern Georgia, where the storm eventually moved on the morning of June 10. Ironically, its center passed directly over Alma, Georgia, as it drifted over the state. It exited into the Atlantic just above Savannah, drifted along the Carolina coast, and briefly regained hurricane status before dissipating over the North Atlantic.

Although the $10 million damage estimate for Florida was not on the same scale as damages in other recent hurricanes, moderate damages were spread from one end of the state to the other. On the east coast, Miami experienced gusts to 65 mph, one person was killed, and a total of about $1 million in damages was reported. Along the Gulf coast, tidal flooding damaged docks, seawalls, small craft, and homes from the Keys to Apalachee Bay. Cedar Key was inundated, and the tidal surge washed out the only bridge to the mainland, stranding some 1,000 residents.

Scattered wind damages were reported all along the coast and were most notable in the Tampa–St. Petersburg area, where gusts reached 95 mph. These damages were rather typical and included downed utility lines and trees, battered residential roofs, and windows shattered by flying debris. In Leon County, according to Weather Bureau reports, "approximately 75 percent of all roads in the county were closed due to fallen trees." Crop damages were concentrated in the northern counties, where farmers suffered losses to corn and tobacco because of high winds and heavy rains. The mango crop in the southwestern counties and the grapefruit crop in Pinellas County were also hit hard by the storm. In addition to the effects of wind, rain, and tide, Alma spawned eight tornadoes in Florida, including two in Dade County, three near Sarasota, one in Jacksonville, and two near Marianna, in Jackson County. No significant damages or injuries were reported as a result of the twisters.

Six deaths were blamed on Alma in Florida, including two heart attacks, two drownings, and two electrocutions. One of the victims was Raymond Willis, a seventeen-year-old Miami youth who was electrocuted when he stepped in a puddle into which a live wire had fallen. Including the deaths in Cuba and Honduras, Alma was responsible for the loss of ninety lives.

INEZ (OCTOBER 3–5, 1966)

One of the most powerful and deadly hurricanes of the 1960s was Inez, which left a trail of destruction across the globe in September and October 1966. This great hurricane, with winds that at one point neared 175 mph, was an unwelcome visitor wherever it went, from the Leeward Islands to Mexico and all points in between. Like other storms tracked by the Weather Bureau in recent years, it followed an unpredictable path. Forecasters struggled to keep up with its twists and turns as it neared South Florida, until it finally dipped over the Keys on its way west. Its passing brought a great sense of relief to many in Florida, especially those along Miami's Gold Coast.

Inez began some 1,400 miles east of Trinidad, far across the warm Atlantic. On September 21, reconnaissance aircraft verified the developing storm and continued to monitor it for the rest of its twenty-one-day existence. On the twenty-sixth, it reached hurricane strength, and the following day it blasted through the Leeward Islands with 120 mph winds. Damages were heavy from Antigua to Dominica, but Guadeloupe was near the hurricane's eye and suffered the greatest losses. The combination of fierce winds, rains, and tides destroyed thousands of homes in the islands, and entire villages were swept away. Inez's first visit left 27 dead, over 600 injured, and $50 million in damages.

As the killer hurricane continued west across the Caribbean, it passed about seventy-five miles south of Puerto Rico, sparing the island its greatest fury. Reconnaissance reports indicated that it was continuing to strengthen, however, its pressure now down to 27.52 inches and its winds estimated at 150–75 mph. Early on September 29, as it was poised just off the southern coast of the Dominican Republic, Inez reached its peak intensity with a low pressure of 27.38 inches. An Environmental Science Services Administration Research Flight Facility aircraft recorded a wind speed of 197 mph at 8,000 feet, the highest hurricane wind speed recorded by a research plane to that date. Over the next few hours, the storm hammered the Barahona Peninsula with ten- to fifteen-foot tides and winds of over 130 mph. It then crossed into Haiti through the "Valley of Death," a deep trough between two mountain ranges on the Tiburon Peninsula where past storms had left tremendous death tolls. According to Weather Bureau reports, it was here that Inez delivered torrential rains and "local winds that may have well exceeded 160 mph." Damages across Hispaniola were massive, and the death count was high—between 75 and 100 died in the Dominican Republic, and 750 were killed in Haiti. In addition, almost 1,500 were seriously injured in the two countries. Many of the island's residents were still recovering from Hurricane Flora, which had killed more than 5,000 in the same region in 1963.

The next stop for Inez was southeastern Cuba. On September 30, the deadly storm came ashore between Guantánamo City and Santiago with sustained winds measured at 138 mph. The U.S. naval base at Guantánamo Bay was hammered by high winds, and tides of six to ten feet swept the beaches. Cuba's Sierra Maestra affected the storm's circulation, causing it to quickly become weak and disorganized. It tracked westward along the island's southern coast and finally crossed toward the north near Santa Clara. On the morning of October 2, the once-mighty cyclone passed into the Straits of Florida as a poorly organized storm of less than hurricane force.

It wasn't long, however, before Inez was once again a hurricane. Positioned about ninety-five miles southeast of Miami, it drifted toward the northeast into Bahamian waters with maximum winds of about 85 mph. It was around this time that the re-formed hurricane spawned a tornado in Nassau that killed a fifteen-month-old child and injured three others. An anemometer in the vicinity of the tornado recorded a rapid increase in wind speed as the twister approached—it lifted to 100 mph within fifteen seconds. By the morning of October 3, gale-force winds were buffeting the Florida coast, and the hurricane began to stall. Seas churned all around the storm, resulting in the loss of a twenty-three-foot boat that sank in high waves about thirty-five miles south of Miami. On board were forty-six Cuban refugees, all but one of whom drowned in the angry waters.

As Inez stalled just east of the Bimini Islands, high tides swelled into the streets of Nassau, where more damages were reported and four lives were lost. After remaining almost stationary for eight hours, the growing hurricane then unexpectedly did an about-face and began drifting toward the west-southwest. Its new course brought it closer to Miami, but it eventually dodged the mainland and slipped over the Keys. While it passed offshore, ships in the area were caught by the turn of events. The Liberian freighter *Verona* was disabled by high seas, as was the 353-foot Panamanian *Freight Transporter*, some ten miles off the coast of Miami.

Also tossed by Inez was the eighty-two-foot Coast Guard cutter *Point Thatcher*, which was grounded by heavy surf just off Miami Beach. As the *Point Thatcher* rolled through the surf at Miami Beach, a crowd of about seventy-five spectators gathered on the shore. By the time it finally went aground on a sandbar less than thirty yards from the beach, an unidentified lifeguard had gathered a rope and entered the water. He fought through huge breakers to reach the stranded crew of nine, who were then helped to the beach by the lifeguard and an assembly of men, women, and children of all ages who formed a human chain. Reporters who witnessed the rescue marveled at how the rescuers disregarded their own safety to save the men. A Coast Guard spokesperson later offered thanks to the rescuers and noted the irony of the fact that the crew was saved by the public instead of the other way around.

At Miami the edges of the hurricane delivered only moderate winds and tides. The Weather Bureau forecast office measured gusts of up to 60 mph, and gales in the Miami area were said to have lasted thirty-five hours. The only sustained winds of hurricane force recorded on the mainland were 81 mph, measured at Flamingo. Unfortunately, as Inez tracked over the Keys toward the west-southwest, it continued to strengthen. Observers noted that its strongest winds were experienced after the passage of the eye. The lowest pressure recorded in the Keys was 29.03 inches at Islamorada, and the highest sustained winds measured were 98 mph at Plantation Key. But according to Weather Bureau records, the storm's most awesome display was at Big Pine Key, where observers estimated sustained winds of 150 mph and gusts of 165 mph. The worst of the hurricane moved through fairly rapidly, though, with hurricane-force winds lasting only four hours. In addition to the forty-five Cuban refugees who drowned off the Miami coast, three other people were reported killed in Florida.

As Inez left the Keys on the morning of October 5, it appeared that the storm would visit Cuba for a second time. Winds near the eye were around 105 mph, and further strengthening was forecast. Fortunately it missed landfall in Cuba and passed just off the northwestern coast early on the sixth. High tides and damaging winds battered the shore, with some locations, like Havana, reporting up to twelve inches of rainfall. In the low-lying sections of Havana Province, 21,000 people were evacuated, and 4 more Cubans died in the storm.

After pummeling Cuba for the second time in four days, Inez continued its southwestward drift and reached the Yucatán Peninsula by October 6. It paralleled the shoreline and lashed the sparsely populated coastal sections with hurricane-force winds and heavy rains. Over the next few days, its course shifted toward the northwest, and its pressure dropped; it now posed a threat to South Texas, with sustained winds of 130 mph. Finally, Inez turned back toward the west on October 9 and slammed the Mexican coast, north of Tampico. Wind gusts were measured up to 127 mph, and tides reached twelve feet above normal just north of the point of landfall. Mexico was not prepared for the storm. Damages exceeded $100 million, 65 people were killed, and 250 were injured.

A survey of the ravages of Inez reveals that although it killed over 1,000 people on its journey across the hemisphere, its impact on crops and property was not as great as that of other storms that have struck such an extensive area. This fact has been attributed to the relatively small diameter of the storm and its arrival late in the season. Total damages from the hurricane were estimated at $200 million, $5 million of which occurred in Florida. Newspapers called it "the most unpredictable storm ever to howl out of the tropics." Even Paul J. Hebert of the Weather Bureau's hurricane forecast office noted that "a path crossing so many countries at different latitudes will have to be consid-

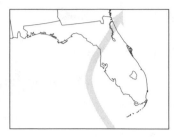

ered somewhat unusual at the very least." Forecasters were given a workout in tracking the storm, as Inez established a new record for warnings—a total of 151 bulletins and advisories were prepared.

GLADYS (OCTOBER 16–19, 1968)

The next hurricane to venture into Florida waters was Gladys, a classic October storm born in the western Caribbean. Like so many other hurricanes of its kind, Gladys developed a predictable course that carried it northward, across western Cuba and into the Gulf of Mexico. Winds of 80 mph and flash floods were reported in the vicinity of Gerona, on Cuba's south coast. Serious crop damage resulted and one death was attributed to the storm, but its overall impact made it a rather unremarkable event in Cuba's hurricane history.

From the time Gladys exited the Cuban coast, forecasters at the National Hurricane Center felt it would eventually affect some portion of Florida. Hurricane warnings were put into effect in the lower Keys and along the southwest Florida coast and were later extended northward to Cedar Key. Its rather casual northward drift carried it just west of the Dry Tortugas on October 16, where its effects were first felt. The highest winds measured on the islands were 64 mph, with gusts to 86 mph. Plantation Key received a gust of 88 mph, the only other wind speed of hurricane force measured in the Keys. Tides were less than two feet above normal, and no significant damages were reported.

Gladys paralleled the Florida coast as it tracked northward and then paused in the Gulf about 120 miles west of Tampa. Wind gusts along the southwest coast were below hurricane force, although tides in some locations ran three to five feet above normal. A slight jog toward the northwest spared coastal communities from Naples to Sarasota any notable damages. After drifting at a snail's pace for several hours, Gladys finally took its expected turn toward the coast on the morning of October 18. It was around this time that the modest hurricane was observed by the astronauts of *Apollo VII* as the spacecraft orbited some 100 miles above the Gulf.

Just after midnight on the nineteenth, the storm moved ashore between Bayport and Crystal River, near Homosassa. Sustained hurricane-force winds were reported along the coast from Bayport southward to Clearwater, with gusts estimated at around 100 mph. Gladys continued its trek inland, passing just north of Ocala and then back out to sea at St. Augustine by daybreak. During its crossing, it managed to maintain hurricane intensity, and once over the warm waters of the Gulf Stream, it further intensified as it sped off toward the northeast. As it passed just off the North Carolina coast on October 20, gusts of hurricane force were felt along the Outer Banks, but only minor damages were reported. Its last gasp came as it merged with a cold front and passed off Nova Scotia as an extratropical storm.

Damages in Florida, which were estimated at $6.7 million, occurred primarily in Pinellas, Hillsborough, Pasco, Hernando, Citrus, and Marion Counties. Extensive wind damages stretched inland as far as Ocala and included dozens of overturned mobile homes. As would be expected, countless trees were uprooted, power lines were downed, and houses were unroofed. At Bayport a weather observer with the Cooperative Hurricane Reporting Network (CHURN) measured winds of 94 mph before his anemometer, along with the roof of his house, was blown away. Air force reconnaissance aircraft reported a low pressure of 28.85 inches as the hurricane was making landfall. The highest tides in the region were measured at between six and seven feet, which brought considerable flooding to low-lying coastal areas. Beach erosion was extensive, and numerous piers, boat houses, and other waterfront structures were damaged.

Pinellas County suffered the most damage from the storm, about $2.5 million, largely because of its population density. Citrus crops across the state were relatively unscathed, although farms near the point of landfall lost as much as 75 percent of their fruit. Two tornadoes were confirmed during Gladys's passage—one near Boca Raton and one at Palatka. Neither caused significant damage. A total of five deaths were attributed to the hurricane—three in Florida, one in Cuba, and one in Nova Scotia. The three Floridians who died were all attempting to escape the storm by car. Two suffered heart attacks while at the wheel, and the third drowned while attempting to navigate a submerged road.

AGNES (JUNE 19, 1972)

One of the greatest lessons that has been learned about the destructive nature of hurricanes is that incredible disasters can result from storms of "minimal" strength. Perhaps no other hurricane illustrates this point as well as the first storm of the 1972 season, Hurricane Agnes. Like Hurricanes Diane in 1955 and Juan in 1985, Agnes ranked as only a category 1 storm on the Saffir-Simpson scale when it made landfall in June 1972. Also like Diane and Juan, it rapidly diminished to tropical storm strength, dumped enormous amounts of rainfall across a broad region, and went on to become one of the most destructive and costly hurricanes in U.S. history.

Like many great hurricane disasters, Agnes had humble beginnings. It was first detected as a small area of circulation over the tip of the Yucatán Peninsula on June 15. By the afternoon of the next day, surveillance by the Hurricane Center indicated that it had grown into a tropical storm, and it was given a name, the first of the season. It continued to develop in size and strength and became a hurricane about 300 miles southwest of Key West on the seventeenth. As it drifted over the western tip of Cuba, heavy rains caused flash floods that claimed the lives of seven Cubans. Weather Service reports noted

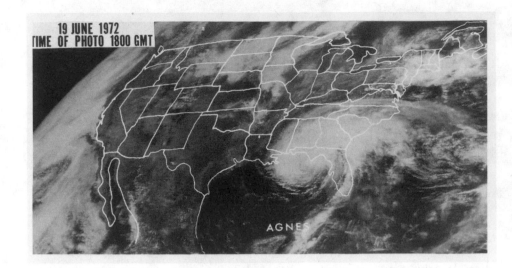

The broad, spiraling storm clouds of Hurricane Agnes in June 1972 dominate this satellite image. Although Agnes made landfall near Panama City, it eventually moved northward through the Carolinas, where it combined with a secondary low from the west to produce record floods in the Northeast. (Photo courtesy of NOAA, National Weather Service)

that by early the next day, "the circulation covered most of the Gulf of Mexico and all of Florida," with gales extending outward 200 miles north and east of the center. Although it was large, its winds remained just above hurricane force as it paralleled Florida's west coast. A barometric low of 28.88 inches was recorded by aircraft just prior to Agnes's landfall, which occurred on the Florida Panhandle around noon on June 19.

The storm came ashore over Cape San Blas, just west of Apalachicola. Sustained winds hovered around 75 mph over a lengthy stretch of coastline, and gusts reached 95 mph. But these winds were not of great consequence, except that they pitched Gulf waters onto the coast, which resulted in some of the highest tides in years. Above-normal tides were experienced along the entire west coast, from the Keys to Panama City. Pinellas County suffered about $12 million in property damages from severe erosion and flooding, more than any other coastal county. Tides rose five feet above normal at St. Petersburg and nearby beaches, and numerous homes and structures were inundated. Panama City suffered little damage, but low-lying coastal communities between Carrabelle and Apalachicola were hit hard by the rise of water, which was also five to six feet above normal. According to local reports, during the storm a group of young boys found a diversion in a street-turned-river in Apalachicola—they caught both freshwater and saltwater fish with their cast nets in front of the Franklin County sheriff's office.

By mid-morning on the day of the storm, Alligator Point was already underwater, and by afternoon, sixteen houses were "washed away" and another fifty or so were heavily damaged. In some cases, pieces of the structures were said to have been carried five miles by the tide. At St. Marks four to five feet of water covered the downtown area. In the aftermath of the storm, reporters from the *Tallahassee Democrat* described the scene: "DeLacy Peavy drove a Democrat reporter and photographer into the area in a huge old farm tractor

with six-foot-tall rear wheels. The water flowed over the hub as the vehicle moved down the town's main street, passed occasionally by motor boats. . . . More than 50 private automobiles were seen parked in front of businesses and homes. Many rocked like boats in the wake of the tractor."

The night before Agnes crossed the Panhandle coast, shelters were established in dozens of schools, churches, county buildings, and National Guard armories. The Red Cross estimated that at least 5,000 people moved into the shelters as the storm drew near, many of whom fled mobile homes at the urging of local officials. According to the *Democrat*, the refugees made the best of the experience—they "played cards, rolled hand-made cigarettes, threw a basketball around and played musical chairs."

Agnes's most deadly spree in Florida had nothing to do with tides, however. Fifteen tornadoes and two events classified by the Weather Service as "windstorms" rocked the state as Agnes churned by. Unfortunately, as so often seems to happen, several of the twisters sliced through mobile home parks with disastrous results. The first twister touched down at Big Coppitt Key at about 2:15 P.M. on June 18 and wrecked almost eighty mobile homes. Forty people were injured, and damages were estimated at almost $350,000. The following morning in Okeechobee City, another tornado carved a path 100 yards wide and 3 miles long. This twister dissected five mobile home parks, killing six people, injuring forty, and causing $500,000 in damages. The greatest destruction, however, occurred in Brevard County, where a string of three tornadoes caused $4 million in losses.

In addition to those killed in Okeechobee City, three other Floridians died in the storm. One was a child who drowned in a rain-swollen stream. These casualties brought the death toll in the state to nine. In addition, there were 119 reported injuries and over $40 million in damages. All of the coastal Gulf counties from Bay to Monroe were declared federal disaster areas after the storm, as were the inland counties that endured tornadoes—Brevard, Okeechobee, Hardee, and Hendry. President Richard Nixon proclaimed these twenty-five Florida counties disaster areas just nine hours after the request was issued by Governor Reubin Askew.

Sadly, as Hurricane Agnes exited Florida and entered southwestern Georgia as a tropical storm on the morning of June 20, its deadly and destructive forces were just beginning. Winds dropped quickly as the storm moved inland, although more tornadoes were spawned in Georgia. After dumping beneficial rains over Georgia and South Carolina, Agnes accelerated across eastern North Carolina and approached Cape Hatteras on the afternoon of June 21. Here the storm's pressure was measured at 29.13 inches. Within hours, it was back over water, bouncing along the Delmarva Peninsula on its way northward. A summary of events in *Weatherwise* described what happened next: "With the Atlantic Ocean now a source of energy, Agnes commenced to increase and expand its already amazing rain-making prowess."

With sustained winds of 55 mph and a falling minimum pressure, the storm turned inland over New Jersey and Long Island, New York, on the afternoon of the twenty-second. Observers in New York City recorded a minimum pressure of 28.99 inches, which broke the 100-year-old June record for that location by the large margin of 0.35 inch. Agnes slowed and became diffuse as it moved inland and soon merged with a broad trough of low pressure from the Ohio Valley. The two systems combined over western Pennsylvania and drifted over Ontario, western New York State, and eventually New England. Throughout this episodic journey from the Carolinas through the Northeast, Agnes dumped record amounts of rain that overfilled countless rivers and claimed scores of lives.

The tragedy was staggering. So many rivers were swollen beyond their banks that over 500,000 people in several states were chased from their homes. In Wilkes-Barre, Pennsylvania, a dike was breached and most of the town was destroyed. The governor's mansion in Harrisburg was submerged. In some cases, the populations of entire cities were evacuated, as in Corning, New York, where 17,000 people fled their homes. In Elmira, New York, half of the city's population of 40,000 was forced to leave because of high water, and 15,000 were removed from Auburn due to the threat of a weakened dam.

Rainfall amounts across a broad area were of record proportions. From ten to nineteen inches of rain fell in many locations in North Carolina, Virginia, Maryland, Pennsylvania, and New York. The Office of Emergency Preparedness calculated that Agnes dropped 25.5 cubic miles of rainwater, or 28.1 trillion gallons. Rivers in several states crested at record levels, and the consequences for structures near their banks were dire. Property damages were staggering, not just to homes and businesses but also to factories, highways, bridges, utilities, and other infrastructure. Cemeteries were submerged, and caskets were said to have floated out of the ground and into the streets. Water seemed to be everywhere it wasn't supposed to be.

Tragically, the storm killed 122 in the United States (including those in Florida), most of whom drowned horribly. Many died trying to escape in their cars, and some were swept under as they waded through neighborhood streets. Helicopter and airplane crashes added to the death toll. Fires broke out in dozens of flooded towns and burned uncontrollably. Hundreds, if not thousands, of residents were rescued by helicopter from their rooftops. Some rescue missions even lifted cows, pigs, dogs, cats, raccoons, and rabbits to safety. The entire Northeast was ravaged by the remnants of what was once Hurricane Agnes.

A summary report, "Hurricane Agnes: The Most Costly Storm," that appeared in *Weatherwise* in August 1972 offered this stark conclusion: "Agnes had been an entity for two weeks. From its humble beginnings in the Caribbean Sea, it had laid waste more of the industrial might and destroyed the home comforts of more Americans than any other storm in history." Agnes caused $2.1 billion in U.S. damages and killed 129, including the 7 people who died in Cuba—an incredible impact for a storm that never strengthened beyond a category 1.

ELOISE (SEPTEMBER 23, 1975)

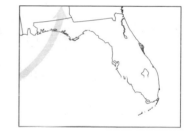

From the late 1960s through the 1970s, the United States was spared the frequent battering of hurricanes it had experienced during previous decades. Notable storms certainly occurred during this period, like Camille in 1969 and Agnes in 1972, but the number of hurricanes that made landfall in the United States was well below the average for the last fifty years. Those hurricanes that did venture near, however, always seemed to find Florida in their path. The 1975 season brought Hurricane Eloise, which crossed the Gulf of Mexico, struck the Florida Panhandle, and went on to flood the Northeast, just as Agnes had done three years earlier. Although the flooding it caused throughout the Northeast was not nearly as destructive as that left by Agnes, Eloise hammered the Florida coast with category 3 winds and tides. It was the state's first major hurricane in ten years.

Long before it came ashore in Florida, Eloise paid a dreaded visit to the storm-weary islands of the northern Caribbean. Although it was only a tropical storm when it passed north of Puerto Rico on September 15–16, its massive

rain clouds covered the island. Rainfall totaled 10–20 inches in many locations, with a maximum of 26.70 inches near Sabana Grande. Even though warnings were issued well in advance of the storm, flash floods raced through several villages, killing thirty-four people. The same fate befell the Dominican Republic and Haiti, where landfall occurred late on September 16. Eloise was only a minimal hurricane when it arrived, but heavy rains flooded the countryside, killing at least thirty.

Over the next four days, the storm drifted along a westward course over southeastern Cuba toward the Yucatán Peninsula, never managing to regain hurricane strength. It was barely a tropical storm by the nineteenth, but it slowly began to intensify as it neared the Yucatán Channel late the following day. An approaching upper-level trough forced it to turn northward into the Gulf of Mexico. It then began to rapidly strengthen and returned to hurricane force in the central Gulf, some 350 miles south of New Orleans. Hurricane warnings were issued for much of the upper Gulf coast, from Louisiana to Apalachicola. By midday on September 22, forecasts suggested that Eloise would hold its course and make landfall near Mobile Bay.

But that's not what happened. Early that evening, Eloise began an unexpected turn toward the northeast as pressures dropped and winds increased. Hurricane warnings were extended eastward to Cedar Key. Residents along much of the Florida coast never heard the news and went to bed that night still believing that landfall would be well to their west. But in the predawn hours of September 23, civil preparedness officials with loudspeakers on their cars combed the streets of Panama City Beach, Apalachicola, Carrabelle, and other coastal towns, urging residents to seek high ground. Most coastal residents west of Fort Walton Beach had fled the night before. According to the Red Cross, because of the frightening intensity of the fast-approaching storm, the evacuation was thorough. The beaches near Pensacola were said to have been "99% evacuated." In all, 100,000 coastal residents from Louisiana to northwest Florida left their homes and businesses.

Eloise continued strengthening until it made landfall between Fort Walton Beach and Panama City at around 7:30 A.M. on September 23. This popular stretch of coast, dubbed the "Miracle Strip" during World War II, had experienced explosive growth in recent years and had become one of Florida's liveliest resort areas. Scores of businesses and homes were devastated by the storm's sustained winds of 130 mph and tides that ran sixteen feet above normal. According to a report in the *Tallahassee Democrat*, "Cottages, motels, restaurants, convenience stores and other beach businesses were strewn across the highway in a tangle of down power poles, lines and busted mains."

Eloise had strengthened to a barometric low of 28.20 inches, which was recorded at Destin. Sustained winds were estimated at around 130 mph near the point of landfall, although few official recordings were obtained. Wind instruments at Eglin Air Force Base were destroyed after a gust of 92 mph. Eglin also recorded the most rain—almost fifteen inches. According to Weather Service records, a gust of 135 mph was measured on a ninety-eight-foot tower near Panama City. Private anemometers reportedly clocked gusts of 140 mph and even an awesome 156 mph. These winds were the highest encountered in this area in the twentieth century. They were strong enough to flip and destroy twenty planes at two local airports. Several cars exposed to the hurricane were said to have been sandblasted down to bare metal. And naturally signs, awnings, utility poles, trees, and countless other objects were shattered and tossed by the storm.

More than 200 commercial buildings were unroofed at Fort Walton Beach alone, and many suffered a similar fate elsewhere along the Strip. Dozens of buildings were blown down by strong gusts and then washed about by the raging storm surge. Local estimates suggested that three-fourths of the structures along the strand received some damage in the storm. Many areas were cleared of trees, and in some locations, deep white sand covered roadways and lawns. The National Guard was called in soon after the storm to prevent looting, and several arrests were made. The Red Cross estimated that in northwest Florida, 8,000 families suffered losses, and 500 businesses were destroyed.

Tides throughout the area were variable, but the twelve- to sixteen-foot tides near Panama City were among the highest ever recorded in that region. Although the winds peeled away many roofs, it was the surging Gulf waters that undermined structures and caused the most serious damage. Structures built on pilings fared relatively well because the surge swept under and around them. But older buildings constructed on concrete slabs and "spread footings" were trapped in the surf and undermined, causing them to collapse. After his tour of the forty-mile-wide damage zone following the storm, Governor Reubin Askew was quoted by the Associated Press: "I think we're going to have to take a long, close look at some of the construction. . . . Some of those structures simply won't be able to be built back in the exact location where they were." A 1971 Florida law establishing coastal-construction setback limits had been enacted too late to help many of the ruined structures along the Miracle Strip.

After blasting the immediate coast, Eloise quickly sped inland. Its forward speed was nearly 30 mph when it entered eastern Alabama, where it rapidly lost strength and was downgraded to a tropical storm. Drier air was drawn into its circulation, and it turned toward the northeast over eastern Tennessee, with winds that still registered as gale force. Rainfall from Louisiana to Florida had ranged from four to eight inches, but the storm became a massive rainmaker as it crossed into Virginia. It combined with a slow-moving frontal zone and went on to cause extensive river flooding and major damage in the Northeast. Also contributing to the heavy rains in the region was Hurricane Faye, which was located at the time far at sea off the coast of Cape Cod. Although the remnants of Eloise did not break the records for rainfall and flooding recently set by Agnes, the dissipating storm caused $300 million in damages and seventeen deaths in the northeastern states. Pennsylvania and New York once again suffered the greatest losses in lives and property. Among the rivers that experienced major flooding were the Chemung, Susquehanna, Potomac, and Shenandoah.

Remarkably, no deaths were directly attributed to the hurricane in Florida. A Fort Walton Beach man died of a heart attack in an emergency shelter, and a Panama City woman also died of cardiac arrest. Scores of injuries were reported, many caused by glass cuts or received during the lengthy cleanup effort. Many deaths resulted in the Northeast, mostly due to drownings and storm-related traffic accidents. According to the Hurricane Center's *Deadliest Atlantic Tropical Cyclones, 1492–1994*, by Edward N. Rappaport and José Fernández-Partagás, Eloise claimed a total of eighty lives, twenty-one of them in the United States. Property losses totaled about $150 million in Florida, and total damages in the United States added up to $490 million. Perhaps the single greatest financial loss was suffered by Marifarms of Panama City, which lost a 2,100-acre, $2 million mass-production shrimp farm to the storm tide and had no insurance to cover the loss.

DAVID (SEPTEMBER 3–4, 1979)

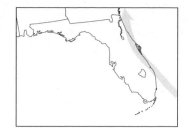

As the 1970s came to a close, the 1979 hurricane season was a bit closer to what meteorologists would consider an "average" year than the years that had preceded it. Relatively few storms had struck Florida and the rest of the U.S. coast during the decade. But in 1979 two hurricanes—David and Frederic—slammed the coast, both having a significant impact on Florida. They were labeled by some as "twin brothers," the first arriving just days before the second. The first was a gruesome killer, and the second broke all records for total damages. But even with David and Frederic on the books, the 1970s still had the lowest number of hurricanes (12) and the lowest number of major (category 3 or greater) hurricanes (4) to make landfall in the United States of any decade of the twentieth century.

The 1979 season also featured a major change in the way hurricanes would be remembered. For the first time, tropical storms and hurricanes were named from an alternating list of female and male names. Hurricane Bob was the first storm given a male name; it eventually struck the Louisiana coast as a minimal hurricane. Ironically, the season's other two hurricanes to make landfall also were named for men, the first of which was David.

David was a classic Cape Verde–type hurricane. Its formation began far across the Atlantic, but it developed explosively as it approached the Lesser Antilles during the last week of August. On Wednesday the twenty-ninth, it tracked through the Martinique Passage as a major hurricane. Dominica was among the hardest hit islands, suffering raging tides, torrential rains, and sustained winds estimated at 145 mph. Thinking that their island would receive some protection from its mountainous terrain, many Dominicans went about their usual business as the storm approached. When it was over, David left 56 dead and some 60,000 of the island's population of 78,000 homeless. Many of the island's lush rain forest–covered hillsides were stripped bare by battering winds and mudslides. Even before David's winds subsided, chaos erupted as a frenzy of looting spread across the island. According to National Weather Service reports, David was the strongest storm to strike Dominica since 1834 and the most costly since Hurricane Inez barreled through in 1966.

David continued its trek toward the west and strengthened even more. It passed eighty miles south of Puerto Rico on August 30 as its central pressure continued to fall. Winds, tides, and rainfall of up to nineteen inches contributed to the loss of seven lives and $70 million in damages in Puerto Rico. At about this time, reconnaissance aircraft measured winds of 150 mph and a low pressure of 27.29 inches. According to Weather Service reports, only six other Atlantic hurricanes had achieved such depth of intensity. Although dangerous before, David was now a monster storm on the verge of category 5 status.

On the morning of August 31, David turned toward the northwest and slammed into the southern coast of the Dominican Republic at full force. Winds were estimated at over 150 mph, but flooding was responsible for the greatest destruction. Landfall occurred just west of Santo Domingo, where all roads were washed out and thousands of structures were blown down. Across the countryside, rain-swollen rivers swept away entire villages, including the mountain town of Padre Las Casas. In this remote village, several hundred people were killed when a church and school being used as shelters were carried away. After the storm had passed, the official death toll in the Dominican Republic was 1,200, over 200,000 were homeless, and damages were estimated at $1 billion. David was the most powerful storm to strike the island since September 1930.

David weakened considerably as it crossed the mountainous terrain of Haiti. Its distorted eye emerged over the Windward Passage on September 1, surrounded by winds of less than hurricane force. Throughout the day, it drifted toward the northwest and traversed the tip of Cuba, then slowly began to strengthen as it moved over warm Bahamian waters. It now posed a threat to the South Florida coast, just as residents and vacationers were settling in to enjoy the Labor Day weekend. It crossed Andros Island the following day, buffeting it with winds of 75 mph. Although it continued to intensify through the night, fortunately David never regained its former strength as it moved closer to the Florida coast.

Hurricane warnings were released for most of the South Florida area, and forecasters suggested that Miami was a likely target for landfall. The Hurricane Center indicated that if the storm held its course, it would strike somewhere between Palm Beach and Key West. Governor Bob Graham urged all residents of the Keys to evacuate their homes, fearing another disaster in that part of the state. Graham, who would later serve in the U.S. Senate, was particularly sensitive to the threat of hurricanes because of his vivid memories of the severe flooding around his family's home in Miami during the hurricanes of 1947.

In the hours just before it arrived, David turned farther northward, missed Miami, paralleled the coast, and finally came ashore north of Palm Beach around midday on September 3. The barometric pressure at the time of landfall was measured at 28.71 inches, far above the intensity recorded near Puerto Rico. Winds gusted to nearly 85 mph from South Melbourne Beach to Jupiter, and tides up to five feet above normal caused considerable damage. Rainfall over most of the area ranged from four to six inches, although some locations near Vero Beach received up to ten inches. The eye passed over a number of coastal communities from Jupiter to New Smyrna Beach, just south of Daytona Beach. It moved almost due north at about 12 mph, and witnesses in some locations reported being in the eye for almost two hours.

After bumping along the Florida coast for several hours, David took another brief trip into the Atlantic before making a second landfall near Savannah Beach, Georgia, on September 4. While over the warm waters of the Gulf Stream, the storm had retained its strength, and it hit Georgia with winds comparable to those in Florida. Savannah recorded a low pressure of 28.65 inches, and winds gusted to 90 mph. Wind gusts up to 70 mph were felt along the coast as far north as Myrtle Beach, South Carolina. David moved into central South Carolina as a tropical storm and tracked northward through North Carolina, Virginia, and the northeastern states. Tornadoes touched down in Virginia, Maryland, Delaware, Pennsylvania, and New Jersey, accompanied by squalls that delivered rainfall of up to eight inches and wind gusts to 55 mph. Power lines and trees were downed throughout the region, and in the New York City metropolitan area alone, over 2.5 million people were without electricity after the storm.

In Florida damages were not particularly severe at any one location, but the cumulative destruction along the coast caused by winds, high tides, and tornadoes was significant. According to surveys conducted by the state after the storm, Brevard and Indian River Counties suffered the greatest losses. In the vicinity of Melbourne, strong winds uprooted trees, twisted power lines, and unroofed buildings. A tornado was believed to have cut across Melbourne Beach, demolishing a condominium under construction and wrecking about a dozen mobile homes. In Indian River County, some of the seventeen public shelters filled with evacuees had windows and doors blown out as the storm rumbled by in the afternoon. Phil Long, the *Miami Herald*'s Vero Beach bureau chief, was frantically typing his report when a strong blast of wind ripped away his office door, causing him to conclude: "To hell with this, I'm getting out of here!"

In St. Lucie County, about 95 percent of the area's residents were without electricity after power lines were tossed into streets "like spaghetti." At Kennedy Space Center winds gusted to 70 mph on the space shuttle's landing strip, but the shuttle itself was safely stored in a nearby hangar. Large waves pounded the beaches and caused severe erosion in some locations. Fortunately, because the eye of the hurricane never moved far inland, David's strongest winds remained over the Atlantic as the storm slipped up the coast. The wind-related damages would have been far greater if the eye had cut across the state.

After David changed course prior to landfall and missed the Greater Miami area altogether, some people criticized the Hurricane Center and its director, Neil Frank, for suggesting that landfall might be in the Miami area. Many people had prepared for the storm or evacuated, only to watch it pass by harmlessly. Forecasters responded that this turn of events was simply a reminder that hurricanes can be fickle and that the stakes remain high. In an Associated Press report published after David had passed, Frank defended the Hurricane Center's position: "We're faced with a very delicate forecasting situation. . . . The threat was there and it was great enough to make it necessary to prepare. If we hadn't and our predictions had been more accurate, the consequences could have been disastrous. We're dealing with something that could be a killer." In Florida alone, some 300,000 residents fled to escape the storm, about 78,000 of whom took refuge in emergency shelters in the coastal counties.

David was clearly a killer. Aside from the great loss of life in the Caribbean, five deaths in the United States were directly attributed to the storm, and at least another fourteen were indirectly caused by the hurricane. In Florida one surfer was drowned while attempting to ride David's dangerous swells, and two residents suffered fatal heart attacks while making storm preparations. One man was killed when his car overturned on a rain-swept portion of I-95, and another was electrocuted when his sailboat mast hit a power line as he towed the boat away from the Keys. An elderly Fort Lauderdale woman was struck by a van as she walked to a hurricane shelter carrying a bag of groceries. Two students who attempted to swim in the pounding surf drowned along the Georgia coast near Brunswick. Other deaths were caused by traffic accidents, heart attacks, tornadoes, and drowning in the Carolinas, Virginia, Maryland, Pennsylvania, New Jersey, and Massachusetts. The total cost of Hurricane David in the United States was estimated at about $320 million, about $80 million of which resulted from damages in Florida.

FREDERIC (SEPTEMBER 12, 1979)

Until Hurricane David's arrival on September 3, 1979, Cape Canaveral had been tied with Mobile, Alabama, for having gone the longest amount of time without being hit by a hurricane of any U.S. coastal location south of Cape Hatteras, North Carolina—fifty-three years. No one could have guessed that Mobile's luck was also about to change.

While David was churning up the Florida east coast on Labor Day, its "twin brother" Frederic was adding insult to injury in Puerto Rico and the eastern Caribbean. Although not the killer storm David had been, Frederic followed a track very similar to that of its earlier sibling and poured additional rains over many of the islands that had been pummeled the week before. Few serious consequences resulted, although twenty-four inches of rain fell on St. Croix, and seven lives were lost when a fishing boat sank near St. Martin. As Frederic's heavy clouds hung over the Dominican Republic on September 5, relief efforts that had begun after David were hampered by torrential rains.

After dragging across the high mountains of Hispaniola, Frederic drifted westward toward Cuba as a weakened depression. It meandered along the Cuban shores, passed over the island twice, and then finally rebounded into the Gulf of Mexico as a reborn hurricane on September 10. Only a few days after the remnants of David had spun off toward the Arctic, Frederic built up steam in the central Gulf and moved into position for a possible strike on the Florida coast. At 9:30 P.M. on September 11, hurricane warnings were issued from Grand Isle, Louisiana, to Panama City, Florida. With David's antics fresh on residents' minds and lingering memories of Hurricane Camille in 1969, few coastal inhabitants ignored the threat. Evacuations along most of the upper Gulf coast moved smoothly and quickly. More than 500,000 people fled the shores, leaving many seaside communities virtual ghost towns as the storm approached.

Frederic intensified as it crossed the Gulf and slammed into the Mobile, Alabama–Pascagoula, Mississippi, area as a category 3 storm. Within one week, both Cape Canaveral and Mobile had experienced direct hits that ended their record quiet spells. This storm was anything but quiet, however. With a central pressure measured at 27.94 inches and sustained winds above 115 mph, Frederic was the most intense storm to strike the Mobile area directly in the twentieth century. As night fell on September 12, the storm pushed an enormous tide, up to twelve feet above normal, over and through the barrier islands that line the coast and into Mobile Bay. At the Dauphin Island bridge, the storm's top gusts of 145 mph were recorded. An eleven-foot surge of water, intensified by the power of frothy storm waves, washed out the causeway leading to the island. Most of the beachfront structures at Gulf Shores, Alabama, were demolished by the surge, and much of the island was wrecked. In addition to the mayhem caused by wind and tide, up to nine inches of rain fell in the Mobile area, and several tornadoes were reported.

After ripping across the Alabama coast, Frederic did what many powerful hurricanes do—it marched inland with diminished strength and dumped heavy rains over several states. Its course carried it along the Mississippi-Alabama border and through Tennessee, Kentucky, and the Northeast. Rainfall amounts were generally two to five inches all along its course, even after the storm completed its extratropical transformation. Winds remained gusty as well, with reports of gusts to 44 mph in Nashville, 46 mph in Latrobe, Pennsylvania, and 50 mph in Bridgeport, Connecticut.

Even though Frederic never passed directly over Florida, it had a significant impact on the state's westernmost counties. As the eye moved inland across Mobile Bay, portions of the powerful eastern half of the storm rocked the Florida coast from Pensacola to Mexico Beach. The Pensacola area suffered heavy losses from the roaring storm tide and damaging winds. Many residents had fled their low-lying homes in advance of the storm and returned the next day to a shocking scene of destruction. Beachfront homes at Grande Lagoon were torn apart by 95 mph winds and punishing waves that collapsed walls of brick and cinder block. At least 120 homes in this exclusive area were inundated by an eight-foot storm tide. Sailboats were tossed into yards and streets and remained high and dry, tilted at crazy angles, when the tides receded. Home furnishings and structural debris littered neighborhood streets the day after the storm. In one yard, a refrigerator was found nestled in the branches of a tree.

At Perdido Key similar destruction befell waterfront homes. Tides swept through a number of houses, carrying with them appliances, furnishings, clothing, and an assortment of personal belongings. One family searched their neighborhood the following day for a baby grand piano swept from their family room by the tide. In one location during the storm, observers watched the surge wash over a strip of land between the bay and a canal, forming a torrent seventy-five yards wide and eight feet deep. In all, officials estimated that at least 515 houses in the Pensacola area were damaged so badly they were uninhabitable.

After the storm, a *Tallahassee Democrat* reporter described Frederic's impact on the Geigel family home at Grande Lagoon:

> The rising tides had filled her house as high as the light switches. Pounding waves in the den apparently slammed furniture through the walls and hurtled pieces of it into the living room and garage. Water poured down walls and doors and scattered them throughout the neighborhood.
>
> The water had carried away a 19-foot sailboat, three sides of the garage and a long bookcase among other belongings of the Geigels. It left behind a slimy layer of silt and dirt on everything it had touched.
>
> "We had no idea it was going to be this bad," Mrs. Geigel said, her voice cracking as she stared at the jumbled mess that was her home.

Throughout Pensacola, damages were widespread. Two feet of sand covered most of the streets of Pensacola Beach, making driving difficult for those who ventured onto the island after the storm. Several mobile home parks were heavily damaged, including one where 150 homes were said to have been "shredded" by winds of nearly 100 mph. Pensacola-area marinas were also hit hard, first by the effects of wind and tide and then by looters. According to the *Tallahassee Democrat*, the Florida Highway Patrol reported that looters had "stolen them blind." Electricity was out all over the city, and trees and utility poles were downed on "virtually every street."

In a Pensacola motel, sixteen people, all members of the same family, were huddled together in one room as Frederic struck the coast. At the peak of the storm, strong winds lifted the motel's floor and tore away its roof, exposing the family to the worst of the wind and rain. Family members erupted into prayer as the roof sailed away, and fortunately their prayers were answered— except for minor cuts from flying glass, no one was injured. Other damages included a Winn-Dixie store that reportedly collapsed, a drive-in theater that

lost its screen, and numerous homes and small structures that lost their roofs.
In addition to strong winds, as many as twelve tornadoes were reported in the
area.

Shelters throughout Pensacola were filled to capacity the night of the storm.
Booker T. Washington High School was one of the most popular sites, where
over 500 residents crowded into the cafeteria to wait out the hurricane. Included in that group were 160 elderly patients from a nearby nursing home,
many of whom were forced to sleep sitting up in chairs in the school library
because of the lack of cots in the shelter. Many of these patients were unaware
of the dangerous storm outside, and some had resisted leaving the nursing
home; Pensacola police had been forced to deliver two patients to the shelter
in handcuffs.

Frederic's destructive effects lessened somewhat east of Pensacola, but high
tides still caused problems at Fort Walton Beach, Panama City Beach, and
Mexico Beach. Fishing piers were destroyed, small docks and fish houses were
washed away, and boats that weren't safely harbored were driven aground. All
along the Florida coast, it was estimated that 200,000 people evacuated their
homes.

Among the strange and tragic events of the storm was a report that a man
in Niceville had been arrested for tying his two young sons to a tree during
the hurricane. According to police records, the father was irritated with the
boys for disrupting his television viewing, so he tied them to an oak tree in
his yard with cargo strapping. There they endured wind gusts of up to 60 mph
and pelting rain, which left them sobbing hysterically. An Okaloosa County
sheriff's deputy discovered the boys, ages seven and ten, while on patrol dur-

President Jimmy Carter surveyed the destruction near Pensacola in the wake of Frederic. (Photo courtesy of the Pensacola Historical Society)

ing the storm. After releasing them from the tree, the officer arrested the father on the charge of aggravated child abuse.

Numerous injuries were reported along the Florida coast, including at least six in the Pensacola area. One of those was an ambulance driver who was hurt when his vehicle was blown off the road during the peak of the storm. Other injuries were caused primarily by flying glass; some of these injuries were apparently the result of tornadoes in the area. In one instance, employees of a Pensacola supermarket were belatedly taping a large window in the midst of the storm when gusting winds caused it to shatter, seriously lacerating one worker. Dozens of injuries were also reported across Alabama and Mississippi.

Thirteen deaths were attributed to Frederic in the United States, although only five were judged a direct result of the storm. Among those was a woman who drowned when eight-foot seas capsized her forty-foot sailboat in the

Intracoastal Waterway near Pensacola. Her companion, a forty-five-year-old Mobile physician, was rescued from the choppy seas by local volunteer fire fighters. Other deaths were caused by heart attacks, drownings, fallen trees, automobile accidents, and the explosion of a kerosene stove. Frederic's death toll was thought to be incredibly low considering the severity of the property destruction along the coast.

After the storm, President Jimmy Carter surveyed the damages left by Frederic by helicopter, along with Florida governor Bob Graham and other top officials. Carter quickly declared thirty counties in Florida, Alabama, and Mississippi major disaster areas, among them Escambia, Santa Rosa, Okaloosa, Walton, and Bay Counties in Florida. Just one week ago, Graham had asked for $95 million in federal aid to relieve the damages left by Hurricane David. It was apparent from the helicopter tour that Frederic's cost in Florida would exceed that amount. The overall price tag for Frederic in the United States was placed at $2.3 billion, eclipsing the $2.1 billion damage figure for Hurricane Agnes and making Frederic the most costly hurricane in U.S. history up to that time.

ELENA (AUGUST 31–SEPTEMBER 2, 1985)

Through the early 1980s, Florida residents, east and west, were spared the anguish of direct hurricane hits. The skies darkened somewhat in 1985, however, when two hurricanes and one particularly destructive tropical storm affected the state's upper west coast. It was a busy year all over, in fact. Out of the season's eleven named storms, a total of six hurricanes and two tropical storms struck the United States—the most to make landfall on American soil since 1916. Among the year's major storms was Hurricane Gloria, which left destruction along the eastern seaboard from North Carolina to Massachusetts and was dubbed "the most intensely-reported weather event in history." But Gloria wasn't the only storm to make coastal residents take to their heels. During the 1985 season, at one time or another, some portion of every coastal state from Texas to Maine was placed under a hurricane warning.

The first hurricane to threaten Florida during the year was Elena. It formed over warm Caribbean waters and became a tropical storm over central Cuba on August 28. As it tracked westward into the Gulf of Mexico the following day, it strengthened to hurricane force and became a source of concern to residents of several states. Hurricane warnings were issued along the Gulf coast from Morgan City, Louisiana, to Pensacola. The storm advanced steadily toward the north-central Gulf and then slowed when high-altitude steering currents collapsed. On August 30, a frontal trough moving in from the west caused Elena to veer toward the northeast. Hurricane warnings were dropped in Louisiana and extended along the Florida west coast as far south as Tarpon Springs.

While making its slow turn toward the northeast, Elena strengthened. As it approached the coast near Apalachicola, reconnaissance aircraft reported that sustained winds topped 100 mph and were climbing. As the storm drew closer, Florida governor Bob Graham called for massive evacuations of much of the Florida Gulf coast. Residents realized that their upcoming Labor Day weekend was about to be spoiled by the first hurricane to strike Florida in six years.

Evacuations all along the coast in Louisiana, Mississippi, Alabama, and Florida were of unprecedented proportions. During the storm's initial approach, low-lying portions of eight Florida counties from Escambia to Wakulla were evacuated, in addition to the coastal regions of Alabama, Mississippi, and Louisiana. Almost 1 million residents and vacationers were affected. Then, as the storm turned and the warnings were shifted toward the east, many more coastal dwellers were asked to leave. In the early-morning hours of September 1, Governor Graham met with Hurricane Center officials to review the latest forecast. Afterward, he ordered mandatory evacuations of about 573,000 people in ten additional Gulf coast counties. Coastal residents from Taylor County to Sarasota awoke to the news and packed their belongings. In Pinellas County alone, some 264,000 left their homes for the safety of inland retreats or local shelters. According to a 1985 report on Elena in *Weatherwise* by Donald E. Witten, the result was "perhaps the most extensive evacuation in the history of the United States."

Some refugees visited friends or relatives in inland sections of Florida and Georgia; others filled virtually every inland hotel room in the region. Many others sought refuge in countless churches, schools, armories, libraries, and other designated shelters. Among the evacuees were patients at nursing homes and hospitals, including those registered at Tampa General Hospital in the low-lying Davis Island area. National Guard troops were called in to assist in the patients' transport to hospitals in central Florida. Officials considered evacuating prisoners from the Pinellas County jail but later decided against it.

As the storm drew closer to Florida, it appeared that landfall was destined for the vicinity of Levy County. The eye of the storm moved to within fifty-five miles of Cedar Key, but it suddenly stalled under the influence of a high-pressure system off the northeast Florida coast. Just as the sparsely populated Cedar Key area was beginning to feel the brunt of the storm, Elena began to retreat. Fortunately for the residents of Cedar Key, the storm had stopped in its tracks short of landfall and spared their community great destruction. Still, high water inundated the town, washing out a primary bridge and leaving heaps of seaweed and shattered lumber in the streets. According to press reports, S.R. 24, the only passage to Cedar Key, was partially washed away, and efforts to repair it quickly with truckloads of gravel were abandoned. Alligators, snakes, rats, and other creatures were said to have been forced onto the roadbed by high waters. Levy County road superintendent J. G. Etheridge reported in the *Tallahassee Democrat* that "boys killed a rattler as big as a man's arm over there."

After putting on brakes just west of Cedar Key, Elena did an about-face and tracked back across the Gulf toward the northwest. Its last-minute turn came as a relief to coastal residents from Cedar Key to St. Petersburg. But the reversal was an unwelcome surprise to residents west of Panama City who were just returning to their homes after the first round of evacuations. Within hours, hurricane warnings shifted westward, and evacuations were reinstated. The warnings stretched back across the upper Gulf coast to Grand Isle, Louisiana. The *Tallahassee Democrat* later reported that Elena had forced "hundreds of thousands of residents from their homes for the second time in three days."

Meanwhile, the erratic storm was inflicting damage along the Florida coast. The *Democrat* reported that in Apalachicola "winds of up to 74 mph trashed the nearly deserted fishing town, tossing trees, signs, and garbage cans all over." Two houses there were crushed by falling hickory trees. High winds peeled open hangars and damaged planes at the nearby airport. Electrical service was shut down over a large portion of the Apalachicola area. Winds whipped away roofs and toppled trees as far inland as Tallahassee. Helicopter surveys later discovered that about twelve to fifteen homes were destroyed between St. Marks and the western edge of Apalachicola. Many more were damaged by tides and winds. High seas battered seawalls and docks along the entire Florida Gulf coast from Sarasota to Pensacola. Erosion was severe on many Florida beaches. Causeways and bridges were undermined and damaged. In Tampa Bay two barges broke free from their moorings, rode eight-foot waves across the bay, and slammed into the Gandy Bridge. High waves washed over its roadway. Tugboats later removed the barges, and the bridge suffered only minor damage.

Near Carrabelle one house built on pilings was ripped from its supports and dumped into the sea. This occurred during the peak of the storm, when winds in Franklin County were estimated at almost 125 mph. One corner of the house remained in place, however, and was spared the worst of the wind and waves. Press reports indicated that when the owners returned to investigate their home's damages, they found only the fractured room remaining. Among the exposed debris were a full set of encyclopedias still sitting on a bookshelf and four decorative mugs hanging on a wall.

In Tallahassee about fifty cars were damaged by fallen trees. One large tree became tangled in a live electrical wire and caught fire in the 500 block of Gadsden Street. The flames were quickly extinguished by Tallahassee fire fighters.

While Elena was poised off the coast, a string of tornadoes swept across central Florida. A twister in Leesburg destroyed thirty-two mobile homes, damaged another twenty-two, and injured at least seven people. Another tornado struck a mobile home park in Marion County and damaged thirty homes. Even NASA's launchpad at Cape Canaveral was struck by a twister, near where the space shuttle *Atlantis* was being prepared for its maiden flight. The shuttle wasn't harmed, but two vehicles parked nearby were damaged. Other tornadoes were reported in New Port Richey and in Sumter County.

Finally, on the morning of September 2, after teasing millions of coastal residents for days, Hurricane Elena made landfall on the Mississippi coast near Biloxi. On its way toward land, its eye passed just thirty-five miles off the coast of Pensacola, and winds of 95 mph pounded the local beaches. Water lines and other utilities were washed out on Santa Rosa Island, and the western end of the island was closed after the storm. Damages in Escambia County totaled almost $2 million, but the overall damages in the Pensacola area were less than those from Hurricane Frederic just a few years before.

Elena hammered the Mississippi and Alabama coasts with extremely high tides and damaging winds. Wind gusts of 135 mph were recorded at Dauphin Island, Alabama, and gusts of 120 mph were observed in Gulfport, Mississippi. In Pascagoula, Mississippi, the barometric pressure reportedly dropped so quickly as the eye approached that car windows were shattered. Tornadoes touched down in Gulfport, ripping away the roof of a local elementary school that was being used as an evacuation shelter. Tides ran eight feet above normal, and heavy damages were inflicted on dozens of oceanfront structures. The category 3 hurricane weakened quickly after striking the coast and drifted toward the northwest, dumping heavy rains over Louisiana and Arkansas on September 2.

Wade Guice, Gulfport's veteran civil defense director, commented in a summary report in *Weatherwise* that "Elena was the most aggravating storm I have ever been associated with in 20 years. She taunted us, she teased us, and then she hit us." The *Tallahassee Democrat* quoted a Gulfport shop owner who summed up many people's feelings about Elena: "I'm sorry it hit here, but I'm just glad it finally hit, period."

Although the storm never made landfall in Florida, it caused substantial destruction to personal property and public structures across the state. According to the Red Cross, well over 17,000 dwellings in Florida, Alabama, and Mississippi sustained damage during the storm. Total damages in the three states were $1.25 billion, making Elena the sixth most costly hurricane in U.S. history up to that time.

Three of the storm's four deaths and many of the twenty-five reported injuries occurred in Florida. A Daytona Beach man was killed when a large tree crashed onto his parked car, pinning him underneath and breaking his neck. Rescue crews worked with torches for more than an hour to free his body from the twisted wreckage. No one knew whether the tree was struck by lightning or leveled by a small tornado. Other fatalities were attributed to heart attacks and automobile accidents, although there was another unusual and gruesome death. A mate aboard the container ship *M. V. Ambassador* was crushed between two unsecured storage containers that shifted when the ship rolled in high seas near the hurricane's eye on August 29.

For many Florida residents, the 1985 Labor Day weekend was ruined by Hurricane Elena. More remarkable than the storm's destructive legacy was the large number of people involved in the agonizing ritual of coastal evacuation. Elena was both powerful and exceptionally unpredictable, and it caused more widespread alarm than any other storm of its time. Those who evacuated their homes twice were no doubt frustrated by the storm's unpredictable movements. Most endured the evacuations as best they could, playing cards in local shelters and watching preseason football on portable televisions. A commercial fisherman from Eastpoint best described the diminished novelty of hurricane evacuations in the *Democrat*: "When you're a kid, it's an adventure. But when you're an adult, it's a headache."

KATE (NOVEMBER 21, 1985)

After the passage of Hurricane Elena, Florida residents put thoughts of hurricanes behind them and enjoyed relatively good weather throughout the remainder of the 1985 summer. But the season wasn't over, as they would soon discover. Two more tropical events would occupy their attention that year; both were late-season storms on the northwest coast.

The first was Hurricane Juan. Although Juan never actually struck Florida as a hurricane, it left its mark on the state. After forming in the central Gulf in late October, it tracked inland over the low, marshy Delta region of southern Louisiana. Sustained winds at the time of landfall were only about 85 mph, and Juan's initial impact was not expected to be catastrophic. But the outlook changed over the next several days, as the minor hurricane drifted in circles over Louisiana, turned back into the Gulf late on October 30, and then tracked over extreme western Florida as a tropical storm on Halloween.

Copious amounts of rain fell across Louisiana, Mississippi, Alabama, and northwestern Florida as the storm shifted. Even though Juan dissipated over northern Alabama the following morning, its atmospheric influences triggered other events that kept the rains falling in neighboring states. A resulting low formed over the Carolinas on November 2 that went on to produce heavy rainfall, up to eighteen inches in some locations, along the eastern slopes of the Blue Ridge Mountains. The Weather Service had forecast possible floods for the region, but the damages that eventually occurred were far greater than anyone could have predicted.

In Florida winds near Pensacola gusted to nearly hurricane force as the storm approached, and seas ran about four to six feet above normal. Only minor damages were reported to small craft, docks, trees, and signs. Many seawalls, still in disrepair after Hurricane Elena, were further damaged. Power was disrupted over portions of several western counties, and some lines were downed as far east as Tallahassee. Rainfall was heavy, with some stations measuring as much as eight inches. Juan's presence produced tornadoes in ten Florida counties—Bay, Escambia, Hillsborough, Lee, Manatee, Nassau, Polk, Pasco, Santa Rosa, and Volusia. The twisters destroyed at least thirty homes but caused no reported injuries. Evacuations were not ordered in advance of Juan's arrival in Florida because tides were not extreme and officials feared that the heavy rains and potential twisters would make the evacuation itself hazardous.

Juan's overall impact on Florida was not severe, but elsewhere it was a deadly menace. Huge offshore oil rigs were sunk off Louisiana, swollen rivers inundated whole neighborhoods, and property damages accumulated from the Gulf of Mexico to Pennsylvania. In all, Juan claimed twelve lives directly, and a total of sixty-three deaths were reported more than a week later, many of which were the indirect result of the storm in flooded regions of the eastern states. Property losses were enormous—about $1.5 billion—surpassing the damages caused by Elena, which made Juan the most expensive hurricane of the year.

The season's last tropical cyclone was Kate, a rare landfalling November storm that was considered the first "shore-incident" hurricane in Florida in ten years. Not since Eloise in 1975 had a hurricane made a direct and intrusive strike on the state's coast. Although they caused considerable distress, Frederic, Elena, and Juan were near misses, and David's glancing blow was not considered a direct blast. Kate's arrival on the northwest coast was indeed a strike, unlike the two wild pitches thrown toward the region earlier in the 1985 season.

Kate formed over warm ocean waters north of the Virgin Islands on November 14 and reached hurricane strength two days later above Puerto Rico. By the time it moved onto Cuba's northern coast on the nineteenth, it was a formidable storm. Cuba's beaches were pounded by huge swells, and high winds rocked the countryside. Across the island nation, over 360,000 residents were forced to flee their homes. Winds well over 100 mph reportedly buffeted numerous cities, including Havana, where gusts were said to have collapsed dozens of buildings. At least ten deaths and fifty serious injuries were reported there after the storm.

While Kate was pounding the Cuban coast, its northern fringes were felt in Dade County and the Florida Keys. Winds were generally less than hurricane force but reportedly gusted to 80 mph in Miami, 78 mph at Conch Key, and

105 mph at a private weather station in Key West. Damages throughout the Keys were slight, mostly downed power lines, signs, and fences. Minor flooding occurred, and seawalls and piers suffered moderate damages. Three mobile homes were destroyed, including two gutted by fires caused by downed power lines. Perhaps the most notable destruction in the Keys was the collapse of the 300-foot WAIL-FM radio tower, which went down during a violent gust on Sugarloaf Key.

As the hurricane rolled off the Cuban coast and entered the southeastern Gulf of Mexico, it intensified steadily. Reconnaissance reports indicated that its barometric pressure was falling at a rate of 1 millibar per hour until it reached its peak intensity of 953 millibars (28.14 inches) on November 20. At about this time, a NOAA data buoy in the east-central Gulf recorded sustained winds of 108 mph, gusts of 135 mph, and sea heights of thirty-five feet. Hurricane warnings were issued for much of the upper Gulf coast, and residents anxiously awaited the arrival of another storm. Kate was now a category 3 and one of the most powerful hurricanes ever observed so late in the season; it was one of only four storms to reach category 3 status in the Atlantic basin during the month of November.

Kate's course across Cuba and into the eastern Gulf was almost identical to that of Hurricane Elena just eleven weeks before. This fact was of little comfort to coastal residents and forecasters who had struggled to anticipate Elena's erratic twists and turns. But as it turned out, Kate stayed on a somewhat more predictable path, completing a gradual curve toward the north and eventually the northeast. By the morning of November 21, residents along the Florida coast had a pretty good idea where the storm was going to land. Fortunately, as Kate moved into the northern Gulf, it encountered cooler sea-surface temperatures and other atmospheric conditions that caused it to weaken considerably and slow its forward speed. It finally made landfall around 5:00 P.M. on Crooked Island, east of Panama City near Mexico Beach.

Kate's most severe effects were felt well to the east of the storm center. The weather station in Panama City reported a maximum sustained wind of only 40 mph, with peak gusts of 78 mph. The station at Apalachicola was within the maximum wind field of the storm and reported sustained winds of 62 mph and gusts to 85 mph. In Tallahassee winds gusted to 87 mph and took down trees and power lines. According to a government report on the storm, "Sporadic heavy wind damage throughout Gadsden and Leon Counties provided evidence of widespread microbursts or downbursts of localized higher wind gusts which may have reached 100 mph."

After passing inland over northern Gulf County, the storm's eye quickly dissolved into the clouds. Rainfall was heavy in some locations, with up to six inches reported at several stations. Over the next twenty-four hours, Kate continued to dissipate in classic fashion and tracked toward the northeast across

southern Georgia and over coastal South Carolina. It finally returned to the Atlantic as a tropical storm on November 23.

Kate's impact on the Florida beachfront was severe. Normally, the highest winds and storm surge would have been expected to occur just to the east of where the eye crossed the coastline, near Mexico Beach. But for some reason, Kate's surge was more destructive well to the east of the center, from Port St. Joe to Apalachicola and beyond. Tides ranged from six to eight feet above normal across the barrier islands and bays that line the coast. U.S. 98 was undermined or washed out in numerous places where Gulf waters rose with pounding force. Many private seawalls and houses not elevated on pilings were no match for the onslaught and were destroyed. At Cape San Blas the exposed southern tip of the cape was reshaped by the storm. About 1,500 feet of sand was lost during Elena, and another 1,000 feet disappeared during Kate. Afterward, a survey of the destruction revealed that 31 major structures (excluding roads) were destroyed in coastal Gulf County, 156 were destroyed or heavily damaged in Franklin County, and 118 homes in Wakulla County became uninhabitable. The total assessment of the destruction in Florida included the loss of over 2,500 feet of bulkhead, almost 6 miles of paved roads, 179 homes, 36 seafood-processing plants, 3 fishing piers, 2 water tanks, 1 radio tower, and 1 poorly located swimming pool.

The county courthouse in Apalachicola suffered extensive damage, including flooded offices, shattered windows, and a wind-torn roof. The city's 100-year-old water tower collapsed, trailers were blown into a storefront, and a boat crashed into a seafood plant. In numerous incidents, high winds toppled large trees, pinning victims in their cars or their homes and sometimes killing them. In Apalachicola Police Chief Lawrence Faircloth was injured when a tree fell on his car. In Tallahassee three police officers were trapped in their cars as high winds dropped trees around them. Some communities were without power for up to eight days.

Kate was responsible for six deaths in the United States, two of which resulted from falling trees. A North Florida man was killed when a tree fell across the cab of his truck, and a twenty-two-year-old Thomasville, Georgia, man died when a large tree smashed his wrecker. An eighty-one-year-old Panama City woman suffered a heart attack and died after evacuating to a hotel in Chipley. The other deaths occurred in the Keys. One man was electrocuted when he stepped on a downed power line, and a man and woman drowned when their small boat capsized and sank. The estimated damage total for Kate in the United States was $300 million, much of which was counted in Florida.

The 1985 hurricane season ended with the passage of Kate just days before Thanksgiving. In Florida Labor Day and Halloween had been spoiled by Elena and Juan, and Kate had almost been the third holiday storm. In many cases, homes, docks, and seawalls had been ripped by the first storm, torn by the second, and then destroyed by Kate. Panhandle residents had endured one of the most active seasons in years. Although they were tired of the evacuations and weary of the cleanup, they were determined to rebuild.

FLOYD (OCTOBER 12, 1987)

Hurricane Floyd hardly deserves mention here since it was a weak category 1 storm that only held hurricane status for twelve hours and left relatively little damage in its wake. It tracked up the Florida Keys and passed below Miami on Columbus Day, October 12, 1987. Winds were generally measured at below hurricane force throughout the Keys, although gusts of 75 and 94 mph were reported. The storm dropped a scant one inch of rain at Key West, but some portions of the coast between Naples and Fort Pierce received between five and nine inches. Overall, though, Floyd was not a great nuisance to anyone. Power was out in a few areas, and numerous boats were misplaced. No deaths or injuries were reported, and damages totaled nearly $500,000. Most of the damages were to crops, utility lines, signs, and trees. One tornado touched down on Key Largo, causing almost $100,000 in damages.

Sightseers gathered in Key West during the storm to hear the wind howl and watch three-to-five-foot waves crash on normally placid South Beach. Others came in hopes of gathering an unusual harvest after the storm. According to a report in the *Miami Herald*, this group of visitors was seeking to assist in an unorthodox version of hurricane cleanup: "A few were hoping that the rough seas—estimated at 15 feet offshore—would send ashore some 'square grouper'—bales of marijuana jettisoned from smuggling boats when under chase by law enforcement. 'We came down to see the bales,' Paul Woode, a tourist from Santa Cruz, Calif., said. 'We have a save the bales campaign. Whatever we can get.'"

ANDREW (AUGUST 23–26, 1992)

"Damn you, Andrew" was crudely spray-painted across the lone cement block wall of a crumbled residence in Homestead, Florida, in late August 1992. The graffitilike message wasn't the mischief of a local gang but was instead painted by a suburban mother of two left homeless after the storm trashed her house and overturned her world. It was a trying time. South Dade County had been overrun by the mother of all hurricanes, a tempest that would be remembered by an entire generation as Florida's Great Storm. Surviving the violence of wind and water on the morning of August 24, 1992, was just the beginning. For thousands of storm victims, the real test came in the weeks that followed as they tried to piece together their lives from their new quarters in the temporary shade of a National Guard tent.

Andrew was certainly a powerhouse when it hit Florida, a category 5 with all the trimmings. With winds that may have gusted to 190 mph, it was less a meteorological freak than a chance encounter since storms of Andrew's magnitude don't often strike the United States. Records were broken when its winds and tides pummeled South Florida, a region quite familiar with the ways of vicious hurricanes. But most Dade residents weren't around for the big storm in 1926 and only knew a few unpleasant stories about the lake victims in 1928 or the Keys in 1935. To those hammered by Andrew, the other storms didn't matter because they saw with their own eyes a seemingly endless display of hurricane destruction that surpassed the limits of imagination. Only two other hurricanes, both category 5—the Labor Day storm of 1935 and Camille in 1969—had been more powerful than Andrew in the United States during the twentieth century. Andrew's power was painfully evidenced in the broken, stripped, and tattered landscape of South Dade County after the storm.

In many ways, the story of Hurricane Andrew is not merely about wind speeds, barometric pressures, and eyewalls. Incidents of miraculous survival and sorrowful loss were scattered through the blasted neighborhoods. Once the scope of the destruction was realized, the massive recovery that ensued was of epic proportions. And in the weeks and months that followed landfall, Andrew's story continued to unfold. Grim scenes of the destruction in Homestead hit the airwaves and helped pique national curiosity about hurricanes. Federal disaster response, construction fraud, insurance exposure, environ-

mental damage, and code enforcement all became front-burner issues in the wake of this thoroughly modern hurricane.

Like most great storms, Andrew was born of humble beginnings. It started, not surprisingly, as a strong tropical wave near the Cape Verde Islands, the same spawning grounds that have produced many of the Western Hemisphere's greatest cyclones. The 1992 hurricane season had been suspiciously quiet through mid-August, until finally the first named storm—Andrew—was identified over the open ocean on the seventeenth. Tropical Storm Andrew tracked toward the northwest for five days with little strengthening, passing well north of Puerto Rico on August 21. The following day, reconnaissance aircraft verified that the storm was "officially a hurricane," with winds of 75 mph Then some 800 miles east of Miami, it ventured over warm Bahamian waters and began a period of rapid intensification. On the morning of August 22, Andrew's winds were 75 mph, and its pressure was 29.35 inches. By eleven o'clock that night, winds were 110 mph and the pressure was 28.32 inches. By noon the next day, winds surpassed 155 mph and the pressure dropped to 27.46 inches; Andrew had exploded from a minimal hurricane to a category 5 monster in just thirty hours.

Later in the day, Andrew reached its peak intensity with 175 mph winds and a low pressure of 27.23 inches. Although forecasters initially estimated these winds at around 150 mph, expert re-analysis of Andrew's wind data in 2002 determined that the storm was indeed a category 5. At the time it reached this peak, it was moving nearly due west at about 15 mph on a course that would carry it straight through the Bahama Islands toward Florida. Warnings were broadcast and largely heeded before a twenty-three-foot storm surge pounded the Bahamian shores.

By this time, residents along the entire South Florida coast, and many people across the nation, had their eyes fixed on the steady stream of storm updates that rolled across their television screens. All of the usual prehurricane rituals were under way—grocery stores overflowed with customers; residents stockpiled food, batteries, and water; nursing home patients were relocated; long lines formed for gasoline; windows were boarded up and boats secured. All day on the twenty-third, the entire coastline from West Palm Beach to the Keys was buzzing with the anxious labors of preparation.

Forecasters at the Hurricane Center, not accustomed to having major hurricanes bear down on *them*, were nevertheless ready in their Coral Gables stronghold. They stockpiled food and water and tested the two emergency generators that had been installed for use when the power failed. The center had been in the area since 1943 but in 1979 had moved to its Coral Gables offices, which had never been tested by a hurricane prior to Andrew. The director, Bob Sheets, and his predecessor, Neil Frank, had worked successfully to have steel shutters installed on the sixth-story windows of the center's offices, overcoming a local ordinance that prohibited them. As Andrew drew closer, the forecasters' work continued around the clock, just as in any hurricane. But as the hours rolled by, they realized that Andrew was not "just any hurricane" and that they were situated at ground zero.

Across South Florida, and especially in Greater Miami, word was out that Andrew was coming—and with frightening strength. Many people packed their families in their cars along with bags, boxes, and pets and left for safer quarters. The total evacuation was estimated at around 700,000 in South Florida, although many of the evacuees moved to areas hit by the storm. On the afternoon of August 23, local highways were jammed with cars leaving the area. With each weather bulletin, the news worsened. The *Miami Herald* ran its now-famous banner headline that aptly described the storm's approach: "Bigger, Stronger, Closer." Across much of the target zone, some residents still wrestled with the question: "Should we stay or should we go?" Of those residents who did remain in their homes through the night, few got any sleep.

Around midnight, while Andrew was still more than 100 miles east of Miami, aircraft reconnaissance reports and satellite images confirmed that the storm's eye was experiencing cycles of eyewall replacement, a phenomenon sometimes seen in intense hurricanes. As the storm strengthened, its eye would contract, followed by the formation of a new outer eyewall that would eventually choke out the inner eye. As this replacement occurred, the storm weakened slightly, then strengthened again when the new eyewall began contracting. In Jack Williams's *Weatherwise* article, "Tracking Andrew from Ground Zero," Hurricane

Center director Sheets commented on these fluctuations in the hours before landfall: "The question is, will it be on an upswing when it hits us?"

As the hours passed after midnight, Andrew moved in on South Florida, and the radar images told the story. It was not a large hurricane; sustained winds of hurricane force extended only about thirty miles in all directions around the eye. This was thought to be good news since this was only about half the size of Hurricane Hugo's area of sustained hurricane-force winds when it struck South Carolina in 1989. Also, forecasters observed that Andrew's rainbands generally lacked the heavy precipitation usually found in hurricanes. This meant that it was a relatively dry storm. But it was also known that Andrew was a very intense hurricane and that winds would be extreme in the vicinity of landfall. Although most Dade County residents had no concept of how destructive sustained winds of over 150 mph can be, the ardent pleas of television newscasters and the stern forecast from the Hurricane Center gave them much to fear.

Finally, about 4:30 A.M. on August 24, the west eyewall of the storm moved over Biscayne Bay on a track that would take it through Cutler Ridge, Homestead, and other portions of South Dade County. Maximum sustained winds were around 165 mph, with gusts that likely exceeded 190 mph. After blasting through marinas, shopping centers, acres of crops, and dozens of neighborhoods, Andrew's doughnut-shaped core rolled over the more sparsely populated mangrove swamps and hardwood hammocks of Everglades National Park. With a forward speed of 18 mph on a due west course, its cruise across the tip of the peninsula took less than three hours. Hurricanes generally lose strength once they make landfall, and Andrew was no exception, but it still managed to maintain category 3 status, with winds of 125 mph and a pressure of 27.91 inches, as it crossed the state.

By 8:00 A.M., Andrew had passed over Naples and was moving offshore, entering the eastern Gulf of Mexico with much of its former integrity. From there, it began to rebuild, sucking energy from the warmth of the Gulf and setting its sights on its next victim. After Andrew's quick predawn pounding of Florida, news of its astonishing destruction and possible future course filled television screens everywhere. Those broadcasts, however, only reached those still fortunate enough to have electric power and a roof over their heads.

Andrew didn't linger along the Florida coast. It moved at a steady forward speed toward the west-northwest into the north-central Gulf. Less than twenty-four hours after leaving Florida, it was back up to category 4 intensity, with sustained winds of 140 mph. The storm continued to move closer to the lower reaches of Louisiana. Forecasters watched its course gradually turn toward the northwest, prompting hurricane warnings and extensive evacuations. It was estimated that 1.25 million people fled the parishes of southeastern and south-central Louisiana, and about 250,000 left Orange and Jefferson Counties in Texas. Shortly after noon on August 25, Andrew was about 150 miles south of New Orleans, poised to strike the Louisiana coast with winds still sustained at 140 mph. Forecasters at the Hurricane Center feared it might strike New Orleans, but thankfully its course carried it well to the west of the city. New Orleans sits below sea level and, as demonstrated after Hurricane Katrina in 2005, remains more vulnerable to hurricanes than any other U.S. city.

For a brief time, Andrew slowed and weakened somewhat, and then it eventually moved inland between New Iberia and Lafayette, Louisiana. Sustained winds near New Iberia were reported to be 115 mph, and gusts reached 160 mph. After making landfall, Andrew tracked toward the north and then northeast, losing energy rapidly and becoming a tropical storm within ten hours. Storm tides in Louisiana were at least eight feet above normal, and flooding engulfed the region from Lake Borgne westward through Vermilion Bay. Damages throughout the area were extensive, although television images of the destruction in the mostly rural parishes were not as dramatic as the video reports that emerged from Homestead.

Andrew and its remnants produced heavy rains that exceeded 10 inches in some portions of Louisiana. The greatest rainfall amount was 11.92 inches, recorded in Hammond. Along with the winds, tidal surge, and heavy rains that hit the region, Andrew also spawned numerous tornadoes. Twisters were blamed for two deaths and thirty-two injuries in the state. As Andrew dissipated, its once mighty central core dissolved into thunderstorms that drifted over a broad region, causing further problems. Tornadoes were suspected to have caused damages in several Mississippi counties, and two twisters in Alabama resulted in property damage. On August 27, two days after Andrew struck the Louisiana coast, two severe tornadoes that touched down in Georgia were blamed on the remnants of the storm.

Louisiana was left reeling in the aftermath of the hurricane, but Andrew's toll was far greater in Florida. Because of the relatively small diameter of the area with the most destructive winds, the heaviest damages in Dade County were concentrated along a thirty-mile-wide path that just missed Miami and zeroed in on the region around Cutler Ridge, Homestead, and Florida City. Although places as far north as Fort Lauderdale suffered wind damages, the area of extreme devastation began just south of Kendall Drive (Southwest Eighty-eighth Street) in Miami. Homestead, a blue-collar farming community of 26,000, was almost razed beyond recognition. Nearby Homestead Air Force Base, an integral part of the Homestead community, was "virtually destroyed," according to Governor Lawton Chiles, who arrived on the scene after the storm. In every direction as far as the eye could see, houses were ripped to pieces; many were roofless shells with barely a wall standing. Wind-shredded debris of every imaginable kind was scattered across streets and lawns. Few

trees were still standing, and those that were had lost all traces of foliage. Power lines and stoplights were nonexistent, ripped away from their supports by wind gusts that topped 175 mph. Entire neighborhoods were destroyed in tornadolike fashion, but the culprit was not a twister—it was a hurricane the likes of which most Floridians had never seen.

Andrew's winds, unquestionably among the angriest to ever blast across American soil, were strong enough to lift large trucks into the air, shred mobile homes, and hurl massive structural components for blocks. After the storm, planks and pieces of plywood were found impaling the trunks of large palms, providing astonishing evidence of their airborne velocities. Eighteen-foot-long steel and concrete tie beams with roofs still attached were carried more than 150 feet. Paint was peeled from walls, and street signs were sucked out of the ground and hurled through houses. Flying diesel fuel drums were a hazard, as were signs, awnings, decks, trash barrels, and fence posts that filled the skies. Mobile homes not only blew apart during the storm but disintegrated into aluminum shrapnel that became embedded in surrounding structures.

The best measurements of Andrew's winds near the time of landfall sug-

This aerial view of Florida City, taken with a wide-angle lens, shows the scope of devastation left by Andrew. (Photo courtesy of AP/Wide World Photos)

gested that maximum sustained winds were 145 mph, but ten years after the storm, Andrew was still gaining strength. In 2002, a team of hurricane researchers at NOAA's Hurricane Research Division completed a re-analysis of all available wind data and came to the conclusion that Andrew was significantly stronger than first imagined. The new data showed that maximum sustained winds were actually 165 mph at the time of landfall, bumping Andrew up to category 5 intensity. According to NOAA researcher Mark Powell, the storm's "strongest, possibly credible" gust was a 212 mph blast recorded by Randy Fairbank at his home near Perrine. Just moments after the gust, a wall of the home collapsed, preventing any further observations. The anemometer was also destroyed. After wind-tunnel testing of similar instruments, however, researchers adjusted this remarkable reading downward to 177 mph, still high enough to be the strongest known gust in the storm.

Forecasters knew Andrew was a very "deep" hurricane as it made landfall because its pressure was extremely low. Survivors reported that their ears popped as the storm passed, and many experienced severe sinus headaches along with their high anxiety. Some also claimed that the reduced air pressure had sucked the water from their toilets. Near Homestead, two neighbors watched their barometers carefully during the storm and noted nearly identical readings. Their homes, built in 1945 of coral and concrete, held steady in the winds and provided a safe haven for their observations. Later testing of their barometers verified their findings, which provided the official low pressure for the storm in Florida—922 millibars, or 27.23 inches. This reading established Andrew as the third most intense hurricane to strike the United States in the twentieth century, after the Labor Day storm of 1935 and Camille in 1969.

Although the damages in Homestead resembled the aftermath of a major midwestern twister, there was little evidence of tornadoes from Andrew in Florida. One theory, however, suggested that some areas had been hit by a suction vortex—a swirl of faster winds up to half a mile across embedded in the hurricane's eyewall. These violent offspring are thought to rotate within themselves inside the hurricane's destructive core. Ted Fujita, tornado expert and professor emeritus of the University of Chicago, theorized that these vortices are similar to eddies in a river. Intense updrafts are believed to stretch them upward, causing them to spin faster. The vortices apparently "spin-up" as the updrafts intensify, resulting in concentrated blasts of wind of up to 200 mph that leave 50- to 300-foot-wide swaths of ruin. Radar images of Andrew near the time of landfall showed a very strong convection cell on the north side of the eyewall. This strong cell swung around the eye as the hurricane moved inland and may have spawned superdestructive vortices over portions of the Naranja Lakes condominiums, one of the hardest-hit developments, and numerous other areas.

For the first time in almost thirty years, forecasters and top officials at the Hurricane Center were exposed to the consequences of a visiting hurricane. Coral Gables was a few miles north of Andrew's path, just out of reach of the nasty northern eyewall. Through the night, Director Sheets and his staff studied their instruments, analyzed radar and satellite data, and relayed information on the storm's progress to an anxious media. They performed their duties with intense dedication, putting aside their own concerns about their families and their homes. Sheets, for example, had been so busy at work that his wife had installed plywood panels on the windows of their home before the storm.

At 4:00 A.M., as the storm drew close to Biscayne Bay, the anemometer atop the IRE Financial Building that housed the Hurricane Center buzzed at a steady speed of 115 mph, with gusts that went much higher. By this time, the center's emergency generators had already kicked in after an exploding transformer a few blocks away had cut power to the building. According to Jack Williams's article in *Weatherwise*, at about this time the center's sixth-floor offices began to rattle: "The building was shaking in an unending earthquake.

Bound volumes of meteorological journals were dancing on the metal shelves in the library." The eerie swaying of the building almost made some staffers seasick. Around 4:45, just after the wind gauge clocked a gust of 150 mph, a loud thud shook the building. The center's massive, 2,000-pound radar dome had been heaved off its rooftop perch and tossed to the ground below. At 4:50 the rooftop anemometer failed under the strain of a 164 mph gust. Soon afterward, the microwave relay equipment used to send out live television and radio reports was also destroyed. Telephone and other communication lines remained intact, however, and radar images from Key West, Tampa, and West Palm Beach were still available to the forecasters. Throughout the remainder of the storm, they were able to maintain contact with news outlets, other meteorologists, and emergency-management officials.

After dawn arrived and the winds subsided, Sheets and the other forecasters broke from their duties long enough to peer outside. Their first sight was rather disturbing—a car had been tossed into the air and had landed on two other cars. This was merely a sample of things to come. Some staff members returned to their homes to assess damages; at least ten found their houses uninhabitable. The destruction was far greater than anything they could have imagined while hunkered down in their Coral Gables offices. The arduous task of cleanup would have to wait, however, because their work at the center was not complete. Andrew was still very much alive, and its dangerous course over the next few days would require their full attention. Millions of Gulf coast residents depended on their forecasts and warnings, so their work continued from offices that had no air-conditioning or running water. The center's famed storm shutters were opened to allow a warm breeze inside.

Across Dade County, countless stories of great personal tragedy and incredible survival unfolded in the wake of Andrew. Whether in sprawling trailer parks or neatly stacked luxury condominiums, people throughout the hurricane's strike zone waged their own personal battles with the storm. Many experienced similar ordeals—struggling to protect their families and themselves in the predawn hours as the eyewall moved over them. At the sound of the first loud crash, most retreated to the smallest rooms in their homes—a closet, a bathroom, a well-fortified bedroom—where they huddled together with family, friends, and pets. Their ears popped and their teeth ached when the pressure rapidly dropped. The deafening roar of the wind was described as louder than a freight train—it was "like having a F-15 fighter parked on top of your house with its engines at full throttle." In many instances, windows, doors, and even walls gave way, letting the vicious winds inside to rip away the roof and totally demolish the home. Miraculously, many survived this offensive by barricading themselves behind mattresses, dressers, and bathroom fixtures.

Stan Goldenberg and his family survived just such an experience. Goldenberg knew more about hurricanes than the average Floridian since he was employed as a meteorologist with NOAA's Hurricane Research Division in Miami when Andrew arrived. But nothing in his years of hurricane analysis had prepared him for the humbling experience of being a victim at ground zero. He described his ordeal in an interview after the storm:

I've flown into over a dozen hurricanes, through the eye of some strong ones and some weaker ones. People used to always ask "How can you fly into hurricanes, isn't that dangerous?" I'd always tell them I'd rather be in the air in a hurricane than on the ground—and after Andrew, I can definitely say I'd rather be in the air.

I live in South Dade at 169th Street near the Metro Zoo, right where the northern eyewall came through, with some of the strongest winds. Unfortunately, I did not make substantial preparations for the storm like people should. I also had one additional thing going, in that as the week approached, my wife Barbara was due with our fourth child, and the due date happened to be August 23.

As we watched this storm early in the week, it didn't look like it was going to threaten our area. Over the next few days, things changed, and by Saturday morning, it started to intensify very rapidly and aim at South Florida. Come Sunday morning, it really looked like this was going to be it—Dade or Broward County. Then, at nine o'clock Sunday morning, the day before the hurricane, Barbara went into labor. Everybody would ask, "Was that due to the low pressure from the storm?," but that's just a theory that has never been proven. Besides, we were not experiencing any effects from Andrew when the baby arrived. I had to drop everything, forget all my preparations, leave the boys with someone else, almost forget about the hurricane, and get over to the hospital where I remained most of that day. She delivered about 4:30 P.M.—twelve hours before the worst of the storm hit us. She and our new-born daughter, Pearl Esther, stayed there through the night.

Our house was not in an evacuation area at all—even when they started anticipating a category 5. Some people from our church brought some boards over and by working until ten or eleven that night, we covered every window, except for one small one. Boards were hammered on the outside with masonry nails, not the best way to do it, I knew at that time, but we had no other choice given the available time. Then we basically buckled down inside the house. I thought "How good it feels to be in a boarded house!" About eleven o'clock, I even went in and slept for a few hours.

Unfortunately, we had no interior, windowless room that we could pick as the hurricane-safe room. The only place we felt we could go was the hall-way, and we were prepared to go there at the appropriate time, and cover with blankets to protect ourselves from flying glass. The electricity stayed on until around 4:00 A.M. or so, and I continued to film with a video cam-era. About four, I started waking everybody up and we went into the liv-ing room. Then about four-thirty, everything revved up. Things went crazy when the eyewall hit. The first thing that happened was that the plywood ripped off the living room window. At that point, I commandeered every-body into the hallway, and shortly after that put the camera away and got serious. I knew the window could go soon. In the house with me were my three sons, Jonathan (6), Aaron (4), and Daniel (2), along with my sister-in-law Ann Bruce, her husband Roger, and their three sons, Joseph (12), Benjamin (7), and Reuben (6), and their small kitten—three adults and six children in all. There we were, in the hallway, with blankets ready and a mattress at the end. Then the window burst and the winds started whip-ping through the house. At that point, we still had a roof, but the open-ing to the attic started flopping. We started to hear other windows break—basically, the hurricane was coming inside the house. The sound just got louder, and louder, and louder.

We stayed under our covers, hugging the kids and covering them. We just couldn't imagine how much worse it could be. Then, Roger finally suggested we move to the garage and get in his car—he had faith in his station wagon, like a good armored truck. We proceeded to cross the house with these winds whipping through. Aaron, my four-year-old, slipped as we crossed the room and the winds started to slide him out the back of the house, until his cousin Joseph grabbed him and pulled him back to safety. When we got to the kitchen and Joseph opened the door to the garage, we realized the main

Andrew survivor Stan Goldenberg poses in front of his demolished home. (Photo courtesy of Stan Goldenberg)

garage door was already gone. We couldn't go any farther—we were just kind of stuck in the kitchen—we didn't want to move any more. We got down on the kitchen floor, put blankets on, Roger had a couch at the end, and we just stayed there. My dear sister-in-law had done great preparations, and she had filled all sorts of pots with water so we would have water after the storm. All these pots started to fall on us—very heavy pots of water pummeled us. I remember telling her "Thanks a lot for filling all of these things!"

In the meantime, things were so bad, we were praying. I don't say that lightly, I am a believer in the Lord and the Bible and I pray all the time. But we prayed much more than we do normally. We were crying out to God— screaming would be more the word, quoting scriptures. We were waiting and hoping for the calm of the eye to come. I kept screaming "Is it calming down yet?" Then, almost simultaneously, something very heavy fell on me, and Roger said that the roof was gone. I thought surely he was seeing things, because I could not fathom in my wildest imagination that our roof would go in this storm. But indeed, the entire roof had flown off! And when it did, the whole kitchen wall fell on us and was propped up on the other side by the counter. That wall had the stove in it, and the stove fell on my back. I was on my knees, crouched over the kids, with my foot extended, in excruciating pain. The wall that fell on us protected us from the rest of the storm, forming a kind of "hiding place." It wasn't comfortable, but we were protected.

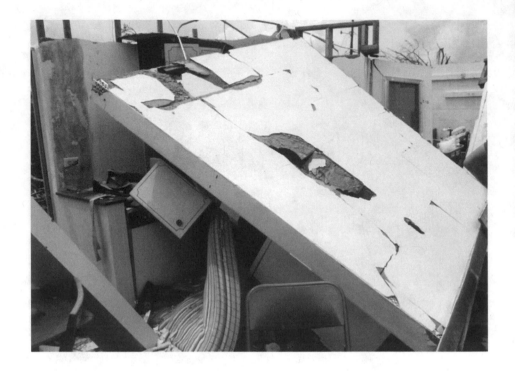

The "hiding place" where Goldenberg and his family were trapped after the destruction of their home. (Photo courtesy of Stan Goldenberg)

One of my sons had his head on the floor, and the water level was rising, both from the rain and from all the water dumped from these pots. I had the presence of mind to periodically check his head with my hand to make sure his nose was out of the water. Everybody was screaming. One of my nephews kept screaming "We're gonna die, I'm gonna die!" I was screaming too because my leg was in so much pain. We all continued to pray-scream. I felt like my leg was crushed, and I also felt like I was suffocating with the stove on my back. The water was rising, and I was under this wet comforter, in a very close space, with the force of the wind pressing everything down on us.

Finally, after what seemed like an eternity, the winds lessened a little bit, and I realized that we weren't going to get the full calm of the eye. Roger pulled us all out. The miracle was that we weren't cut to pieces—there was broken glass all over the floor and we were smashed there on our knees. One of my stupidest mistakes was that none of the kids had shoes on, I had flip-flops on—absolutely ignorant. But fortunately, we were ok, we all got out, and when the wind abated, they were able to move the wall a little bit. They cut the comforter open and got me out, and I was just grateful that I could stand up. The tops of my feet were numb and that lasted for three or four months.

We later went and got into Roger's car in the garage and put carpet over our heads, in case any windows shattered during the next part of the storm.

As we sat in that car and prayed and wondered what to do, our neighbor came from across the street, risking his life, wading through knee-deep water in the street, and asked us if we all wanted to come to his house. We all said YES! We spent the remaining part of the storm in the safety of our neighbor's house.

Although there were many remarkable feats of survival, there were also countless stories of tragic loss. Many lost all of their possessions; some lost family members or their own lives. Neighbors tried to convince sixty-seven-year-old Mary Cowan to leave her Naranja Lakes home before Andrew arrived, but she insisted on remaining to care for her five cats. Naranja Lakes, located between Cutler Ridge and Homestead, was one of the communities where visible "damage streaks" were caused by the storm's most violent gusts. Her home survived the initial impact of Andrew's winds but succumbed to gusts from the opposite direction that arrived with the backside of the eye. When her house collapsed, she was impaled through the chest by a two-by-four piece of wood. Amazingly, the timber missed her heart, and she lay on her bathroom floor for hours waiting for the storm to subside. After the winds retreated, neighbors found her barely alive in her demolished home. They discovered that the telephone in her kitchen still worked and called 911 but couldn't get through—the lines were either destroyed or jammed with calls in the Miami area. For hours they comforted her, hoping that somehow rescue teams would find them. Soon after she died, her phone rang; her daughter was calling from up north to see if she was alright.

In his 1993 article, "Andrew Aftermath," in *National Geographic*, Rick Gore chronicled some of the storm's other tragedies: "Twelve-year-old Naomi Browning also was killed—by a beam that fell on her head in her bedroom. Andrew Roberts, 25, was crushed by his collapsing home. So were Claude Owens, Harry Boyer, and Natividad Rohena. Robert Ramos, 49, was killed by flying debris after his house collapsed. Eighty-year-old Gladys Porter refused to leave her mobile home and was later found in its debris. Jesse James, 47, was crushed in his truck while seeking refuge. As far away as north Dade, Anthony Margiotta, 78, died after falling off a balcony whose railing had been blown away. He was blind."

In addition to the great losses suffered by humans, animals of all kinds were tormented by the storm. It was reported that hundreds of horses were killed or wounded by wind-thrown debris. Because emergency shelters would not take pets, thousands of cats and dogs were left behind in homes that were dismantled by the hurricane's winds. Some died when the houses collapsed, but after the storm, many more roamed the streets with assorted injuries, searching for their missing owners. Declawed cats cowered under piles of debris to avoid roving packs of dogs. After the storm, some of the more fortunate pets were taken to an emergency hospital that was set up in an empty field outside Homestead. There they were treated by veterinary doctors and students, given food and water, and held in portable kennels until they could be reunited with their owners.

At the Miami Metro Zoo, Andrew's winds flipped trailers, peeled away roofs, destroyed an aviary containing over eighty species of birds, and generally traumatized the animals. Chain link fences were torn apart by flying debris, freeing hundreds of birds, a tapir, a gibbon, a herd of antelope, and several 500-pound Galápagos tortoises. The tortoises were later returned with the aid of a forklift. Many of the larger animals—like the rhinoceroses and giraffes—stayed in their torn enclosures and were miraculously unharmed. Others, like lions, tigers, bears, and gorillas, survived the storm in the safety of their concrete and steel night houses.

Among the zoo's most fragile inhabitants were three koalas, who were terrorized when the roof of their air-conditioned enclosure was blown away. Koalas are very sensitive to heat and humidity, and their welfare became one of the zoo staff's primary concerns in the torrid days that followed Andrew. Fortunately, after a passionate radio appeal, a local pilot volunteered to come to the aid of the panting marsupials. After the National Guard cleared a debris-strewn runway at the Tamiami airport, he flew the koalas to a temporary home at Busch Gardens in Tampa.

Countless other volunteers came to the aid of zookeepers by working to clear downed trees, rescue missing animals, and restore what they could of the heavily damaged 290-acre park. The zoo's curatorial staff were grateful for the support, but they maintained a healthy perspective on their own problems. In a *People* magazine article following the storm, Assistant Curator Ron McGill talked of priorities: "While we all love animals, we need to take care of people first. I don't want anyone to bring us water if it takes away from a family that needs it."

The scale of the disaster in South Dade was enormous. The zone of destruction left by Andrew's winds was larger than the city of Chicago, and virtually every structure in the zone was damaged. It was estimated that over 350,000 people lived within this area, and during the peak of the storm, about 1.4 million people were without electricity. Almost 80,000 homes were heavily damaged or destroyed, and another 52,000 received some damages. Besides churning over the more populated region surrounding Homestead, Andrew ravaged many of South Florida's wondrous natural ecosystems. *National Geographic* described the defoliated islands of Biscayne National Park—Elliott, Adams, and Boca Chita Keys—as looking like they had been "drenched with Agent Orange." Thousands of acres of mangroves and hardwood hammocks in the Everglades were stripped of their leaves and severely damaged. Although the natural vegetation in these regions had been affected by many hurricanes through the years, after Andrew experts felt that some areas might take decades to return to their former natural state. Wildlife throughout the Everglades took a beating as well, but most species were believed to have survived the storm. The endangered Florida panther apparently fared well, since soon after the storm it was reported that all twenty-three cats equipped with radio collars had survived.

Andrew was unique in that the majority of the damages it caused in Florida resulted from its incredible winds. It was a relatively dry hurricane, although some areas near the storm center recorded up to seven inches of rain, and localized flooding due to rainfall was of minor consequence. But even though news reports focused primarily on the freakish winds, Andrew created a storm surge of record proportions. The surge crested at 16.9 feet, the highest storm tide ever recorded in southeastern Florida. This peak was measured at the edge of Biscayne Bay, very near the Burger King world headquarters. Like most structures along the bay, this sleek corporate office complex was hammered by both wind and tidal surge. Windows were shattered, office furnishings were destroyed, and portions of the building were simply blown or washed away. According to a report from the Federal Emergency Management Agency (FEMA), Andrew's massive surge pushed the waters of Biscayne Bay inland for several hundred yards in some areas.

Marinas, docks, and pleasure craft of all kinds were rocked by the hefty tide. In South Coral Gables it was widely reported that "powerboats were stacked like dominoes." Many large boats were carried onto highways, over lawns, and into mangrove thickets. One vessel, the forty-four-foot sloop *Pourquoi Pas*, was swept inland from a Homestead marina for more than a half mile, finally landing on its port side deep in the mangroves. It was one of an estimated 15,000 pleasure boats in Dade County damaged or destroyed by the storm. This figure represented about one-third of all pleasure boats registered in the county. The losses from wrecked vessels alone totaled around $500 million, which is more than the total dollar losses for many hurricanes.

The swirling tides brought other problems as well. South Florida's extensive artificial reefs, placed to boost fishing in the area, were pounded and shifted about, even though most sat in over sixty feet of water. The *Belzo Barge*, a 350-ton vessel that rested on the ocean floor in sixty-eight feet of water with more than 1,000 tons of concrete on its deck, was one of those affected. After Andrew, it was found 700 feet farther west with less than 100 tons of concrete still in place. In FEMA's *Interagency Hazard Mitigation Team Report for Hurricane Andrew*, the following account touched on some of the storm's other impacts: "Artificial reefs, which stretch 36 nautical miles from the Broward-Dade line to south of Homestead, were severely damaged, making diving hazardous and ruining habitat for various species of commercially important fish. Approximately 75% of the lobster traps in the area were demolished. Hurricane Andrew damaged thousands of acres of productive mangrove forest, destroyed forests and parks, encouraged invasion of natural areas by alien waters and caused tons of marine debris to be deposited along pristine shorelines. These damages affect the area's economy and quality of life, which are largely dependent on pristine beaches, clear waters and abundant natural resources."

In the hours before the hurricane blasted ashore, thousands of residents in South Dade County scrambled to avoid the storm. Many jammed the highways and headed north; others took refuge with friends and relatives across town. Forty-eight emergency shelters in the metropolitan area quickly filled to capacity. At nearby Baptist Hospital, a flood of phone calls poured in from people with heart problems, diabetics, and others begging to be admitted. There was no room for those who had no medical emergency, however, and most were directed to alternate locations. The hospital staff did allow over 200 expectant mothers to camp out in an auditorium so that any who went into labor during the storm would have access to medical attention.

Soon after Andrew's heavy clouds rolled away from Dade County, thousands of bewildered residents stumbled or crawled out of their homes and shelters and emerged into the streets. The immensity of the destruction was impossible to comprehend, even though they had listened intently the night before to Bob Sheets, television newscaster Brian Norcross, and others who had honestly told them what to expect. (Norcross had courageously stayed on the air nonstop for over twenty-four hours during the storm and undoubtedly saved many lives by offering timely instructions on how to "hunker down" during the hurricane's peak.) But now they could see for themselves, most of them for the first time in their lives, the aftermath of one of nature's most awesome forces.

Insult soon followed injury as hundreds of businesses and homes fell victim to looters in Andrew's wake. At eight o'clock on the morning of the storm, metropolitan police director Fred Taylor issued a warning that police would be out in force patrolling the affected area and that looters would be arrested and prosecuted. But chaos prevailed through much of the morning, and by eleven o'clock, almost fifty people had helped themselves to recently exposed merchandise at the Cutler Ridge Mall. They burst through the shattered storefronts of a Peaches music store and a Payless shoe store, taking with them all their arms could carry. As the looters were fleeing the scene, trucks filled with National Guard troops arrived, and one of the soldiers managed to tackle a man who had stolen a pair of shoes and a bag of socks. Soon thousands of business owners were forced to leave their damaged homes and stand guard over their businesses with shotguns. Most stayed around the clock, some turning away as many as fifty potential looters in the first day. Many unsuspecting homeowners were also hit hard by thieves. In Rick Gore's *National Geographic* article, "Andrew Aftermath," storm victim Mildred Gray expressed a familiar

sentiment as she sifted through the remains of her Homestead mobile home: "I think the looters were as bad as the storm. They took all my husband's clothes and left their dirty jerseys. Took our TV and VCR."

It didn't take long, though, for the National Guard to move into action. At around 1:00 P.M., Governor Lawton Chiles and National Guard adjutant general Ronald Harrison left a North Miami airport for a helicopter flyover of the strike zone. Although they were equipped with headsets that allowed them to communicate with each other, the two sat in profound silence as they toured South Dade and looked down at the wreckage below. The governor then wasted no time in directing the National Guard to fan out over the region and begin work. They stood sentry over countless banks, stores, and shopping centers whose structures had been peeled open by Andrew's winds. They also helped clear debris, distributed emergency medical supplies, provided much-needed water, enforced curfews, and directed traffic in major intersections. Some traffic signals were out because of a loss of electricity, but many had simply disappeared, further casualties of Andrew's ferocious winds.

At about 6:00 P.M., *Air Force 1* touched down at the Opa-Locka airport, and President George Bush and other top officials then motored south toward the hardest-hit areas. They stopped briefly to examine a fallen tree, then visited a shelter, and finally stopped at the wrecked and looted Cutler Ridge Mall for a brief press conference. The president could clearly see the gravity of the situation and stated that federal assistance would be part of the solution. Soon afterward, the tour ended, and they returned to their awaiting plane. Although the president's visit was brief, his compassion for the stricken people of Dade

Many structures near Homestead were completely leveled by Andrew's ferocious winds. (Photo courtesy of the Florida Army National Guard)

County was sincere. Unfortunately, though, the wheels of government turned slowly during the next few days, and the storm's many desperate victims received little attention.

Three days later, one of this disaster's heroes emerged. Kate Hale, the director of Dade County's Office of Emergency Management, had weathered the storm in a war room where she had maintained telephone contact with all of the key players in the recovery. She was there when President Bush held his press conference, and she had immediately asked the appropriate agencies in Tallahassee to "send us everything you've got." But three days after the storm, she was still waiting for the help that had been promised. Although the National Guard troops were greatly appreciated, the immensity of the destruction was overwhelming. In *The Florida Hurricane and Disaster of 1992*, Howard Kleinberg described the effect of Hale's famed press conference on August 27: "Hale is Dade County's emergency director. Today she held a press conference and stood tall. Before live radio mikes and video cameras, she challenged the federal government. 'Where in the hell is the cavalry?' she demanded to know in an emotional and angry appeal. She woke up a lot of people in Washington with that one. Before the day was over, Army troops by the thousands would be flying into Miami, Navy ships were on their way with tons of food supplies. Did Kate embarrass the feds? I think she did. Did Kate save some lives in South Dade? I'm sure she did!"

Soon afterward, relief efforts became better organized, and food, water, shelter, and medical supplies began to pour into the area by land, sea, and air. Military convoys clogged the highways, and helicopters delivered slingloads

The National Guard played a critical role in the aftermath of Andrew by providing victims with much-needed water, shelter, and first aid. (Photo courtesy of the Florida Army National Guard)

of supplies to distribution centers in the strike zone. The Red Cross, the Salvation Army, the Southern Baptist church, and numerous other groups set up mobile kitchens, distributed clothing, and administered first aid to those in need. But by far the greatest aid was provided by the military, which had not been challenged by any undertaking of this scale since Operation Desert Storm. One military commander, using a cliché from the Gulf War, referred to the effort in South Florida as "the mother of all relief operations."

Like refugees from a bizarre civil war, residents of South Dade lined up at various distribution points to pick up bottled water, food, and other basic necessities. Many of those in line had few remaining possessions beyond the clothes on their backs. Some nursed the wounds of their battle with Andrew—the cuts, scrapes, and bruises they received either during the storm or while sifting through the wreckage afterward. Against a backdrop of blasted buildings and military checkpoints, many likened the scene to war-torn Beirut.

Nearby, opportunistic entrepreneurs sold portable generators out of the backs of vans, raking in substantial profits. Roadways were jammed throughout South Dade as astonished residents who had evacuated the area attempted to find their old neighborhoods. This was not an easy task because few signs, trees, and recognizable landmarks remained standing. Also clogging the streets were hoards of tourists who came to photograph and videotape the wreckage. In some areas where downed trees blocked major thoroughfares, gracious residents redirected traffic through their own yards!

As the sun beat down on the debris-filled communities, tempers also flared among residents struggling to pull their lives together. At first, a great spirit of

THE MODERN ERA   279

cooperation prevailed, but as the days passed, the gravity of the ordeal began to sink in. Petty thefts continued, the number of domestic-violence incidents soared, and many—especially children—suffered severe emotional stress. The South Dade Safespace for battered women was destroyed in the storm, making it difficult for abused women to seek help. The lack of sleep, excessive heat, inability to bathe, and absence of conveniences of modern life contributed to the stress. Adding to the anxiety were summer thunderstorms that frightened many who associated their noisy approach with Andrew's roar. And with each rain shower, exposed furnishings and personal belongings were drenched once again. Fortunately some tried to make the best of the situation. On Sunday, August 30, many residents paused to count their blessings, including a group of Mennonites in Florida City who gathered for an open-air service at the site of their former church, which was now a pile of debris thanks to Andrew's winds.

Two weeks after the storm, 22,000 National Guard troops and other military forces were in the South Dade area, and the basic needs of most storm victims for food, water, and shelter were being met. "Tent City" had been erected at Harris Field in Homestead, housing refugees for weeks after the storm. The focus then became the massive cleanup and rebuilding effort that would eventually take years. But as the recovery was getting under way, a critique of the organized response to the disaster was offered by the press and by people on the street. FEMA, so roundly criticized for its poor performance after Hurricane Hugo struck South Carolina in 1989, was once again charged with bu-

Andrew's emotional toll on Dade County victims lasted far beyond the first few days of cleanup. (Photo courtesy of the Florida State Archives)

reaucratic sluggishness. The local and national press reported extensively on the disaster and also devoted considerable attention to FEMA's management efforts following Andrew and the slow federal response. In the election year of 1992, President Bush and opponent Bill Clinton were both armed with their own ideas for improvements. Like Hugo just a few years before, Hurricane Andrew focused the nation's attention on the government's response to natural disasters. In the case of Andrew, however, criticism of the relief effort helped bring about changes that have significantly improved FEMA's response to the worst of hurricanes. Still, great disasters like Katrina in 2005 have shown that good communication and coordination among government agencies should not be assumed.

The degree of destruction in the South Dade area was far greater than the destruction that had been experienced in other Florida hurricanes, and the winds were among the worst in the state's history. Soon after the storm passed and damage assessments were estimated, questions were raised about the extent of the destruction: Why hadn't South Florida's tough building codes prevented much of the loss? The answers were not simple, but shoddy building practices and inadequate inspections took much of the blame. The explosion of growth in recent years had brought countless new developers and contractors into the area, and county inspectors hadn't kept up with code enforcement. As a result, flimsy roofs, inferior craftsmanship, and poor designs caused some recently constructed structures to fail. In other cases, however, buildings that met the codes were still destroyed. After all, codes required that homes be built to withstand winds of 120 mph, well below those experi-

enced at the hurricane's core. Homeowners who had inadequately protected their property also bore some of the responsibility. Even those who diligently boarded up their doors and windows overlooked a key weakness in their defense against the wind—garage doors. Inadequately braced garage doors were in many cases peeled open, allowing winds to penetrate a home's interior and lift away the roof.

For homeowners who lost everything, the next ordeal was the all-important insurance settlement. Most homes that had walls still standing were adorned with spray-painted policy numbers that at first resembled a blight of urban vandalism. As the insurance companies paid up, new construction commenced, and homes and businesses were slowly put back on their foundations. For many, the reconstruction experience was said to have been "far worse than the storm itself." Countless homeowners struggled with "roofers from hell," unscrupulous contractors who charged exorbitant prices for shoddy work. In the meantime, the insurance companies took a beating, paying out record amounts and in some cases going broke. State Farm Insurance, for example, paid out close to $4 billion, an amount over seven times greater than the previous record for payments by a single insurance company. As a direct result of Andrew, eleven insurance companies failed, and another forty either pulled out of Florida or severely limited their underwriting of property in the state.

The damages racked up by Andrew are both staggering and elusive. Years after the storm, estimates of its total cost were still climbing, some surpassing $30 billion. This figure was far beyond the damage estimate for any other hurricane or any other single natural disaster in U.S. history up to that time. It wasn't until 2005 when Hurricane Katrina devastated the Louisiana and Mississippi coasts and flooded New Orleans that Andrew's economic impact was surpassed. The four hurricanes of 2004 topped Andrew in total damages, but Andrew remains Florida's single most expensive storm. Andrew's other vital statistics are equally astounding. The following is a tally of losses based on best estimates by NOAA, FEMA, and the *Miami Herald*:

43 deaths in Florida, 15 directly, 28 indirectly
over $30 billion in damages
700,000 people evacuated
175,000 people homeless
80,000 people housed in shelters
25,000 homes destroyed, 100,000 damaged
8,000 businesses damaged or destroyed
278 K–12 schools damaged, 23 heavily, 9 destroyed
2,300 signal lights destroyed
50,000 street signs destroyed
29,300 troops deployed
100,000 people forced to leave Dade County permanently
$70 million donated to the Red Cross for relief
35 million tons of debris, more than 30 years' worth
6,382 construction fraud complaints, 1,125 charges filed
9 deaths in Louisiana and the Bahamas
$1.5 billion in damages in Louisiana

Andrew's impact on Florida will continue to be measured for years to come. The lessons learned were many, and the experience of the disaster will remain with those who lived through it for the rest of their lives. Andrew had the positive outcome of bringing South Florida neighbors together. But those who searched for a silver lining to its darkened clouds had to look long and hard because its legacy for many remained grim. Businesses failed, marriages were destroyed, and the Dade County version of the American Dream took it on the chin. But with the passage of time, trees were replanted, homes were rebuilt, and lives were reassembled. Prosperity slowly worked its way back into the strike zone, nurturing a new generation of hurricane watchers.

ERIN (AUGUST 1–3, 1995)

Even before the 1995 hurricane season was under way, forecasters and veteran storm watchers looked to the coming months with heightened interest and apprehension. They knew that atmospheric indicators suggested the season would be a busy one. William Gray, professor of atmospheric sciences at Colo-

rado State University, issued his annual forecast for cyclonic activity, and the numbers were well above average. Gray, who had been predicting the number of tropical storms and hurricanes since 1984, was guessing that twelve named storms would swing through the Atlantic, Caribbean, and Gulf of Mexico during the year, including eight hurricanes. By August 1, he shifted his prediction upward to sixteen named storms, including nine hurricanes. Gray accurately predicted a busy season, but the actual numbers surpassed even his estimates. By the time the season was over, the Hurricane Center had identified nineteen tropical storms, eleven of which became hurricanes. This total makes 1995 the third most active Atlantic hurricane season of record; only 2005 (27) and 1933 (21) scored more storms. And the year's total of eleven hurricanes was third only to 1969, when twelve hurricanes formed, and 2005, when fifteen were recorded.

As would be expected considering the activity in the Atlantic, it was a record-breaking year in Florida as well. Two tropical storms and two hurricanes struck the state, the most since 1953, when four tropical storms and one hurricane made landfall. The first event was Hurricane Allison, which spawned in the western Caribbean on June 3, just days after the opening of the season. It ventured northward into the Gulf of Mexico and became a hurricane on the fourth, threatening the Florida Panhandle with 75 mph winds. More than 5,000 residents throughout the Panhandle and Big Bend area evacuated as the storm approached, with about 3,000 spending time in forty emergency shelters around the state. But fortunately Allison lost energy prior to its landfall near Apalachicola on June 5. It arrived as merely a tropical storm, with winds of 65–70 mph. No deaths were reported, and damages in Florida totaled about $1.7 million. Much of the dollar losses were from damages to a recently completed million-dollar roadway at Alligator Point.

The next storm to visit Florida was Hurricane Erin, which churned across the Bahamas on August 1 on a track toward the southeast coast. For a while, it appeared that the category 1 storm might enter South Florida, and an estimated 500,000 Andrew-weary residents packed their cars and fled. But Erin moved farther north and struck Vero Beach with maximum sustained winds of 85 mph. Fewer mid-coast residents heeded the evacuation order, complacent about the storm's modest winds. In Miami some residents were furious about the hurricane warnings and vowed not to be fooled by them again. Listeners on Dade County radio talk shows chided forecasters and television reporters for misreading the storm's track and accused them of hyping the potential threat to gain ratings. Officials at the Hurricane Center responded with what by now should have been common knowledge—hurricane forecasting is an inexact science, and residents should take every hurricane warning seriously.

Erin's strength continued to wane as it crossed the Florida Peninsula. Trailing rainbands dumped up to eight inches of rain in Brevard County, causing

extensive flooding around Melbourne and Palm Bay. Many neighborhoods
were swamped by floodwaters that reached their doorsills. Handmade signs
that read "No Wake, Please" were taped onto speed-limit signs, urging drivers to move slowly through flooded areas to avoid pushing waves into nearby
living rooms. Electricity was out to over 1 million people, forcing many to
leave their homes in search of malls and fast-food restaurants that still had
air-conditioning. Minor roof damage occurred across the state, and dozens of
cars and homes were struck by fallen trees.

As Erin left the coast and entered the Gulf, it held its course and threatened
Florida's northwestern counties. Although it was now only a tropical storm,
forecasts suggested that it would likely return to hurricane strength before
again striking land. The Hurricane Center placed the Panhandle coast under
a hurricane warning on the afternoon of August 2 but suggested that the
storm might only brush the coast on its way toward New Orleans. Many went
to bed that night unprepared for Erin's next move. It was estimated, for example, that only about 40 percent of Escambia County's residents evacuated,
and only about 600 were housed in shelters across the Panhandle. At four
o'clock the following morning, the Hurricane Center reported that Erin was
once again a hurricane and that its course was turning more toward the
northwest. By this time, it was too late for many to leave. Erin came ashore at
Pensacola about 11:30 A.M. with sustained winds of 85–100 mph.

As the storm cleared, residents emerged to survey the damages. Around

480,000 people lost power, and downed trees and power lines filled streets and yards. At Navarre Beach it was estimated that almost one-third of the structures sustained roof damage. Around Pensacola church steeples were toppled, countless windows were shattered, and signs and awnings were broken and crumpled. The city's gravity-fed water-supply system suffered when lines were ruptured by uprooted trees, causing water to boil out of the ground and mix with standing rainwater. Erosion was severe along the beachfront, where dunes crumbled and older homes were undermined.

In the storm's aftermath, truckloads of generators, food, clothing, water, and other necessities were brought into the region to aid victims. Some arrived from great distances, including one tractor trailer full of supplies from Oklahoma City, donated by Dallas Cowboy Emmitt Smith, a Pensacola native. Relief stations were established to serve those in need. Florida's westernmost counties were hardest hit, including Escambia, Santa Rosa, and Okaloosa. Florida governor Lawton Chiles requested a federal-emergency declaration from President Clinton and made preparations to seek disaster assistance.

Many along the coast felt they had been ambushed by the storm. Because of the storm's relatively modest impact on the east coast and its loss of strength as it crossed the peninsula, thousands of West Florida residents ignored the hurricane warnings, thinking that Erin would likely be a weak storm that would pass them by. Some called 911 in panic when the hurricane arrived the following morning, begging authorities to come to their rescue. Afterward, some criticized the Hurricane Center and local officials for not specifying the danger. But once again forecasters defended their actions. In an Associated Press report after the storm, Hurricane Center forecaster Ed Rappaport noted that "people are focusing too much on a particular track or point. It doesn't take much of an angle change to make a big difference."

Few lives were lost on land, but Erin did cause several fatalities at sea. The 240-foot cruise ship *Club Royale* left Palm Beach well before the hurricane arrived, and its captain and ten crew attempted to outrun the storm off Cape Canaveral. Unfortunately a shift toward the north brought the hurricane directly over the ship. The floating casino went down, taking its captain and two crew members with it. Eight others managed to escape in life rafts and were picked up later by the Coast Guard. A tugboat also sank off the Georgia coast, but all five of its crew were brought to safety. Near Cape San Blas a father and his nine-year-old daughter were lost and presumed dead after they ventured into the Gulf in a twelve-foot inflatable raft, just hours before Erin's approach began to churn the seas. Rescue efforts were hampered over the next two days by the storm's high winds and waves. Three other deaths were attributed to the hurricane in Florida. A seventy-five-year-old woman died of a heart attack after she was evacuated to a Tampa shelter, a surfer drowned in a rip current off Palm Beach County, and a Palm City man was crushed under a stack of plywood as he was boarding up his home. Erin delivered about $700 million in damages during its visit to Florida.

Three weeks later, as repairs from the storm were commencing, Florida braced for another weather event. Tropical Storm Jerry, the tenth of this remarkable season, developed from a depression off the Miami coast and drifted up the Florida mainland during the third week of August. Jerry was a weak storm whose winds were inconsequential, but it produced extremely heavy rains from South Florida through the Carolinas. Ironically, even though its storm center tracked some 240 miles to the north, Jerry gave Collier County its worst flooding in modern history. Rain gauges overflowed, with some areas receiving up to fifteen inches in sixteen hours. The heaviest concentration was around Naples, where officials reported that 90 percent of the city's streets were "nonfunctional." More "No Wake" signs were posted throughout area neighborhoods. According to the *Naples Daily News*, "Drivers taking on the flooded streets from Central Avenue in the city to Golden Gate Parkway a little further east bailed water out of their cars with coffee cups." Up to twenty inches of rain fell in northwestern South Carolina. Jerry was blamed for six deaths in the Carolinas and $21 million in U.S. damages.

OPAL (OCTOBER 4, 1995)

Two months after Allison and Erin hit Florida and just weeks after Luis and Marilyn sliced through the Leeward Islands, Hurricane Opal emerged out of the Gulf to become the season's most menacing storm. Although it had almost achieved category 5 status at one time, it struck the Florida Panhandle as a category 3. It came ashore on October 4 and was the strongest October hurricane to hit Florida since King in 1950. Because the 1995 season was the most active since the naming of hurricanes began, Opal was the first Atlantic cyclone to begin with the letter O.

Although it first became organized over the Yucatán Peninsula on September 30, Opal originated as a tropical wave that emerged from the west coast of Africa on September 11. The wave drifted steadily westward for days and was slow to develop once it reached the western Caribbean. Steering currents were weak, but eventually the budding storm moved into the Bay of Campeche and was given a name. On October 2, aircraft reports indicated that Opal had become a hurricane and was turning toward the north. The following day, it began to strengthen and accelerate toward the northeast, moving into the central Gulf of Mexico. By midday on the third, its winds were at category 2 strength, and hurricane watches were extended from Morgan City, Louisiana, to the mouth of the Suwannee River in Florida. What happened next was every forecaster's nightmare. As Opal bore down on the Florida Panhandle, it rapidly blossomed into a category 4 monster with maximum sustained winds of 150 mph.

As emergency planners well know, the timing of a hurricane's approach and subsequent landfall can make or break an evacuation plan. Opal was almost a worst-case scenario because it intensified very rapidly while coastal residents slept. Some had wisely abandoned their homes during the afternoon of October 3, even before the official evacuations were announced. Officials in the affected coastal counties issued evacuation orders at different times, some choosing to get things started during the evening, and others waiting until morning. Hurricane warnings were issued at 10:00 P.M., but Okaloosa County had already started evacuations at 6:00 P.M. Escambia and Santa Rosa Counties began evacuations at 10:00, and Walton County started at 11:00. Many residents were contacted by a computerized telephone notification system and advised or ordered to evacuate. Residents were asked to contact any Jewish neighbors since Yom Kippur had begun at sundown and many Jewish families were away at synagogues. In most cases, local officials scrambled to get their messages on the eleven o'clock news. Many residents, however, had either already gone to bed or were out and missed the news. And even those who were watching television might have disregarded the warnings because the threat of the storm was overshadowed by other late-breaking news—the sensational verdict in the O. J. Simpson murder trial. Amazingly, because of the media attention on the infamous verdict, no representatives from the news media were at the Hurricane Center the night Opal intensified—they had to be called! For whatever reason, most people waited until morning to pack their cars and leave.

These events created what could have been a recipe for disaster. In the hours before landfall, not only was Opal strengthening explosively, but its forward speed increased as well. At 4:00 P.M. on October 3, it was moving 12 mph, but by 10:00 P.M., it had sped up to 21 mph. This rapid acceleration effectively cut the evacuation time in half and set the stage for a mad scramble to leave the coast. Thousands of residents jammed the highways during the morning of the fourth, only hours ahead of the rapidly approaching storm. The highways couldn't handle the enormous number of vehicles, and many evacuees sat in their cars for hours in a bumper-to-bumper exodus that at times was motionless. They tuned in their radios to hear the frightening 8:00 A.M. report that Opal had grown to become a category 4 hurricane with 150 mph winds and was located just 210 miles south-southwest of Pensacola. Local officials were horrified since the storm was now moving faster than the traffic.

A sense of panic overcame many who found themselves trapped in automotive gridlock. Those who persevered later reported that it took them seven hours to travel 100 miles. Rains moved in on the fleeing motorists, and many were forced to return to their homes. The traffic was severely congested on parts of I-10, especially where construction narrowed the road to a single lane. Some evacuees sought local shelters, while others searched desperately for vacant hotel rooms. Competition for Tallahassee's 5,000 hotel and motel rooms was made even more fierce by another bout with hurricanes—fans had filled the city for Florida State University's football game against the University of Miami Hurricanes.

As Opal drew nearer, officials established numerous "refuges of last resort" near the highways but had difficulty convincing motorists to abandon their plans for escape. Some kept driving, while others pulled into rest stops along the highways and sought shelter in public restrooms. At one point, panicked motorists abandoned their cars on the bridge along a section of I-10 that crosses Pensacola Bay. They left their vehicles amid the traffic and ran to the nearest end of the bridge, creating chaos for police, who summoned tow trucks to clear the cars.

Local shelters quickly overfilled with evacuees. Several shelters in Escambia County reported food shortages, and one shelter designed for 500 took on more than 900. To make matters worse, the sewage systems in several shelters backed up. State officials later reported that at least 15,000 people took refuge in forty-two shelters. Finally, with the storm already striking land and its center just hours away, officials announced that the evacuation was "called off" and that those who had not yet found refuge should either return home or seek shelter immediately.

During the early-morning hours of October 4, the meteorologists following Opal's progress were alarmed by the storm's rapid deepening and faster pace. When it reached its peak with winds of 150 mph, its eye shrank to less than ten miles across, and its barometric pressure dropped to 916 millibars, or 27.05 inches. This reconnaissance report, taken at 4:45 A.M., indicated that Opal was more intense than Hurricane Andrew had ever been.

Fortunately, over the next several hours, Opal's small inner eyewall diminished, and an outer eyewall became more dominant. An infusion of cold, dry air into the storm's circulation, combined with cooler sea-surface temperatures in the northern Gulf, caused Opal to weaken before landfall. At 4:00 P.M., the hurricane moved inland over Navarre Beach, east of Pensacola Bay, as a marginal category 3. Ironically, this was almost exactly the same point of landfall as that of Hurricane Erin two months before. Opal's strongest winds were confined to a narrow region east of the storm center, about midway between Destin and Panama City. The highest official wind readings were taken at Hurlburt Field in Okaloosa County, where sustained winds of 81 mph and a peak gust of 144 mph were recorded. Incredibly, because the storm lost strength before it hit, most areas received winds that were well below category 3 strength. Many observers reported that the winds were "not as bad as Erin."

The tides were a different story. Opal was a large storm, and its tidal surge had a tremendous impact on a wide portion of the Panhandle coast, damaging or destroying nearly every structure on the immediate beaches from Pensacola Beach to Mexico Beach—a distance of about 120 miles. Some surge-related damages occurred as far east as Wakulla County, over 180 miles from Pensacola. By comparison, Hurricane Andrew's swath of destruction was only about thirty-five miles wide. Twenty-foot sand dunes, built up over a period of decades, were completely flattened along the hardest-hit beaches. The lower floors of some beachfront homes were filled with three to five feet of sand. A half-mile stretch of U.S. 98 near the Eglin Air Force Base Officer's Club was destroyed by the tide and actually became an inlet of Choctawhatchee Bay.

A poststorm high-water survey conducted by the U.S. Army Corps of Engineers and the U.S. Geological Survey revealed the true extent of Opal's destructive tide. Still-water-mark elevations measured inside buildings and tide-gauge maximums, which limit the effects of breaking waves, ranged from 5 to 14 feet above mean sea level. These measurements indicate Opal's storm-surge elevation. The height of water marks on the outside of buildings and debris lines on sand dunes near the Gulf shoreline ranged from 10 to 21.5 feet above sea level. These measurements are a record of the storm surge plus the wave heights. According to a summary report from the Hurricane Center, a tide gauge at the Panama City Beach Pier recorded a maximum surge of 8.3 feet, and a debris line at the end of the pier measured 18 feet. Battering waves on top of the storm surge added the difference of about 10 feet.

Heavy rains followed the storm inland, contributing to the flooding of coastal rivers and bays. The Blackwater River in Santa Rosa County crested fourteen feet above flood stage, flooding over 100 homes northeast of Milton. Moderate flooding was reported on the Escambia, Yellow, and Choctawhatchee Rivers, as well as Big Coldwater Creek. Even in Lee and Collier Counties in southwest Florida, feeder bands from Opal were responsible for rain-induced flooding that forced thousands from their homes. These were the same areas hit by record floods from Tropical Storm Jerry in August. Opal deposited from five to ten inches of rain over portions of the Florida Panhandle, Alabama, and Georgia.

As the storm tracked inland, the combination of gusting winds and heavy rains caused significant damage and several deaths far from the coast. Countless trees were downed all along the storm's course, knocking out power to nearly 2 million people in Florida, Alabama, Georgia, and the Carolinas. The Robert Trent Golf Course in Opelika, Alabama, lost over 7,000 trees in just a few hours. Acres of timberland were scoured as far away as North Carolina, where two people were killed by falling trees. Isolated tornadoes were another hazard of the storm. Two twisters were confirmed in Florida, including one that touched down in Crestview, killing a seventy-six-year-old woman in her

home and injuring two others. The tornado damaged several other homes, as well as a building and two portable classrooms at Crestview High School, which was in use at the time as a shelter for the elderly and infirm. Another tornado injured several people and demolished a number of structures as it ripped through portions of Maryland.

Tangled utility lines and deep sand covered Gulf Shore Drive on Holiday Isle after Opal. (Photo by David Lee Hartlage, courtesy of the Northwest Florida Daily News)

In Destin harbor Opal left cars submerged and boats high and dry. (Photo by Devon Ravine, courtesy of the Northwest Florida Daily News)

The most striking damages, however, occurred along the coast. The rolling surge crumbled piers, wrecked water and sewer systems, and buckled roadways. Almost 3,500 homes were totally destroyed, and another 5,300 suffered major damage. Seventeen Florida counties were declared disaster areas by President Clinton, the hardest hit being Escambia, Santa Rosa, Okaloosa, Walton, and Bay. Hundreds of fishing boats and pleasure craft were destroyed, and marinas were filled with wreckage. Among the losses were a radio tower at

Miramar Beach that toppled to the ground, the roof of the Museum of the Sea and Indian, the showroom and repair shop at Gary Smith Ford, and countless other devastated businesses and local landmarks. This portion of the Florida coast had not experienced such destruction since Hurricane Eloise struck the area twenty years before in September 1975.

Immediately after the hurricane passed, the usual poststorm events began to unfold. Assessment teams sprang into action. The Red Cross, Salvation Army, National Guard, and other relief agencies went to work, and residents scurried to return to their homes. Curfews were put into place, and coastal residents were prohibited from returning to areas where downed electric lines and broken highways prevented safe passage. Heated discussions erupted as some residents challenged police blockades preventing reentry onto the barrier beaches. Governor Chiles and FEMA director James Lee Witt led a convoy of choppers and small planes on a tour of the heavily damaged area surrounding Panama City Beach and Fort Walton Beach. Other top government officials on the tour included U.S. transportation secretary Federico Pena, Florida senators Connie Mack and Bob Graham, Florida representative Joe Scarborough, and Red Cross president Elizabeth Dole. After the tour, all of the officials pledged support, and the cleanup began. No one wanted to allow a repeat of the belated response that had occurred after Andrew.

In the days following the storm, utility crews repaired downed lines and restored services, and heavy-equipment operators cleared the streets of debris. One new aspect of the recovery effort was the use of "comfort stations," a concept developed in the wake of Hurricane Andrew to better serve the needs of storm victims. These rapid-response units manned by the Salvation Army and the National Guard provided shelter, food, first aid, toilets, and showers—the basic necessities—all under one tent. Twenty five comfort stations were in operation during Opal and were well received by those most affected by the hurricane. Relief supplies were donated by countless churches, charities, and individuals and at least eight major corporations. In all, the Salvation Army estimated that over 300,000 storm victims received aid.

As the damages were surveyed and the losses counted, it quickly became apparent that Opal's toll would be high. Most of the destruction was along the shore, where the hurricane tide had bashed some structures and undermined others. But as engineers and government officials studied the losses, a pattern soon emerged. Newer structures survived, and older ones didn't. Their recommendation to Governor Chiles was simple and direct: communities should enforce tough building standards to reduce losses in future storms. In an Associated Press report on the losses, Florida insurance commissioner Bill Nelson agreed: "Wherever you would see a structure of the vintage of the 1970s it was totally destroyed. Standing next to it would be another structure built to the new code, on the pilings, and it was undamaged." As FEMA representatives

put it, Opal's positive legacy was that it had given some Panhandle communities "the opportunity to rebuild to a higher code."

One dramatic exception to the many beachfront communities whose dwellings were hammered by Hurricane Opal was the smartly tucked-away community of Seaside. This resort village of some 280 homes near Panama City was well within the hurricane's strike zone but managed to survive relatively

unscathed. The reason was simple: its developer maintained careful planning, sound construction, and a healthy respect for Mother Nature. Unlike most nearby resort communities that were paved and built right down to the shore, the Victorian homes of Seaside developer Robert Davis were constructed behind the dunes, taking advantage of the barrier island's natural storm-buffering features. The dunes were severely eroded by Opal, but the homes they protected were untouched by the tides. Developers in Florida have historically shunned this approach in favor of down-by-the-water construction in order to obtain maximum profits. Typically, these developers have unleashed their lawyers whenever resistance slowed their progress. As a result, condominiums and homes that were normally lapped by high tides were wrecked by Opal. The wisdom of Davis's design was evident after the hurricane and serves as a lesson for all who plan, build, and live on barrier islands.

Remarkably, no deaths were associated with Opal's storm surge. Two people were killed in Florida—one person by a falling tree during the cleanup and the other by the tornado in Crestview. At least nineteen others were reported killed in the United States, most of whom were victims of falling trees, including eleven in Georgia, six in Alabama, and two in North Carolina. At least fifty people died in Guatemala and Mexico due to flash flooding during the hurricane's formative stages. It was also estimated that hundreds of residents of Florida, Georgia, and Alabama received minor injuries, ranging from lacerations from broken glass to venomous snakebites.

Like most major hurricanes of the modern era, Opal exacted a high cost in dollars. Final estimates of the losses were placed near $3 billion, making this hurricane the fourth most expensive in U.S. history up to that time. But measuring the economic impact of a storm like Opal is a very complex task. Aside from the insured losses, the uninsured losses, damages to public infrastructure, and other measurable items, major hurricanes that strike populated areas leave behind economic consequences that are more difficult to quantify. Some can only be measured over time, like the setbacks suffered by commercial fisheries and the diminished influx of seasonal tourist dollars. Hurricanes sometimes accelerate the need for expensive beach renourishment and can influence the distribution of public funding for erosion-control projects, highway construction, and bridge replacement. Some businesses struggle to recover after a storm, while others—like roofing contractors, for example—prosper from the repair efforts. Because most coastal areas depend heavily on tourism, livelihoods are jeopardized when hurricanes strike. Vacationers will likely pass over storm-battered resorts in favor of those untouched by recent hurricanes. Hurricane Opal, with its wide swath of destruction, only affected a small portion of Florida's extensive shoreline. But bad news travels fast, and Florida tourism officials were quick to respond on behalf of their economic priority. One week after Opal, they purchased a $38,000 ad in the weekend edition of *USA Today* that reminded hurricane-shy tourists, "We're still open."

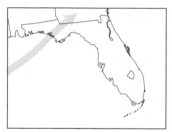

EARL (SEPTEMBER 3, 1998)

Florida was burdened with disasters in 1998 when an assortment of calamities occurred across the state that forced five presidential disaster declarations. First came winter flooding that affected several counties. Then in February a deadly tornado spun across central portions of the state, killing forty-two people. That summer, Florida experienced one of its worst wildfire outbreaks in history. Nearly 2,200 fires burned as many as a half-million acres across the state, destroying at least 342 homes and killing three people. Finally, in September government officials and disaster planners turned their attention to hurricanes.

Warmer than normal sea-surface temperatures in the Atlantic contributed to another above-average hurricane season in 1998. Fourteen storms were named, including two hurricanes that affected Florida—Earl in early September and Georges later in the month. But the 1998 season would be remembered as one of the deadliest in history largely because of Hurricane Mitch's devastating impact in Honduras and Nicaragua in late October. The category 5 hurricane caused more than 9,000 deaths, most resulting from flash flooding and mudslides.

Earl was not nearly so lethal. It formed from a strong tropical wave that emerged off the African coast on August 17. It passed through the Lesser Antilles on August 23 as a tropical wave, its formation partially held in check by the upper-level outflow of Hurricane Bonnie to the northeast. When it finally reached the Gulf of Mexico, it began to take shape as a tropical depression. It finally reached tropical storm strength and was named on August 31 while some 500 miles south of New Orleans.

The warm waters of the Gulf fed the storm, and it reached hurricane intensity on September 2. Even so, Earl was not well organized and did not exhibit classic hurricane symmetry. The strongest winds remained well to the east of the storm center. Hurricane watches and warnings were issued across much of the central Gulf coast, and the storm briefly attained category 2 status. Finally, at 1:00 A.M. on Thursday, September 3, Earl made landfall near Panama City. After quickly losing strength, it spun across Georgia, skirted the Carolina coast, and moved over Atlantic waters as an extratropical system.

Because the hurricane's greatest energy was well to the east of its center, the strongest winds and highest storm surge landed along Florida's Big Bend region. As is often the case with minimal hurricanes, there were no reports of sustained hurricane-force winds from any land stations. Around the time of landfall, amateur radio volunteers relayed unofficial observations to the National Hurricane Center, including a 91 mph gust measured on St. George Island. A C-MAN automated weather station at Cape San Blas recorded a gust of 70 mph. Storm surges of just under 8 feet were reported in Franklin, Wakulla, Jefferson, and Taylor Counties, and tides reached about 6.5 feet in Dixie County. Some news reports placed the surge at St. George Island at 12 feet. Rainfall amounts were generally 4 to 6 inches, though one reporting station at Panama City recorded a storm total of over 16 inches. A minimum central pressure of 29.09 inches was measured by aircraft just prior to landfall.

As with most hurricanes, Earl dished out a variety pack of destruction across the affected area. At Panama City Beach and Shell Point, rising water flooded homes, hotels, and restaurants. Homes on St. George Island suffered heavy damages, and many were occupied at the time. About 150 island residents ignored evacuation orders and barricaded themselves in their homes with food, water, and pets. As surging waters washed over the only bridge onto the island, they were temporarily trapped. Some of the homes were hit even before Earl's arrival when a tornado tore open the roofs of six houses. Portions of U.S. 98 and Alligator Point Road were washed away, docks were destroyed, trees were uprooted, 2,000 people moved into public shelters, and over 20,000 area residents lost power.

The St. George Island twister was not the only one reported along Earl's path. In Brevard County, 300 miles southeast, a tornado peeled open two restaurants in Port Canaveral, and a total of seventeen buildings in the area were damaged. In Citrus County, north of Tampa, a couple in a mobile home heard the roar of an approaching twister, grabbed their daughter, and jumped into a bathtub. Moments later, their roof was torn away, leaving the family frightened but uninjured.

Others were not as fortunate. As Earl's remnants tracked across Georgia and the Carolinas, several more tornadoes touched down. Mary Lou Seabrook, sixty-six, was huddled with her daughter on St. Helena Island, South Carolina, when a tornado shredded her mobile home. Seabrook was killed. Another twister lifted a South Carolina couple and their pickup truck off the ground and spun them around. In Georgia, another touched down and injured five people. Heavy rains fell across the region too, which Georgia authorities blamed for traffic accidents that killed four.

One of the greatest tragedies associated with Earl was the loss of two fishermen who drowned in the Gulf as the hurricane approached the coast. Paul Pence, sixty-eight, and Kalvin Fountain, thirty-four, died when Pence's fishing boats, *Can-Too* and *Me-Too*, capsized about 100 yards apart in twenty-foot waves in the hours just before the storm's arrival. Three of the vessels' crew were rescued by a Coast Guard helicopter several hours later, and a fourth crewman was found in a life raft just before dawn. The fishermen had ignored hurricane warnings and remained at sea because they believed the storm would track to the west. As Earl edged closer to Panama City Beach, they made a dash for port but were overcome by the hurricane's winds and waves.

According to reports from the National Hurricane Center and the *Tampa Tribune*, Earl damaged more than 1,300 homes and 70 businesses, resulting in almost $80 million in property damages.

One of the most unusual stories that emerged from this hurricane happened on the night of Earl's arrival at about 8:30 P.M., when "Oyster Radio" fell silent. According to the *Tampa Tribune*, WOYS news director Michael Allen had been busy throughout the evening providing critical updates to anxious listeners across the Big Bend area when suddenly the station went dead. A backup generator had failed, and emergency batteries lasted only minutes. But by 10:00 P.M., Allen's voice was back on the air. "We're operating on Ford power," he told his listeners. The station's owner and general manager had rigged a set of jumper cables to run their equipment off the battery of a van parked outside. Every fifteen minutes, they would crank up the van to recharge the battery. St. George Island resident Susan Hudson stopped by the station after the storm to thank Allen for his ingenuity. "You all kept us going," she said.

GEORGES (SEPTEMBER 25, 1998)

Most residents of Florida's Keys know that when it comes to hurricanes, there are high stakes associated with living along the narrow chain of islands. But they gladly exchange the risk for the sun-drenched life-style they enjoy. They know that every so often, they will face an approaching storm that will force them to either retreat to the mainland or, as many do, hunker down.

Hurricane Georges was such a storm. Following a classic Cape Verde pattern, it formed in mid-September from an African wave, reached hurricane strength in the open Atlantic, and pushed westward, where it eventually reached category 4 strength. Eventually, it made eight different landfalls and claimed over 600 lives.

Georges became the seventh named storm of the 1998 season on September 16 when it reached tropical storm strength some 600 miles west of the Cape Verde Islands. As it drifted westward over the next several days, it continued to intensify, becoming a hurricane on September 17 and then a category 4 hurricane on the nineteenth. Hurricane-hunter aircraft confirmed the intensification and determined that the storm reached its peak the following day with winds of 155 mph. At the time, it was only about 285 miles east of Guadeloupe in the Lesser Antilles.

Fortunately Georges weakened considerably before making its first landfalls on Antigua, St. Kitts, and Nevis on September 21. As it passed through the islands, maximum sustained winds were 115 mph. Later that evening, it moved inland over Puerto Rico, weakened slightly, and tracked into the Mona Passage on the twenty-second. While over water, it regained some strength and then made landfall in the Dominican Republic with estimated sustained surface winds of 120 mph. Over the course of the day, it weakened as it dragged its heavy clouds across the rugged mountain terrain of the Dominican Republic and Haiti, unleashing torrential rains that brought deadly flash floods and mudslides. As the storm left the island and moved into the Windward Passage on the morning of the twenty-third, it was barely of hurricane strength. Later that day, it made landfall again in Cuba, just east of Guantanamo Bay, and then skirted along the northern Cuban coast.

When Georges was finished with Cuba, it moved out over the warm waters of the Florida Straits and began to reintensify. On the morning of September 25, a band of deep convection developed east of the center, which grew throughout the day. By this time, thousands of Keys residents had heeded hurricane warnings and fled, but many remained in Key West, where they watched Georges make landfall with sustained winds of 100 mph. According to the National Hurricane Center, the minimal central pressure at landfall was 28.97 inches.

As Georges tracked across the Gulf, the active 1998 season tied an 1893 Atlantic basin record when four hurricanes occurred in the same day. Hurricanes Georges, Karl, Ivan, and Jeanne were all churning about on September 26. Then Hurricane Georges's westward journey continued for one last landfall. On the morning of the twenty-eighth, Georges struck the Mississippi coast near Biloxi as a category 2 storm. Soon afterward, it stalled out and

Over fifty Carribean flamingos took shelter in a men's room at Miami Metrozoo during the passage of Hurricane Georges in September 1998. (Photo by Max Trujillo, courtesy of Getty Images)

drifted over southern Mississippi and eventually turned eastward. For two more days, it spun itself out as a tropical depression as it tracked along the Florida-Georgia border. Finally, after seventeen days and eight landfalls, Hurricane Georges dissipated in the Atlantic off the Georgia coast.

Hurricane-hunter and NOAA aircraft flew twenty-three reconnaissance missions into the storm and recorded winds as high as 175 mph. The highest unofficial wind report from the Caribbean was a 176 mph gust measured on the island of Saba in the Netherlands Antilles. In Puerto Rico, gusts were measured to 130 mph, and in Cuba, the peak gust was 92 mph. By the time the storm struck the Keys, it was not the powerful storm it once had been. At Key West, a barometric low of 29.00 was recorded along with a peak gust of 87 mph. Apparently, a power failure at the Key West station kept it from measuring higher winds. In Marathon, a weather gauge at the Monroe County Emergency Operations Center reported a peak gust of 110 mph. And in Biloxi, where Georges made its final landfall, the barometer measured 28.47 inches and winds gusted to 117 mph.

Tides ranged from 12 feet in Mississippi to 10 feet in Puerto Rico to 5 feet along the Florida Panhandle. Storm surge was carefully measured in many locations. The still-water level found inside a structure is regarded as the storm-surge level, and the tide's highest debris line, usually measured on the outside of a structure, is created by the storm surge plus wave action. In the Keys, surveys completed after the storm showed still-water marks that measured 7.5 feet, whereas the debris lines reached 10.8 feet.

Georges produced significant and sometimes deadly rains on its trek across the globe. One station in the Lesser Antilles reported over twenty-eight inches, but the heaviest amounts probably fell across the Dominican Republic and Haiti. Although no weather station data was available from the island, aircraft reconnaissance indicated that more than thirty-nine inches of rain fell in twenty-four hours over portions of the island's upper elevations. These tremendous rains spelled disaster for hundreds of residents in mountain villages that were swept away by gusherlike floods and mudslides. In the Keys, rains were far less threatening. Key West reported 8.3 inches. But once the storm struck the Mississippi coast, stalled, and dissipated, heavy rains fell again across portions of Mississippi, Alabama, southern Georgia, and northern Florida. River flooding across the region forced evacuations in many communities. Elgin Air Force Base in Florida recorded 24.3 inches of rain, and 29.6 inches were reported in Bay Minette, Alabama. Mobile, Alabama, received 13 inches of rain, which brought its monthly total to 23 inches and broke a 100-year-old record. In addition to the wind, surge, and rain it delivered, Hurricane Georges spawned twenty-eight tornadoes, including two in Puerto Rico.

In the hurricane's wake, the heaviest toll occurred in the islands struck before the storm reached the United States. In Antigua, where Georges first made landfall, there was major structural damage across the island, severe coastal flooding, and two reported deaths. In St. Kitts and Nevis, three were killed and 3,000 were left homeless. It was estimated that 85 percent of all homes on the islands were damaged. In Puerto Rico, Georges was considered a major disaster. Over 33,000 homes were destroyed, and another 50,000 suffered heavy damages. Twelve deaths and numerous injuries were reported. The Arecibo Observatory radio telescope was knocked offline when high winds damaged the reflector plate of the 1,000-foot-wide dish. Cuba was hit hard as well, with devastated crops, thousands left homeless, and five reported deaths.

But by far the greatest tragedy occurred when Georges raked across Hispaniola. The storm dumped pounding rains across the Dominican Republic and Haiti, washing out bridges and highways and sweeping homes and villages down mountain slopes. The impact was greatest in the Dominican Republic, where over 185,000 lost their homes, at least 210 died, and more than 500 were reported missing. In Haiti, 165,000 were left homeless, at least 94 were killed, and another 60 were reported missing.

As Georges approached the United States, its stronger northern side spun over the lower Keys, where 1,500 homes were damaged and 173 were completely destroyed. Mobile homes were particularly hard-hit, but many other structures suffered significant damages as well. Among the homes destroyed were about seventy-five houseboats docked on Key West's "Houseboat Row." Other islands that were hit hard included Big Pine Key and Kudjoe Key, where a high storm surge swept into homes and businesses. On Lower Sugarloaf Key, roofs

Brian Goss, George Wallace, and Michael Mooney held on to each other as they battled 90 mph winds along Houseboat Row in Key West during Georges. The three had sought shelter behind a Key West hotel when Georges's winds and tides forced them to flee. (Photo by Dave Martin, courtesy of AP/Wide World Photos)

were sheared from homes and boats were tossed over highways. Utility poles were snapped and trees were blown down. One house burned when a generator caught fire. At Ramrod Key, waves drove a sixty-two-foot sailboat one mile inland into the backyard of a home with a missing roof. Up and down the Keys, Georges left debris rafts of splintered lumber, twisted aluminum, and strands of pink insulation.

Before the storm's arrival, Monroe County Emergency Management had issued a mandatory evacuation order for the Keys, and some 35,000 residents fled. But about 40 percent of Keys residents decided to stay, a fact that was disturbing to emergency planners—given that Georges had been forecast to strike the Keys as a major hurricane. In total, almost 900,000 residents had evacuated from South Florida in advance of the storm. Another 400,000 Tampa Bay residents were ordered to leave coastal areas and mobile homes when it appeared that Georges's track might sweep Florida's western coast. It was the biggest evacuation in Pinellas County since Hurricane Elena had forced 500,000 to leave in 1985. But as Georges passed the Keys and its track became more clear, evacuation orders around Tampa Bay were lifted and residents were asked to leave low-lying areas in Mississippi, Alabama, and the Florida Panhandle.

After Georges made its final landfall on the Mississippi coast, authorities surveyed the damages and were surprised by the extent of the destruction. In

Pascagoula, where floodwaters covered some homes and left four to five feet of water in others, Jackson County administrator George Touart told USA *Today*: "I've never seen anything like it in more than fifty years." The roof was torn off a gymnasium at Mississippi Gulf Coast Community College in Gautier, where over 400 people were seeking shelter from the storm. Another shelter was damaged in Pascagoula, apparently by a tornado. Across a broad region, National Guardsmen and local firefighters were busy rescuing trapped residents from flooded homes. In Moss Point, Mississippi, emergency workers rescued a man in a wheelchair whose home was flooded up to his lap. In downtown Mobile, Guardsmen waded through chest-deep water to carry children out of a flooded housing project. One man was washed out of a flooded building and climbed up a tree, where he held on for hours before finally swimming to another structure where he was found the next day. Along Florida's Panhandle, 200 people were rescued from flooded homes by National Guard troops and local firefighters.

In New Orleans, authorities feared a direct hit from Georges, but the city was spared. About 10,000 residents spent the night in the Louisiana Superdome, but the storm's winds and rains caused only minor damages to signs, power lines, and awnings. Bruning's, a 139-year-old restaurant, collapsed into Lake Pontchartrain, and several planes were flooded at Lakefront Airport. The biggest problem seemed to be the massive traffic jam that occurred after the storm as residents poured back into the city.

Tornadoes spawned by Georges added to the destruction. One touched down in the north-central Florida town of Live Oak, destroying six homes and sending five people to the emergency room. Twisters were also reported near Miami, north of Mobile, and in Georgia, where over forty workers in a manufacturing plant in Cuthbert went diving for cover. Another South Georgia tornado nearly sucked Richard Lynch right out of his pickup truck as he was driving through Mitchell County. Lynch told the *Atlanta Journal-Constitution*: "I lay across the front seat and locked my legs on the back side of the steering wheel and held onto the door. The wind was trying to pick the truck up. It sucked out the windshield and even took my windshield wipers."

According to the National Hurricane Center, Hurricane Georges was directly responsible for 602 deaths, making it one of the twenty deadliest Atlantic hurricanes of the twentieth century. The large loss of life was attributed to devastating flash floods that swept the Dominican Republic and Haiti. In the United States, five fatalities were connected with the storm. The only "direct" death occurred in Mobile when a forty-three-year-old woman was returning after checking on her parents near the Mississippi line. Her car apparently hydroplaned on a flooded highway, sending her into a ditch where she drowned. In Escambia County, Florida, three deaths were indirectly related to the storm. One woman died when her house went up in flames after a candle was left burning, and an elderly couple were killed when they were hit by a car as they drove through an intersection where stoplights were not working. In New Orleans, a man died in a house fire when candles burned his home. And an eighty-six-year-old woman died while waiting to be relocated after her nursing home was evacuated.

As deadly and destructive as Georges was, it was soon overshadowed by one of the deadliest and most powerful hurricanes on record. Hurricane Mitch formed in late October, attained category 5 status with sustained winds of 180 mph, and then stalled over Honduras, Nicaragua, and Guatemala, where it unleashed unimaginable rains that swept the region. Some rainfall reports included storm totals exceeding seventy-five inches! Massive mudslides and flash floods scoured the hillsides, washed away entire villages, and killed thousands. Mitch's actual death toll may never be known, but some estimates put the losses at more than 11,000. The U.S. Agency for International Development placed the official death toll at 9,086. Either of these figures ranks Mitch among the deadliest Atlantic hurricanes in history, along with the Great Hurricane of 1780 (22,000 deaths across the Caribbean), the Galveston hurricane of 1900 (8,000 deaths), and Hurricane Fifi in 1974 (8,000 deaths in Honduras).

But after Mitch's lethal sweep across Central America, the dying storm turned northward and headed for the warm waters of the Gulf of Mexico. It crossed the Yucatán Peninsula and reemerged as a tropical storm—on a course that would take it into the Florida Keys. On November 4 and 5, Mitch pounded Key West with tropical storm–force winds and heavy rains. Many homes ripped open by Hurricane Georges were further damaged by Mitch. At Fowey Rocks Lighthouse, just southeast of Miami, a wind gust of 73 mph was reported. Tornadoes triggered by the storm ripped through several communities in South Florida, including a mobile home park in Key Largo that was heavily damaged. In all, twisters spawned by Mitch injured sixty-five Floridians and destroyed 645 homes.

IRENE (OCTOBER 15–16, 1999)

The active Atlantic hurricane season trend that began in 1995 continued in 1999, with twelve named storms for the year. Several were quite potent; five reached category 4 strength (Bret, Cindy, Floyd, Gert, and Lenny)—the most to reach that intensity in a single season since 1886. In mid-September a monstrous Hurricane Floyd threatened Florida's east coast with 155 mph sustained winds and was for a time as powerful as Hurricane Andrew but three times its size. Floyd eventually weakened and turned northward, missing Florida altogether, but not before triggering what was believed to be the largest evacuation in U.S. history. Over 2 million residents from the Florida Keys to Norfolk, Virginia, boarded up and fled their homes. Floyd struck North Carolina as a category 2 storm, unleashing heavy rains that produced widespread river flooding across eastern North Carolina and central Virginia. Floyd still stands as North Carolina's greatest hurricane disaster, swamping the Tar Heel state with $6 billion in damages and leaving behind over fifty fatalities.

Although Hurricanes Dennis and Floyd both turned and missed Florida, Hurricane Irene did strike in mid-October. Irene was what meteorologists call a "classic October hurricane," fitting a pattern of development and track similar to numerous October hurricanes in the past, particularly those from the 1930s and 1940s. Born from a broad low-pressure area in the southwestern Caribbean, it was named on October 13 before striking western Cuba on the following day. It became a minimal hurricane on October 15 and then passed over Key West, making landfall near Flamingo in Everglades National Park. It tracked across Southeast Florida and exited the Atlantic coast near Jupiter. It then briefly threatened the Carolina coast but turned northeast and missed land. After passing by North Carolina's Outer Banks, the storm briefly reintensified over the Gulf Stream before tracking out into the North Atlantic.

Since Irene was a minimal hurricane when it struck the Keys and Florida mainland, high winds were not a tremendous threat. The highest official wind speeds were on Big Pine Key, where sustained winds of 79 mph and gusts to 102 mph were recorded. Miami International Airport recorded a gust of 70 mph. Irene is remembered not as a windstorm but as a prodigious rainmaker. Most locations recorded storm-total rainfall exceeding ten inches. Storm total amounts included 17.45 inches at Boynton Beach, 14.57 inches at Homestead, and 13.38 inches at Fort Lauderdale. These rains filled ditches, streets, and yards across the region, and the high water was slow to recede, lingering in many neighborhoods for more than a week. The National Weather Service described reports of "serious urban flooding" across most of Southeast Florida. State flood-control managers knew the storm was coming but did not have enough time to react. Normal wet-season weather in the preceding weeks had filled Lake Okeechobee and the Everglades system to levels above normal. Forecasters said Irene was a once-in-twenty-five-year rain event. National Weather Service meteorologist Jim Lushine told the *Miami Herald*: "This will be one for the record books."

The widespread flooding caused lots of problems. Highway intersections disappeared under the floods, cars floated in parking lots, and hundreds of residents from Key West to Palm Beach County were trapped in their homes and businesses, unable to go anywhere. The Miami River overflowed its banks, leaving cars on Southwest Second Avenue completely submerged. In addition to swamping hundreds of automobiles under water for days, floodwaters gushed into homes, shops, and factories. In Palm Beach County, fish from overflowing canals swam up and down the streets. Sewage overflowed on Dinner Key in Coconut Grove, along the Rickenbacker Causeway, and near

Jose Marti Park in Little Havana. Power was out for over a million people across the region, including forecasters at the National Hurricane Center, who switched to emergency generators when the lights flickered out. Power lines were downed in many neighborhoods and were often submerged, making travel treacherous.

Ironically, many South Florida residents said they were caught off-guard by Hurricane Irene, even though the storm had been accurately forecast and the media broadcast numerous warnings. So many people had been frightened by the warnings of Hurricane Floyd's ominous approach in the weeks before that they paid little attention to the weaker Irene when it came ashore. "They got so scared at Floyd," George Jacome told the *South Florida Sun-Sentinel*. "Since Floyd never actually hit us, people were taking this one as just a lot of rain." Jacome was assistant manager at Home Depot in Boynton Beach, where plywood had nearly sold out in advance of Floyd. With the approach of Irene, few bothered to board up their homes.

In Key West, where residents ignored a citywide curfew and paddled rafts down Duval Street, there was also a feeling of surprise. Residents of this resort town are sometimes known for their defiance, and most had not seen the storm as a great threat. Even mayor Jimmy Weekly, who was still dealing with recovery from Hurricane Georges from the year before, said he was surprised by Irene. "It's very unusual to have two in two years," he told the *South Florida Sun-Sentinel*. "Just last week I said to myself, "We made it through the season.""

Any time a hurricane strikes a heavily populated region, there is great potential for loss of life. Even a minimal hurricane like Irene can quickly turn into a deadly event. Eight deaths were indirectly blamed on the storm, including five deaths by electrocution and three drownings. Mary Ann Ruda, forty-eight, died in a brave attempt to save her eleven-year-old twin sons, Mike and Max, and their friend Douglas Hemphill, fourteen, when she saw them being electrocuted the night of the storm. They had been walking the family dog near their Broward County home when they apparently stepped into a puddle that concealed a downed power line. Aaron Crompton, thirteen, also was electrocuted when he tried to pick up a fallen live wire near his Cooper City home. In addition, three people drowned when they drove their cars into flooded canals, two in Broward County and one in Palm Beach County. Damage estimates for the storm in Florida totaled $800 million.

THE NEW MILLENNIUM,
2000–2006

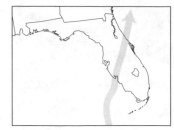

CHARLEY (AUGUST 13, 2004)

You might say that Friday, August 13, 2004, was an unlucky day—unlucky for Southwest Florida residents who braced for the arrival of Hurricane Charley, the strongest hurricane to strike the state since Andrew landed in 1992. It was bad for all of Florida since Charley's appearance on that Friday the thirteenth began what would become a record-breaking year for hurricanes in the Sunshine State. It was even a bad day on the Chinese coast, where Typhoon Rananim, the most powerful to strike China in seven years, roared ashore, killing hundreds. But in Florida, all attention was on Charley, the first major hurricane to smack the state's southwestern edge in over forty years.

Charley formed from a fast-moving tropical wave that crossed the Atlantic and moved southeast of the Dominican Republic on August 10. It continued westward across the Caribbean, reaching category 2 strength on the twelfth as it passed near Jamaica. It turned northwest and passed over western Cuba, then emerged in the southeastern Gulf of Mexico on the morning of the thirteenth. It passed by the Dry Tortugas by mid-morning on a northerly course that appeared to track toward Tampa. Sometime just after noon, a slight increase in southwesterly winds in the upper atmosphere nudged Charley to the right, sending it on a new course that would take it into Charlotte County. Mysteriously, a rapid intensification occurred just prior to landfall, as the storm's central pressure fell 0.65 inches in a matter of hours. Charley's small but powerful core made landfall at 3:45 P.M. at Cayo Costa and then again at Mangrove Point, just southwest of Punta Gorda. Satellite and reconnaissance reports indicated that the eye was only five miles in diameter at the time of landfall. By 5:30 P.M., the storm center was five miles west of Arcadia. At 9:15 it passed over Orlando International Airport, and before midnight Charley was passing off the coast near Daytona Beach, still maintaining hurricane strength. After a brief run up the Atlantic coast, Charley made landfall again near McClellanville, South Carolina, on August 14. It landed with sustained winds that were still hurricane force, and on the following day, it continued to buffet the Atlantic Seaboard with tropical storm–force winds and rains as far north as coastal New England.

When Charley exited western Cuba and approached Florida on August 13, forecasts called for the hurricane to spin up the coast to Tampa. Evacuations got under way, and almost 1.5 million people were asked to leave their homes. Even MacDill Air Force Base, the U.S. nerve center for the war in Iraq, was evacuated except for essential personnel. But the storm's early turn toward the northeast took it into Port Charlotte, and once again the Tampa metro area was spared. Many who fled Tampa traveled inland only to move into the path of the storm near Orlando.

It took just over seven hours for Charley to spin across Florida, leaving behind a long, relatively narrow wake of wind-blown wreckage. The National Hurricane Center's official report on the storm suggests that sustained winds at landfall may have been over 145 mph with a pressure of 27.79 inches, based on satellite and aerial reconnaissance. The lowest barometric pressure officially measured on land was 28.47 inches recorded at the Charlotte County Airport in Punta Gorda, where a peak gust of 112 mph was also measured before the anemometer was destroyed. Unofficial recordings from a private mobile weather unit in Punta Gorda measured a low pressure of 27.86 inches and a gust of 127 mph. All along the hurricane's path, new wind records were set as Charley carved its way across the peninsula. Wind gusts were measured to 104 mph in Arcadia and 109 mph in Wauchula, but in many locations, no peak readings were available because high winds damaged or destroyed wind instruments. Orlando International Airport, some 175 miles inland from Charley's landfall, recorded sustained hurricane-force winds of 79 mph and a new record peak gust of 105 mph—a testament to the storm's enduring intensity.

Because of Charley's fast pace and relatively small size, rainfall was not a serious threat to the affected region. Most stations reported less than 3 inches of rain, although over 5 inches were recorded in Sanford and over 6 in Gardner. The storm-surge effect, so often a deadly force in category 4 hurricanes, was modest along much of the southwest Florida coast. This was likely due, again, to the relatively small diameter of the hurricane and the fact that it had intensified so quickly that seas did not have time to build. Storm surges ranged from six to seven feet on Sanibel and Estero Islands. Tide gauges on the Caloosahatchee River near Fort Myers generally ran three to four feet above normal. Tornadoes were also a threat across much of Florida during Charley's passing. One touched down in South Daytona Beach in advance of the storm, producing a quarter-mile-long track that destroyed one home and heavily damaged several others. It also tore the roof off of a strip mall and started a petroleum fire when it ripped out two pumps at a gasoline station. One woman was injured. According to National Hurricane Center reports, at least five other weak tornadoes likely touched down in Charley's path, but assessing their impact was difficult because of the other wind damages caused by the hurricane.

Charley's overall impact in Florida was immediately compared to that of Hurricane Andrew. Although Charley's winds were not as powerful as the category 5 blasts that leveled portions of Dade County back in 1992, scenes of devastation in Port Charlotte and Punta Gorda resembled the earlier storm's aftermath in Homestead. And like Andrew, Charley had picked a busy spot—nearly 1 million people lived within thirty miles of the hurricane's landfall. Hardest hit and the subject of most video news reports were the mobile home parks and RV resorts so common across much of the area. In some parks, virtually every mobile home was torn to shreds. Those that were not ripped apart

Mobile home owner Al Wheeler was surrounded by the remains of his residence following Hurricane Charley in August 2004. Nearly every mobile home in the Riverside Drive area of Punta Gorda was destroyed by the hurricane. (From Direct Hit, photo by Jonathan Fredin, courtesy of the Charlotte Sun)

were often flipped on their sides or smashed by flying debris. Among those parks hardest hit were several in Charlotte County, including one on Carl Avenue in Punta Gorda where two residents were killed. The park contained several dozen trailers, but only a handful were standing after the storm. At Maple Leaf Estates off of Kings Highway near I-75, virtually all of the 1,100 trailers were destroyed or heavily damaged. At Port Charlotte Village, dazed residents wandered about after the storm, searching for clothes, furniture, and other belongings that had been sucked out of their homes by the storm's fierce winds.

Port Charlotte and Charlotte Harbor were where Charley's intense eyewall reached land, and the community of over 46,000 was pummeled by the storm. Thousands rode it out crammed in darkened closets, bathtubs, and hallways while ear-popping winds shrieked overhead. After it was over, many emerged to find their houses torn apart, no emergency services available, and mountains of debris in every street. Even Governor Jeb Bush, who visited shortly after Charley passed, was "stunned" by the devastation he saw. The heaviest damage was south of Toledo Blade Boulevard, down to Charlotte Harbor and the Peace River, extending northeastward past I-75. The Charlotte County Sheriff's Office, which served as the county's emergency-management headquarters, lost its roof during the storm, forcing emergency managers to scramble to meet immediate needs in the hot days that followed. Charlotte County sheriff Bill Cameron and twelve others took cover inside a closet, hoping the county's administration building would not completely lose its roof. Firefighters took shelter in the bathroom at Station 1 as it lost its roof, and an-

other group of firefighters and their families were huddled under mattresses at Station 12 when that building's roof went flying. It landed several hundred yards away across 1-75. All three hospitals in the county suffered damages, including Charlotte Regional Medical Center, where over 200 ambulances had to be called in from across South Florida to transfer the entire patient population to other locations. The facility's windows were blown out, part of the roof was missing, and there was no electricity or phone service. Residents had poured into the hospitals throughout the night with cuts, bruises, and broken bones, many sustained when the roofs of their homes collapsed. DeSoto Hospital treated 350 injured storm victims in the first forty-eight hours after the hurricane.

At the Charlotte County Airport, high winds tore apart small planes and sent others sailing as though they were flying. Wind gusts spun cars around, overturned four semitrucks, and peeled back the roof on an 80 by 100–foot building. Charlotte High School was also left in bad shape. The main building had roof and window damage, portable classrooms were destroyed, the roof was blown off the weight room, and several large light towers were toppled on the athletic fields. At a Port Charlotte nursing home, Charley shattered windows and ripped off portions of the roof. Although they were horrified by the ordeal, none of the 100-plus residents were injured. Home administrator Joyce Cuffe told the Associated Press about the experience: "The doors were being sucked open. A lot of us were holding the doors, trying to keep them shut, using ropes, anything we could to hold the doors shut. There was such a vacuum, our ears and heads were hurting."

In Punta Gorda, Charley's destruction was evident in every neighborhood.

Charley's category 4 winds mangled power lines in Punta Gorda. (From Direct Hit, *photo by Jonathan Fredin, courtesy of the* Charlotte Sun)

Don Patterson was one of many who tried to brave the storm in his mobile home. The Associated Press reported that Patterson "got beaned by a flying microwave oven as his home was demolished. His refrigerator fell on him, and he spent the rest of the storm sheltering behind a lawnmower." "Happy Friday the 13th" was his comment to reporters. Others in Punta Gorda saw their homes and businesses crumble in Charley's violent winds. WBBH television news reporter Amy Oshier was trapped inside the office building that housed her news bureau after its walls and windows blew in. All four walls of one local service station were leveled; the only thing left standing was a Pontiac on a hydraulic lift. Power lines were wrapped and tangled around trees, and most roadsides were littered with puffy pink shreds of insulation from disintegrated homes. According to the Red Cross, more than half of the 12,000 houses destroyed by Charley were in Charlotte County, and three-quarters of the 16,000 homes with major damage could be found there as well.

On Boca Grande, the narrow swath cut by the storm was evident. North of 29th Street, tree damage was relatively minor and isolated. South of that location, evidence of the storm was more apparent, all the way to the end of Gasparilla Island. Numerous homes had extensive roof damage, and thousands of trees were broken and tangled with power lines. In some areas, storm debris formed ten-foot-tall mounds that blocked the streets.

Charley's winds had hardly diminished by the time it tracked a few miles inland to Arcadia. Most of the town suffered some degree of structural damage as the storm passed just to the west. One fire tower was blown down, the town's water tower collapsed, and numerous homes and businesses suffered significant roof damage. Mobile home communities and RV parks were, again, the hardest hit, especially those just west of U.S. 17. The storm blew some houses off their foundations, shredded metal agricultural buildings, and snapped power poles down long stretches of highway. Several dead cows were seen wrapped in barbed wire along one roadside. Buildings collapsed along Main Street in the historic downtown, and a fruit-packing business lost a wall and its roof. About 1,400 people seeking refuge in the Turner Civic Center were shaken but not injured when Charley's winds tore the roof off the shelter. Many had evacuated to Arcadia, thinking it would be a safe haven from the storm. Witnesses told the Associated Press they saw the roof shiver and shake and lift away from the building, letting more and more light pour in and making "a zipping noise like a giant Ziploc bag." Officials scrambled to move the frightened evacuees underneath the facility's metal bleachers, where some said they were "packed like sardines."

Farther along the hurricane's course, winds caused similar damages in Wauchula, Lake Wales, and other inland areas. Overall, Charley's greatest toll was in Lee, Charlotte, De Soto, Hardee, Polk, Osceola, and Orange Counties.

Parts of Sarasota, Highlands, Seminole, and Volusia Counties were affected to a lesser degree. Damage assessments suggested that the storm's swath over the state was about forty miles across. Charley tore through the heart of the state's citrus industry, causing heavy damages to groves and facilities. Estimates put the losses at about 20 percent of the total year's harvest, or about $150 million. In Orlando, high winds forced the closure of Walt Disney World, Universal Orlando, and SeaWorld Orlando. The only previous time the parks had closed for a hurricane was in 1999 when Hurricane Floyd threatened the area. Vacationers in the city were told to stay in their rooms for the day. Tupperware's headquarters in south Orange County was heavily damaged, as were hundreds of homes, screen porches, awnings, and billboards.

Florida governor Jeb Bush, along with his brother, President George W. Bush, arrived in Punta Gorda just two days after Charley made landfall. Together they surveyed the scenes of destruction throughout the city. They talked with local officials and offered comfort to homeless victims of the hurricane. The Bushes pledged federal and state assistance to help the hardest-hit communities, and the people they encountered in Charlotte and De Soto Counties were appreciative of their visit. Russell Lee of Charlotte Harbor told the *Charlotte Sun* that he felt the president's concern was genuine. "He was very concerned, and it was a true concern," he said. Senator John Kerry, President Bush's opponent in the approaching 2004 election, also toured Punta Gorda and sur-

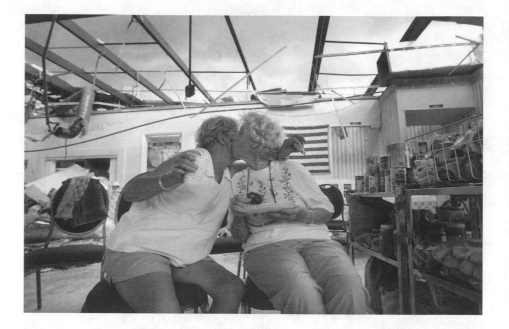

rounding areas to meet with people and see the damages for himself. Neither Kerry nor Bush gave any speeches, but instead they spent their time meeting and talking with people.

In the days that followed the hurricane, as residents began to try to recover, many were anxious about finding food, water, and shelter. Thousands in Charlotte County were homeless, many of them elderly. At night, streets were darkened because of power outages, and looting became a serious threat. In some neighborhoods, men slept with shotguns by their beds, posting signs to warn potential thieves. "You loot, we shoot" was spray-painted at the entrance to one neighborhood. Looters took computers from Fire Station 8 in Port Charlotte. Some victims reported that thieves weren't looking for TVs and stereos but were taking generators, fuel, food, and water—the basics needed for survival. Authorities arrested more than a dozen suspected looters, including some who were believed to have taken small boats into the county's canals to plunder homes.

Emergency relief of all kinds poured into the devastated communities where Charley had been. Governor Jeb Bush deployed National Guard troops to the region, and FEMA resources moved into place. Red Cross and Salvation Army units were on the scene quickly, setting up relief stations and serving hot meals to homeless refugees. Tractor-trailer loads of ice, food, water, and generators arrived in nearby distribution centers to provide residents with basic needs. Across Florida, churches of every denomination took up special collections and sent caravans of workers to help with the cleanup. FEMA estimated that about 77,000 families registered for disaster relief in the first week after

the storm. Debris removal was a major issue, as mountains of wreckage piled high on every street corner in Port Charlotte and Punta Gorda. The recovery was made more taxing by the lack of electricity in many communities through the hot August days and dark humid nights that followed the storm.

The unpredictable nature of hurricanes is well documented, and Hurricane Charley was a prime example of that unpredictability. Hurricanes like Charley that rapidly intensify and abruptly change direction just hours before landfall are a forecaster's worst nightmare. At 10:30 A.M. on August 13, the National Hurricane Center reported that Charley was a category 2 hurricane headed north toward Tampa. In an article in *TV Technology*, Claudia Kienzle described how a group of brave television meteorologists offered forecasts that differed from the Hurricane Center's official track:

> "There's just no doubt in my mind that our live weather reports saved lives. Our experience, especially in the coverage of Hurricane Charley, proved the case for why we still need powerful local affiliates in each market," said Steven Pontius, executive vice president and general manager of Waterman Broadcasting, the licensee of WBBH-NBC-2 in Ft. Myers. . . . "At 11 A.M., the NHC was sticking to their Tampa trajectory," said Pontius. "But our guys were certain that the storm now presented a danger to our market, so we immediately decided to go with it." In their live report, WBBH chief meteorologist Robert Van Winkle and WZVN meteorologist Jim Reif explained to viewers that while the NHC had the storm heading for Tampa, they believed that Charley (now a Category Four) had taken an obvious and distinct turn to the northeast, making it a serious threat to their area. "Our report gave

Roofers from Miami set up a bucket brigade–style line while removing damaged roof tiles from the Aztec Realty building in Port Charlotte after Charley. (From Direct Hit, *photo by Paul Schmidt, courtesy of the Charlotte Sun)*

our viewers a one and a half hour 'heads-up' in which they could evacuate or hunker down, before the storm knocked the power out," said Pontius.

At WFTV-TV, the ABC-9 affiliate in Orlando, Chief Meteorologist Tom Terry had a similar experience. . . . "At 11 A.M., we had to break into the ABC News Special Report where anchor Elizabeth Vargas was reporting that the NHC advisory had the storm headed for Tampa and that Tampa had been evacuated. We broke in and said, 'Folks, what you just heard was incorrect. Charley's coming to Orlando,'" said Terry. "We took a big risk here because the NHC continued to report the storm as headed to Tampa. In fact, our local emergency operations center was planning to dismiss everyone for the afternoon until they saw our report." . . . "It was a very trying time because we were going against the NHC advisory. A lot was at stake, but we stuck to it because we knew we were right," said Terry. By 2 P.M., the NHC had corrected its track to show Charley's new northeasterly direction, but WFTV viewers already had a three-hour advance warning to hunker down or evacuate.

As might be expected from a category 4 hurricane, Charley was responsible for scores of deaths. The National Hurricane Center's report of the storm suggested that only ten deaths in the United States were directly attributed to Charley, nine of which were in Florida. A couple were killed in Punta Gorda when their mobile home collapsed, two men died when they were struck by flying debris, and a North Fort Myers man was killed when he went outside during the storm to smoke a cigarette. A De Soto County man was killed when his toolshed collapsed on him. One man died after he fell from a tree. Others were killed in traffic accidents, drownings, electrocutions, and carbon monoxide poisonings. According to a Florida State Emergency Response Team report, Charley was directly or indirectly responsible for thirty-three deaths in Florida, including six each in Polk and Lee Counties; five in Charlotte County; three each in Orange and Collier Counties; two each in Sarasota, Hardee, and Volusia Counties; and one each in De Soto, Osceola, Highlands, and Brevard Counties.

In all, Charley damaged tens of thousands of buildings, destroyed more than 12,000, and cut electrical service for more than 2 million people. Twenty-five of Florida's sixty-seven counties were declared disaster areas. According to the Insurance Information Institute, insured losses from Charley totaled $7.4 billion, making it the second most costly hurricane in U.S. history at that time, with a total damage toll of $15 billion.

Many stories of heroism were told in the weeks after Hurricane Charley struck. People did wonderful and miraculous things to help their neighbors survive and cope after the ordeal. Many Charlotte County residents whose homes were livable took in families and senior citizens who had lost everything. Church groups, youth programs, and volunteers from more than two

dozen states came to toil in the hot Florida sun. Some children and grandchildren took weeks away from their work to travel to Punta Gorda, Port Charlotte, and other hard-hit communities to help their relatives recover from the disaster.

In its post-Charley publication *In the Eye of Charley,* the *Charlotte Sun* told the story of one inventive Port Charlotte survivor who was a hero of sorts to his neighbors. Before the storm's arrival, Cliff McMahon had gone door-to-door in his Moore Haven Court neighborhood warning his friends of the pending disaster. McMahon and his wife, Joanne, barricaded themselves in their own home with sofas and mattresses as their windows blew out upon the arrival of Charley's fierce eyewall. They thought their roof would go next. Twice during the ordeal, McMahon tried to write his name and social security number on his arm with a marker in case his body was later found and needed identification. When the storm passed, McMahon and his wife were thankful that their roof was still intact, and he scrambled out into the street to check on neighbors. They took in the family across the street whose home had partially collapsed.

With no electricity, McMahon knew that cleanup after the storm would be a miserable experience. He soon came up with a scheme to provide much-needed electrical power to his neighborhood. He cranked up the generator onboard his nearby boat, the *Elizabeth Fisher,* and connected cables to eight different homes on his street. Each homeowner was allowed to power a refrigerator, a fan, and one light in the evenings. For three days, he ran the generator and helped restore some sense of normalcy to his cul-de-sac. Then, when the generator broke down, McMahon drove fifty miles to Fort Myers to retrieve a part, came home and fixed his generator, and cranked the power back on again. On his way back home, he even stopped to change a flat tire for an elderly woman on I-75. By all accounts, McMahon deserved the smiles and thanks he received from his friends and neighbors in the aftermath of Hurricane Charley.

FRANCES (SEPTEMBER 5–6, 2004)

While victims of Hurricane Charley were still lining up for food and water in parts of Southwest Florida, another storm was brewing across the Atlantic. The potent 2004 season was just getting cranked up. A vigorous tropical wave that moved westward off the African coast on August 21 was carefully monitored by forecasters at the National Hurricane Center. They watched as it gathered steam, finally becoming a named tropical storm on the twenty-fourth. Within two more days, it was Hurricane Frances, spinning across the Atlantic and edging closer to the Caribbean. It reached a peak intensity of 145 mph late on August 31 as it veered north of the Leeward and Virgin Islands. It moved into Bahamian waters in early September, still maintaining category 4 strength. Along the way, it experienced a series of concentric eyewall-replacement cycles, a phenomenon often observed in powerful cyclones as their intensities fluctuate. Then high-altitude shearing winds affected Frances's progress, causing the storm to weaken considerably over the northwestern Bahamas on September 3. It was then a challenge to monitor its changes in intensity as it drifted slowly westward toward the Florida coast.

Frances finally came ashore as a category 2 over the southern end of Hutchinson Island early on September 5. It pushed slowly across the state on a west-northwest course, weakening along the way. By the time it exited Florida and moved out over the Gulf, it had diminished to tropical storm intensity. Early the next day, the storm center made landfall again near the mouth of the Aucilla River along Florida's Big Bend. Winds during its final landfall were less than hurricane strength. Remnants of the storm then drifted northward over the next few days into the Appalachian Mountains, where heavy rains totaling up to twenty inches spawned flash floods that caused significant damage in North Carolina. Frances then further degraded and became extratropical over West Virginia but still brought gale-force winds to parts of New York and southern New England.

Needless to say, Florida was not ready for another hurricane disaster. Massive evacuations, described as the largest in Florida's history, were launched on September 2 when Frances was still a category 4 some 375 miles southeast of West Palm Beach. Some news reports put the number of evacuees at 2.8 million. Hurricane warnings extended along much of the state's eastern coast, all the way from Florida City to Flagler Beach, north of Daytona Beach. The Kennedy Space Center at Cape Canaveral was completely evacuated for the first time because of the double threat of high winds and storm surge. The nuclear plant on Hutchinson Island was briefly shut down as a precaution, even though it was built to withstand winds of 195 mph. Posh oceanfront hotels in Miami Beach and Fort Lauderdale were emptied when almost 900,000 residents and guests in Miami-Dade, Broward, and Palm Beach Counties were asked to leave. Traffic jams clogged northbound I-95 and I-4, the primary artery connecting Daytona Beach, Orlando, and Tampa. Thousands sat in slow-moving bumper-to-bumper traffic as they tried to find refuge inland, away from the coast. Shelters were opened in forty Florida counties and at their peak housed over 108,000 people. By Friday, September 3, it was clear that for millions across the state, Frances had already ruined the upcoming Labor Day weekend.

It wasn't just the hurricane's intensity that got everyone's attention—it was the size of the storm. At several hundred miles across, Frances was at least twice the size Charley had been when it struck near Punta Gorda just three weeks before. Millions of Floridians watched anxiously for each update from the Hurricane Center, and fortunately the news was good for a change. They watched hour-by-hour as Frances weakened from category 4 to category 2 strength. This was a welcome development since television news images of Charley's wind-ravaged destruction were still fresh on their minds.

NOAA aircraft flying into the storm recorded a minimum low pressure reading of 27.61 inches on September 1. But by the time of landfall in Florida on the fifth, the hurricane's pressure had risen to 28.32 inches, as measured by a storm chaser on Hutchinson Island. A peak gust of 120 mph was measured on San Salvador in the Central Bahamas, but the highest winds in Florida were somewhat weaker. An Army Corps of Engineers station at Port Mayaca reported maximum sustained winds of 85 mph, and a peak gust of 108 mph was recorded at Fort Pierce on a portable instrument operated by the Florida Coastal Monitoring Program. Peak gusts in other areas near landfall were generally 85–95 mph.

Frances produced moderate storm surges along Florida's Atlantic and Gulf coasts. The National Weather Service office in Melbourne estimated that storm surges reached eight feet near Vero Beach and six feet at Cocoa Beach. Tides were as much as two feet above normal as far north as the Georgia coast. In the Gulf, a storm tide of six feet was estimated in Pinellas County, and tides in the Big Bend area were three to five feet above normal. In the Bahamas, where Frances was a more potent storm, significant storm surges swept several islands, flooding airports in Freeport and Marsh Harbor, Abaco.

Many sections of the eastern United States reported extraordinary rainfall amounts after the storm. The greatest measurement was a report of 18.07 inches in Linville Falls in the North Carolina mountains. Several locations in western Georgia and North Carolina recorded rainfall amounts exceeding ten inches. Rainfall exceeding ten inches also poured over much of the northern and central Florida Peninsula and southeastern Georgia. A storm total of 15.84 inches was reported in High Springs, Florida, and 15.81 inches were measured in Chassahowitzka, Florida. In addition to the flooding rains, gusting winds, and storm surges, Frances also produced 101 tornadoes, including 23 in Florida.

Bahamians were the first to suffer from Hurricane Frances. The northern island of Grand Bahama was especially hard-hit. Winds gusting to more than 120 mph ripped away roofs, toppled power poles, and mangled trees across the normally picturesque island. Two people were killed, and several more were injured. Winds tore at many structures, and others were flooded by ocean waters that ran waist-deep through living rooms. Resort hotels were not spared either. Large plate glass windows shattered in the lobby of the Crowne Plaza Resort in Freeport. More than a thousand residents and vacationers rode out the hurricane in public shelters. Most described the storm as far worse than Floyd during its visit in 1999.

As Frances came ashore across Florida's central east coast, preparations were in place and the entire state seemed to hunker down to ride it out. Knowing that it had weakened to category 2 intensity seemed to offer some comfort, but residents still braced for the worst. Once again, the Orlando theme parks were closed, Kennedy Space Center was shut down, and about seventeen hospitals along the east coast closed their doors. As Frances tracked inland across the densely populated eastern counties, gusting winds toppled power poles and twisted lines in countless communities. Florida Power and Light, the state's largest electric company, said power outages affected more than 5 million customers. Entire roadways were submerged, rooftops were blown off, and traffic signals swung dangerously close to the ground. Frances may have weakened before it hit, but it still packed a punch that seemed to leave destruction at every street corner. Just a few weeks after Hurricane Charley rocked the state, Frances gave even more Floridians a hurricane story to tell.

The damage was widespread. Like Charley, Frances was particularly brutal to manufactured housing. Several mobile home parks were razed, others had just a few torn trailers. Marinas and the boats moored in them took a beating from lofty storm tides and high winds. In some marinas, like the one in Belle Glade, scores of pleasure craft were tossed over their docks or onto each other. In Palm Beach County, a section of I-95 was closed when a massive sinkhole ate huge chunks out of the northbound lanes. Farther north, about two dozen large trees fell and blocked portions of the interstate over a fifty-mile stretch. Citrus crops were blasted (again), and flooding took the lives of over twenty cattle across the state.

With some areas along the coast recording over thirteen inches of rain, deep water poured into streets and homes. Danger lurked everywhere. Live power

lines were downed over fences and yards and in some places were submerged under several feet of water. In Martin County, over 600 evacuees at a school had to leave during the storm when the shelter's roof was torn off. On Hutchinson Island, near where Frances came ashore, the Royal Inn lost its entire roof and part of a wall collapsed. The storm's ocean surges caused heavy erosion at Boca Raton, where waves ate away three-fourths of the recently widened central beach. Palm Beach County's courthouse and administrative buildings had water damage in dozens of offices. Nearby, two people were killed when the roof of their home collapsed. In all, Frances was directly responsible for seven deaths and indirectly responsible for another forty-two. The fatalities included deaths from wind-thrown debris, collapsed structures, drownings, electrocutions, traffic accidents, heart attacks, carbon monoxide poisonings, and lightning. The total cost of the storm was placed at over $9 billion.

In Orlando, as if authorities didn't have enough to contend with, police were busy arresting criminals as the hurricane tracked to the south. Thieves used a stolen car to crash into a clothing store and steal over $10,000 worth of garments. Two other men were arrested when they tried to cut apart an ATM machine with a chain saw during the storm. At the Palm Beach County Jail,

The steeple of the First Baptist Church of Cocoa Beach blew off and pierced the roof near the church's choir loft during Frances's visit to central Florida. (Photo by Tom Burton, courtesy of the Orlando Sentinel)

power outages and minor flooding triggered a tense situation in the days following the hurricane. Fights broke out among the inmates as temperatures climbed. Authorities had to release about 200 curfew violators and other non-violent inmates to ease overcrowding and reduce tensions at the jail. As local governments tightened their security in the hurricane's aftermath, hundreds of curfew breakers were arrested. Looters were also captured in several counties. In Boca Raton, police arrested one man for impersonating a police officer. He was trying to slip out onto the beach to surf.

While Frances whipped trees and power lines outside a Red Cross shelter at Fox Trail Elementary School in Davie, the lights flickered on and off over the evacuees inside. After the storm, a classical pianist who happened to be staying there entertained the crowd to break up the monotony. Following that, a musician from New Jersey performed a free concert since his engagement to record a CD had been postponed. At a middle school in Weston, the entertainment took on an international flavor. A multinational troop of gymnasts and acrobats that had evacuated to the shelter began performing shows for the people staying there.

Along the eastern beaches, most residents had heeded warnings to evacuate and left for inland areas. A few stuck it out in their fortresses on the oceanfront. Professional golfer Greg Norman and his wife decided to stay in their Jupiter Island estate; they were among the few who remained on the island. On Cocoa Beach, Paul Jutras and his family stayed in their "hurricane house," a home built to a far higher standard than regular building codes. Jutras, a retired Defense Department engineer, built the house to withstand hurricanes, and at least during Frances, it measured up pretty well. There were no damages to report.

While Frances was still churning across the Gulf, Florida governor Jeb Bush and an entourage of twenty state and federal officials began their tour of the damaged areas. They flew into West Palm Beach on Sunday afternoon, met with local officials, and urged residents not to venture out into the streets. With Bush were FEMA director Michael Brown, Florida's chief financial officer Tom Gallagher, Major General Douglas Burnett of the Florida National Guard, and Craig Fugate, director of Florida's Division of Emergency Management. Bush assured local officials that even though many state and federal resources had been devoted to Charley, there were more than enough in reserve to send to the area. The governor told the *South Florida Sun-Sentinel*: "We have the resources. We have a great partner in FEMA."

Florida launched a massive relief effort soon after Frances moved northward toward the Carolinas. Within three days of the storm's arrival, over fifty distribution centers in sixteen counties had handed out millions of pounds of ice, almost 5 million gallons of water, and over half a million ready-to-eat meals. But the demand was overwhelming, and in some locations, rations ran out. Traffic was jammed along expressways, hampering the arrival of supplies. In fact, three FEMA supply trucks had Frances-related accidents in Martin County, slowing the delivery of goods. Armed National Guardsmen stood watch over long relief lines, where frustrations ran high and tempers often flared among overheated storm victims. The more aggressive people in line for food and water were threatened with arrest. Frustrations mounted for weeks in some communities when supplies of food, gasoline, and other essentials could not keep up with the staggering demand.

One disturbing report printed in the *South Florida Sun-Sentinel* revealed the downside of the flowing river of federal aid that usually follows hurricane disasters. According to the report filed in late November 2004, over $28 million in federal disaster relief was awarded in Miami-Dade County following Hurricane Frances, even though most damages in the area were limited to downed trees and power lines. Still, claims were paid for over 5,000 televisions and over 1,400 air conditioners. FEMA paid for lawn mowers, vacuum cleaners, cars, and even one man's funeral. The report generated an outcry from local readers. "Either this is significant negligence on behalf of FEMA or there is fraudulent or possibly criminal activity going on," U.S. Representative Robert Wexler of Boca Raton told the paper. "Either one is very disturbing."

After just witnessing the wreckage from Charley, President George W. Bush returned to Florida to survey the damages left by Frances—one of many such trips that would be necessary during the tumultuous 2004 hurricane season. In Fort Pierce, he handed out bags of ice to residents who waited in line for hours. He toured the coastline by helicopter and then flew down for a visit to the National Hurricane Center in Miami. It was the first time a president had ever visited the center, and Bush had nothing but praise for the men and women who put out the forecasts. He thanked director Max Mayfield and the Hurricane Center staff for their long hours in such busy times. Busy indeed. While there, the president got a glimpse of a dangerous Hurricane Ivan churning across the Caribbean toward Jamaica.

IVAN (SEPTEMBER 16, 2004)

Never before had anyone in Florida seen anything like it. After suffering through back-to-back hurricanes that crisscrossed most of the state and with floodwaters from Hurricane Frances still lingering in many areas, Florida residents and the entire Southeast were threatened by another killer storm emerging from the Caribbean in early September 2004. Before it was all over, Hurricane Ivan would span more than three weeks and track more than 6,000 miles; reach category 5 strength three times; kill dozens of people in South America, Central America, the Caribbean, and the United States; and land Florida its third hurricane strike in five weeks.

Ivan's journey through the Western Hemisphere was quite remarkable. Fueled by the warm sea-surface temperatures that prevailed throughout the 2004 season, Ivan was a classic Cape Verde hurricane that strengthened at very low latitudes, charted a familiar course, and then refused to die. The large tropical wave that initiated the hurricane emerged from the African coast on August 31. By September 2, a tropical depression was born thanks to favorable conditions for intensification across the Atlantic. Despite its relatively low latitude (only 9.7 degrees north), Ivan became a named tropical storm the following day and then a hurricane by September 5. Then the storm began a period of rapid intensification, the first of several such episodes that would later become its trademark. On September 6, Ivan became a category 3 hurricane while still at only about 12 degrees north latitude, making it the southernmost major hurricane ever observed in the Atlantic basin.

Ivan weakened soon afterward, only to restrengthen very quickly the following day. Aircraft reconnaissance reported that it was a strong category 3 when its center passed just six miles south of Grenada on September 7. Powerful winds on the storm's stronger northern side swept over the southern portion of the island, causing considerable structural damage. Soon afterward, the hurricane weakened and then restrengthened again, this time reaching category 5 intensity with sustained winds of 160 mph. The storm's forward speed slowed a bit, and it began a gradual turn toward the west-northwest that took it across the Caribbean toward Jamaica. Ivan made a short westward jog, which spared Jamaica a direct hit. It dropped down to category 4 strength, wobbled away from Jamaica, then regained category 5 status on September 11 with sustained winds of 165 mph. It was then that the National Hurricane Center reported that Ivan had become the sixth most intense hurricane ever recorded in the Atlantic basin, with a barometric low of 26.93 inches. But it could only muster that intensity for six hours, dropping back to category 4 that evening. It was back up the next day, reaching category 5 intensity for the third time while only about eighty miles west of Grand Cayman Island. Winds approaching 150 mph blasted Grand Cayman, and a giant storm surge completely overswept the island, except for the extreme northeastern portion.

Fortunately Ivan's next moves carried it through the Yucatán Channel and into the Gulf of Mexico off the extreme western tip of Cuba, sparing major land areas the devastating winds that had rocked Grenada, Jamaica, and Grand Cayman. And it was good timing, too, because instead of dropping intensity again like it had done several times before, Ivan went on to hold its category 5 power for an amazing thirty-hour period. By this time, on September 14, it was clear that Ivan would make landfall somewhere on the Gulf coast of Louisiana, Mississippi, Alabama, or Florida and that even if the storm weakened again, it would still likely come ashore as a major hurricane—category 3 or greater. From New Orleans to Pensacola and across the Florida Panhandle, large-scale evacuations got under way.

Ivan did weaken somewhat as forecasters had predicted. Its track turned more northward, and then in the early-morning hours of September 16, after making a slight jog to the east, it barreled ashore just west of Gulf Shores, Alabama. Although landfall was technically in Alabama, the storm's fifty-mile-wide eye meant that some of the strongest winds and highest tides were projected across the beaches on the Alabama-Florida border. Ivan was a strong category 3 upon arrival. It marched inland and turned somewhat to the northeast, passing over eastern Mobile Bay and weakening to a tropical storm twelve hours later over central Alabama. It continued its gradual turn to the northeast, eventually tracking across eastern Tennessee and central Virginia before passing into the Atlantic off the Delmarva Peninsula as an extratropical low on the eighteenth. But even as the diminished storm drifted across the east, it caused widespread destruction as a memorable rainmaker and tornado producer.

Most hurricanes, after expending their energy over land and dissipating across the Northeast, would simply be absorbed by some passing weather system somewhere over the North Atlantic. But not Ivan. As an extratropical low, it reached the Atlantic and abruptly turned southward, drifting past the Carolinas and Georgia and back into Florida waters. It turned and crossed the southern Florida Peninsula on the morning of September 21 and by afternoon had emerged in the eastern Gulf of Mexico. It soon began to redevelop tropical characteristics as thunderstorms grew around its well-defined low-level circulation. By the following day, Ivan was a tropical depression again, tracking slowly westward across the Gulf. Soon it was upgraded to Tropical Storm Ivan as it passed about 100 miles south of the Louisiana coast. On the twenty-fourth, Ivan made its final landfall as a tropical depression in extreme southwestern Louisiana. From start to finish, it had logged more than 6,000 miles in twenty-two days and twelve hours.

When Ivan first threatened the United States, rounding the corner of Cuba and entering the Gulf of Mexico on September 14, emergency managers in four states went on high alert. They were weary from the progression of storms that had already tracked toward them, and now this one appeared to be the fiercest of all. Evacuation plans were launched, sending over 2 million people running for cover. Hurricane warnings were posted for a 300-mile stretch, from Grand Isle, Louisiana, to Apalachicola, Florida. The greatest exodus was in New Orleans, where 1.2 million residents were ordered to leave town. New Orleans, of course, was most vulnerable, especially if Ivan decided to zig to the left of the Hurricane Center's projected path and strike the city head on. Oil and gas rigs in the Gulf were evacuated, chemical plants and refineries around Mobile Bay were closed, and major evacuation routes like I-65 in Alabama were converted for northbound traffic only. Deputies went door-to-door along the Alabama and Florida Panhandle beaches, warning residents not to stay. This one, they said, would likely be worse than Opal—the 1995 hurricane that most beachfront residents could identify with.

At landfall, Ivan had a forward speed of around 15 mph. The minimal central pressure, as measured from NOAA aircraft, was 27.85 inches. Official reports place the sustained wind speeds at landfall near 120 mph, though as usual, most reporting land stations recorded significantly lower wind speeds. The highest official winds were measured at Pensacola Naval Air Station, where sustained winds of 87 mph and a gust of 107 mph were recorded. However, unofficial reports from storm chasers and other locations yielded some more impressive figures. A wind gust of 145 mph was observed on the sailboat *Odalisque* while anchored in Wolf Bay, north of Orange Beach, Alabama. A storm chaser near Gulf Shores recorded sustained winds of 89 mph and a peak gust of 114 mph. An instrument on an oil-drilling platform located some seventy miles south of Mobile measured a gust of 155 mph, though it was positioned nearly 400 feet above sea level, which escalated the reading. Most amazing was a wind report from Grand Cayman, where sustained winds of 150 mph and a gust to 171 mph were recorded.

Storm-surge levels likely ranged from ten to fifteen feet on the beaches between Mobile Bay and Destin. Combined with the gusting winds, Ivan's destructive force was described as "historic." According to one report from the Mobile/Pensacola Forecast Office of the National Weather Service,

> Preliminary damage and destruction over Baldwin County Alabama and Escambia and Santa Rosa counties of northwest Florida likely exceeded that of both Hurricane Frederic (September 1979) and Hurricane Opal (October 1995). Additionally, Hurricane Ivan may rival the magnitude of damage and destruction caused by the Hurricane of 1926 which ravaged the aforementioned counties east of Mobile Bay. . . . The surge along this stretch of coastline was likely at least as high as 10 feet and possibly 12 feet. Fortunately, for downtown Mobile, Alabama, the center of Ivan passed to the east preventing nearly 16 to 18 feet of devastating storm surge, which is what would have happened if Ivan would have made landfall west of Mobile Bay.

Weather buoys positioned along the U.S. coast have become an increasingly important component of NOAA's weather-reporting system, and they have proven especially useful in analyzing hurricane landfalls. As Hurricane Ivan was bearing down on the Alabama coast, NOAA buoy number 42040 recorded a wave height of 52.2 feet while positioned in the north-central Gulf about seventy miles south of Dauphin Island, Alabama. Soon after the measurement was made, the buoy went adrift from its mooring. According to the U.S. Geological Survey, Ivan set several hydrological records, including what was

described as possibly the largest ocean wave ever recorded. A wave measuring 91 feet was reported, but it may have been as high as 131 feet.

Although rainfall was not Ivan's greatest threat at landfall, localized flooding did occur in some areas after six to ten inches of rain fell across southern Alabama and western Florida. The highest official storm totals in the region were 11.66 inches in Millers Ferry, Alabama, and 11.31 inches in Milligan, Florida. In Pensacola, a television station recorded 15.75 inches. These rains overfilled ditches and made driving hazardous immediately after the storm. But the ten to twelve inches of rain that fell across parts of the Tennessee and North Carolina mountains created flash floods that swept away homes, flooded entire neighborhoods, and claimed several lives. A landslide brought on by the heavy rains killed two in Macon County, North Carolina, one of whom was an expectant mother. Like Frances a few weeks before, Ivan brought devastation to portions of western North Carolina, flooding crops and causing millions of dollars in damages.

Tornado activity associated with Ivan was widespread and deadly. On September 15, just prior to the storm's arrival, Florida was hit with a brutal attack of F2 tornadoes that left seven dead. One struck Panama City Beach, killing one resident and injuring seven. About an hour later, two more people were killed when a twister landed across West Bay in Panama City. Another tornado plowed through a mobile home park near Blountstown in Calhoun County, killing four residents and injuring another. And just like Hurricane Frances, Ivan was an active tornado producer throughout its journey northward. It spawned a total of 117 tornadoes in the United States, including 37 in Virginia, 25 in Georgia, 18 in Florida, and 9 in Pennsylvania. Of these, most were spotted on September 17, the day after Ivan made landfall. These tornadoes, combined with the 101 that had been reported during Hurricane Frances, helped set a new September record for tornadoes in the United States. NOAA's Storm Prediction Center reported that 247 were recorded for the month, topping the old record of 139 set in 1967. The average number of tornadoes in the United States during September is 47.

Everywhere Ivan went, it left behind smashed buildings and troubled lives. Across the Caribbean, it blew down homes and flooded beaches on every island it came near. In Grenada, high winds knocked out power on most of the island, and over 14,000 homes were damaged or destroyed. Many houses lost their roofs. Hundreds were reported injured, and thirty-nine people were killed. At the height of the storm, a seventeenth-century prison was damaged, allowing prisoners to briefly escape. Early in its trajectory, Ivan had also pummeled other low-latitude islands and was responsible for deaths in Barbados, Tobago, and Venezuela.

Jamaica, an island of over 2.5 million, was spared a direct hit when Ivan's center wobbled westward and passed it by. But the storm's far-reaching impact was still tremendous. Almost 6,000 homes were totally destroyed, and nearly 14,000 were damaged. Power was knocked out over most of the island, and trees and power poles were snapped like toothpicks. There were seventeen reported fatalities. In Negril, a resort town in northwestern Jamaica, waves over thirty feet high smashed over a seawall and damaged shops and hotels. Large pleasure yachts were swept inland and stacked atop each other. Helicopters were later used to rescue residents trapped in mountainous areas where mudslides covered roads. Mounds of debris, mixed with lumber, rocks, and coconuts, covered miles of beachfront in several resort communities.

In the Cayman Islands, many fled on chartered planes before the storm arrived. Residents of Little Cayman were brought to the big island, and about 3,000 people filled evacuation shelters on Grand Cayman. Hundreds of residents on Cayman Brac fled into ancient caves that have historically provided residents with shelter during major hurricanes. The islands were walloped with fierce winds that topped 150 mph and shredded thousands of rooftops. As many as half of the island's homes and businesses were damaged, many of which were constructed under building codes as tough as those in South Florida. Reporters flying over the island after the storm reported that most of the island appeared to have been overwashed by storm surge. Century-old trees, some three stories tall, were uprooted and blown down. In fact, virtually every tree on the island appeared denuded, the leaves swept away by the storm's ferocious gusts. The airport runway was flooded, windows were shattered in the control tower, and a hangar roof was missing. The Caymans suffered heavy losses, including the lives of two more people. Reuters published an online news report from the *Cayman Net News* describing the flooding at the local office: "The glass doors at Cayman Net News thankfully resisted the worst of the flooding, even though at times it was like looking at an aquarium (complete with tadpoles) as the water rose some three feet (1 meter) outside."

In the United States, though Ivan's trail of destruction stretched across the South and into the mid-Atlantic, it was the Alabama and Florida coastline that caught the full fury of the storm. On Dauphin Island, Alabama, at least forty-four houses were completely destroyed, and over a hundred more suffered extensive damages. Most were homes on the front row facing the Gulf, where Ivan's seven-foot storm surge and fifteen-foot waves pounded the shoreline. Almost all of the lost homes were on the island's western end, where the land is low and narrow and had experienced rapid erosion in recent years. After the storm, some suggested that property owners should not be allowed to build back along that vulnerable stretch. None of the destroyed homes were constructed after 2003, when contractors began building to a tougher building code that requires stronger materials and sturdier framing.

Not since Hurricane Frederic in 1979 had the Alabama Gulf coast taken such a brutal hit from a major hurricane. From Perdido Key and Orange Beach to Gulf State Park and Gulf Shores, dunes were wiped away and structures were pounded by waves and storm surge. Ivan's strike was particularly fierce at Gulf Shores, where waves washed across the streets and multistory beachfront condos were undermined. One five-story condominium that collapsed in Gulf Shores was described by the U.S. Geological Survey as "the largest building to fail during a hurricane in United States History" (at least until Katrina struck Mississippi in 2005). Beach erosion in this area was dramatic. The U.S. Geological Survey's Center for Coastal and Watershed Studies reported that Ivan carved away an average of 42 feet of beach between Mobile Bay and Pensacola Bay, with some stretches losing as much as 164 feet. This was terrible news for residents of Baldwin County, Alabama, who had just completed a $2.5 million beach erosion repair project prior to Ivan's arrival. Still, local officials believed the storm's impact could have been far greater had they not renourished the beaches.

One bit of good news came a few days after the hurricane when "Chucky," a fourteen-foot-long, 1,000-pound alligator, was captured in a Gulf Shores ditch and returned to the Alabama Gulf Coast Zoo from which it had escaped. Floods during Ivan had floated Chucky and eight other gators out of the zoo during the storm. It took more than a half-dozen people, including state troopers and workers from Gatorland in Orlando, to wrestle him out of the ditch. Witnesses said that nearby cleanup crews couldn't resist stopping their work and gathering around to watch the capture.

In Escambia County, the home of Pensacola and some 300,000 residents, Ivan was blamed for seven deaths. Pensacola was hit hard by the hurricane, and the twisted evidence was scattered in every corner of the city. Ivan's powerful eastern eyewall raked directly over it, knocking out power and sending residents deep into their closets. Huge oaks were toppled, historic buildings collapsed, neighborhoods became knee-deep ponds, and bridges, roads, and power lines were sliced in two. More than 1,600 residents fled to the Pensacola Civic Center, which served as a Red Cross shelter. But during the storm, evacuees had to be moved from floor to floor after wind-driven water seeped through the walls and partially flooded the arena. More than 100 large boats at the Palafox Pier marina were tossed in a pile at one end of the marina. Several large historic buildings along the waterfront, some dating back to the early 1800s, crumbled into piles of bricks. After the storm passed, hundreds of urban search-and-rescue workers with trained dogs were called in to dig through demolished neighborhoods to search for victims along the city's flooded riverbanks.

Some of the most dramatic evidence of Ivan's fury could be seen in the broken and missing sections of the I-10 bridge that crosses Escambia Bay. Winds and waves tore huge concrete segments away from the bridge, eliminating access along that portion of the interstate. Unfortunately the collapsing bridge caught a truck driver by surprise, sending him and his cab plunging into the bay below. After the storm, his tractor-trailer was found dangling on the edge of the broken roadway. The next day, divers recovered the body of Robert Alvarado, forty-six, from Brownsville, Texas. Avarado had been hauling a load of fruits and vegetables from Texas to Miami when he apparently came to a stop on the bridge during the height of the storm. The roadway collapsed underneath him, and he became another of the hurricane's victims. Other damaged bridges in the area included the U.S. 98 bridge from Pensacola to Gulf Breeze and a bridge on U.S. 90. The damaged bridges forced traffic to detour, creating bottlenecks and transportation delays throughout the region.

At Pensacola Naval Air Station, home of the famed Blue Angels, Ivan struck with full force, causing millions of dollars in property damages. Although none of the station's jets were harmed, many vintage warplanes at the National Museum of Naval Aviation were badly damaged or destroyed. Nearby Warrington, Gulf Breeze, and Pensacola Beach were slammed by Ivan's surge, which washed away docks and piers and flooded beachfront homes. Milton, just northeast of Pensacola, was among the hardest-hit communities. There, an eight-year-old girl was killed when a large tree came crashing into her home. Down the coast at Fort Walton Beach and Destin, storm tides of ten to twelve feet battered the beachfront, and winds gusting over 100 mph blew away roofs and knocked over billboards. Farther east at Panama City Beach, the surge was not as great, but at least two tornadoes struck the area, killing three people and injuring almost a dozen. In one way or another, almost all of Northwest Florida was impacted by the storm.

According to the National Hurricane Center, Ivan was directly responsible for 92 deaths, including 39 in Grenada, 25 in the United States, 17 in Jamaica, 4 in the Dominican Republic, 3 in Venezuela, 2 in the Cayman Islands, and 1 each in Tobago and Barbados. Of the deaths in the United States, 14 were in Florida, 8 were in North Carolina, 2 were in Georgia, and 1 was in Mississippi. Among those killed in Florida were truck driver Robert Alvarado, who died in Escambia Bay; Robert Krause, who died when a tree struck him in his Navy Point yard; second-grader Roxane DeLoach, who was killed by a tree in her Milton home; Joseph Greenblatt, who drowned in floodwaters at Grande Lagoon; Arvie Jernigan, who drowned on Grande Lagoon Drive; and Lois Zaragoza-Goode, who drowned near Gulf Beach Highway. As is quite common in the days following major hurricanes, additional fatalities were reported across the affected area as the cleanup got under way. As many as thirty-two more people died. On September 23, four members of Pace Assembly of God died in a plane crash near North Airport Road. They were taking an aerial survey to determine which areas most needed relief assistance. Others were killed in accidents or by heart attacks.

As Ivan pushed inland and dumped heavy rains over Georgia, Tennessee, and the Carolinas, the destruction and death continued. A six-year-old girl was swept away by floodwaters in Georgia, and eight people died in western North Carolina in flash floods and mudslides. One entire community of twenty to thirty homes was swept away by a landslide in Macon County, North Carolina, killing four. Haywood County, North Carolina, reported over 400 structures either damaged or destroyed. In Virginia, where thirty-seven tornadoes were sighted, there were no fatalities, but there were several injuries. Across West Virginia, about 290 homes and over 30 businesses were destroyed. In Pennsylvania, at least 14,000 residents were forced to evacuate their homes because of flooding. Even in southeastern Ohio, Ivan produced storms that pushed the Ohio River to its highest level in forty years. The 126-year-old Rinard Covered Bridge over the Little Muskingum River was said to have "disappeared" in the flooding. Winds and rains knocked out power and washed out roads, stranding students and teachers in one elementary school overnight.

When Hurricane Ivan approached the Gulf of Mexico on September 13 and evacuation orders were first issued along the Gulf Coast, the city with the most at stake—New Orleans—took it very seriously. As was seen during Hurricane Katrina's deadly visit in 2005, New Orleans was vulnerable to Ivan, especially if the city were to take a direct hit. Mayor Ray Nagin asked 1.2 million New Orleans residents to leave, and a massive evacuation got under way. Highways were jammed for hours with fleeing residents who headed inland in search of hotel rooms and refuge. The Louisiana Superdome became a shelter, and some 100,000 residents who either couldn't or wouldn't leave stayed in the city. Fortunately for them, Ivan's course shifted to the east, and New Orleans

only received brisk winds, two-tenths of an inch of rain, and a few downed tree limbs. Many residents who encountered stressful traffic during the evacuation and then again as they returned were bitter about the evacuation order. "I know I'm going to hear from the Monday morning quarterbacks," Mayor Nagin told *MSNBC News*. "But look at the scenes from Mobile and Pensacola—that could have been us."

In Florida, state officials were struggling to organize and pay for the cleanup of Hurricanes Charley and Frances when Ivan added to their burden. Mountains of debris began to form, the largest of which was in Escambia County. This heap of lumber, tree limbs, appliances, and other debris was seventy feet tall and over three-quarters of a mile in length. At the time of Ivan's landfall, utility workers across the state were working to restore power to over 160,000 residents still without electricity after the first two storms. Then Ivan struck, putting an additional 345,000 Floridians in the dark. Utility crews and emergency workers poured in from other states and worked long hours to make repairs and help those in need. FEMA distribution centers soon emerged, just as they had in areas affected by Charley and Frances. Food, water, ice, and other essentials once again rolled in by the truckload, but again residents were frustrated by long lines as they waited to pick up supplies. Some residents gave up rather than wait in the miles-long line of cars that formed on U.S. 90 for FEMA's distribution of ice and water. Gas was also in short supply, and so was patience. Fights broke out at several gas stations in Crestview when people attempted to cut in line. One station nearly faced a riot when it ran out of fuel while scores of people still waited in line. In Niceville, one FEMA distribution center worked hard to keep the ice and water flowing and the lines moving. Charles Hamilton, an emergency coordinator from New York State, told the *Orlando Sentinel*: "We moved 900 cars through in 45 minutes, and I think we can do even better. Is there a Guinness record for disaster relief lines?"

Rumors about the hurricanes swirled in the days that followed, often fueled by lack of information and excess imagination. After Charley, a story was told that corpses were stacked high inside refrigerated tractor-trailers in South Florida, which was similar to a myth that was spread after Andrew in 1992. As Ivan churned in the Gulf, a rumor hit the Tampa area that gasoline was going to be rationed. That led to a rush on the pumps that forced Governor Jeb Bush to go on TV and debunk the story as "urban legend." After Ivan, a rumor circulated that three sisters had perished behind a house on Perdido Key, when actually the entire family had evacuated and the sisters were alive and well. According to another story, a local hospital lost its roof to a tornado, and scores of patients were killed. As with other disasters, emergency operations centers and local news media devoted many hours to quelling rumors and sorting out facts.

Ivan's economic impact in the United States was staggering. Damages were heaviest along the coast, but the toll also mounted across inland portions of Florida, Alabama, and Georgia and throughout the storm's northward jaunt. Millions of board feet of timber were lost, including more than $600 million worth in Alabama alone. Agriculture in the region suffered large losses, and the offshore oil industry was hurt as well. Twelve large oil and gas pipelines were damaged. Seven oil-drilling platforms were destroyed, and another six suffered major damages. These kinds of losses can be measured directly, whereas losses of revenue from tourism and other businesses require a more detailed analysis and are not factored into most hurricane-damage records. In the United States, Ivan was reported to have generated $14.2 billion in damages, or twice the amount reported as insured losses. Eight billion of that amount was credited to damage in Florida. Thanks to this figure, Ivan joined an elite group, nearly reaching Charley's recent toll to become the third costliest U.S. hurricane disaster up to that time.

In its storm summary, the National Hurricane Center concluded that "Ivan was the most destructive hurricane to affect this area in more than 100 years." So it was not surprising that in 2005, at the annual meeting of the World Meteorological Organization, the name "Ivan" was retired from the rotating list of names used for Atlantic hurricanes. It was replaced with "Igor," which was put in place for possible use in 2010.

JEANNE (SEPTEMBER 25–27, 2004)

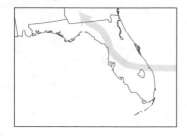

The last straw. Insult to injury. These were some of the ways people in Florida described their ordeal with Hurricane Jeanne, which hit the state late in September 2004. Jeanne topped off a brutal year that set new records for hurricane destruction and tested the wills of millions of Florida residents. Never before since record keeping began had anyone seen four hurricanes (three of them major) strike Florida in such a short period of time. Although it was neither as large as Hurricane Frances nor as powerful as Charley and Ivan, Jeanne was still a formidable hurricane that added to the state's misery. Landing at nearly the same spot as Frances had twenty days earlier, Jeanne was a category 3 that smacked many homeowners and businesses that were still recovering from the earlier storms. For many, Jeanne delivered an emotional and economic blow that left them wondering if their lives or their communities would ever be the same. And in a year when Atlantic hurricanes would claim so many lives, Jeanne was the deadliest, killing more than 3,000 people in Haiti alone.

While Hurricane Ivan was rounding the Yucatán Channel on September 13 on its way toward the Alabama coast, Tropical Storm Jeanne was forming east of the Leeward Islands. It tracked slowly toward the west-northwest, passing over the Virgin Islands and reaching Puerto Rico on the fifteenth. It made landfall over the eastern tip of the Dominican Republic the following day as a minimal hurricane and then raked along Hispaniola's rugged northern coast. It weakened to become a tropical depression just north of the Haitian coast, briefly lost its center of rotation, and then formed a new center well to the northeast. Its slow, drifting motion during this period contributed to the torrential rains that fell across the Dominican Republic and Haiti, where thousands died from flash floods and mudslides.

While rains from Jeanne were creating chaos in Haiti, Hurricane Ivan was moving inland over the southeastern United States and merging with an extra-tropical trough. Ivan's movements to the northeast set up an erosion of the high-pressure ridge north of Jeanne, creating a weak steering pattern that left Jeanne drifting northward for the next five days. Jeanne then turned in a large clockwise loop about 500 miles north of Hispaniola and finally regained hurricane strength on September 23. From there, it began a westward track that carried it over warmer waters, and it reintensified to become a category 3 hurricane.

By the morning of September 25, it was clear that Jeanne was destined to strike the Florida coast. Hurricane watches were upgraded to hurricane warnings from East Cape Sable to Anclote Key. Along the barrier island beaches of St. Lucie County, residents hit by Frances who had only recently patched their roofs with blue tarps prepared to evacuate once again. As the hours ticked by and the Hurricane Center continued to update forecasts, it became clear

The 2004 hurricane season delivered an unprecedented four hurricanes to Florida. Hurricanes Charley, Frances, Ivan, and Jeanne all made landfall within a six-week period.

that Jeanne would soon strike right on top of where Frances had come ashore. And it did. Just before midnight on September 25, Jeanne's fifty-mile-wide eye crossed the southern end of Hutchinson Island, only about five miles from where Frances had landed.

After landfall, the storm weakened rapidly as it tracked across central Florida. But it never moved into the Gulf of Mexico like Frances. It dropped to tropical storm strength just north of Tampa and curved toward the northwest, passing just east of Cedar Key and Tallahassee on its way into southern Georgia. By the morning of the twenty-eighth, Jeanne was only a tropical depression, dumping heavy rains across northern Georgia and the Carolinas. The dying storm eventually tracked through Virginia and exited the coast off the Delmarva Peninsula, becoming extratropical on the following day.

The *South Florida Sun-Sentinel* summarized the similarities between Hurricanes Frances and Jeanne:

> In an eerie tropical two-step, both hurricanes hit almost the exact same spot on the Treasure Coast, with their cores making landfall less than five miles apart—Frances hit Sewell's Point while Jeanne hit the southern end of Hutchinson's Island, just east of Stuart. For two hurricanes to strike that close in a decade is remarkable, let alone in less than three weeks, hurricane experts say. Frances arrived on Sept. 5 and Jeanne 20 days later, on Saturday. Such coincidences have happened before: in 1928, before hurricanes were given names, two systems struck near the Palm Beach–Martin County line 40 days apart, with the second of those being the infamous storm that killed about 2,500 people around Lake Okeechobee. . . . The bizarre similarities between Jeanne and Frances go deeper. Both made landfall late at night, Frances at 1 A.M. and Jeanne at 11:50 P.M. Both grew to be expansive systems, about 400 miles in diameter, and both had huge eyes: 45 miles across for Frances, 40 miles for Jeanne. Both were rainmakers, causing severe flooding along their immediate paths. Both slammed the Bahamas on their way to Florida. Both angled northwest and sideswiped Orlando, which was a very unusual twist by itself. In the past 50 years, the popular tourist destination has suffered one direct hurricane hit, Donna in 1960. Yet this year, the city was socked by three storms: Charley, Frances, and now Jeanne.

The National Hurricane Center reported that Jeanne had a central pressure of about 28.06 inches at landfall. Sustained winds of 120 mph may have battered a small area of the coastline near Sebastian, although there were no surface observations to confirm the estimate. The highest sustained winds observed were at the Melbourne office of the National Weather Service, where winds were clocked at 91 mph. The highest wind gusts reported were 128 mph measured at Fort Pierce Inlet and 122 mph recorded at Vero Beach. Sustained hurricane-force winds likely extended about halfway across the Florida Peninsula as the storm tracked inland and began weakening.

In Haiti, where heavy rains spurred deadly flash floods, no reliable rainfall reports were available after the storm. It is likely, however, that given Jeanne's lingering movements over the island, rainfall totals exceeded twenty inches or more. In Florida, the rains were not as deadly, but they still caused widespread flooding in many communities. Along a narrow band through Osceola, Brevard, and Indian River Counties, rainfall amounts totaled between eleven and thirteen inches. Other areas in Florida near the storm track received up to eight inches, while four to seven inches accompanied Jeanne as it crossed Georgia and the Carolinas. Storm-surge flooding along the ocean beaches just north of landfall was likely up to six feet above normal. Interestingly, along Florida's Gulf coast on Cedar Key, offshore winds generated by Jeanne's passing created a negative surge of 4.5 feet, meaning that the water receded by this amount during the storm's approach. After Jeanne passed and the winds shifted, a positive surge of about 3.5 feet above normal was recorded on these Gulf beaches.

When news reports of Jeanne's approach first hit the airwaves, millions of Florida residents took a deep breath and began to make plans. Many were already familiar with the evacuation drill, having just come home from extended stays in hotels and Red Cross shelters a few days before. Many did not even have to pack—their most valuable possessions were still stuffed into boxes or wrapped in plastic bags. In Martin, St. Lucie, and Indian River Counties, storm-weary residents ventured back to shelters they had just left to wait it out again. This time, many carried luxuries with them like air mattresses and DVD players, as long as shelter managers would allow them. At Central High School in Wellington, about 3,000 people crammed into the shelter, though the capacity was limited to about 2,700. Normally, the school would house 5,000, but damages to the auditorium and other buildings forced Red Cross officials to limit the numbers. In some communities, people found refuge in unofficial shelters like private clubhouses and churches. Florida Emergency Management reported that in all, about 59,000 Florida residents were huddled in schools, civic centers, and other public shelters on the Saturday night that Jeanne arrived.

But government officials also said that evacuations for the storm were far less complete than those for Frances. During Frances, communities like Stuart were said to be like "ghost towns," whereas during Jeanne, many residents stayed home. Many felt they needed to stay to protect their already damaged roofs from further wind and rain. Others were apparently disgusted with the evacuations and emotionally drained; they were tired of moving in and out of their homes. On Hutchinson Island, where the hurricane made landfall, about 200 residents refused to evacuate and decided to ride out the storm.

While anxious Floridians were waiting in shelters for Jeanne to strike, government officials and relief organizations in Haiti were updating news reporters on the horrific tragedy that had befallen that impoverished nation. In a matter of hours, Jeanne had wiped out generations of villagers and become one of Haiti's worst natural disasters. Final figures are purely estimates, but it is believed that over 3,000 lives were lost when the storm's heavy rains fell across the mountainous regions along the island's northern peninsula. Mudslides washed away homes in dozens of villages, but the greatest losses were in the coastal city of Gonaives. Initially, casualty figures were thought to be around

1,500, but the discovery of hundreds more bodies outside the city raised the figure substantially. Over 300,000 Haitians were left homeless by the disaster. In the days and weeks that followed the flooding, relief efforts were hampered by the inaccessibility of many remote villages since entire road systems had been washed away. But a greater difficulty faced by relief workers was the political unrest that erupted into violence about the time of the storm. Haitian police arrested the president of the country's senate and two others following a six-hour standoff at a local radio station, and at least fourteen others were killed in political violence. Riots later erupted when large mobs stormed United Nations food trucks that finally made their way into the hardest-hit areas.

Across Florida, damages left in Jeanne's wake were widespread and significant. In almost every neighborhood along its path, residents told stories of damages from Frances or Charley that were made much worse by Jeanne's visit. In fact, it was often difficult to tell what damage was caused by which hurricane. Many homeowners had just completed temporary repairs, in particular the installation of bright blue roof tarps that were intended to hold back the weather until insurance claims could be settled and shingles replaced. Jeanne sent the tarps flying and then wreaked its own havoc on thousands of roofs across the state. Some of those who were unlucky enough to suffer damages from two or more storms later found themselves tangled in a sticky web of insurance-claim disputes. In the weeks and months that followed, they discovered that finding someone to make repairs and then getting insurance claims settled to pay for them would be an enduring struggle.

Again, some of the worst damages could be found in mobile home communities along the coast. At Barefoot Bay, a sprawling community of 4,900 mobile homes north of Stuart, dozens of trailers were crushed and most others were damaged in some way. Large crumpled sheets of aluminum littered the streets and, along with tangled power lines, blocked intersections throughout the community. Five hundred of the park's homes were totally destroyed. The scene was similar in Palm Bay, where nearly all 252 mobile homes in the park were damaged. Many had their roofs peeled back like aluminum cans. At Ocean Breeze trailer park in Jensen Beach, it was more of the same, with many homes damaged beyond repair. Debris piles left over from Frances became airborne during Jeanne, sending dangerous missiles whirling into car windows and homes. One resident who was in her trailer during the storm told her story to the *South Florida Sun-Sentinel*. Mary Musser moved into her mobile home just three days after Hurricane Charley crossed the state. She had evacuated for Frances but said she "didn't have the strength" to do it again. She was alone in her two-bedroom unit when the power went out. The *Sun-Sentinel* wrote: "She said she lit a candle, held a flashlight and read the Bible. At one point, she called 911 for help, but it was too late to try to rescue her. 'So I said

that if the good Lord wants me, he can take me,' said Musser, standing in the rubble of her front porch, one foot on the shattered front door. 'I was feeling the wall, and I said, "Dear God, please don't let the wall fall."' It didn't. But parts of her roof peeled off and many of her windows shattered. 'This is catastrophic,' she said."

Residents of Stuart gave vivid descriptions of the eerie calm that came over them when Jeanne's eye passed in the night. They woke the next morning to witness the wind-torn damages around them. Trees and power poles were tilted and wrapped with stray electric lines. The Stuart police station was abandoned and condemned because portions of the roof collapsed after taking a beating from both Frances and Jeanne. The Martin Memorial Medical Center lost half of its roof after having sustained similar damages in Frances. About fifty patients were relocated, but none were injured. Stuart City Hall and other city facilities were also damaged. One person had to be rescued during the storm when portions of a condominium roof collapsed. At the nearby Indiantown Marina, one of the largest in the area, at least twenty-five boats were damaged. On Hutchinson Island, where Jeanne came ashore, ocean surges flooded the first floor of the Atlantis condominiums and piled sand up to the kitchen cabinets. Windows in the top-floor restaurant of the nearby Marriott Courtyard Hotel were blown out. Parking lots were covered with five feet of water and sand. Both the Stuart Causeway and the Jensen Beach Causeway bridges were wedged open by the hurricane's fierce winds and tides, forcing officials to close them to traffic after the storm. Emergency 911 dispatchers received reports of one car that had broken through a guardrail and plunged into the waterway during night. Indian River Drive lost huge chunks of pavement to the bashing waves, just as it had during Frances. The day after the storm, Stuart mayor Jeff Krauskopf told CNN reporters how local residents felt about Jeanne: "It just doesn't stop. It's like that song, Frances to the left of me, Ivan to the right, and Jeanne, I'm stuck in the middle with you."

In Jensen Beach, a waterfront drive was undermined by high waters after having been paved just a few days earlier. The new asphalt had been put down to repair washouts that occurred during Frances. The town's community center was destroyed, and streets were blocked by fallen palm trees and signposts. In Fort Pierce and Port St. Lucie, several people were rescued from their homes during the calm of the hurricane's eye. Police in St. Lucie rescued five families during the eye, including a wheelchair-bound elderly couple whose mobile home collapsed on top of them. Many others endured terrifying experiences during the night. In northern St. Lucie County, a crowd gathered in the Pennwood Motor Lodge because they knew it had survived Hurricane Frances. But Jeanne tore its roof off in one fierce blast that shell-shocked the evacuees huddled inside. About ten people were crouched under mattresses in one Fort Pierce home when its ceiling began to peel back from the walls. Its roof was also destroyed, but everyone inside was unharmed. Nearby, about 100 special-needs patients had to be transferred from a shelter when its roof began leaking. In the lower-income portions of north Fort Pierce, made up of mostly smaller, older homes, Jeanne tore some structures down but left others untouched. Along the city's upscale Indian River waterfront, docks and seawalls were washed out, but most of the well-built homes were unscathed.

On Vero Beach, a foot of seawater filled the streets, flooding homes and businesses and floating boats off their trailers. Even emergency vehicles on patrol after the storm were flooded out and had to be towed. One resident found a big surprise in his badly eroded driveway: the storm had unearthed a live rocket warhead that had likely been buried there since World War II. U.S. Army munitions experts safely detonated the rocket. In St. Augustine, rangers at Anastasia State Park discovered the remains of an eighteenth-century shipwreck newly exposed on the beach. Beach erosion was dramatic in some areas. Oceanfront swimming pools tumbled into the surf at Satellite Beach. In Sanford, surrounded by rivers and lakes like several other inland communities near Orlando, wind-driven water piled onto streets near the lakeshore. Many rural inland roads were washed away or blocked with debris, making driving after the storm impossible. Sewage lift stations were without power in most counties, and there were several reports of overflowing sewage. Four

Donely Gorges paddled a canoe through her yard near Lake Jessup in Seminole County after Jeanne swept across the state. She also put up a fence to keep alligators away. (Photo by Hilda M. Perez, courtesy of the Orlando Sentinel)

hundred evacuees were moved from a shelter at Sherwood Elementary School in Melbourne when strong gusts tore away sections of the school's roof. Small planes flipped over at Palm Beach International Airport. NASA's giant shuttle-assembly building at Cape Canaveral lost more wall panels after having suffered earlier damages from Charley and Frances. But despite widespread damages and the loss of power to almost 2 million people, there was some good news during the storm. An Indiantown woman who was unable to get to a hospital the night of the hurricane gave birth to a healthy baby boy in her home with the help of 911 dispatchers.

Although Jeanne's heaviest toll was in east-central Florida, it caused other calamities on its trek inland across the southeastern United States. A Coast Guard helicopter had to rescue two fishermen from a life raft in the Gulf of Mexico when their boat sank in the storm. In Georgia, Jeanne washed out dozens of roads, toppled tall pines, damaged a courthouse roof, and floated a handful of coffins out of a flooded cemetery. The storm's remnants spawned tornadoes in Georgia and South Carolina, where one ripped through a mobile home park, injuring a dozen people and killing one.

The Hurricane Center's records show that Jeanne directly caused three deaths in Florida. They included a Clay County boy who was hit in the head by a falling limb while playing outside during the storm; a Brevard County man whose truck was swept into a canal; and an elderly Indian River County woman who died of complications a few days after she was knocked down by gusting winds while on the way to a shelter. But according to a Florida State Emergency Response Team report, Jeanne caused thirteen hurricane-related deaths in Florida. They included two in Palm Beach County, two in Polk County, and one each in Brevard, Clay, Dade, Hardee, Lake, Orange, Pasco, Pinellas, and St. Lucie Counties. For those families who lost loved ones to the storm, Jeanne was a true catastrophe. But this hurricane will always be remembered for its merciless toll on Gonaives, Haiti, where as many as 2,900 died.

Since Charley, Frances, Ivan, and Jeanne all struck within such a short period of time, local, state, and federal officials faced an unprecedented challenge in providing an immediate response for hurricane victims and orchestrating effective recoveries. There were so many storm-related priorities spread around the state that significant outside support was needed. FEMA was pushed to its limits as well and executed what director Michael Brown described as the largest disaster-relief effort in history, surpassing the agency's responses to the 1994 Northridge, California, earthquake and the 2001 terrorist attacks in New York City. In early October 2004, just days after Jeanne but weeks after Charley, "boil water notices" were still in effect in thirty-six Florida counties. Mountains of disaster aid and thousands of volunteer relief workers poured into Florida in caravans of trucks, ready to provide basic necessities to homeless and battered people around the state.

The following statistics were compiled in 2005 by Florida's State Emergency Response Team for all four hurricanes in 2004:

- More than 700 volunteer organizations responded to the four hurricanes.
- At the peak of the disaster-recovery operation, more than 2,600 FEMA personnel were deployed to Florida in support of state and local response and recovery efforts.
- Disaster medical teams treated more than 9,600 patients for storm related injuries.
- More than 200,000 volunteers from across the United States came to help Floridians. Thousands continue to repair and rebuild homes as part of the statewide long-term recovery.
- More than 368,000 residents stayed in shelters during and after the four hurricanes.
- More than 1.2 million Floridians applied for federal and state assistance through FEMA's registration system, setting an agency record. On September 28, 2004, FEMA took a record 44,800 applications nationwide in a single twenty-four-hour period.
- More than 9.5 million people evacuated Florida during the historic hurricane season.
- Over 14 million MREs (Meals Ready to Eat) were supplied to Floridians in the immediate disaster response, along with 10 million gallons of water and 59 million pounds of ice.

- Florida received more than $5.9 billion in federal disaster assistance, more than the average annual federal disaster assistance nationwide.

Total damages caused by Jeanne were estimated to be just over $7 billion, but added to the losses from Charley, Frances, and Ivan, the 2004 season set new records for hurricane-related losses. According to the Insurance Information Institute, the four storms caused $20.5 billion in wind insured losses in the United States. This tops the $20 billion in wind insured losses from Hurricane Andrew (adjusted to 2004 dollars), to make 2004 the costliest year for hurricanes on record, at least up until that time. That record was shattered in 2005, of course, when $52 billion in insured losses were recorded, $40.6 billion of which came from the record-breaking Hurricane Katrina. In fact, when the cost figures were compiled in 2005, the ranking showed that eight of the ten most costly hurricanes in U.S. history affected Florida, and six of the ten were in 2004 and 2005 (see the appendix for a chart of the costliest U.S. hurricanes). Undoubtedly, this ranking will continue to change in the future as other destructive hurricanes generate more billion-dollar disasters.

The 2004 damage figures were staggering for Florida. Not only had the state suffered from four potent and destructive hurricanes, but in their aftermath, there were widespread fears for the health of the state's economy. In the end, it turned out that many economic sectors, like banking, construction, and retail, actually got stronger in the months after the hurricane season ended. But agriculture had been hit hard, millions of residents were out of work while they struggled to repair their homes, and tourists thought twice before traveling to Florida's sun-drenched resorts. The board and staff of Visit Florida, the agency that markets Florida's $52 billion tourism industry, launched an aggressive advertising campaign to lure tourists back. Ads placed in *USA Today* told readers, "We're Still Here. Naturally."

One Miami woman had an interesting story to tell about Jeanne, even though her home was far from the destruction zone. Jeanne Van Wyck told the *Miami Herald* how Hurricane Jeanne came to be named after her. "Half the people don't think of me, they just think it's the name of a storm," said the seventy-five-year-old grandmother of two. It seems that Jeanne and her family were longtime close friends of senior hurricane forecaster Gilbert Clark and his family. Their families sometimes vacationed together. Clark retired from the National Hurricane Center in 1990, but back in 1979, he had the opportunity to suggest names for the rotating lists used for each new season. Clark contributed many suggestions that made the list, including the names of his wife, Nancy, and two of their children, Roxanne and Allen (Hurricane Roxanne struck the Yucatán in 1995, and Allen was an intense storm that struck Texas in 1980). But he also suggested the name Jeanne after Van Wyck, as well as the names of her two children, Diana and Beryl (Hurricane Diana's name was retired after it caused ninety-six deaths in Mexico in 1990, and Beryl was a tropical storm in 2000). Jeanne Van Wyck gets a chuckle out of knowing her name finally became recognized. "But my heart is with those people," she said. Clark's colleagues also added Gilbert to the list in his honor. In 1988 Hurricane Gilbert became the most intense Atlantic hurricane of the twentieth century.

DENNIS (JULY 10, 2005)

At the end of the 2004 Atlantic hurricane season, storm-weary Florida residents tried to enjoy the Thanksgiving and Christmas holiday season and put hurricane recovery out of their minds. It wasn't easy, though, because in many neighborhoods the evidence still surrounded them. Broken trees, bright blue tarp-covered roofs, and debris piles still lingered in the hardest-hit communities. And those storm victims lucky enough to have moved back into their damaged homes were still wrestling with insurance claims and piles of unpaid bills. In early December 2004, they were reminded that the next hurricane season was just a few months away. William Gray of Colorado State University issued his annual extended-range forecast for the 2005 season and called for another above-average year—not exactly what dispirited Florida residents wanted to hear.

Of course, the 2005 season turned out to be an all-time record setter, and it didn't take long for things to get cranked up. After three early tropical storms, Tropical Storm Dennis formed near the Windward Islands on July 5, marking the first time in history that four storms had been named by that date. Dennis moved west-northwestward through the Caribbean and was a hurricane by July 7. It quickly intensified into a category 4 storm with winds of 135 mph and slammed into the southeast Cuban coast on the eighth. During this period of rapid intensification, hurricane-hunter aircraft measured a pressure drop of 0.91 inches in twenty-four hours. Dennis weakened slightly and then regained category 4 strength while moving parallel to the south Cuban coast. It struck land again near Punta Mangles Altos, Cuba, and passed over the island, emerging in the Gulf of Mexico just east of Havana early on July 9. Along the way, it destroyed 120,000 Cuban homes and caused sixteen deaths. Dragging across the Cuban countryside, Dennis weakened considerably and was only a category 1 as it entered the Gulf.

As the storm continued its steady arc over increasingly warmer waters, it began another cycle of rapid intensification. Early on July 10, it reached category 4 strength again, with sustained winds of 145 mph and a barometric pressure of 27.47 inches. This time, its rapid drop in pressure measured 1.09 inches in twenty-four hours. It was at this point that Dennis set a record as the most intense Atlantic hurricane ever observed before August. Unfortunately this

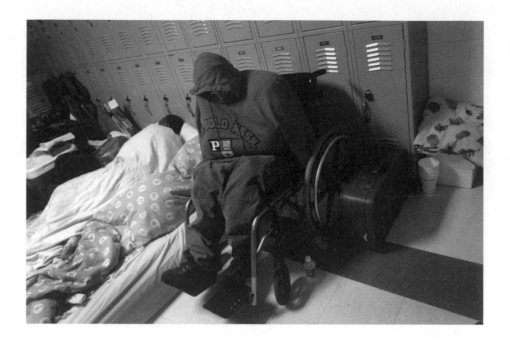

period of rapid strengthening came as the storm was bearing down on the Florida coast near Pensacola, the same area slammed by Hurricane Ivan just nine months before.

While Dennis was blasting Cuba, Florida governor Jeb Bush was taking the all-too-familiar action of declaring a state of emergency. Hurricane warnings were issued for the Keys, and a steady stream of cars fled the island chain. Naval air stations in Key West and Pensacola sent planes to safer quarters, and oil rigs in the Gulf evacuated again. As Dennis passed by the Dry Tortugas and left the Keys unscathed, evacuations spread to the Mississippi, Alabama, and Florida Panhandle coasts, where thousands relived their Ivan experiences by packing their cars and hitting the roads. After witnessing Ivan's destruction in 2004 and then watching the frightening weather updates as Dennis approached, it was an easy decision to make. More than 9,000 people spent the night in shelters in Florida alone.

But fortunately Dennis weakened considerably before making landfall on the afternoon of July 10 at Santa Rosa Island, Florida, between Gulf Breeze and Navarre Beach. According to National Hurricane Center reports, Dennis was a category 3 at landfall, with sustained winds of 120 mph and a central pressure of 27.94 inches. The highest wind measured in Florida was a 120 mph gust recorded in Navarre. Dennis pushed inland quickly through the city of Milton, across Santa Rosa County, and into southwestern Alabama. It then dissipated rapidly, tracked across northern Mississippi and western Tennessee as a tropical depression, and became a meandering, rain-producing low over western Kentucky, Indiana, and Ohio.

Since Dennis struck the coast only a few miles east of where Ivan hit and since both were category 3 hurricanes, news reporters and local residents were quick to offer comparisons between the two storms. The result: almost everyone agreed that Ivan was far, far worse. This was especially true in Pensacola, where Dennis passed just to the east and Ivan landed to the west. Just a few miles made a big difference. During Dennis, the Escambia Bay Bridge was shut down but didn't suffer damages like it did during Ivan, when giant waves washed away entire sections and sent a trucker plunging to his death. Officials were fearful of massive storm-surge destruction on the beaches, but the damages just didn't stack up to what Ivan had done. Roof-ripping winds were also expected but were not as widespread as Ivan's. Some credited the fact that Dennis was more compact and moved through more quickly. Hurricane-force winds extended only forty miles from the center, compared with 105 miles with Ivan. And Dennis sped through at nearly 20 mph, whereas Ivan's motion was about 13 mph. "I've seen worse," Navarre Beach condo owner Jessie Brown told a group of story-hungry reporters the morning after the storm. "And I've only been here three years." Margie Wolfgram, another Navarre resident, told *USA Today*: "We had 22 inches in [the house] last time and nothing in it this time. We did real good. We've lived in this house 18 years. Ivan was the worst."

Still, there was plenty of evidence of Dennis's visit all around. On Pensacola Beach, the Holiday Inn lost its roof, as did the Crabs restaurant. Several Emerald Isle condos were peeled open, and tangled power lines were wrapped around utility poles across Via de Luna. On Navarre Beach, a television-news satellite truck was overturned and half-buried in the sand. Milton was hit hard, as it had been during Ivan. The Santa Rosa Medical Center had windows blown out on two floors, and the nearby Santa Rosa Courthouse lost its roof. Most of the roof was found strewn across a lawn on Elmira Street. Huge trees in front of the courthouse were toppled over too. Several homes lost their roofs in Villa Venyce, east of Gulf Breeze, targets of a possible tornado. Water was standing in many parking lots, and a few houses were under water on Oriole Beach. At Tiger Point, high waters lapped at doorsteps of recently renovated homes that had been flooded by two feet of water during Ivan. Farther inland across Santa Rosa County, huge trees covered roadways and rows of utility poles were leaning. As with most hurricanes, power outages followed the storm, and almost 700,000 customers lost electricity in Florida, Alabama, and Georgia. Sadly, some of Dennis's heaviest rains and winds battered over 3,000 families across the region who were weathering the storm inside the government-issued trailers they'd lived in since Ivan.

East of landfall, high waters flooded roads and homes in several communities. U.S. 98, the major east-west route along the Panhandle, was flooded in many locations but not completely washed out as it had been during Ivan in 2004 or Opal in 1995. In Okaloosa County, Davidson Middle School lost a portion of its metal roof, and there were scattered reports of wind damages in Fort Walton Beach, Destin, and Niceville. Strangely, some of Dennis's worst flooding occurred far to the east in Apalachee Bay, where homes and businesses in St. Marks were inundated by tides six to nine feet above normal. Among the damaged sites was a marina that was wrecked. According to the National Hurricane Center's report on Dennis:

> This surge was higher than currently known wind reports would support for that area, and roughly 3.5 feet higher than the surge forecast from the Sea, Lake, and Overland Surge from Hurricanes (SLOSH) model. This surge was likely triggered by an oceanic trapped shelf wave that propagated northward along the Florida west coast. Modeling results from the Center for Ocean-Atmospheric Prediction Studies at Florida State University suggest that although Dennis was roughly 150 n mi west of the area, this remotely generated sea-level rise added 3–4 ft to the surge in and around Apalachee Bay.

Dennis was blamed for 41 deaths—22 in Haiti, 16 in Cuba, and 3 in the United States. The deaths in the United States included a surfing-related drowning at Dania Beach, Florida, a drowning on a sunken boat in the Florida Keys, and a Decatur, Georgia, man who was killed when a forty-inch-diameter tree fell on his home while he slept. However, more than a dozen additional deaths in the United States were indirectly blamed on Dennis, most of which happened in Florida. Two days after the storm, a utility worker died in Flomaton, Alabama, when he touched a live electric cable he was trying to repair. Utility officials concluded that Ronnie Adams of Winterville, Georgia, was electrocuted because someone nearby had improperly connected a home generator and it back-fed the line. In Walton County, Florida, a three-year-old boy died on Friday before the storm when he apparently fell out of a van while his family was making evacuation preparations. Others died from carbon monoxide poisonings, automobile accidents, electrocutions, natural causes exacerbated by "storm stress," and rooftop falls as they attempted to make roof repairs.

Property damages from Dennis totaled about $1.8 billion in the United States, about half of which were determined to be insured losses.

Following the passage of Hurricane Dennis and with Tropical Storm Katrina looming in the Atlantic, thousands of Florida residents were emotionally drained by the continuous string of hurricane disasters that had swept over them. Many felt their lives had become entangled like power lines twisted by the wind. In an effort to ease their distress, the Florida Department of Children and Families (FDCF) extended its counseling program, Project Hope. In coordination with FEMA and local nonprofit organizations, Project Hope was designed to provide short-term crisis counseling to hurricane victims "to help reduce situational stress, anxiety, and depression." The FDCF estimated that 153,000 Floridians were affected by the strains of the 2004 season and that the program had proven beneficial in more than two dozen hurricane-stricken counties. By the end of July 2005, calls from across the Panhandle were pouring in to the program's toll-free hotline. Dennis-weary callers were able to talk through their fears. But the 2005 hurricane season was just getting started.

KATRINA (AUGUST 25–29, 2005)

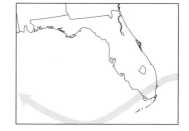

As with most great hurricane disasters, it is impossible for mere words and photos to convey the complete story of Hurricane Katrina. Although it undoubtedly received more worldwide media coverage than any hurricane in history, the round-the-clock television reports, radio talk-show diatribes, emotional photo essays, and sharp-tongued newspaper editorials that followed the event offered only a passing glimpse of its complexity. Those who survived the storm in Louisiana's hard-hit parishes, the Mississippi coast's obliterated communities, and New Orleans's sunken streets endured an unprecedented catastrophe that could not truly be captured on paper, film, or videotape. Their misery was complete, their cumulative losses far beyond anything witnessed in U.S. history. Their stories played out over weeks and months on *Oprah!* and *Larry King Live* to a sympathetic nation. Families were broken, children were missing, and people moved away never to return, expanding the storm's impact from Louisiana and Mississippi to states such as Texas, Florida, Michigan, and California. As the floodwaters receded, questions about governmental response and dubious leadership soon took center stage. FEMA's quarterback lost his job, and the U.S. president's approval ratings plummeted. Oil prices skyrocketed, and supplies ran short. New Orleans's public policies and engineering strategies became topics of debate at watercoolers around the country. The gap between rich and poor was exposed. People were angry. Underlying societal ills floated to the surface. Complex questions begged for rapid and thorough answers. What should be built back, how, when, and where? Who will pay for it? Katrina was simply a modern hurricane disaster that trumped all others. It knocked us all down a notch, reminding us of our true vulnerability to the forces of nature. Was it a worst-case scenario for hurricane forecasters and emergency planners? No, because as bad as it was, it could have been worse. Still, it stands as this nation's most costly natural disaster ever and our most deadly hurricane since the Lake Okeechobee hurricane of 1928.

Hurricane Katrina is included here because before it wreaked havoc on the upper Gulf coast, it crossed South Florida as a minimal hurricane. Its impact on the Sunshine State hardly compares with the catastrophe described above. Nevertheless, it will be remembered by Florida residents for what it could have been and later was—a deadly monster storm that captured the full attention of a nation.

Katrina's origins, like those of many tropical cyclones, were brought on by a complex combination of forces. The busy 2005 season was well under way when Tropical Depression 10 encountered strong shearing winds on August 14 that caused it to degenerate some 800 miles east of Barbados. As it dissipated, it left behind a middle tropospheric circulation that then interacted with a passing tropical wave near the Leeward Islands on August 19. This system drifted north of Hispaniola and eventually grew into Tropical Depression 12 in the southeastern Bahamas on the twenty-third. Convection deepened throughout the night as it tracked to the northwest near Nassau. Finally on the twenty-fourth, the National Hurricane Center identified the system as Tropical Storm Katrina, the eleventh named storm of the year.

Katrina strengthened rapidly, and a hurricane watch was issued for Southeast Florida on the afternoon of August 24. By 11:00 P.M., the watches had changed to warnings, and residents from Key West to West Palm Beach tuned in late-night news reports to see exactly where the storm was heading and how strong it was going to be. The Keys were not evacuated, and most residents in Miami-Dade and Broward Counties just hunkered down for what was expected to be a minimal hurricane landfall. At 5:00 P.M. on the twenty-fifth, Katrina became a hurricane while just fifteen miles east-northeast of Fort Lauderdale. It turned toward the west-southwest and continued to strengthen, making landfall between Hallandale Beach and North Miami Beach at around 6:30 P.M. with sustained winds of 80 mph. Although it couldn't be seen on conventional satellite images, a well-defined eye was observed on the Miami National Weather Service Doppler radar as the storm made landfall. Interestingly, the eye became even more well defined and remained intact as the category 1 hurricane churned across the lower peninsula. When Katrina moved over land, it was rather asymmetrical, with the strongest winds and heaviest rainbands south of the center in Miami-Dade County. It tracked west-southwestward over the Everglades and lost hurricane strength, emerging in the Gulf near Cape Sable as a tropical storm just six hours after making landfall.

Fed by very warm waters in the southeastern Gulf of Mexico, Katrina quickly regained hurricane strength. Even though the storm was now moving away from Florida, a large and potent rainband swirled back around toward the Keys, delivering tropical storm–force winds throughout the day on August 26. Sustained hurricane-force winds were briefly measured on the Dry Tortugas late that afternoon. While the Keys were still catching Katrina's backside, National Hurricane Center director Max Mayfield was holding a press conference in Miami, talking about the future of the storm. The news was not good, as forecasters could see favorable conditions for Katrina's strengthening as it pushed westward into the Gulf. "I just don't see any reason why this will not become a very, very powerful hurricane before it's all over," he told reporters from CNN. "Everybody from southeast Louisiana through the Florida Panhandle really needs to pay attention to this one."

Churning across the Gulf over the next two days, Katrina transformed from a small, minimal hurricane to a massive and powerful cyclone. It reached category 3 strength with winds of 115 mph early on the twenty-seventh and grew tremendously throughout the day. According to Hurricane Center reports, it nearly doubled in size that day, expanding its tropical storm–force wind field to 280 miles across. Weather patterns over Texas and the southeastern United States shifted on August 28, allowing the storm to turn toward the northwest and eventually shift northward. Extremely warm sea-surface temperatures in the central Gulf provided plenty of fuel. At this time, Katrina was experiencing eyewall-replacement cycles, and early on the twenty-eighth, its eyewall contracted and became a sharply defined ring. This was followed by a period of rapid intensification—Katrina exploded from a low-end category 3 to a category 5 in less than twelve hours. Its pressure dropped to 26.64 inches, the fourth lowest pressure ever measured in the Western Hemisphere up to that time (just weeks later Rita bumped it to fifth place, and then Wilma later knocked it back to sixth). Katrina's maximum sustained winds peaked at 175 mph, but just as impressive was the size of the wind field: tropical storm–force winds extended 230 miles from the center, and hurricane winds extended outward up to 105 miles. The prospect of a hurricane this big and this powerful coming ashore was terrifying. So with forecast models showing an inevitable strike somewhere on the upper Gulf coast, millions of people from Louisiana to the Florida Panhandle jumped in their cars for another all-too-familiar exodus to safety. In New Orleans, Mayor Ray Nagin ordered his city evacuated. Most did leave, but as many as 90,000 New Orleans residents stayed behind, either unable or unwilling to flee their below–sea level neighborhoods. Thousands evacuated to the Louisiana Superdome and the New Orleans Convention Center to wait out the storm.

It was about this time that a courageous National Weather Service meteorologist in New Orleans put out a public statement that is perhaps the most chilling ever issued by the service:

8/28/05. MOST OF THE AREA WILL BE UNINHABITABLE FOR WEEKS . . . PERHAPS LONGER. . . . THE MAJORITY OF INDUSTRIAL BUILDINGS WILL BECOME NON FUNCTIONAL. . . . HIGH RISE OFFICE AND APARTMENT BUILDINGS WILL SWAY DANGEROUSLY . . . A FEW TO THE POINT OF TOTAL COLLAPSE. . . . ALL WINDOWS WILL BLOW OUT. . . . AIRBORNE DEBRIS WILL BE WIDESPREAD . . . AND MAY INCLUDE HEAVY ITEMS SUCH AS HOUSEHOLD APPLIANCES AND EVEN LIGHT VEHICLES. . . . SPORT UTILITY VEHICLES AND LIGHT TRUCKS WILL BE MOVED. . . . POWER OUTAGES WILL LAST FOR WEEKS . . . AS MOST POWER POLES WILL BE DOWN AND TRANSFORMERS DE-

STROYED. . . . WATER SHORTAGES WILL MAKE HUMAN SUFFERING INCRED-
IBLE BY MODERN STANDARDS. . . . NEW ORLEANS MAYOR: "EVERY PERSON
IN THE CITY OF NEW ORLEANS IS HEREBY ORDERED TO LEAVE THE CITY."
. . . MAXIMUM SUSTAINED WINDS ARE NEAR 175 MPH . . . GUSTING TO 210
MPH. . . . KATRINA IS A CATASTROPHIC CATEGORY FIVE HURRICANE ON THE
SAFFIR-SIMPSON SCALE. . . . NHC WARNS: ALREADY 26.75" PRESSURE, EX-
PECT 15" RAIN, 25 FOOT STORM SURGE. . . . ON AIR METS QUOTING 40 FOOT
WAVES ON TOP OF THAT! . . . LAST WORD FROM BUOY BEFORE SILENCE WAS
35-FOOT WAVES. . . . 17-FOOT WAVES APPROACHING COAST ALREADY.

The eyewall that formed on August 28 began to erode late that evening,
and throughout the early-morning hours of the twenty-ninth, Katrina weakened considerably. By the time it made its next landfall near Buras, Louisiana,
at around 6:10 A.M., internal structural changes caused the winds to drop to
category 3 strength, about 125 mph. Also contributing to the weakening were
slightly cooler sea-surface temperatures and the entrainment of some dry
air into the central circulation. This loss of intensity was welcome news and
somewhat expected. According to National Hurricane Center reports, most
intense hurricanes moving into the northern Gulf of Mexico tend to weaken
somewhat during the last twelve hours before landfall.

Katrina continued its northward track and made a final landfall at the
mouth of the Pearl River on the Louisiana/Mississippi border. It was still
a category 3 with sustained winds of 120 mph, but after moving inland, it
weakened rapidly. Tracking northward over central Mississippi, it degraded to
category 1 and then tropical storm strength, then shifted toward the northeast. It continued to dissipate over central Tennessee and Kentucky and finally
evolved into an extratropical low over the eastern Great Lakes on August 31.

It is interesting to note that Katrina's category 3 winds at landfall in Louisiana hardly seem to correspond to its extremely low barometric pressure measured at the same time. In its report on the storm, the National Hurricane
Center explained:

> The estimated Buras landfall intensity of 110 kt [125 mph], just beneath the
> threshold of Category 4, is quite low relative to many other hurricanes with
> a comparable minimum central pressure. In fact, the central pressure of 920
> mb [27.17 inches] is now the lowest on record in the Atlantic basin for an
> intensity of 110 kt, surpassing Hurricane Floyd (1999) that at one point had
> a central pressure of 930 mb with an intensity of 110 kt. The 920 mb pressure
> is also the third lowest at U.S. landfall on record, behind only Hurricane
> Camille in 1969 (909 mb) and the 1935 Labor Day hurricane that struck the
> Florida Keys (892 mb). The relatively weak winds in Katrina for such a low
> pressure are the result of the broadening pressure field on 29 August that
> spread the pressure gradient over a much larger than average distance from
> center, as confirmed by both surface and aircraft observations.

As a result, category 3 Katrina had a lower barometric pressure at landfall (27.17 inches) than did category 5 Andrew in 1992 (27.23 inches).

In Florida, the highest winds measured included gusts of 82 mph at Fort Lauderdale, 87 mph at the National Hurricane Center in Miami, and (unofficially) 97 mph at Homestead General Airport. An automated reporting station at the Dry Tortugas, about sixty miles west of Key West, recorded sustained winds of 82 mph and a gust of 105 mph. Storm surge on the Southeast Florida beaches and through the Keys was generally less than two feet. But surges of over four feet affected Flamingo in Monroe County and the Everglades National Park. Several trailers were flooded, along with Park Service quarters and over a dozen vehicles. Heavy rains poured over the southern half of the storm's track, while lesser rainfall was seen along the northern side. Miami-Dade, Monroe, and Collier Counties received the largest amounts. Homestead Air Force Base recorded 14.04 inches, Florida City reported 12.25 inches, and 11.13 inches were measured in Cutler Ridge. These rains flooded streets, warehouses, vehicles, and a few homes and caused numerous problems across the region. As Katrina made landfall in Louisiana and Mississippi, its massive size generated wind and surge effects that spread eastward into Florida's Panhandle and upper west coast. On Pensacola Beach, the surge measured over five feet, and a wind gust of 71 mph was recorded at the Pensacola Naval Air Station.

But Katrina will always be remembered for the catastrophic effects of its wind and surge in Louisiana and coastal Mississippi. At first, meteorologists reported that winds were 140 mph at landfall there, but after later analysis of aircraft data, they concluded that winds were sustained at 125 mph. The strongest sustained winds measured on the ground were 87 mph recorded in Grand Isle, Louisiana, but the automated instrument that made the recording failed about two hours before the closest approach of the eye. That was a problem with many reporting stations that took a pounding from the storm. The highest gust, though unofficial, was 135 mph in Poplarville, Mississippi, at the Pearl River County Emergency Operations Center (EOC). The Jackson County EOC in Pascagoula recorded a gust of 124 mph.

Because of its intensity and large size, Katrina was able to generate a storm-surge effect of record proportions along the northern Gulf coast. Unfortunately precise measurement across the affected area was complicated by the failure of many tide gauges and the loss of structures to use in measuring the surge after so many buildings were completely destroyed. One of the highest recordings was made at the Hancock County, Mississippi, EOC, where a storm tide of 28 feet was measured, suggesting that storm surge may have been as high as 27 feet at that location. Similar surge effect would have been expected throughout the area around Gulfside, Waveland, Bay St. Louis, Pass Christian, Long Beach, Gulfport, and Biloxi. In Gulfport and Biloxi, surge levels were said to have been five to ten feet higher than those measured after Hurricane Camille in 1969. Southeast of New Orleans, surges that may have exceeded 25 feet obliterated Delta communities in Plaquemines and St. Bernard Parishes. The unprecedented surge pushed the Gulf as much as six miles inland along portions of the Mississippi coast and up to twelve miles inland along bays and rivers. The tide crossed I-10 in many locations. Although not quite as high, the surge along the Alabama coast was also dramatic. Homes were destroyed in Bayou La Batre, where the surge reached 13 feet, and the Mobile State Docks in Mobile Bay reported a surge of 11.45 feet, nearly breaking the record of 11.60 feet set back in 1916.

In addition to high winds and surge, there were other notable weather effects in Louisiana and Mississippi. While Katrina was churning into the northern Gulf of Mexico, it generated huge sea swells that were some of the highest ever observed. The National Data Buoy Center's buoy 42040, positioned about sixty-four miles south of Dauphin Island, Alabama, recorded a peak wave height of 55 feet on August 29 that matched the highest ever recorded by that program. The giant swells, coupled with the elevated effect of the storm surge, generated most of the coastal destruction that was later found. Rainfall was generally eight to twelve inches along a large band just west of the storm track in southeastern Louisiana. The combination of rising waters from the Gulf and persistent heavy rains caused Lake Pontchartrain to overflow, breaching the famous dike system that keeps water out of New Orleans. Within hours, floodwaters filled the streets of the city. And thirty-three tornadoes were associated with the hurricane, including one that touched down in the Florida Keys on the morning of August 26. Once Katrina made landfall in Louisiana and Mississippi, more twisters were spotted in Mississippi, Alabama, and Georgia.

Katrina produced a nearly endless tally of destruction. In Florida, where it arrived as a category 1 hurricane, the scope and severity of damages were predictably mild, especially when compared to what would follow. Power was out for about 1.3 million South Florida residents because electric lines, poles, and transformers were jostled or knocked down by the wind. There were many reports of damages to nurseries and vegetable crops. Some homes were flooded, a few lost parts of their roofs, and trees were toppled in many neighborhoods. In Broward County, three people were killed in accidents involving falling trees. Also among the damages was a partially constructed highway overpass that collapsed on U.S. 836 west of Miami.

Destruction in several parishes in Louisiana, in the city of New Orleans, and along the Mississippi coast could only be described as epic. Storm tides wiped out entire communities and either swept them into huge piles of rubble or left them deeply submerged. Nowhere was the scene of destruction more gripping than in St. Bernard Parish, Louisiana, where entire towns were temporarily covered under twenty feet of water. Gulf-front communities like Waveland, Gulfport, and Biloxi resembled war zones where miles of coastline had been bombed. Structures nearest the Gulf simply disappeared, leaving only concrete-block outlines of where they once stood. Floating rafts of debris from demolished homes became battering rams that crushed and damaged more homes. And it wasn't just houses that were obliterated; government buildings, historic structures, schools, and even offshore oil rigs were also destroyed. Huge floating casinos on the Mississippi coast were smashed by waves and sent sailing down the beach. The surge-related damages extended well eastward into Alabama too, where many Dauphin Island homes were damaged or destroyed and a new channel was cut across the island's western end.

New Orleans, of course, sits below sea level, so the flood that occurred in the days following Katrina was one that had long been feared. For decades, hurricane forecasters and emergency planners had warned that the city would one day be inundated by a major hurricane. Katrina fulfilled that prophecy, flooding more than 80 percent of the city after the system of dikes and levees built to protect it failed in more than a dozen places. Some streets and neighborhoods were submerged in up to twenty feet of water. Tens of thousands of the city's trapped residents scrambled onto rooftops or floated around on anything they could find—from rubber inner tubes to trash cans. Thousands more residents were trapped in the Louisiana Superdome and the New Orleans Convention Center, where they had sought refuge. Hospitals and other downtown buildings were also flooded, and many lost large windows to 100-plus mph gusts. New Orleans, though on the somewhat weaker western side of the hurricane, became the epicenter of human misery and destruction to a nation of people who sat glued to their televisions watching it all unfold.

Hurricane Katrina ranks among the deadliest hurricanes in U.S. history. According to a National Hurricane Center report revised in August 2006, Katrina was responsible for 1,833 deaths, including 1,577 in Louisiana, 238 in Mississippi, 14 in Florida, 2 in Alabama, and 2 in Georgia. These numbers may be adjusted upward in years to come, but the sheer number of deaths was overwhelming by modern standards in the United States; Katrina was the most lethal weather event since the Lake Okeechobee hurricane in 1928 and the third deadliest since 1900, when over 8,000 lives were lost in the Galveston hurricane. As is often the case with disasters of its scope, counting the deaths was an inexact process. Discerning between deaths directly caused by the hurricane and those indirectly related was not easy. Even so, over 1,500 people in four states were believed to have been directly killed by the storm.

Among the dead were about a dozen killed in Florida, a significant number for a category 1 hurricane. Two boaters anchored off Dinner Key Marina drowned when the storm turned their way on August 25. A Fort Lauderdale man was crushed by a falling tree as he drove his Cadillac Escalade along

Riverside Drive during the storm. Two other Broward residents were killed by falling trees, and a nearby Cooper City man died when his car struck a tree. Others died from automobile accidents, carbon monoxide poisonings, and debris-removal accidents.

The following are some of Katrina's more notable statistics, compiled from reports by the National Climatic Data Center, FEMA, the American Red Cross, CNN, and the Associated Press:

- Katrina was the third most deadly hurricane in the United States since 1900, with an estimated death toll of over 1,500.
- Its barometric low of 902 mb (26.64 inches), measured on August 28, was for a short time the fourth lowest pressure ever observed in the Atlantic basin. After having been surpassed by Rita and Wilma later in the 2005 season, Katrina ranks as having the sixth lowest pressure ever recorded.
- Its barometric low of 920 mb (27.17 inches) at landfall in Louisiana is the third lowest on record in the United States. Only the Labor Day hurricane of 1935 (892 mb or 26.34 inches) and Hurricane Camille in 1969 (909 mb or 26.85 inches) had lower barometric pressures at landfall.
- Katrina ranks as the most destructive hurricane in U.S. history, though total damage estimates vary considerably. The American Insurance Services Group placed the figure for insured losses at $40.6 billion in the United States. Conventional methodology assumes that total damages are roughly twice insured losses, therefore Katrina's total estimated cost is $81 billion. Even after adjusting for inflation, Katrina's costs are more than double those of Andrew in 1992, the United States' second costliest hurricane disaster. Note that some news agencies frequently report that Katrina's damages exceeded $100 billion.
- Over 1.2 million people were under evacuation orders along the Gulf coast when Katrina arrived in Louisiana, although estimates vary on how many people actually fled.
- Storm surges approaching 30 feet affected portions of the Mississippi coast, perhaps the highest ever seen in the United States.
- As a result of Katrina, oil production in the Gulf was reduced by 1.4 million barrels per day or approximately 95 percent of the daily Gulf of Mexico production. Gasoline prices reached record highs in the days following the hurricane.
- Over 1.7 million people lost electrical power in the Gulf states due to the storm, and many were without power for weeks. About 1.3 million customers in Florida lost power during Katrina's initial landfall.
- In Louisiana alone, as many as 5,000 people were rescued by helicopter and boat in the first few days after the storm.

- The Red Cross estimated that more than 220,000 volunteers from all fifty states participated in its relief efforts. It operated over 1,100 shelters and temporary housing facilities in 27 states. The Red Cross provided financial assistance to 1.2 million families or 3.7 million hurricane victims. Donors contributed almost $2 billion through the Red Cross, a figure that does not include gifts given through other charitable organizations.
- FEMA issued more than 1.4 million checks to Katrina victims, including over $3.1 billion for Louisiana victims alone.
- The Congressional Budget Office estimated that Katrina may have cost the United States more than 400,000 jobs and shaved up to 1 percent off the nation's economic growth in the second half of 2005.

WILMA (OCTOBER 24, 2005)

In September 2005, while the nation watched the unfolding tragedy in New Orleans and Mississippi in the aftermath of Hurricane Katrina, forecasters at the National Hurricane Center were busy working overtime observing a string of additional storms. Among them was Hurricane Ophelia, a category 1 that inched slowly along the North Carolina coast through the middle of the month, pounding the state's barrier islands with hurricane-force winds for two days. Another was Hurricane Rita, a record-setting category 5 that barely missed landfall in the Florida Keys and went on to strike the Texas-Louisiana coast. Rita formed on September 19 in the southeastern Bahamas and tracked westward through the Florida Straits the following day as a category 2 storm. It delivered tropical storm–force winds to Key West, with gusts up to 76 mph. Once over the superheated waters of the central Gulf of Mexico, Rita exploded into a category 5 with sustained winds of 165 mph, the second storm of the 2005 season to reach that intensity. As it strengthened even further to 175 mph, its pressure dropped to 26.49 inches, the third lowest barometric pressure ever measured in the Atlantic basin (surpassing the low-pressure mark set by Katrina just weeks before). It briefly threatened a direct hit on the already wrecked and flooded New Orleans area but instead forced a massive evacuation in Galveston, Texas, and eventually made landfall as a category 3 on the Texas-Louisiana border. Some portions of New Orleans were flooded once again by Rita's rains. It was a close call for Florida and for thousands of Katrina victims in Louisiana and Mississippi, but Rita still left behind a multi-billion-dollar disaster along stretches of the northwestern Gulf coast.

The incredible 2005 season rolled on into October, when six more tropical storms were named, four of which became hurricanes. As the Hurricane Center identified each new storm, the list of available names became shorter. Hurricane Stan struck portions of Mexico and Guatemala, killing hundreds in flash floods and mudslides. Tropical Storm Tammy formed off of Cape Canaveral on October 5 and drifted northward over the northeast Florida coast, striking Mayport with sustained winds of 50 mph but causing minimal damages. Hurricane Vince formed far out in the Atlantic and turned eastward to strike the coast of Spain as a tropical storm—the first known tropical cyclone to make landfall there. But the wacky 2005 season was far from over. On October 17, the Hurricane Center finally exhausted its prescribed list of names when Wilma was born in the western Caribbean Sea. With more than a month left in the official season, Wilma became the twenty-first named storm, tying a record set back in 1933 for the most storms in one year.

Wilma drifted westward and became a hurricane the next day, on October 18, the twelfth storm of the year to reach that threshold. This tied the record for the most hurricanes in a season set in 1969. But as forecasters at the Hurricane Center in Miami gathered reconnaissance reports on Wilma over the next day, it became clear that this hurricane was setting even more important records. They watched in amazement as the hurricane exploded from tropical storm to category 5 intensity in just twenty-four hours. Its maximum sustained winds jumped from 70 mph on October 18 to 175 mph on the nineteenth, a gain of 105 mph. This established Wilma as the most rapidly intensifying Atlantic storm on record. At one point around midnight on October 18, Wilma's winds increased from 110 mph to 150 mph in two hours and then from 150 mph to 175 mph in just ninety minutes. When sustained winds reached 175 mph, NOAA aircraft reported that the storm's eye was less than four miles across. By reaching that intensity, it became the third category 5 of the year, the first time three storms of that strength had ever been observed in the Atlantic in one season. At its peak, the minimum central pressure dipped to 26.05 inches, setting another new record—Wilma is the most intense hurricane on record in the Atlantic basin, surpassing the 26.22 inch mark measured during Hurricane Gilbert in 1988.

Soon the monster storm experienced an eyewall-replacement cycle, and some weakening occurred over the next day. Meanwhile, vacationers and business owners in Cozumel and Cancun, Mexico, scrambled to prepare for its arrival. On the twenty-first, a slightly weaker Wilma rolled into Cozumel packing 140 mph winds and pushing a massive storm surge into the beachfront hotels and resorts that line the island. Cancun was next, where the hurricane also struck as a category 4. Unfortunately many vacationers, including thousands of Americans, were caught off-guard by the hurricane's rapid development and were unable to escape their resorts. Flights were cancelled, and thousands of American tourists were bused to shelters where some waited for weeks to leave. Damages were heavy throughout the region: power was out, streets were blocked by piles of debris, and dozens of large hotels were flooded and battered by high winds. According to the National Climatic Data Center, in Mexico the storm damaged over 700,000 dwellings and left some 300,000 homeless. Interestingly, this same stretch of the Mexican coast was hit earlier in the year by category 4 Hurricane Emily, though Wilma was far more destructive.

Wilma was moving slowly at the time of landfall, dragging across the Yucatán Peninsula at only 5 mph while dumping up to five feet of rain. It drifted northward across the northeastern tip of the peninsula and emerged in the Gulf of Mexico late on October 22. Even though it had weakened considerably over land, it was still a category 2 with winds of nearly 100 mph when it moved back over water. It was about this time that Florida residents began to take notice of the hurricane since forecasters felt that it was likely to turn their way. And it did. The projected track turned toward the northeast, and Wilma accelerated toward Florida on the twenty-third. Along the way, it punished Havana, Cuba, as it passed nearby, sending huge swells over the city's protective seawall and flooding city streets with six feet of water. Thousands were caught off-guard because evacuations were not ordered in Havana until after midnight, when most residents were already asleep. With its wind field expanding and its eye growing to more than fifty miles across, it regained category 3 strength and spun dangerously into Florida waters.

About the time Wilma turned away from the Yucatán, officials began broadcasting a clear message to millions of South Florida residents: get ready for another hurricane, a strong one, and prepare for more major destruction. Some residents were fed up with all the storms, gnashing their teeth at newspaper headlines that announced: "Seventh Hurricane in Fourteen Months." Hurricane warnings went up for the Keys and for the east coast as far north as Titusville and the west coast as far north as Longboat Key. Evacuations got under way, but again Governor Bush was forced to make urgent pleas for coastal residents to evacuate their homes, especially in the Keys, where Wilma was expected to produce a large storm surge. The surge was of particular concern to Hurricane Center forecasters, who feared that thousands could be trapped if they remained in homes at low elevations. Comparisons soon emerged with another recent storm, 2004's Hurricane Charley. Ed Rappaport, deputy director of the Hurricane Center, told CNN: "This is going to be a much more significant event, more widespread for Florida even than Charley was. We think it will be category 3, moving about 20 to 25 mph by the time it hits Florida."

The Red Cross sprang into action, opening over 100 staffed shelters with a total capacity of 160,000 across Florida and South Georgia. Unfortunately very few residents in the Keys took the storm seriously, according to Monroe County Emergency Management director Billy Wagner. No shelters were opened in the Keys because of the lack of sizable structures built to withstand winds and storm surge. Many residents along Florida's southwest coast did evacuate, but the large majority of people in the hurricane's projected path simply hunkered down, not sure where they would go even if they were to leave. Finally, Wilma behaved as forecasters had predicted, picking up both speed and strength just before making landfall at Everglades City at 6:30 A.M. on October 24.

Tracking inland as a category 3 with maximum sustained winds of 120 mph, Wilma raced over the lower peninsula at 25 mph, crossing Big Cypress National Preserve and spinning through the densely populated Miami–Fort Lauderdale region with what seemed like lightning speed. Its exceptionally large sixty-mile-diameter eye could easily be seen on local radar. The storm exited Florida's east coast just above Palm Beach as a category 2 just over four hours after making landfall. Once in the Atlantic, Wilma briefly reintensified and became a strong category 3 as it tracked away from Florida's central east coast and out to sea. It gradually weakened over the next day and eventually lost tropical characteristics southeast of Halifax, Nova Scotia, on October 25. About that time, a powerful nor'easter over New England drew strength from Wilma's demise, creating nearly a "perfect storm" that churned up twenty-foot waves and gusts to 70 mph at Cape Cod, Massachusetts.

Most areas in the storm's direct path experienced extreme winds as the eye-wall barreled through. Around 10:30 A.M., a meteorological field station at the south end of Lake Okeechobee measured sustained winds of 103 mph and a gust of 112 mph. Gusts were recorded to 101 mph at Palm Beach International Airport, 99 mph at Fort Lauderdale, and 92 mph at Miami International Airport. Four reporting stations measured peak gusts just before their instruments failed: Opa Locka (105 mph), Pompano Beach (98 mph), Tamiami (83 mph), and Naples (82 mph). In its summary report on the storm, the National Weather Service Forecast Office in Miami noted a significant phenomenon regarding Wilma's winds:

> An interesting and revealing aspect of Wilma was the wind field in the eye wall. The winds on the back (south/west) side of the eye wall were as strong, if not stronger, than those on the front (north/east) side. This goes against the common, but sometimes erroneous, belief that the strongest winds in a hurricane are always in the right-front quadrant of the storm. This occurred over much of South Florida, except for central and southern Miami–Dade County which barely missed the southwestern portion of the eye wall, and likely contributed to the heavier damage across Broward and Palm Beach counties, compared to slightly lesser damage across much of Miami-Dade and Collier counties.

Storm surge throughout much of South Florida was significant, but the most severe flooding occurred in the sparsely populated portions of mainland Monroe County south of Everglades City. The storm surge in Chokolos-

Glen Bierman and Julia Hamel rowed through the downtown streets of Key West in a homemade rowboat during Hurricane Wilma in October 2005. Bierman built the rowboat following the approach of Hurricane Rita the month before. (Photo by Josh Ritchie, courtesy of Getty Images)

kee was seven feet, but along the coastal mangrove swamps to the south, the surge was estimated to be thirteen to eighteen feet. Marco Island reported a surge of seven feet, and tides in some areas of the Keys were estimated at five to seven feet. Large portions of Key West were submerged during the storm, but the water receded quickly and there were only minor reports of damage. Even Florida's southeast coast didn't escape the wrapping effects of Wilma's surge—a tide gauge at Virginia Key measured a surge of four feet, and there was minor tidal flooding in downtown Miami and Coconut Grove. Rainfall amounts of two to four inches fell across much of South Florida, with up to six inches reported in western Collier County and in areas around Lake Okeechobee. A few stations recorded up to nine inches, even though the storm spun rapidly across the state.

Wilma's quick trip over Florida from west to east left shattered glass and tangled power lines in almost every neighborhood along the way. Residents in Naples and Marco Island said it was "far worse" than Hurricane Charley in 2004. Broken roof tiles and toppled palms littered the streets of many resort communities on the lower southwest coast. High-rise condominiums lining the Naples beach lost rows of windows, allowing piercing winds to blow through their upper floors. Ninety percent of the mobile homes in East Naples were destroyed. Along the densely developed southeast coast, large population centers like Miami, Hialeah, Hollywood, Fort Lauderdale, and West Palm Beach caught the brunt of the storm. Winds topping 100 mph whipped through downtown high-rise buildings, popping out rows of windows and

A downtown Miami bank building was one of Wilma's many victims as the storm marched across South Florida. Dozens of large plate glass windows were shattered by gusting winds. Several million residents in the hurricane's path were without power for days. (Photo by Roberto Schmidt, courtesy of Getty Images)

peeling away huge chunks of the structures' facades. Among the hardest-hit areas was downtown Miami's financial district near Brickell Avenue. One of the best accounts of the destruction came from the *South Florida Sun-Sentinel*:

In South Florida's sprawling suburbs, the blue glow of exploding transformers illuminated the pre-dawn sky, and the storm stirred whitecaps even on neighborhood lakes. . . . More than 200 people stood next to the Colonial Bank Building where it appeared the entire southern facade peeled off. Fire officials tried to move the crowd away as shards of glass came crashing down. Office documents from different buildings swirled in the wind gusts while many others floated in the floodwaters. Curtains were flapping through the blown out windows of the ritzy JW Marriott Hotel and water poured into the hotel's marbled lobby. More than a dozen windows were blown out from the Four Seasons Hotel, among the most luxurious hotels in downtown Miami. Nearby, a green Toyota hatchback appeared stuck in the raging floodwaters in the middle of Brickell Avenue, all of its windows smashed in. Over at the Miami Police Department, the building had lost some letters on its sign. "It was a wild and crazy night," police Lt. Bill Schwartz said. "This building, built in 1976, shook like it was 1876."

Broward County faced some of Wilma's fiercest winds, and the outcome was evident on every street corner. The landscape was littered with the usual hurricane flotsam of downed trees, shingles, lampposts, utility poles, signs, and awnings. Trees blocked side streets and major expressways, including Federal Highway through Fort Lauderdale. Huge branches crushed the hoods of cars and light trucks, and smaller ones smashed their windshields. Over 800 mobile homes were damaged or destroyed. High-rises lost their windows, paving the streets below with shattered glass and scattered office supplies. Among the buildings most visibly damaged were the Broward County Courthouse and the fourteen-story Broward School Board office building.

In Key West, where more than a third of the city was flooded and water filled some homes to a depth of five feet, witnesses said the tide rose so fast they didn't have time to move their cars. One local said the water surged four to five feet within forty-five minutes. Others added that their decision to ride out the storm was a big mistake. Still, since the waters receded quickly, residents and visitors soon flocked to local watering holes that somehow managed to reopen even though power was out across the island chain.

One of Wilma's most memorable effects across South Florida was its decimation of the region's electrical power system. From Key West northward to Daytona Beach, Wilma knocked out transformers, toppled utility poles, flooded substations, and whipped miles of power lines onto the ground. In some areas of Broward County, even concrete power poles were snapped by the hurricane's winds. The Florida State Emergency Response Team reported that at its peak, the storm cut power to over 6 million people, creating the most widespread power outage in Florida history. In some areas, the outages lasted for weeks, though thousands of utility workers quickly arrived on the scene to restore power. The lack of electricity shut down factories and large corporations, disrupted school schedules, left busy intersections without traffic signals, and caused millions of hurricane-weary Floridians to bump through their homes in the dark. In addition to losing power, most people also lost cable television, telephone service, and Internet connectivity, and many did not have these services restored for more than two months. Emergency generators became a hot commodity, and people found inventive ways to cope without ice, lights, and electric ranges for cooking. Fortunately the lack of air-conditioning wasn't a big problem after Wilma because the strong cold front that had helped steer the storm over Florida plunged temperatures into the upper forties in the evenings that followed.

The scope of the disaster presented huge challenges to Florida's emergency-response and -recovery officials, as well as to the much-maligned FEMA bureaucracy. The plans were well laid: thousands of relief workers and National Guard troops and countless tons of food, water, and ice were all ready for distribution across Wilma's destruction zone. In the first days after the storm, many received what they needed to survive, especially the food and water that are so critical after any major disaster. But in heavily populated cities and scattered towns across the region, many tired, hungry, and thirsty storm victims became outraged when distribution stations didn't fulfill their expectations. While FEMA asked for their patience, residents stood in lines for up to twelve hours in North Miami to receive a bag of ice and three bottles of water. In Hollywood, an incorrect distribution time was announced, adding several hours to the wait. A similar fiasco occurred in Naples, where relief workers didn't show up to distribute supplies when they said they would. But with such a huge number of people in need, officials conceded that glitches, shortages, and inconveniences were inevitable. Food, water, and ice were not the only commodities worth waiting for—long lines formed at many gas stations across the state, partially due to restricted supplies and a lack of stations with power to run their pumps but also due to post-Katrina rumors of gas-rationing schemes that turned out to be urban legends. The long waits were made even more frustrating by surging gas prices that exceeded $4 per gallon.

According to the National Hurricane Center, Wilma was directly responsible for 25 deaths, including 12 in Haiti, 6 in Florida, 6 in Mexico, and 1 in Jamaica. Among the deaths in Florida were two in Collier County and one in St. Johns County. In Coral Springs, a man reportedly was killed when he was struck by a falling tree. In Palm Beach County, a man was crushed by a tree when he went outside to move his car during the eye of the storm. A Boynton Beach woman was found dead in her home surrounded by broken glass, the victim of an apparent heart attack, and a Miami–Dade County man apparently drowned when his boat capsized on Maule Lake. Some newspaper reports suggested that over thirty-five Florida fatalities were related to the storm, including victims of accidents during the storm and in the cleanup afterward.

The Insurance Information Institute reported $6.1 billion in insured losses for Wilma, which puts the total damages for the storm at over $12 billion. Wilma was the last hurricane of the 2005 season to make landfall in the United States, and it capped off an incredibly deadly and expensive two-year run for cyclone activity. With over $12 billion in losses, it joined five other hurricanes from the 2004 and 2005 seasons—Charley, Frances, Ivan, Katrina, and Rita—that all vaulted into the top ten most expensive hurricanes in U.S. history (see a ranking of the twenty costliest storms in the appendix).

The incredible 2005 hurricane season went far beyond Wilma, of course, setting additional records with more storms through November and December and finally ending in January 2006 with the demise of Tropical Storm Zeta. For the first time since naming began in the early 1950s, the National Hurricane Center exhausted its annual name list and began using letters of the Greek alphabet. Alpha, Beta, Gamma, Delta, Epsilon, and Zeta, when added to the twenty-one on the list, brought the season total to twenty-seven, shattering the old record of twenty-one storms set in 1933. Some blamed global warming. Most NOAA researchers, however, suggested that the increase in activity had more to do with a natural decadal cycle that shifted climatic conditions. Either way, with sea-surface temperatures in some parts of the Tropics averaging two to three degrees Fahrenheit above normal, the record-breaking 2005 Atlantic hurricane season became a benchmark that meteorologists would continue to study for years to come.

The following are a few highlights and new records from the 2005 Atlantic hurricane season, as compiled by the National Climatic Data Center, the Florida Division of Emergency Management, William Gray, and Colorado State University:

- Twenty-seven named storms formed during the 2005 season, the most named storms to develop in a single season. The old record of twenty-one was set in 1933.
- Fifteen hurricanes formed in 2005, the most ever observed in a single season. The old record was twelve hurricanes in 1969.
- Seven major hurricanes (category 3 or greater) formed in 2005, tying the record for the number of major hurricanes set in 1950.

- Three category 5 hurricanes formed during the 2005 season (Katrina, Rita, and Wilma), the most ever observed in a single season. Two formed in 1960 and 1961.
- Seven named storms made landfall in the United States in 2005 (Arlene, Cindy, Dennis, Katrina, Rita, Tammy, and Wilma). This puts 2005 in a tie for third place in the number of landfalling storms behind 1916, when eight storms made landfall, and 2004, when nine storms struck. Hurricane Ophelia would have been the eighth of 2005 but barely missed landfall in North Carolina.
- The 2005 season was the most destructive in U.S. history, with well over $100 billion in total damages. Hurricane Katrina, the eleventh storm of the season, became the most expensive disaster of any kind in U.S. history, with total damages estimated at over $81 billion. Some estimates are even higher.
- Five named storms occurred in July (Cindy, Dennis, Emily, Franklin, and Gert), the most ever observed for that month.
- Hurricane Dennis, with a barometric pressure of 27.47 inches, became the most intense hurricane ever observed before August. Then just days later, Hurricane Emily, with a barometric pressure of 27.44 inches, eclipsed the record set by Dennis and became the most intense pre-August storm.
- Hurricane Katrina's central pressure fell to 26.64 inches, the fourth lowest pressure recorded up to that time in the Atlantic basin. Hurricane Rita's pressure dropped to 26.49 inches, the third lowest pressure measured up to that time in the Atlantic basin. Then Hurricane Wilma broke all records when its pressure dropped to 26.05 inches, making it the most intense hurricane ever observed in the Atlantic basin, surpassing Hurricane Gilbert's barometric low of 26.22 in 1988.
- Katrina's central pressure at landfall in Louisiana was 27.17 inches, the third lowest pressure ever measured at landfall in the United States, behind the Labor Day hurricane of 1935 (26.35 inches) and Hurricane Camille in 1969 (26.84 inches).
- Six named storms formed in October (Stan, Tammy, Vince, Wilma, Alpha, and Beta), tying the record for the month set in 1950. Four of these became hurricanes (Stan, Vince, Wilma, and Beta). Only 1950 had more hurricanes form during October.
- Hurricane Vince formed farther east and north than any other storm in the Atlantic basin. It is the only tropical cyclone in recorded history to have struck Spain.
- Hurricane Epsilon was the sixth hurricane to ever form in December.
- Florida was struck by three hurricanes (Dennis, Katrina, and Wilma) and affected by three more tropical storms (Arlene, Rita, and Tammy)

during the 2005 season. In 2004 and 2005, Florida was hit by seven hurricanes (Charley, Frances, Ivan, Jeanne, Dennis, Katrina, and Wilma) within fourteen months. Five were major hurricanes (Charley, Ivan, Jeanne, Dennis, and Wilma). In Florida alone, total damages from the seven hurricane landfalls were estimated at over $50 billion.

- During the 2005 season in Florida, hurricane volunteers logged more than 4.7 million hours of service, and organizations donated more than $18 million worth of food, ice, and water. The Florida Hurricane Relief Fund, established in August 2004, raised over $20 million in private contributions during its first year to assist with unmet needs and other expenses in the hardest-hit Florida counties.

THE NEXT GREAT STORM

When *Florida's Hurricane History* was first published in 1998, it was clear that Hurricane Andrew was the measuring stick by which modern U.S. hurricane disasters should be compared. Its impact on South Florida in August 1992 not only astounded seasoned weather watchers and broke numerous records for destruction but also focused national attention on the monumental challenges we face in responding to and recovering from large-scale disasters. It was a metro-catastrophe. The onslaught of category 5 winds over a semi-urban landscape was followed by an unprecedented and complex cleanup and recovery effort that at times was also rather stormy. Following Andrew, our understanding of the social, political, environmental, and economic aspects of disaster recovery was forever changed. "Emergency management" became a buzzword and federal and state politicians poured new money into mitigation and response programs as, rather suddenly, Andrew spawned a newfound respect for the awesome destructive forces of hurricanes.

Today, almost fifteen years later, the Andrew experience seems to have faded into history as more recent destructive hurricanes have captured our full attention. Through the 2004 and 2005 seasons, warmer-than-normal sea-surface temperatures and other global weather factors turned the waters of the Atlantic, Caribbean, and Gulf of Mexico into a cyclone machine, cranking out potent hurricanes as fast as forecasters could track them. These were record-setting years in which each successive storm seemed to top the one before. Four barreled through Florida in 2004 and hit almost every corner of the state. And, of course, Hurricane Katrina topped them all in 2005 when it slammed into Louisiana and Mississippi, flooded New Orleans, and became the most destructive disaster of any kind in U.S. history. By the time Wilma struck in October, Florida had been pummeled by seven hurricanes in only fourteen months. Five of those seven were major hurricanes, category 3 or greater. It was a flurry of activity never before seen since record keeping began in the mid-1800s.

It is unlikely that the flurry has ended. The Sunshine State remains vulnerable to more deadly and destructive hurricanes, especially since forecasters believe that active hurricane seasons may continue for years to come. Sooner or later, another big storm will make landfall. Atmospheric scientists and emergency planners agree that it's just a matter of time before some portion of Florida is hit by another one. Perhaps it will be a category 4 like Charley or even a category 5 like Andrew. It could strike this year or next year, or it could come thirty or more years in the future. It could land in downtown Miami, track across Tampa Bay, or even pass right over Jacksonville. No one knows when or where it will strike, but we do know that eventually it will blast ashore somewhere and cause massive destruction—perhaps even greater than that caused by Katrina. Since there is nothing anyone can do to alter that foreboding reality, the question is: Are we ready for the next great hurricane?

Since Andrew, we have entered a new era in hurricane disaster management—the organized effort to prepare for and recover from major hurricanes. With every storm, hard lessons are learned, operational plans are tweaked, and new initiatives are put to the test. Coordination and communication between various agencies on the federal, state, and local levels have improved substantially in recent years, despite the meltdown so widely reported in New Orleans following Katrina. Governments have pumped billions of dollars into relief efforts, but significant resources have also been funneled into emergency planning to better equip and train personnel and reduce the impact of future storms. Chuck Lanza, Miami–Dade County's former director of emergency management, saw great improvements after Andrew: "We lacked a lot of money in the old days. There were very few areas of this country that had good emergency plans or organizations because there wasn't the money—people didn't see the threat as clearly. On the east coast, hurricanes were infrequent, and when they did hit, it was usually someplace else. They weren't the magnitude, in our memory, of a Hurricane Andrew. That really was the defining

No one knows which portion of Florida will be the next to fall victim to a powerful and destructive hurricane.

moment—it changed emergency management—from the east coast all the way through to Texas."

Although a few breakdowns in coordination occurred along the way, Florida's overall response to the string of storms in 2004 and 2005 was well planned and effective. Never before had the state's emergency planners been tested by so many major disasters over such an extended period. From Charley in August 2004 through Wilma in October 2005, the network of local, state, and federal agencies that deal with disaster response and recovery never got a break. FEMA and its partners on the federal level never left the state. Nonprofit organizations like the Salvation Army and the American Red Cross brought in volunteers from across the nation who fanned out over Florida to help meet immediate needs. Countless church groups, civic clubs, and other nongovernmental organizations also came to rebuild homes, help with repairs, and provide other general support. Governor Bush and members of his administration were forced to make hurricane recovery their top priority. Craig Fugate, director of Florida's Division of Emergency Management, described the state's efforts: "After September 11, some people thought we'd have to change everything in emergency management. In Florida, we demonstrated it works. You can respond to these challenges. Emergency management works, but it is an active process. And it isn't government by itself. It takes a community effort to respond and recover from these storms."

Some of the initiatives that Fugate and his agency applied during the 2004 and 2005 hurricanes had never been tried before. "September 11 crystallized some thinking about disasters," said Fugate. "You have little time to react, and you have to move fast. We used to send reconnaissance teams in after a storm and wait for their reports back to determine what the needs are. But that's not good enough. We wanted to send in supplies early, and not wait for the winds to stop blowing. In Charley, we tried it out. Food, ice, water, National Guard troops—all were stood up early, as fast as we could. We set aggressive goals. That's how you can change outcomes."

We will rely on the forecasters at the National Hurricane Center to warn us when the next great hurricane heads toward the Florida coast. Technological advancements have given meteorologists better tools for analyzing storm movements, and forecasts have become much more accurate over the last several decades. Computer models used to predict hurricane landfalls have improved, and the implementation of new programs like the use of a Gulf Stream IV jet for high-altitude reconnaissance has enhanced the Hurricane Center's capabilities. The center is in a state-of-the-art facility in Miami and has earned a reputation for issuing timely, life-saving warnings to those facing an approaching storm. But as demonstrated with Hurricane Charley in 2004, predicting exactly when and where a hurricane will strike and how strong it will be remains an elusive goal. The Hurricane Center's average forecast error in a twenty-four-hour period is now less than 70 nautical miles, down from around 120 nautical miles in 1960. Neil Frank, director of the National Hurricane Center from 1974 to 1987, summarized the problem: "While I was at the Hurricane Center, there was only a 10 percent improvement in forecast error in twenty-five years. During this time, the population of Florida's coastal areas was exploding. The increase in population far exceeded any small improvement we made in our ability to forecast hurricanes."

Hurricane forecasting is about predicting not just where a storm will go but also how strong it will be when it gets there. Intensity forecasting is particularly tricky because of the unpredictable nature of tropical cyclones. Max Mayfield, former director of the National Hurricane Center, knows how much is at stake when a hurricane approaches the coast: "On average, we do OK with intensity forecasting. But we don't catch the rapidly changing hurricanes. Wilma went from a tropical storm to a cat 5 hurricane within twenty-four hours. Fortunately, that happened over the open waters of the Caribbean. Someday, it will happen as a hurricane makes landfall in the U.S. The NHC has identified intensity forecasting, especially rapid intensification, as our number one need in the research community."

For many reasons, Florida remains vulnerable to the next great hurricane. Because of its large coastal population, continuing growth, heavily developed barrier beaches, and limited arteries for evacuating traffic, large numbers of residents and tourists could find themselves trapped within the core of the next major storm. Every year, as the state's population grows, the problem becomes larger. Evacuation studies in recent years, combined with observations

Clyde Avenue resident Charles Wolf was distraught after Hurricane Charley destroyed his family's mobile home. The Punta Gorda resident was forced to live under a tarp next to the pile of rubble that used to be his trailer. (From Direct Hit, *photo by Sarah Coward, courtesy of the Charlotte Sun)*

from recent storms, have depicted dire scenarios. Out of a total population of more than 18 million, the number of Floridians vulnerable to storm surge (and mobile home residents vulnerable to wind) is estimated at over 8 million. With regional clearance times that may exceed fifty-plus hours and a state-wide shelter deficit, emergency planners fear a worst-case scenario in which thousands of motorists are trapped in expressway gridlock just as category 5 winds and deadly storm surge sweep over them. This mass-casualty scenario could happen anywhere in Florida. Such a storm could be especially deadly along the heavily populated Miami–Fort Lauderdale coast; around Tampa Bay, where storm surge could spread inland for miles; or in the Keys, where the only escape route is vulnerable and residents are often reluctant to leave.

In response to these gloomy scenarios, the Florida Division of Emergency Management has examined numerous ways to minimize the risks for Florida residents. Through their public education efforts, state and county emergency planners have encouraged nonvulnerable residents to remain at home rather than attempt to evacuate and further clog already congested highways. Another approach has been to promote early evacuations and evacuations of minimal distances whenever possible. The message has been frequently stated: "Go 2 miles or 10 miles, not 200 miles." Other plans include the staggering of evacuation times in adjoining counties with high populations. This procedure allows evacuation traffic to flow more smoothly, preventing much-feared logjams. But most important, emergency planners advise each family or individual to have a personal evacuation plan in place long before the hurricane season begins and to contact emergency-management offices for information

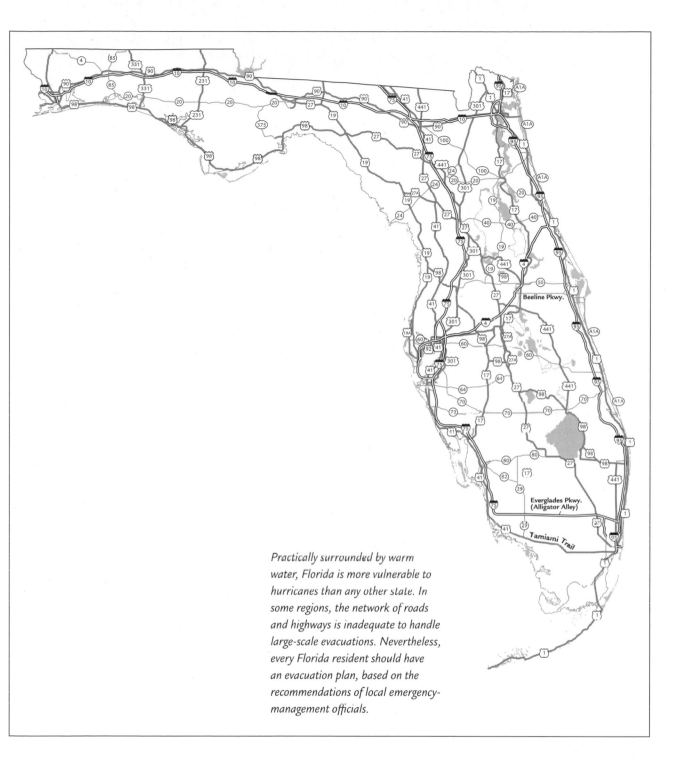

Practically surrounded by warm water, Florida is more vulnerable to hurricanes than any other state. In some regions, the network of roads and highways is inadequate to handle large-scale evacuations. Nevertheless, every Florida resident should have an evacuation plan, based on the recommendations of local emergency-management officials.

on hurricane evacuations. "The battle against the hurricane is won outside the hurricane season," says former Hurricane Center director Max Mayfield. "Everyone needs to take that personal responsibility to develop their own hurricane plan and know what to do in advance."

It is conceivable that Florida's next great hurricane could bring about catastrophic loss of life, causing perhaps more deaths than the 1,500-plus reported after Hurricane Katrina. It is almost a certainty, however, that powerful hurricanes in the future will continue to deliver enormous property destruction. It may not be just one big storm. As seen with the hurricanes of 2004 and 2005, the cumulative economic impact of multiple strikes within a short period of time is staggering. But sooner or later, a category 4 or 5 hurricane will set a new standard. Depending on which region of the state is affected and the severity of the storm, it is likely that Andrew's $30 billion–plus price tag will be eclipsed by some future cyclone. And it's even possible that Katrina's record-breaking toll in Louisiana and Mississippi could also be surpassed. All it would take would be a monster hurricane striking one of Florida's major cities and then tracking over other population centers across the state. Should a storm rapidly intensify and strike Miami as a category 5, then quickly track northwest over Tampa–St. Petersburg and then Pensacola, who knows what the cost would be. Emergency planners have no choice but to envision these kinds of dire scenarios so they can better prepare for such a disaster. They know that their worst-case hurricane would bring far-reaching economic consequences. One study completed in the mid-1990s concluded that if Hurricane Andrew had made landfall just twenty miles farther north in Miami, the economic losses could have totaled $60-100 billion. In addition to virtually wiping out some insurance companies, financial shock waves would have occurred on an international scale due to the disruption of banking, exports, commerce, and other services based in the city.

Much of the economic equation is tied to the insurance industry. After Andrew, a crisis emerged in the Florida insurance industry as numerous companies went belly-up after making enormous payouts. In 1995, the Florida legislature launched a task force to study the problem of insurance risk in the state. Included in the task force report was this grim reminder of how serious the hurricane problem had become in Florida: "As bad as it was, hurricane Andrew was not the 'Big One.' . . . The real 'Big One,' or worse—two 'Big Ones' hitting major metropolitan areas within a few years of each other—could bankrupt insurance companies, builders, Realtors, the State of Florida, hundreds of thousands of Florida's homeowners, and the banks which financed their homes. That's how big the potential of this problem is."

After Andrew and through the rest of the 1990s, Florida transformed its insurance industry by stepping in to provide governmental support. Legislatively created joint underwriting associations (JUAS) were developed to back

A liquor store in Port Charlotte was one of many businesses that were totally destroyed by Hurricane Charley. (Photo by Mario Tama, courtesy of Getty Images)

homeowners who otherwise could not find insurance for their homes. Citizens Property Insurance Company was developed to provide coverage until the private sector could take over, but it has been difficult to attract and keep insurance companies in Florida. More pulled out in 2004 after issuing payouts through four hurricanes. Instead of being the insurer of last resort, Citizens has taken on over $1 trillion in exposure, and without it, over one-fourth of Florida residents would have no insurance. In January 2006, Tom Gallagher, Florida's chief financial officer, told the *Insurance Journal*: "Without Citizens, where would we be? There would be no mortgages, there would be no real estate closings, there would be nothing else. . . . Nobody ever expected to have $32 billion worth of losses in 15 months. The best thing we can do is take care of insurance rates and availability, and stop having hurricanes."

But the problem has expanded. For the average Florida homeowner, insurance has become hard to find and very expensive to keep. Most of the state's major insurers were allowed to raise their premiums after the 2004 and 2005 seasons, and some rates jumped more than 30 percent. Thousands of homeowners also lost their coverage in 2005 when their insurance carriers scaled back their Florida exposure and refused to rewrite their policies. With higher rates, shocking surcharges, and limited availability, it is no wonder that homeowners are looking for government to step in and support their insurance needs. One proposal called for the state of Florida to take over all windstorm risk, which would probably not reduce costs for homeowners but might encourage more insurers to come to Florida. Another proposal called for the creation of a national catastrophe fund, which might help spread the risk—

though ultimately the charges would come back to the homeowner. Craig Fu-gate, director of Florida's Division of Emergency Management, sees a future where risk is more fairly distributed: "I think you've got to reward good behavior, and enforce good building codes. . . . And if you want to build in a coastal high-hazard zone, that's fine. But why am I assuming their risk? Why should my tax dollars subsidize their exposure to hurricanes? You're not going to ever stop coastal development, but we should put the onus back on those who profit from it."

In recent years, much attention has been focused on disaster mitigation—planned efforts to reduce the destructive impact of future storms. Fortunately, building codes in Florida are good and getting better. The South Florida building code, the standard in Miami-Dade and Broward Counties, has long been one of the toughest in the country. In 2001, a new unified code was put in place in all sixty-seven counties, strengthening construction standards across the state. Newer homes and buildings have been built to that higher standard, and the result has been very positive. Just a few days after Hurricane Charley struck in 2004, President George Bush joined his brother, Governor Jeb Bush, and Craig Fugate for a walking tour of Punta Gorda and saw for himself the difference the new code made. "We walked together down a long block with rows of destroyed homes, and there at the end was a house that was untouched," remembered Fugate. "It looked like it had been built after the storm. It didn't have a scratch on it. The president asked me about it, and I told him it was there 'cause it had been built to the better code. . . . It's a tool that will help us in the future. The code is paying for itself."

In the mid-1990s, atmospheric scientists and hurricane researchers delivered an unwelcome message about the future: expect more storms. Beginning with the 1995 season, an upswing in hurricane activity was documented over the next decade. According to William Gray and his colleagues at Colorado State University and others at NOAA who study hurricane climatology, the Atlantic basin is experiencing a period of increased activity that produces more tropical storms and hurricanes than average, as well as more intense storms. Scientists also believe this trend might continue through a natural cycle, perhaps a decade or two into the future. Decadal cycles of hurricane activity have been recorded in the past, followed by similar periods of relative inactivity. Gray's research, which considers such factors as sea-surface pressures in the North Atlantic, rainfall in Africa's Sahel region, and the effects of El Niño, has enabled him to produce an annual prediction of Atlantic hurricane frequency since the early 1980s. His track record is pretty good. In 1996, he coauthored "Discussion of Atlantic Basin Seasonal Hurricane Activity in 1995 and Prospects for 1996," along with Christopher Landsea, Paul Mielke Jr., Kenneth Berry, and John Knaff. In this report, the authors prophetically wrote: "There has been a great lull in the incidence of intense category 3-4-5 hurricanes

striking the U.S. East Coast, Florida and Caribbean basin (except for 1995) during the past 25 years. . . . Both historical and geological (proxy) records indicate that this lull in major hurricane activity will not continue very long. A return of increased major land-falling hurricane activity should be expected within the next decade or so. When this happens, the upshot of large coastal development during the last 25–30 years will very likely include hurricane destruction as never before experienced."

Some link the increase in hurricane activity to global warming, but many scientists feel the jury is still out on that notion. "It is a fair question," says former Hurricane Center director Max Mayfield. "But I personally think that the active period of hurricanes that we are currently in can be explained by natural variability, without invoking global warming. The scientific community is divided about this issue, and it will continue to play out in the referred journals." Nevertheless, the media has helped promote the global-warming issue whether real or not. Even Hollywood weighed in with its portrayal of mega-cyclones in 2003's *The Day after Tomorrow*. And cable television's version of the next great storm took an eerie twist in 2005. The first episode of the Weather Channel's new show, *It Could Happen Tomorrow*, had to be remade when reality caught up with the script. It seems that the pilot episode, about a major hurricane striking Louisiana and flooding New Orleans, was filmed one year before Hurricane Katrina engulfed the city. Now known at the Weather Channel as the "lost episode," it was replaced by another "what if" catastrophe when the series was aired. Terry Connelly, senior vice president

WHEN A HURRICANE THREATENS

KEEP YOUR RADIO OR TV ON...AND LISTEN TO LATEST WEATHER BUREAU ADVICE TO SAVE YOUR *LIFE* AND POSSESSIONS

and general manager of the Weather Channel, told the *TV Times*: "This is not science fiction. It's scientific fact. It sends chills up our spines when you think we produced this episode on the potential of a hurricane hitting New Orleans and it all came true."

Although we could see active hurricane seasons for years to come, it is the powerful storms that concern hurricane experts the most. "Plans are good to have, but no one is ready for a category 5," said Neil Frank. "The real question is: Are we improving our preparedness activities, are we anticipating the new problems that emerge, and are we improving the awareness of people who live along the coastline? No single community in this nation is ready to deal with a category 5. No matter where it lands, it's going to take a lot of outside help to survive. Our greatest concern is that when the next 5 does come, at least we don't have people in harm's way."

Many Floridians who endured the hurricanes of 2004 and 2005 learned valuable lessons and came away with a better understanding of the storms' impact. Experience is a great teacher when it comes to hurricane disasters, and many portions of the state may strangely benefit in the future by having gone through the toils of surviving and rebuilding. But public education is still a critical need if we are going to become more hurricane resistant and protect lives and property in the future. In 2005, the *Orlando Sentinel* published a quick summary of lessons learned that should be useful to all property owners and visitors in the Sunshine State for years to come:

THE STORM TIDE

MAY BE A HURRICANE'S GREATEST KILLER

TAKE PRECAUTIONARY MEASURES PROMPTLY WHEN THE WEATHER BUREAU ISSUES
HURRICANE WARNINGS

10. *Know your insurance policy.* Many homeowners faced financial ruin after their homes were damaged in 2004 and 2005—often because their coverage was inadequate. Know your insurance options.

9. *Stock up on the right things.* Prepare yourself long before hurricane season starts in June. Then add supplies to your stockpile that will help you survive for days, if needed.

8. *Trim your trees before the storm hits.* This sounds like simple advice, but removing just one or two limbs could save your roof and a lot of damage.

7. *Forget about that skinny forecast line.* Beware of track changes as the hurricane approaches the coast that could dramatically alter the storm's impact on you.

6. *Gas up and protect your vehicle.* Depending upon the severity of the storm, your car might be your lifeline as you recover from a disaster. Gasoline may be unavailable in your location.

5. *Don't flee too far—or at all, in some cases.* Know the elevation of your home. Make sure you and your family have a clear evacuation plan, if you do need to leave. Seek the advice of local officials in determining your evacuation priority.

4. *Know your workplace policies.* If you're thinking of skipping work during a hurricane, check with your employer first.

3. *Don't panic—learn to cope with boredom.* If you have sought safe shelter, try to maintain calm throughout the experience. Be prepared for no electricity for weeks, and make plans for how you will use your time.

2. *Do some quick emergency repairs.* If you are capable, making fast repairs on a tree-damaged roof could prevent significant water damage later on.

1. *Don't be a fool—and you'll live to tell the tale.* Respect the awesome power of the storm, and don't venture into danger—on foot, or by car or boat. Heed evacuation orders and leave mobile homes. Use extreme caution in the hours immediately following the storm, as dangers lurk in many places.

No one can say exactly when the Florida coast will be hit by the next great storm. Most people generally accept the risk, just as midwesterners accept tornadoes and Californians live with earthquakes. Vast improvements have been made in hurricane forecasting, warning, communications, and recovery, but Florida still remains vulnerable. The problems faced by the state today are rooted in meteorology, geology, economics, and population. Evacuations are a grave concern because even when the best information is available, human nature sometimes causes us to wait to do something until it's absolutely necessary. But common sense is the ultimate weapon against the hurricane threat, and well-prepared coastal residents know that lost property is replaceable whereas lost lives are gone forever. If a major hurricane threatens, they pack their cars and secure their plans to escape the approaching storm. They know that sooner or later, *the big one* will come.

APPENDIX

HURRICANE	YEAR	CATEGORY	DEATHS
Galveston, Texas	1900	4	8,000+
Lake Okeechobee, Florida	1928	4	2,500
Cheniere Caminada, Louisiana	1893	4	1,100–1,400
Sea Islands, South Carolina; Georgia	1893	3	1,000–2,000
Katrina (Louisiana, Mississippi)	2005	3	1,500+
Georgia, South Carolina	1881	2	700
Labor Day hurricane, Florida Keys	1935	5	408
Last Island, Louisiana	1856	4	400
Audrey (Louisiana, Texas)	1957	4	390
Miami, Florida; Alabama; Mississippi	1926	4	372
Grand Isle, Louisiana	1909	3	350
Florida Keys; South Texas	1919	4	287
Galveston, Texas	1915	4	275
New Orleans, Louisiana	1915	4	275
Camille (Mississippi; Louisiana; Virginia)	1969	5	256
New England	1938	3	256
Diane (Northeast U.S.)	1955	1	184
Georgia; South Carolina; North Carolina	1898	4	179
Texas	1875	3	176
Southeast Florida	1906	3	164

THE TWENTY DEADLIEST MAINLAND UNITED STATES HURRICANES, 1851–2006

Source: NOAA, National Hurricane Center.

HURRICANE	YEAR	CATEGORY	DAMAGES[a] (BILLIONS)
Katrina (Louisiana; Mississippi; Alabama)	2005	3	$81[b]
Andrew (Florida; Louisiana)	1992	5	43.7
Charley (Florida)	2004	4	15
Ivan (Alabama; Florida; North Carolina)	2004	3	14.2
Hugo (South Carolina; North Carolina)	1989	4	12.8
Wilma (Florida)	2005	3	12.2
Agnes (Florida; Northeast U.S.)	1972	1	11.3
Betsy (Florida; Louisiana)	1965	3	10.8
Rita (Texas; Louisiana)	2005	3	9.4
Frances (Florida; North Carolina)	2004	2	8.9
Camille (Mississippi; Louisiana; Virginia)	1969	5	8.9
Jeanne (Florida)	2004	3	7
Diane (North Carolina; Northeast U.S.)	1955	1	7
Georges (Florida; Mississippi)	1998	2	6.7
Frederic (Alabama; Florida)	1979	3	6.3
New England	1938	3	6
Allison (Texas)	2001	Tropical storm	5.8
Floyd (North Carolina; Virginia)	1999	2	5.8
Northeast U.S.	1944	3	5.4
Fran (North Carolina)	1996	3	4.5

Source: Insurance Information Institute; NOAA, National Hurricane Center.
[a]Damage estimates are adjusted to 2004 dollars. Total damages are represented as twice the amount of insured losses.
[b]Total damages for Hurricane Katrina may be higher.

HURRICANE	YEAR	CATEGORY	PRESSURE (MILLIBARS)	PRESSURE (INCHES)
Labor Day hurricane, Florida Keys	1935	5	892	26.35
Camille (Mississippi)	1969	5	909	26.84
Katrina (Louisiana; Mississippi)	2005	3[a]	920	27.17
Andrew (Florida)	1992	5	922	27.23
Indianola, Texas	1886	4	925	27.31
Florida Keys; South Texas	1919	4	927	27.37
Lake Okeechobee, Florida	1928	4	929	27.43
Donna (Florida Keys)	1960	4	930	27.46
New Orleans, Louisiana	1915	4	931	27.49
Carla (Texas)	1961	4	931	27.49
Last Island, Louisiana	1856	4	934	27.58
Hugo (South Carolina)	1989	4	934	27.58
Miami, Pensacola, Florida	1926	4	935	27.61
Galveston, Texas	1900	4	936	27.64
Florida; Georgia	1898	4	938	27.70
Hazel (North Carolina)	1954	4	938	27.70
Florida; Louisiana	1947	4	940	27.76
Texas	1932	4	941	27.79
Charley (Florida)	2004	4	941	27.79
Gloria (North Carolina; New England)	1985	3	942	27.82

Source: NOAA, National Hurricane Center.

Note: "Most intense" means lowest pressure at landfall.

[a]Hurricane Katrina measured 920 mb at landfall, but with category 3 winds.

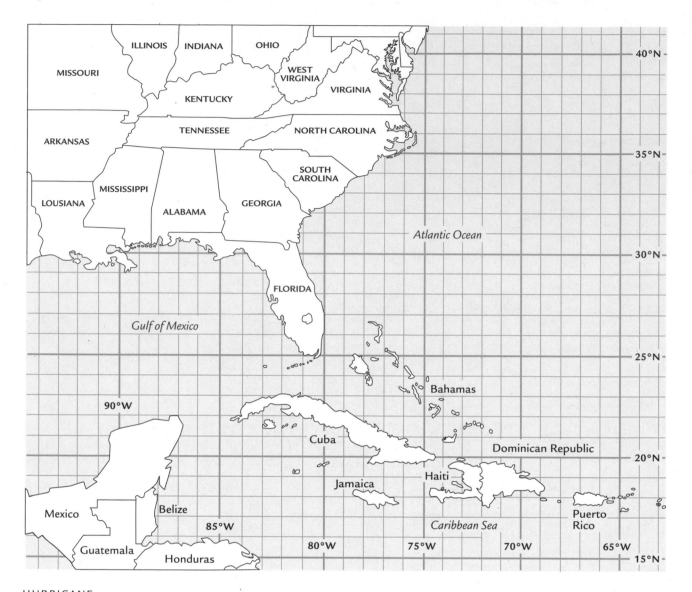

HURRICANE

TRACKING MAP

ACKNOWLEDGMENTS

This book was prepared with the outstanding cooperation of many individuals and organizations. I owe special thanks to those who assisted me in collecting the stories, weather reports, historical information, and photographs. Whenever possible, appropriate credit for photographic sources has been provided in the captions.

Several key historical and meteorological works were consulted frequently in the preparation of the text. Extensive use was made of technical memorandums and booklets published by NOAA, the parent organization of the National Weather Service; the Tropical Prediction Center/National Hurricane Center; and the National Climatic Data Center. Among these are *Tropical Cyclones of the North Atlantic Ocean, 1871–1995*, by Charles J. Neumann, Brian R. Jarvinen, Colin J. McAdie, and Joe D. Elms; *The Deadliest, Costliest, and Most Intense United States Hurricanes of This Century*, by Paul J. Hebert, Jerry D. Jarrell, and Max Mayfield; *The Deadliest Atlantic Tropical Cyclones, 1492–1994*, by Edward N. Rappaport and José Fernández-Partagás; *Florida Hurricanes*, by R. W. Gray, revised by Grady Norton; *Florida Hurricanes*, by Gordon Dunn; *U.S. Weather Bureau, Monthly and Annual Reports*; *Some Devastating North Atlantic Hurricanes of the Twentieth Century*; numerous issues of the *Monthly Weather Review*; and a variety of hurricane summary reports issued by the National Hurricane Center.

Other major publications referenced throughout the text include *Early American Hurricanes, 1492–1870*, by David M. Ludlum; *Hurricanes: Their Nature and History*, by Ivan R. Tannehill; *Atlantic Hurricanes*, by Gordon Dunn and Banner Miller; *The Hurricane and Its Impact*, by R. H. Simpson and H. Riehl; *Florida Hurricanes and Tropical Storms, 1871–2001*, by John M. Williams and Iver W. Duedall; *Hurricane*, by Marjory Stoneman Douglas; and numerous summary articles in *Weatherwise*.

Booklets, pamphlets, and technical memorandums produced by NOAA were among the primary resources for chapters 1, 2, and 3. These excellent publications were useful in providing information on the formation, tracking, and intensity of tropical cyclones. In addition to the publications listed above, other sources include *Florida Weather*, by Morton Winsberg; "A Comparison of Six Great Florida Hurricanes," an article by Donald C. Bunting in *Weatherwise*; *Weather Is Front Page News*, by Ti Sanders; *Hurricane Survival Guide*, by Leslie R. Crown; *Weather Sourcebook*, by Ronald Wagner and Bill Adler; *Living with the East Florida Shore*, by O. H. Pilkey; *Violent Storms*, by Jon Erickson; Everything Weather, software by the Weather Channel; *West Indian Hurricanes*, by E. B. Garriott; and *American Weather Stories*, by Patrick Hughes.

Chapter 4 relies heavily on Ludlum's *Early American Hurricanes, 1492–1870*; Tannehill's *Hurricanes: Their Nature and History*; and Douglas's *Hurricane*.

Other sources include "A History of Hurricanes in Eighteenth Century West Florida," an article by Thomas Muir Jr. in *Pensacola History Illustrated*; *A Concise Natural History of East and West Florida*, by Bernard Romans; a 1980 article in the *Stuart News*; "Hurricane History" and "Hurricanes: A Devastating History," articles by Jerry Wilkinson in the *Reporter*; "Blasts from the Past," an article in the *Associate*, published by the Florida History Associates; "Development of the Plan of Pensacola during the Colonial Era," an article by Robert B. Lloyd Jr. in *Florida Historical Quarterly*; a column by Ernest Lyons in the *Stuart News*; "New Light on Galvez's First Attempt to Attack Pensacola," an article by Everett C. Wilkie Jr. in *Florida Historical Quarterly*; "Historic Hurricanes of South Florida," an article by Don Gaby in *Update*; *The Weather Factor* and *The American Weather Book*, by David M. Ludlum; and *Spanish Treasure in Florida Waters*, by Robert F. Marx.

Many of the above works were also sources for chapter 5, along with "Storm Stalking with a Hurricane Historian," an article by William Brennan in *NOAA Magazine*; *Tampa*, by Karl H. Guismer; *Tampa: A Pictorial History*, by Hampton Dunn; *The Scariest Place on Earth: Eye to Eye with Hurricanes*, by David E. Fisher; *The Hurricane Handbook*, by Sharon Carpenter and Tonie Carpenter; *Origin, Progress, and Conclusion of the Florida War*, by John T. Sprague; a letter from S. R. Mallory of the Key West Collector's Office to the secretary of the treasury; and various articles from the *Delray Beach News*, *Miami Herald*, *Pensacola Gazette*, *Stuart Times*, *Tallahassee Democrat*, and *Tampa Morning Tribune*. Several articles published in *Florida Historical Quarterly* were also helpful in preparing chapter 5: "Pioneer Florida," by T. Frederick Davis; "Apalachee," by the Tallahassee Historical Society; "Survival of a Frontier Presidio," by William R. Gillaspie; and "St. Joseph: An Episode of the Economic and Political History of Florida," by James Owen Knauss.

Primary sources for chapters 6 and 7 include various issues of the *Monthly Weather Review* and reports from some of the books and newspapers listed above. Other sources include *Florida: A Pictorial History*, by Hampton Dunn; *Pioneer Commercial Photography*, by Robert E. Snyder and Jack B. Moore; *The City of Cocoa Beach: The First Sixty Years*, by Glenn Rabac; "Palm Trees, Public Relations, and Promoters: Boosting Florida as a Motion Picture Empire, 1910–1930," an article by Richard Alan Nelson in *Florida Historical Quarterly*; *Florida Hurricane and Disaster 1926*, by L. F. Reardon; "The Hurricane of 1926," an article by Carl Wernicke, and "Hurricane Interrupted Wedding," an article by Katherine Carlin, both in *Pensacola Historical Illustrated*; *Miami: The Magic City*, by Arva Parks; *Lake Okeechobee, Wellspring of the Everglades*, by Alfred J. Hanna and Kathryn A. Hanna; *Okeechobee Hurricane and the Hoover Dike*, by Lawrence E. Will; *Pioneers in Paradise: The First One Hundred Years of West Palm Beach*, by Jan Tuckwood and Eliot Kleinberg; *The History of Martin County*; "Surviving the Horrific Hurricane of 1935," an article by Gene Burnett in *Florida Trend*; "Report of Hurricane Victims, 1935, Florida Keys," by Monroe County coroner George J. Rawlins; "Who Murdered the Vets?," an article by Ernest Hemingway in *New Masses*; a letter from Ernest Hemingway to Maxwell Perkins, in *Ernest Hemingway: Selected Letters, 1917–1961*; *The Day of the Seventh Fire*, by James Leo Herlihy; *The Railroad That Died at Sea*, by Pat Parks; a report on Hurricane Donna in *Florida Health Notes*; "Donna," an article by LaTelle Dixon in *Naples Now*; *Hurricane Donna in the Florida Keys*, published by the *Florida Keys Keynoter* and *Florida Keys Sun*; "Hurricane!," an article by Ben Funk in *National Geographic*; "Hurricane Kate," a report by the Florida Department of Natural Resources; "Andrew Aftermath," an article by Rick Gore in *National Geographic*; *Interagency Hazard Mitigation Team Report for Hurricane Andrew*, published by FEMA; *Florida National Guard Official History, Operation Andrew*, published by the Florida National Guard; *The Big One*, published by the *Miami Herald*; *Hurricane Andrew: Images of a Killer Storm*, published by the *Palm Beach Post*; "Zoo Story," an article by Ron Arias and Cindy Dampier in *People*; "What Went Wrong," an Andrew summary article in *Newsweek*; *Florida Hurricane and Disaster of 1992*, by Howard Kleinberg; *Nature on the Rampage*, by H. J. de Blij; "Hurricane Opal Synopsis," a report by the Florida Division of Emergency Management; and "Public Response to Hurricane Opal: Preliminary Findings," by Jay Baker.

In addition to the newspapers listed above, reports used in chapters 6, 7, and 8 were obtained from the *Asheville Citizen-Times, Atlanta Journal-Constitution, Big First, Brandenton Herald, Charlotte Sun, Collier County News, Florida Keys Keynoter, Ft. Myers News-Press, Home News, Martin County News, Miami Beach Daily Tribune, Miami Daily News, Miami Herald, Naples Daily News, Naples Star, Northwest Florida Daily News, Orlando Sentinel, Palm Beach Post, Pensacola News Journal, St. Augustine Record, St. Petersburg Independent, St. Petersburg Times, Seminole Tribune, South Florida Sun-Sentinel, Stuart News, Tampa Daily Times, TV Technology*, and *USA Today*. Also critically important were a variety of online news reports from CNN News, MSNBC News, and the Associated Press and Reuters news agencies. Supporting information for chapter 8 was obtained from the American Red Cross, FEMA, the Florida Division of Emergency Management, the Insurance Information Institute, the National Climatic Data Center, the National Hurricane Center, the National Weather Service, and William Gray and his colleagues at Colorado State University. Among the articles referenced from *Weatherwise* are "Hurricanes David and Frederic," by Dick DeAngelis; "The Return of the Hurricane," by Bob Case; "Open Season on Hurricanes," by D. C. Cameron; "Hurricane Donna in Florida," by Keith Butson; and "Tracking Andrew from Ground Zero," by Jack Williams. Other publications used in chapter 8 include *Direct Hit* and *In the Eye of Charley*, published by Sun Newspapers; "Key Facts from Florida's 2004 Hurricane Season," published by the National Association of Mutual Insurance Companies; various press releases from the Florida Hurricane Relief Fund and Volunteer Florida; and numerous situation reports from Florida's State Emergency Response Team (SERT).

Chapter 9 is based on some of the publications mentioned above, as well as the following: *What? Another Florida Insurance Crisis?*, a report by the Florida Academic Task Force on Hurricane Catastrophe Insurance; "Discussion of Atlantic Basin Seasonal Hurricane Activity in 1995 and Prospects for 1996," a report by William M. Gray, Christopher W. Landsea, Paul W. Mielke Jr., Kenneth J. Berry, and John A. Knaff; "Mean Season," an article by Daniel Pendick in *Earth*; *Florida Hurricane and Disaster of 1992*, by Howard Kleinberg; "Candidate Forum," an article in *Insurance Journal*; "Ten Lessons Learned," a report by the *Orlando Sentinel*; and "It Could Happen Tomorrow," an article by Nancy McAllister in *TV Times*. The Florida Division of Emergency Management, the Florida Governor's Office, the Florida Department of Insurance, and FEMA provided crucial information for chapter 9, especially on issues relating to hurricane evacuations, disaster recovery, mitigation, and property insurance. Of particular help were Chuck Lanza, former Dade County emergency management director; Craig Fugate, director of the Florida Division of Emergency Management; Neil Frank, former director of the National Hurricane Center; and Max Mayfield, former director of the Hurricane Center. Each kindly took time from their busy schedules to provide interviews.

Special recognition and thanks are due to many others who assisted in the completion of this publication. They include former National Hurricane Center director Max Mayfield; former Hurricane Center director Neil Frank; former Hurricane Center director Bob Burpee; former Dade County Emergency Management director Chuck Lanza; Weather Channel hurricane expert Steve Lyons; and NOAA hurricane researcher Stanley Goldenberg. Others who deserve special thanks include Ed Rappaport, Chris Landsea, Brian Jarvinen, Frank Lepore, and the staff of the Tropical Prediction Center/National Hurricane Center; Joe Pelissier of the National Weather Service; William Gray of Colorado State University; Noel Risnychok and the staff of the National Climatic Data Center; Monroe County Emergency Management director Billy Wagner; former Hurricane Center director Bob Sheets; Julia Hesson and the staff of the Museum of Florida History; Jody Norman of the Florida State Archives; Paul Camp of the University of South Florida; Cynthia Wise of the State Library of Florida; Frank Orser of the University of Florida; Annette Davis of Carteret Community College; Elizabeth Hooks of the American Red Cross; the staff of the Collier County Museum; Shirley Bland of the Historical Society of Martin County; Marc Wolfson of FEMA; Helen Twedell of the Coastal Engineering Archives; Crystal Sauls of the Army National Guard of Florida; Gail Shackleford of the Pensacola Historical Society; Lynne Robertson of the T. T. Wentworth Museum; Susan Freeman of the *Daytona Beach*

News-Journal; Mark Kulaw of the *Northwest Florida Daily News*; Liesette Nabut of the *Miami Herald*; Paul Schmidt of the *Charlotte Sun*; Bob Shaw and Linda George of the *Orlando Sentinel*; and the staffs of the National Archives and the U.S. Naval Historical Center.

Others who deserve special thanks are Arva Parks, Jerry Wilkinson, Don Gaby, Joe Myers, Noel Risnychok, Scott Taylor, Gregory Salyer, Craig Fugate, Skip Waters, Chris Landsea, and especially my wife Robin, my daughters Heather and Lindsey, and my mother Kathleen. Extra thanks are reserved for Steve Lyons, Neil Frank, Max Mayfield, Stan Goldenberg, and David Perry and the staff of the University of North Carolina Press.

INDEX

Page numbers in italics refer to illustrations.